Manchester United: Tragedy, Destiny, History

For Brooklyn, Harrison, Lyle,
Nicky and Matthias, the latest addition to the family,
and in memory of the Busby Babes

MAINSTREAM / SPORT

MANCHESTER UNITED IN EUROPE

TRAGEDY, DESTINY, HISTORY

KEN FERRIS

MAINSTREAM
PUBLISHING

EDINBURGH AND LONDON

First published in Great Britain in 2001 by
MAINSTREAM PUBLISHING COMPANY
(EDINBURGH) LTD
7 Albany Street
Edinburgh EH1 3UG

ISBN 1 84018 897 9

A catalogue record for this book is available
from the British Library

Typeset in Stone and Frutiger
Printed and bound in Great Britain by
Cox & Wyman Ltd

Contents

Book Two: Destiny

Book Three: History

Acknowledgements

I would like to thank John Bartram, my former editor at Reuters and a Manchester United fan, for reading the proofs and suggesting various changes.

I would also like to thank Mainstream Publishing, especially Deborah Kilpatrick, Jess Thompson and Tina Hudson who expertly handled the production, as well as Bill Campbell for his support.

Many people have helped me to tell the remarkable story of Manchester United's search for Europe's Holy Grail, many of whom wished to remain anonymous. I would like to thank everyone who provided valuable insights into the club's pursuit of European glory.

I would also like to thank the staff in the Editorial Reference Unit at Reuters whose files on the Munich disaster proved to be invaluable.

I wish to acknowledge the first-hand account of the Munich disaster *The Day A Team Died* by Frank Taylor. It remains the most immediate version of the events at Munich and was a very useful reference. Special mention goes to John Buckley, his son John and Garry Dann. Their enthusiasm for United (and Ludlows FC) has sustained my interest in the Reds over the years. I hope they have as much fun reading the book as I had writing it for fans like them. My partner Nicky, and my mother Sadie also deserve credit for giving me support throughout what must at times have seemed like a never-ending project. Thanks.

Finally, I would like to thank Charles Frewin of sportsbooksdirect.co.uk for having faith in my first football project and for giving me encouragement ever since.

Ken Ferris,
London, September 2001

Foreword

The year 1999 was amazing for me and United. In the 1960s everyone thought the double was impossible until my old team Tottenham managed it under the leadership of Danny Blanchflower in 1961. But the treble. Now that really was fantasy football.

I'd had my ups and downs at United and being classed as a super-sub wasn't a label I wanted. But all my dreams came true that season. I'd played my part in capturing the premier league title and scored in the FA Cup final. During the Champions League final in Barcelona I was just itching to get involved in the action.

When I came on we were a goal behind but I still felt sure we could pull something out of the bag. The rest, as they say, is history. My first goal was by no means a classic but it got us on level terms as Bayern were preparing for a victory they thought was already done and dusted.

My header to set up Ole Gunnar Solskjaer for the winner rocked the Germans to the core but was the icing on the cake for us. It was such a sweet feeling as we picked up the Champions League trophy to emulate the great United team of 1968 and honour the players from the 1950s.

I've achieved a lot in my career since I started out at Millwall and

I've been lucky enough to play at the World Cup and in domestic cup finals with United and even at Spurs. But nothing can compare to that balmy night in Barcelona when we conquered Europe.

Teddy Sheringham,
July 2003.

Book One
Tragedy

One

Munich

It was close to 1400 hours when Captain Kenneth Rayment was once
again ready to fly the *Lord Burleigh* home. The plane was returning
to Manchester from Belgrade, but the full distance was beyond its
range. The British European Airways (BEA) aircraft therefore had to
stop in Munich to refuel before the last leg of the journey. Heavy
snow was falling. It was a bitterly cold day in the city famous as the
site of British Prime Minister Neville Chamberlain's phoney peace
deal with German Chancellor Adolf Hitler before the start of the
Second World War. The Elizabethan, BEA's name for what was
known in the industry as the Air Ambassador, had a good safety
record: none had ever crashed and they were used to flying Queen
Elizabeth around the world, earning their name. The plane was
therefore perfectly suited to transport Manchester United's party of
players and officials to Yugoslavia for their European Cup quarter-
final second-leg tie against Red Star Belgrade. United were now
returning to Manchester via Munich, where they stopped to refuel
at Reim Airport, outside the city.

At 1419 hours on a dismal and windy afternoon under grey
skies, Captain Rayment, at the controls and sitting in the left-hand

seat, asked for permission to taxi for take-off. He was cleared.

Some of the players were already shuffling cards in the centre of the plane. Bill Foulkes, who faced the back of the plane in a window seat, sat next to Ken Morgans. David Pegg sat opposite Foulkes next to Albert Scanlon. They were at a four-seater card table. United manager Matt Busby and chief coach Bert Whalley sat behind them facing Foulkes. Roger Byrne, Billy Whelan, Dennis Viollet, Ray Wood and Jackie Blanchflower occupied a six-seater card table across the gangway. They wanted goalkeeper Harry Gregg to take the vacant sixth seat, but Gregg had done well at cards the night before and decided to continue a little private joke he'd started on the first leg of the journey from Belgrade. He told them he had no intention of ending up poor and they'd have to manage without him. He moved into a backward-facing seat just under the wing, although he intended to join them as soon as the plane had taken off. The Elizabethan's wings were joined to the fuselage right above the card players, which meant they could see the wheels of the plane below them as the aircraft took off and landed. Mark Jones, Tommy Taylor, Duncan Edwards and Eddie Colman were at the back of the plane, along with most of the journalists.

The stewardesses checked that all cigarettes had been put out and everyone was safely strapped in, and the pilots made their routine pre-take-off checks, which included revving up each engine in turn. When they were satisfied, Rayment opened the throttles. As they moved along the runway Radio Officer William Rodgers told the control tower the plane – code-named '609 Zulu Uniform' – was rolling. The time was 1430 hours and 40 seconds.

Next to Captain Rayment, in the First Officer's seat on the right-hand side of the flight deck, was his friend, Captain James Thain, commander of the plane. Thain had flown the outbound leg of the trip to Belgrade with Rayment as his co-pilot, and had followed the usual custom of inviting Rayment to share the flying by exchanging roles with him for the return to Manchester. A captain could allow his First Officer to act as 'pilot-in-charge' and fly the plane, while he took the role of co-pilot, as long as the First Officer was fully qualified. The captain, of course, always remained in command. Thain and Rayment were both fully qualified pilots and captains. In fact, Rayment was slightly senior in length of service, with more experience of flying Elizabethans than Thain (3,143 hours against Thain's 1,722).

It had been towards the end of January when Thain received a telephone call from the Administrative Officer of the Elizabethan, offering him a 'plum trip' as commander of a return flight to Belgrade. It was a dream assignment for any football supporter, because the plane had been chartered by the famous Manchester United. But Thain wasn't into football – in fact, he knew little about United apart from the name of Matt Busby, and even that required a great deal of thought.

Thain was 36 years old and one of BEA's senior pilots. He'd served in the RAF during the war with the Empire Air Navigation School. After being demobbed in 1946 he went to Southampton University to study navigation and qualify for a civil flying licence. Thain applied to BEA in October of that year and was taken on by them as a pilot. He spent four years as a First Officer before taking full command as a captain. He flew Vikings but transferred to Elizabethans as soon as he got the chance. Thain liked Elizabethans – because of their pressurised cabins, they could rise above the 10,000-feet ceiling that restricted other aircraft and thereby avoid most of the bad weather. The planes were also fast and comfortable, and had extra navigational aids.

Thain lived in Berkshire and had recently bought a small poultry farm in a nearby village, which he ran with local assistance. When he was offered the Belgrade trip he'd just ordered a large shed for the farm, which he was anxious to see put in place. Poultry farming was popular among pilots because it gave them a hobby during the periods of compulsory rest between flights. Thain's success interested Rayment, one of his colleagues at BEA.

Rayment had been off duty for a while after a hernia operation, but now, at the start of February 1958, he was back at work. Rayment was keen to follow in Thain's footsteps as a poultry farmer and had called his friend to see if he could meet up with him to discuss the business and seek some advice. Thain agreed, and at that point asked Rayment to join him as First Officer on the flight to Belgrade. They'd have plenty of time to talk about poultry farming during the layover in Yugoslavia, and it would help relieve the boredom of waiting to return to England. He asked the Flight Officer to roster Rayment on the trip.

There were some administrative obstacles to overcome, but luck and the help of an official were on hand, and when Thain reported for duty at London Airport he was pleased to find his co-pilot was not First Officer Hughes, as stated on the roster, but his friend Captain Rayment.

The first leg of the journey was from London to Manchester to collect the passengers. They had then flown to Belgrade for the match. So far the trip had been a success, and the friends had time to discuss the poultry business before the return flight. Now, as Rayment taxied to the take-off point at Munich's Reim Airport, they were about to begin the last leg of the journey to Manchester.

The plane's throttles were on the central column between the two pilots. As Rayment gradually opened them with his right hand Thain followed with his left, one of his routine duties as co-pilot. The engines began to purr gently. When the throttles were fully open Thain lightly tapped Rayment's hand while still holding the levers open. Rayment moved his hand and Thain called, 'Full power'. 'Full power,' confirmed Rayment. The engines took on a deep-throated roar. 'Temperatures and pressures okay and warning lights out,' said Thain, looking at the instruments in front of him. He called out the speed in knots as the twin-engine aircraft accelerated along Munich's runway 24/25.

Everyone on board was quite happy as the plane sped down the runway. Foulkes could see *Daily Mail* photographer Peter Howard nearby with Ted Ellyard, the man who helped Howard wire his pictures. Ellyard had been an RAF pilot during the Second World War. Frank Taylor, a journalist with the *News Chronicle*, looked out of his window to watch the port wheel retract; then he'd know they were in the air. But all he could see was slush and snow being thrown back, just like when the plane had landed. Gregg, too, watched specks of snow dance by his window as the wing wheel threw up slush.

In the cockpit, Thain noticed an uneven note from the engines and watched the needle on the port pressure gauges start to fluctuate. Rayment also saw the needle wobbling, and took the split-second decision to shut off the power and slow the aircraft down while there was still time. Thain felt a stinging pain in his left hand as Rayment whipped the throttles back and called out, 'Abandon take-off!'

In the cabin, Frank Taylor was shocked when the port wheel didn't slide smoothly into the engine's outer casing, known in the aircraft industry as the nacelle. But Thain asked no questions as he gripped the control column and helped to hold it fully forward while Rayment throttled back and applied the brakes. Suddenly, the plane juddered and lost speed; the passengers felt it slow a little, then more, as the engines lost their powerful roar.

Frank Taylor heard a clatter behind him and turned to see the steward, Tommy Cable, drop into a seat beside a passenger called N. Tomasevic and begin to fasten his belt. 'What are you doing that for, Tom?' Taylor asked. 'You'll give us heart failure. Anyone would think that something had gone wrong with the works.' Taylor had met Cable before on these kinds of trips. The steward was a cheery, efficient type, and very keen on sport. The usual formalities between passengers and crew were often waived on such goodwill journeys; that's why Taylor called him by his Christian name. Cable grinned. 'I got stranded up here in the galley on take-off when I should have been in the tail.' Taylor didn't know whether Cable had fallen into the seat with the sudden braking, or had intended to sit there. He would never find out.

Gregg, sitting under the wing, felt the wheels locking. The moments that followed were frightening. The aircraft seemed to go into a skid as it slewed around before grinding to an almost complete stop just 40 seconds after the start of its run. Thain sucked his knuckles and swore. Rayment apologised. He had not had time to shout a warning.

It was now 1431 and 20 seconds. The passengers didn't panic, but there were lots of frowns and puzzled looks. Since there was no immediate explanation as to why this had happened the inevitable questions and theories were bandied about. 'Why hadn't the plane taken off?' 'What was the hold-up? Engines misfiring?' 'Didn't we reach take-off speed in time?' 'Had an engine suddenly cut?'

'Perhaps the water or slush had been thrown back into the electrical system and caused a short circuit?' Frank Taylor thought that since the lights were still on, the latter surely couldn't be the cause.

The problem, in fact, was power surging, more commonly known as boost surging, in the engine manifold. This occurred when an over-rich mixture of fuel affected the full distribution characteristics of the engine, causing certain cylinders to operate in an over-rich state and making the engine over-accelerate. This caused uneven engine running, boost pressure surge and sometimes rpm fluctuation. If the port pressure soared off the gauge on take-off, something was seriously wrong. It could even lead to an engine seizure in mid-air.

Boost surging was quite common in Elizabethans and was more likely to happen at airports well above sea level, like Munich. Although the engines sounded uneven, there wasn't much danger that take-off power would be affected; Elizabethans were powerful planes and could get off the ground on one engine. But the nature of boost surging gave the impression of unsatisfactory engine performance. No pilot launching himself, 40-odd other people and several tons of metal and machinery into the sky could be happy with the suspicion, however unfounded, that the engines weren't doing their job. This was why Rayment had abandoned take-off. Thain agreed with the decision.

The pilots discussed the problem. They decided that if Air Traffic Control agreed, they'd taxi back down the runway and try again. One cause of boost surging was opening the throttles too quickly. Rayment therefore told Thain on the way back to the take-off point that at the start of the next attempt he'd open the levers gradually before releasing the brakes, and would continue to open them more slowly as he moved to full power.

The crew informed the control tower that take-off had been abandoned and asked for permission to try again. Three minutes after the first attempt, permission was granted for a second take-off. It was now 1434 and 40 seconds. Captain Thain finally told the anxious passengers there was a technical fault and apologised for the delay, adding that he'd be attempting another take-off immediately.

Rayment opened the throttles to 28 inches of boost, pushed the levers forward slowly and released the brakes. The *Lord Burleigh* began rolling. Thain's left hand followed this manoeuvre until the throttles were fully open. Halfway down the runway he saw the starboard engine steady itself at 57.5 inches, but the port pressure ran to 60 inches and beyond. It was the same boost surging problem.

In the cabin, Gregg again watched the slush spewing up by the wing wheel. He sensed they were travelling an awfully long way without leaving the ground. This time, though, Thain abandoned take-off even earlier than on the last run. The plane shuddered again as the brakes were applied, although to Gregg the skidding and slewing seemed less pronounced. The engines dropped their revs until the props were just ticking over. The standard corrective action – slower opening of the throttles – had failed.

Many passengers, including Foulkes, began to think something was wrong. The *Daily Mail*'s wireman, Ted Ellyard, looked out of the window. 'The engine looks as if it could have done with a little more elastic,' he joked. It was the typical stiff-upper-lip attitude you'd expect from a former pilot. Big Frank Swift, the former Manchester City goalkeeper who now worked for the *News of the World*, jumped up at the back of the plane. 'What the hell's going on here?' he roared.

Thain wasn't happy. He got permission from Air Traffic Control to return to the tarmac – he wanted to discuss the problem with BEA Station Engineer William Black. It was 1435 and 20 seconds. The aircraft taxied back down the runway for the second time and when it was clear Thain took the controls.

For the passengers it was becoming a familiar and unpleasant routine. They sat back feeling worried. Questions and theories were once again thrown about in the cabin. Rayment ended the anxiety, giving his bewildered passengers some reassurance by again announcing that there was a technical fault. He'd let them know as soon as possible what the outcome was likely to be. Stewardess Margaret Bellis told the passengers they'd be returning to the terminal while the plane was checked and the problem fixed. There would be a slight delay, but the crew still hoped to take off soon. The passengers should be ready to be recalled.

It was still snowing. Thain could barely see the edge of the runway. Rayment took the controls again and taxied the plane back to the terminal buildings just 20 minutes, almost to the second, after it had first left. The prospect of reaching Manchester that afternoon was fading.

Two

The Busby Babes

Many people believed Matt Busby had assembled the most talented group of players ever seen at one club. The popular view was that his team of young stars, dubbed the Busby Babes, were likely to dominate English football for the next decade.

Busby, known to his staff as the Boss, hated the Babes tag because he thought it implied innocence, naivety and inexperience. He preferred the nickname Red Devils, which the Continentals had given his young team.

The players, not one of them over 30, were already famous around the world and worth a fortune. They were widely viewed as the greatest representatives so far of the most consistently successful football club in post-war British football.

The squad included Duncan Edwards, 23, a Midlander who became the youngest-ever England international at only 18; Roger Byrne, 28, England's star Manchester-born full-back, United's captain and one of the more experienced players, who'd recently married; David Pegg, 22, the son of a Doncaster miner and another England international; Bill Foulkes, once a miner himself; a lad called Bobby Charlton who was just getting into the first team;

Dennis Viollet who, like Charlton, would go on to play for England; goalkeepers Harry Gregg, recently bought from Doncaster, and Ray Wood from Darlington; a splendid 24-year-old centre-half called Mark Jones, a schoolboy discovery from Barnsley; wing-half Eddie Colman, 21, also signed as a schoolboy from across the Irwell in Salford and famous for his wiggling hips; Northern Ireland international Jackie Blanchflower, brother of Tottenham and Northern Ireland captain Danny; wingers Johnny Berry from Birmingham City, and Albert Scanlon who'd joined United as a schoolboy; Tommy Taylor, the most expensive player in the squad having signed four years ago for £29,999 from Barnsley, who'd recently got engaged; Liam Whelan, a Republic of Ireland international; and a brilliant prospect at left-back called Geoff Bent. Other rising stars who hadn't made the trip to Belgrade included Nobby Stiles, Johnny Giles, Nobby Lawton, Alex Dawson and Mark Pearson. They were all part of what Busby called his 'priceless collection'.

Manchester had a traditional image of shabby back-to-back houses with slate roofs and cobbled streets, and the suburbs flanking most routes into the city weren't much better. It certainly wasn't the prospect of living in Manchester that attracted young players to Old Trafford. 'When I joined Manchester United the city was a gruesome place,' says Charlton, 'but one shining light was Manchester United and particularly the young players.'

There was very little money to buy proven, quality players when Busby started his Old Trafford reign. His thoughts immediately turned to the youngsters coming through the ranks. United had won the Central League under assistant manager Jimmy Murphy just after the War. Busby went to Murphy's house for a celebratory drink and told him he'd done a remarkable job. Murphy said that while he was delighted, he didn't feel he had anyone good enough for the first team. It was then that they hit on the idea of a youth development scheme. Busby decided to find the best boys for Murphy to nurture to maturity.

The new policy began in the back streets. Busby recruited schoolboys in his own image, lads hungry for success. The Boss wanted to start a family. It was a tremendous challenge for Murphy, who had to spot the youngsters and bring them to Old Trafford fresh from school, but he was just the man to put into practice Busby's far-sighted philosophy. Two masterly assistants helped Murphy: Bert Whalley, the chief coach, and Joe Armstrong, the club's highly intuitive chief scout. Whalley, a respected and well-loved coach and nurturer of young talent, had been at Old Trafford for more than 25 years. Murphy was lucky to have the big, burly Whalley. Together they set out to find their young team and coached them until they blossomed.

The old United players who'd won the FA Cup in 1948 began to give way to the brilliant boys Murphy and Whalley managed to find over the next three years. This 'new look' team began to develop, not only as good club footballers, but also as world-class players. Whalley, a former United centre-half, was a talented coach and a great judge of football. He had a terrific flair for spotting young footballers and coaching them into great players. He did a magnificent job and was ready to help in anything, both on and off the field.

Charlton was one of United's budding stars. Like many of Busby's Babes he wasn't a local lad but was born in Ashington, Northumberland. Bobby was picked for his school team at the age of 10. United first heard about him from a local teacher. 'They did not make an approach . . . but there were plenty of signs that they were interested,' says Charlton.

United's early interest was crucial. It left Charlton with a soft spot for the club. Once he got into the England schoolboys' team and scored a couple of goals from inside-left at Wembley the scouts began to line up for his signature. They descended on Charlton's home in Ashington to tell him he couldn't do better than join their club. Sometimes there were two scouts from different clubs in the house at the same time – one in the front room with his mother and the other at the back of the house with his father. They even had tea from the same pot without realising it!

But it was United who'd caught the imagination of the country with their youth policy. Seventeen- and 18-year-olds were regularly appearing in their League team and every other club in the country wanted to get in on the act. Clubs that had lived by the chequebook and the transfer market suddenly discovered the raw material was lying around in England's schools.

It had taken them a long time to wake up to the fact. The old system of ignoring the stream of school players and concentrating on works' teams and local junior sides for players was wasteful. Under that system, a youngster had often picked up so many bad faults in a couple of seasons that too much damage had been done. Others had had their skills knocked out of them by full-backs who were seemingly intent on kicking them into the back of the stands. The clubs had now decided to start their search for talent at the very beginning of the players' careers. Their approaches to Charlton were part of this new trend.

About 18 clubs were after him, including the top Northern teams from the area – Newcastle, Sunderland and Middlesbrough – plus Bolton, the two big Manchester clubs and a few others. Wolves came up from the Midlands and Arsenal from London. Charlton sought his mother's advice as he tried to make a decision. She said he should join Manchester United. His mother was worried about what would happen if he didn't make it in football. She'd been around the game too long and knew the dangers. To put her mind at rest United arranged for Charlton to attend a grammar school in Stretford. 'She wanted to see me right – and she did,' says Charlton. But training and school didn't mix well so he went into engineering and moved into digs with some United players. It was then that he started to become a Busby Babe.

Busby, who would become known as the 'Father of Football', made sure his young recruits lived in a cosy environment. United hired an army of carefully selected landladies to look after them as if they were part of the family. They provided the youngsters with the basics such as hot meals and a bed for the night.

Most of the Babes lived in suburban Burnage, among the fans who followed their progress with mounting interest and not a little pride. Winger Kenny Morgans, for instance, stayed with Mrs Evans, who worked at United. He was there for two years before signing as a professional at 17.

When Charlton arrived he lived at Mrs Watson's.

'There were about 12 of us in one digs, a great big old house, and we shared it with travelling salesmen and people like that,' he remembers. 'But it was quite close to the ground, so it was all right, and it was good fun because you never got away from talking about football . . . everybody ribbed everybody else and gags rattled off like machine-gun fire. But this was something more than a hostel for high-spirited youths. This was where the real business of becoming a United player began. You see, we weren't just a gang of kids thrown together to enjoy ourselves. Fourth and fifth teamers straight from school shared those digs with men from the League side. Jackie Blanchflower, Duncan Edwards, Mark Jones and the rest – we all shared the same table and the same conversation, which was invariably about football. Without knowing it, we were learning our business the painless way.'

Charlton was the new boy in the house but he soon made friends, and he, Tommy Taylor and David Pegg all became close pals. Pegg also struck up a friendship with Dennis Viollet and Mark Jones. Viollet, Charlton and Taylor would all go across to Manchester to visit Mr and Mrs Pegg and their two daughters. When Liam Whelan arrived at Old Trafford he went into lodgings with Charlton, and they too became very close. Modesty was their pride; Pegg did the washing-up in his digs. Charlton recalls how well they all got along together. 'We didn't think of ourselves as Busby's Babes but as young people growing up together,' he says. 'A team of lads, a team of pals.'

The family atmosphere Busby wanted to create was built on within the club as well as in the digs to create a sound basis for the fresh-faced boys to develop their football skills and character. Murphy and Busby dealt with the youngsters very firmly, but they always had a friendly word for them and were available to listen to their problems. At first the new recruits did odd jobs like cleaning boots. There was no apprentice-professional scheme in those days and the ground staff lads spent much of their time sweeping the ground or cleaning the toilets. 'That wasn't my mother's idea of how to earn a living,' says Charlton, 'so I promised her I would take a second job in case I flopped at football.' It was then that he began working in engineering. Every morning as he left the house, Edwards, who could enjoy another two hours in bed, would shout,

'Don't slam the door.' 'If making the grade meant the luxury of lying in bed until nine,' recalls Charlton, 'I was going to make the grade.'

Training began five weeks before the start of the season. From about 12 July the boys would train for close to two hours each morning and afternoon. For the first two weeks they'd be as stiff as boards. They trained at the Manchester University ground, where they ran laps of the track. After two weeks, when they were fit, they'd be given a ball for the first time. The emphasis was on fitness, which would build a sound foundation for the rest of the campaign.

During the season the youngsters only trained in the mornings under the experienced men at United. Johnny Carey and Jimmy Delaney looked after the likes of young Blanchflower. The two trainers, Tom Curry and his assistant Bill Inglis, were a great double act and testimony to Busby's ability in selecting his lieutenants. He knew how to use their individual talents to the greatest effect. Curry had been the club's trainer since the 1930's. 'For some unknown reason Tom and Bill always wore ice-cream coats,' remembers Gregg. 'I suppose it was part of the set up.'

On Tuesday and Thursday evenings, Murphy and Whalley took the boys to train on their own. There was lots of trapping, turning, heading, twisting and eliminating faults, and they also played lots of five-a-sides. 'In the practice games there was plenty of needle between us as each of us was playing for a place in the team,' says Blanchflower. 'No one was ever certain of his place. The club always promoted this competitiveness, Curry or Busby sometimes stopping the match to discuss particular points. There was a lot of one-upmanship, but never any animosity.'

Monday was the only day United didn't train. Instead, they played golf virtually all day. Blanchflower's handicap was an impressive four. 'This was all part of the club's idea of keeping the players together,' he says, 'keeping the "family" intact.' Busby was a golfing fanatic and enjoyed the Monday sessions, but he was always very much the Boss.

Senior pros like Carey, Jack Rowley, Stan Pearson and Charlie Mitten all mixed with the youngsters who always called the senior players 'mister'. They were all very much a team. Training could sometimes be a grind, but to break the monotony Curry organised games of hide-and-seek, especially when it was foggy. They played until the last one was found. 'We didn't train very hard in those days because we were playing two to three games a week,' says Gregg. 'We didn't need to train. Some of those lads, especially the internationals, were playing 65 to 70 games a season. They never got stale. They were playing for different reasons in those days. We felt it was a privilege to be playing for United, although they did work us very hard.'

The players would be sent 'up the back' to a stretch of concrete interrupted by electricity pylons. If they could play football on that, they could play on anything. Kenny Morgans was always the best on that surface. 'I think it was Matt's way of keeping us at a basic level so that we never forgot what type of team we were meant to be,' says Gregg. 'We were never spoilt; our training equipment and match gear were never flashy.'

There was a particular greatness in United at that time and the players all had tremendous talent and ability. Charlton's strong feelings for the club were based on its spirit. 'We know at United what it [spirit] is all about because we've had it injected into our bloodstream,' he said. 'It became our reason for living the moment we signed on as United players . . .'

United were not so much a team as a breed. The youngsters were training not just to become footballers; they were being prepared to become members of Manchester United. 'It didn't matter whether we were playing for the youth side in some scruffy park on a foggy afternoon, or in a floodlit European Cup match before 60,000 howling fans – we were simply playing for the reputation and success of Manchester United,' says Charlton.

Viollet agrees.

'For me the thing that really made us a great team was the bond, the team spirit that kept us all together,' he says. 'So many of us had grown up together in the United nursery teams. I had been at Old Trafford since I was 16, playing with lads like Roger Byrne and Eddie (Colman) and big Duncan (Edwards). We were all kids together and had a great relationship. It was more than just team spirit. We would have run through a brick wall for United. You could almost say we had a love for one another.

'To be one of the Busby Babes was one of the greatest things a guy could wish for. Nothing can compare with the enormous feeling of camaraderie we had. It wasn't just that we looked up to Matt. We looked up to everyone, and they looked up to us. There was always a particular understanding between us, with wonderful men like Jim Murphy and Bert Whalley who did so much for us all. Jim especially had a knack for instilling great enthusiasm in everyone. Another lovable man who did so much was Walter Crickmer, who could never do enough to help.'

Crickmer had been club secretary for more than 30 years. Wood's wife, Elizabeth, also remembers how close the players were at that time. 'They had such feeling for each other. They were all brilliant players but none of them ever thought of themselves as a star. There was such a collective bond.'

When Charlton changed digs he shared with Billy Whelan, a first-team regular and a brilliant inside forward. When Charlton got into the first team he took Whelan's place. 'Living with him might have been uncomfortable,' says Charlton, 'but it wasn't.'

Busby's goal was to build the best team possible.

'Matt and Jimmy were hard taskmasters but fair,' says Gregg. 'Matt was the great diplomat, keeping any trouble within the club and allowing only good news to filter through to the outside. No one ever crossed Matt. You adhered strictly to the rules so that everyone knew exactly where they were. You certainly never swore in front of the Boss. As he always said, "If they act like men, I treat them like men. If they act like boys, I treat them like boys."'

In Charlton's early days at Old Trafford as a youth player, when he was at that delicate stage where his talent might either fade or take him through to become a professional, he saw little of Busby. His world was dominated at that time by the dedicated duo of Murphy and Whalley. 'The Boss, as he was called even at that level, was somewhere up there with the first team,' says Charlton. 'He was part of a world we never ceased to think about.'

Now and then the Boss would appear at a youth team match. When he did the air would electrify. Murphy, who'd seen the same phenomenon with every new intake, would come up to the youngsters and say encouragingly: 'Come on, lads, the Boss is here.'

Then they'd tear into action like a pride of young lions. It was the greatest tribute Busby could have had. 'We kids, who had had little personal contact with him, would have run until we blew our boilers just to please him,' says Charlton.

A good deal of Busby's strength sprang from Murphy. The two were a pair, the best in football. The success of one was balanced by the success of the other. They consulted closely on every aspect of the game. Murphy was brilliant at coaching young players and building them up for an important match. Charlton thought he'd get to hate the sound of his voice. Week after week he'd have Charlton running up and down the field doing things he knew very well how to perform. Charlton would clench his teeth and think, 'He must be mad. Can't he see I'm doing it all right?' Still Murphy would go on. But eventually Charlton would realise just how good a job Murphy had done instilling the basics of the game into him. From trapping and controlling the ball well occasionally, Charlton was soon doing it instinctively all the time. That was Murphy's secret; he made these things a natural part of Charlton's game.

The set-up both inside and outside the club was unique and it was to prove very successful; the formula would produce some of the best players the game has ever seen. England manager Walter Winterbottom claimed he could pick out a United player without seeing him as long as he could hear him. 'They have a walk of their own up there,' he explained. 'They've all got it – a kind of Manchester United stomp. You can hear their assurance in it.'

But Busby didn't just set out to build a great team. His horizons were much wider than that, the task correspondingly bigger. 'What I really embarked upon was the building of a system which would produce not one team, but four or five teams, each occupying a vital rung on the ladder, the summit of which was my first XI, representing Manchester United in the Football League.'

Busby's youngsters were part of the most successful youth team England had ever seen. When Charlton got into the team for the FA Youth Cup the tournament was fairly new and the games were very important. The competition had only been going a few years and it was the only international tournament for young players since the winners represented England on the Continent. At Old Trafford it meant everything. United won it for the first five years and crowds of 20,000 came to watch them. It was one of the foundations on which the club's youth policy was built. 'Not only did outsiders expect us to win it,' says Charlton, 'but we looked upon it almost as our own trophy.'

Charlton found himself in the same team as Edwards, who was also playing regularly for the first team. He was a phenomenon. 'I think the sight of him in those youth matches used to put the fear of God into some sides,' says Charlton. 'Even if he did nothing in the game (and that was never the case because he always gave 100 per cent no matter what the game), he still had the ability to put us halfway along the winning path just by pulling on the number six shirt.' Just seeing Edwards on the pitch was enough to upset the other team. They'd think about him playing in the First Division a couple of days before and their imagination would do the rest. Edwards' presence had the opposite effect on United's players; it showed them that if you were good enough you'd get your break. Age didn't matter. 'Here was living proof that we could all make the grade,' says Charlton, 'and we would go like hell to prove it.'

The youth team gave Charlton his first trip abroad. United went to Zurich as England's representatives in the European Competition. Most of the Continental sides, apart from those behind the Iron Curtain, were there. United won easily enough but even then, when Charlton's football education was in its infancy, it was plain to him that the European approach to the game was miles away from United's and England's.

Perhaps the most significant part of the trip for Charlton was finding out that United's players were at least as good, and in many cases better, than the foreign youngsters. United's youth team was the best because the top youngsters in the country wanted to join their crusade. Players gave up the chance of joining their local clubs because they knew from the papers that at Old Trafford they'd be regarded as VIPs. They were so good that if they won 3–0 they considered it a close game.

Busby never expected to be lucky enough or clever enough to find 11 great players for one team at one time. He knew he'd have to get the chequebook out to supplement the club's natural talent. Goalkeeper Ray Wood had arrived from Darlington in 1950 for £6,000, Johnny Berry from Birmingham in 1951 for £25,000 and Tommy Taylor from Barnsley in 1953 for £29,999 and a back-hander of two Cup final tickets. Matt claimed it was really £30,000, because he tipped the tea lady £1 after the deal was struck, but didn't want Taylor to carry the burden of a £30,000 price tag. The success of Busby's youth system meant Taylor was the last player United bought in four years.

Busby and Murphy understood their players well, but they each had a very different approach. Gregg explains:

> At the team talk Matt would tap the table with two fingers, reinforcing his comments. He would point out the characteristics of the opposition, which he knew in great detail. He would tell us to watch a certain player who came inside the back or one who was slightly suspect down his left side. He would never say a player was either good or bad, but merely gave you a clear picture of him before you went out on to the field. He always said that if we were not capable of beating the team we were up against we would not have come through those big gates to join United in the first place. We used to smile at this, because there had never been big gates in our time! Finally, he would tell us to go out and enjoy ourselves and just play football, because that way the results would come. This was always done in a quiet tone. Jimmy's approach could not have been more different. His talks were full of passion backed up by a repertoire of colourful language and unrepeatable expletives . . . Some people regarded Matt and Jimmy as gods, but they were basically wonderful, warm people, full of an emotion which they cloaked – and we respected that.

Charlton was eventually a reserve for the 'B' team. Each time he advanced to a better side he had the same doubt: 'Will I be good enough to stay in this class?' With every step the game was harder and faster, yet, without realising it, he was being shifted through a carefully planned schedule so that he was always ready for the next step, providing he could learn to adjust his play.

Charlton was yet to arrive in the first team but the impact of the young players who had was incredible. The Reds won the League title by 11 points in 1956 with a team whose average age was 20. Thousands had flocked to Old Trafford as the fans got caught up in the excitement and drama of Busby's experiment. Brian Hughes was one of them. 'There was a wonderful spirit, believe me. People said it was religious. It was nothing to do with religion, believe me. It was a religion, but it was a Manchester United religion.'

Jimmy Savile, who would become a famous disc jockey on BBC Radio One, was assistant manager at a Manchester nightclub called the Plaza, which was popular with some players. There had, of course, been famous teams in the past, but Savile sensed times were changing. This side was different from those that had come before.

'It was the birth of the teenager and there was the phenomenon of instant stardom. A boy could get hold of a guitar in the afternoon; by night time he could be a star with somebody looking for his autograph. In the football world we had this amazing team Manchester United. They were a charismatic group of guys and, what wasn't obvious at the time, but I tippled to it, they were the first non-musical megastars.'

Eddie Colman, Old Trafford's own, was born at 90 Archie Street in the terraced row with outside toilets that inspired *Coronation Street*. He was the trendy one of the team and certainly looked the part. 'He was the first I'd seen in drainpipe trousers and winkle-picker shoes,' says Charlton. 'He also had sideburns and was never without a comb to tidy his hair.'

In those days few people had a car and so, when David Pegg arrived at his parents' home late on a Saturday in his Vauxhall Victor, it created a good impression among the neighbours. They were even more impressed, though, when Tommy Taylor, United's hang-in-the-air header of goals, turned up in his car and left it outside the Peggs' house. David's sister Irene polished the cars and smiled at the envious neighbours.

Three

The European Cup

Busby had great ambitions for his young team. They'd won the Championship – now he wanted to scale new heights. United were invited to compete in the European Cup, a new competition open to elite clubs on the continent. It started in 1955, after an article was published in the French daily sports newspaper *L'Equipe* in December 1954, reviving a proposal first laid before FIFA's executive committee in 1927. One of the most fervent supporters of the idea in the late '20s was Henri Delauney, mastermind of the European Championships and Secretary of the French Football Federation. But while there was widespread support for the proposal it never got off the ground in the 1920's, mainly because of concerns about fixture congestion.

After the Second World War, advances in air travel and the growing use of floodlights made the competition more feasible. It was Gabriel Hanot, *L'Equipe*'s football editor, who really got the ball rolling when he invited the delegates of 18 leading European clubs to a meeting in Paris four months after the article in his newspaper. Among those represented were Chelsea, then on the way to winning the League Championship, and the Edinburgh team Hibernian. All the clubs wanted to take part, UEFA was notified and FIFA gave its blessing.

In England, the Football League Management Committee saw the European Cup as a threat to the domestic game. Some officials believed that once supporters saw the skills of the continental players they'd expect higher standards from English clubs. 'I think that a lot of chairmen, and particularly the management committee, lived in their own little world,' says former *News Chronicle* journalist Frank Taylor. 'They were Euro-sceptics and I think they didn't want to be bothered with a lot of foreigners coming over here trying to be clever. They just didn't have the vision to see that it could show our lads the technical skills they needed and could also be a marvellous moneyspinner for the best clubs.' Chelsea were informed that their participation might interfere with their domestic commitments. Under pressure from the Football League, the London club eventually turned down their invitation to take part in the first European Cup.

After Manchester United won the title in 1956, the Reds duly received an invitation from UEFA to compete. Busby was very keen on the idea and at a board meeting early in May 1956 chairman Harold Hardman asked him whether it was wise to take on the extra commitment. 'Well, Mr Chairman, football has become a world game,' Busby told him. 'It no longer belongs exclusively to England, Scotland and the British Isles. This is where the future of the game lies.' 'All right,' said Hardman, 'if that's what you really feel.' 'I do,' replied Busby. 'Anyway, let's just try it.'

The Football League Management Committee wrote to United advising the club not to compete, but Busby wouldn't be intimidated. He felt his squad was big enough and good enough to take on the best teams in Europe and help restore pride to the English game. The country that gave football to the world had suffered two heavy defeats at the hands of the mighty Hungarians and put in a dismal performance at two World Cups, including a 1–0 defeat by the amateurs of the United States in a first-round match at Belo Horizonte in 1950.

Busby felt very strongly about the need to take on the rest of Europe. 'After two World Cup failures, prestige demanded that the

Continental challenge should be met, not avoided,' said Busby. United's players were right behind their boss. 'It was a natural progression; it had to go that way, so I never doubted for a moment that it was right,' says Bobby Charlton.

At United's next board meeting Busby repeated his keenness for the challenge and once more proposed that if the Football Association were willing to accept and back United then the club should enter. So Busby did the unthinkable. He took on the Football League. Busby accompanied Harold Hardman to a meeting with Stanley Rous, the Secretary of the Football Association and a member of UEFA. They found that an English club could not be prevented legally from taking part in a European competition. At a United board meeting on 22 May 1956 Busby persuaded his directors to politely reject the League's advice not to take part. United were to become the first English club to enter the European Cup.

'I found it a tremendous and exciting prospect,' said Frank Taylor. 'And I felt, as Northerners do, that London was way behind the times. It took a northern team to have the bravery to do it.'

Bobby Charlton also recalls the sense of anticipation:

> I remember everybody was really excited about the fact that they were going to play overseas, because it was completely strange. There was no television; we didn't see Spanish football or French football or German football, or whatever. So the only way you could find out [about them] was to play against them. It was just a great adventure.
>
> Matt Busby pioneered going into Europe and he created a great spirit at the club. With Manchester United we went on the great adventure into Europe. We played in the most adventurous matches, which was something that we responded to, and in doing so we lit up this great city. That team set Manchester United on a path which made the club the most popular in the world. Manchester United always had flair; Matt wanted flair and he wanted style. He would say, "Go out and enjoy yourself and if you enjoy yourself you will play well and the public will enjoy watching you".

United's impact in the European Cup was frightening. They started by disposing of Belgian champions Anderlecht by an aggregate score of 12–0, including a 10–0 demolition in the home leg, played at Maine Road because the Old Trafford floodlights weren't quite ready. Viollet scored four and Taylor struck a hat-trick. The crowd was a very respectable 43,635.

Busby, not a man to make rash statements, later called United's performance 'the finest exhibition of teamwork I have ever seen from any team, club or international. It was as near perfect football as anyone could wish to see.' Charlton reckoned it was 'one of the most outstanding performances ever put on by a British club'.

Next came a 3–2 victory against Borussia Dortmund with all the goals in the first leg at Maine Road in front of a staggering 75,598.

United were drawn to play Atletico Bilbao in the quarter-finals. The first leg was in Bilbao and United were to fly out via Bordeaux. The idea of flying to Bilbao for a match seemed incredible. It was another world for both players and supporters.

It turned out to be a terrible journey. Mark Jones and Billy Whelan were ill on the flight, Foulkes accidentally turned off the heating with his feet while he was sleeping, leaving everyone shivering, and the plane made a nightmare landing at a deserted, snowbound airport. United lost 5–3.

The snow made it look as if United would be stranded on the northern coast of Spain. Instead, the players had to help sweep the wings of the plane before they could fly home to England. 'It was treated as a big joke,' recalls Frank Taylor. 'Everybody was laughing and smiling, "Ah, right, skipper", and all that kind of thing. We didn't think anything of it at the time but it was exactly a year before Munich.'

Bill Foulkes got on top of one wing and brushed it down along with Eddie Colman, Bobby Charlton and Duncan Edwards. They eventually cleared all the snow and ice off the wings and posed for a picture holding their sweeping brushes. After the snow and ice in Bilbao, the plane was forced to land in bad weather much closer to home, at Jersey airport in the Channel Islands.

Goalkeeper Ray Wood remembers the importance of returning to Manchester on time. 'We knew that we had to be back because otherwise the League would have been down on the club and the players.' So many times on European trips Busby and Murphy talked about the problems of an English club trying to compete in Europe with such a tight League programme to fulfil. They wished there was more flexibility to give an English club breathing space to go into Europe and win the European Cup. But there was always a mad dash to leave England on a Monday after a hard League match the previous Saturday, a European Cup game in mid-week and then another hectic scramble to get home, usually on Thursday, so the players could prepare for another tough League match on the Saturday.

The second leg against Bilbao was played on 6 February – one year to the day before they'd find themselves trying to take off in the snow at Munich. There were still no floodlights at Old Trafford so the match was again played at Maine Road. Charlton was a soldier at the time and not in the team, but he joined more than 70,000 people at Manchester City's ground to watch the match.

United scored a few minutes either side of half-time to draw level on aggregate. Charlton had seldom known such tension in a ground. United scored again just before the end to win 3–0 on the night and 6–5 on aggregate.

The match touched off a mania for the European Cup in the northwest. The supporters had tasted a new experience. Football would never be the same again; the fans had seen their side give one of the top Continental teams a two-goal start and still beat them. Their attitude to the game changed. Suddenly the local derbies were no longer the focus of interest in their season. They looked across the sea with the challenge, 'Bring 'em all on – we can beat the world.' These were the pioneering days of British interest in the European Cup.

United were through to a semi-final against Real Madrid. The Spanish champions had won the European Cup in its first season. Their forward line included the great Argentine striker Alfredo di Stefano, nicknamed the White Arrow, an expensive little French winger called Raymond Kopa, and Mateos, Rial and Gento. Those five forwards alone were worth about £250,000. Behind them was a solid halfback line of Munoz, Marquitos and Zarraga.

Busby had been to see Real play in the previous round in Nice and brought back hints and tips about their style. He was full of enthusiasm for their players, saying that a lot of them – Gento, Di Stefano, Mateos, and Kopa – were absolutely fabulous. Busby was particularly impressed with Gento. 'He is the fastest man I have seen,' he said. Charlton reserved his judgement. He wanted to see for himself.

Charlton was again a spectator, but this time as a reserve. The Bernabeu Stadium in Madrid was awe-inspiring. The air seemed to have a dull roar of tension in it. When United saw Gento in action, they knew what Busby meant. He was unnaturally fast, his feet hardly seemed to touch the ground and he laid on a couple of goals as Real beat United 3–1.

Still, two goals wasn't an impossible margin to pull back. Now United knew what they had to beat and they reckoned they had enough talent to do it. If the players were confident then the Manchester public was wildly optimistic. For days nobody talked about anything else. 'The build-up for the match was like a thunderstorm that starts low on the horizon and keeps coming at you,' says Charlton. In Madrid the atmosphere was the same. Having seen what United were capable of, the Spanish fans became victims of a similar nervous anticipation.

Inside Old Trafford the tension was nearly as great as at the Bernabeu. It was the first game under United's new floodlights and a great occasion. The start was so promising for the Reds. They attacked and dominated. Charlton, playing at inside-left, felt as if he was running on steel springs. This was United making the game. Real pulled their players back into defence. Nothing was going to keep United out. The exhilaration lasted even when the Spaniards started to move out of defence – and they counter-attacked with bewildering speed.

Then suddenly, after about half an hour, Kopa put the ball in the net. It was unbelievable. You could almost feel the shock spread across the packed mass of spectators onto the pitch and through the players. A few minutes later Real scored again. United were now four goals behind, and the game wasn't even half over. The one thing they hadn't contemplated had happened – Real had destroyed them. United, who had spent all their time thinking about outwitting the Spaniards' defence, had themselves been outwitted.

The Reds fought back to draw 2–2 with goals from Taylor and Charlton, but it wasn't enough. When Real's fans learned the result they danced in the streets in joy and relief. Busby was philosophical in defeat. 'It was a contest between two great teams – a mature side and a young side and, of course, experience told. But our time will come.' The average age of United's side was 21, against 28 for Real's team.

There was still much to play for, though, as United closed in on the elusive League and Cup double. Nobody had managed it since Aston Villa in 1897. The Reds won the Championship for the second year running with eight points more than Tottenham Hotspur, the runners-up. They also reached the FA Cup final.

When United walked out at Wembley for the final, ironically against Villa, they were 90 minutes from the first double of the twentieth century. Unfortunately, after just six minutes tragedy struck. Villa's Irish left-winger Peter McParland charged in and United keeper Ray Wood went down. He had a depressed fracture of the cheekbone. As the stretchers came out United's captain, Roger Byrne, signalled for Jackie Blanchflower to take the keeper's shirt. Wood's injury virtually put him out of the game. In those days there were no substitutes and so from that moment on United didn't have a chance. No team could win a tense match like the Cup final on Wembley's holding turf with just ten men.

Duncan Edwards moved to centre-half and eventually Wood came back and played on the wing, more to make up the numbers than to play any decisive part. For 75 minutes United hung on without being very convincing. Eventually, they cracked. McParland scored twice before United pulled one back through Tommy Taylor. At 2–1 Wood went back in goal and United created more chances, but it wasn't enough. Apart from McParland, the pick of the Villa side was Stan Crowther at wing-half. He created an impression in United's mind that would stay with the club.

Despite the Cup final defeat, it was with justifiable pride that United looked back on their achievements during the 1956–57 season: League Champions; FA Cup runners-up; European Cup semi-finalists; winners of the FA Charity Shield; winners of the FA Youth Challenge Cup for the fifth year in a row. And they made a profit of nearly £40,000. But, most important of all, the title gave them another crack at the European Cup.

Four

Europe Beckons Again

Towards the end of 1957 Matt Busby travelled to Paris for the European Cup draw. When he arrived, Busby was approached by a representative from Real Madrid who asked if he'd like to become their manager. Busby was flattered, but Old Trafford was in his veins. Besides, he still had many things to achieve with his young United team. Before the start of the 1957–58 season Busby had been asked to outline his goals for the future. 'We would like to win the European Cup, of course. But above all I would like to win the English League Championship for the third year in succession. Herbert Chapman achieved this with Arsenal, and it is the ultimate peak for any manager.'

United were in high spirits at the start of the season. They were once more England's representatives in the European Cup. Despite the commitment and efficiency of Wolves, the Reds were again favourites for the League Championship. They were also expected to progress to the final stages of the FA Cup.

Busby's young men were maturing rapidly as they became more experienced. Ray Wood, Johnny Berry and Roger Byrne had played more than 200 games for the first team; Jackie Blanchflower, Bill

Foulkes, David Pegg, Tommy Taylor, Dennis Viollet, Mark Jones and Duncan Edwards had all played over 100 matches.

As summer moved into autumn the team was revelling in beating the also-rans of the First Division by three clear goals. In late October, however, a United team weakened by a sudden bout of flu were humbled 3–1 by their main rivals, Wolves, at Molineux. Meanwhile, United's reserves, playing as methodically and attractively as the first team, were top of the Central League.

In Europe, United disposed of Irish League side Shamrock Rovers by an aggregate score of 9–2 after a 6–0 win in Dublin and a 3–2 victory at Old Trafford. In the next round the talented Dukla Prague were beaten 3–0 at home, with two goals by Colin Webster and one by Tommy Taylor. But Wolves and West Bromwich Albion were making the running in the League and, after unexpected defeats at home and too few points picked up away, United were well behind.

The Reds lost 1–0 in the second leg of the European Cup tie against Dukla in Prague to advance 3–1 on aggregate. But the journey home was long and confused. They were held up at the airport because of fog in London and there was even some doubt about whether they'd arrive in time to play their next League match. Eventually seats were found on a KLM flight via Amsterdam after which they took a boat from the Hook of Holland before boarding a train for London and finally Manchester. Busby was worried about failing to return in time for the next Saturday's League fixture and wanted to avoid the embarrassment that would cause the club in the eyes of the Football League. By the time the United party got back a day late, everyone was totally exhausted.

In those days if a club wanted a first-team player they simply bought one and hoped he'd fit in. Busby had different ideas. When he felt they were ready, he threw his young players into the first team. In the run-up to Christmas 1957, Busby had a shake-up. United had not been playing well, particularly in attack, and a few changes were on the cards. For the match against Leicester City on 21 December Busby replaced five internationals, including David Pegg, Johnny Berry and Billy Whelan, with his new boys. It was Harry Gregg's first game for United.

It was also to be a revolution.

'He [Busby] had a purge,' recalls Charlton. 'He would pull out about five recognised players – you know, really famous players – and then bang five youngsters in, which at that time was unheard of. You never played young players. This was a hard, tough man's game. Put young players in amongst all these big rough diamonds? And suddenly the attention of the whole country was on Manchester United. The Busby Babes can't possibly win anything. But it exploded and it just went on.'

United settled into a good run. The old rhythm and certainty came back. Charlton liked the feeling. He knew he was in a great side because he could feel it in the play: he didn't need results to make him aware of it. The speed of the game was breathtaking, and United were faster than most because they had so many good players. Their play knitted together as if it was the most natural thing in the world.

In the European Cup quarter-final United were drawn against another well-drilled Eastern European side, Red Star Belgrade. The only survivor from the team that had played against the Reds in 1951 was Rajko Mitic, then inside-right but now right-half. Nevertheless, with 11 internationals in their squad Red Star were formidable opposition. United, boasting ten internationals, scraped a 2–1 win in the first leg at Old Trafford, thanks to goals from Bobby Charlton and Eddie Colman. It was less than they'd hoped for ahead of the return in Belgrade.

Before the trip to Eastern Europe United crushed Bolton 7–2 in the League and beat Ipswich 2–0 at Old Trafford in the FA Cup, with both goals scored by Charlton. Then the club suffered the shock of losing director George Whittaker, who died in his bed at the Russell Hotel, United's regular accommodation in London. It happened on 1 February, the night before a game against Arsenal at Highbury just three days before the trip to Belgrade.

More than 60,000 packed into the Arsenal Stadium. Despite the setback of losing George Whittaker, or perhaps because of it, United won 5–4 in one of the greatest matches ever played. Scanlon was man of the match. '. . . the Sunday newspapers could not find enough exclamation marks to do it justice,' said Charlton.

United that day were unbeatable. They felt all the better for playing so well because on the Monday they were off to Belgrade. The Yugoslav capital was difficult to reach in the late 1950s and the country was seen as a hostile Communist place. The Busby Babes were now part of the Cold War.

After their terrible experience getting back from Prague, it was decided that such confusion should never happen again. Walter Crickmer decided to charter a private plane for the second leg so the whole party could travel together on its own schedule. That way they would avoid changing planes in London. But some of the squad weren't keen on going behind the Iron Curtain, whatever the travel arrangements. Eddie Colman certainly wasn't very happy about the trip and made his feelings clear to his girlfriend, Marjorie English, on the eve of the journey. 'I wish I didn't have to go,' he kept telling her. 'I can't believe it,' she said. 'You've got this fabulous job, you can go all over the place.' 'Marje,' he replied, 'I don't want to go.' When Colman left for Belgrade he bent down to kiss his mother goodbye. 'I'm going now, Lizzie,' he said. 'Oh, don't kiss me, Edward, I've got a cold,' she told him.

Unusually, none of the United board would travel with the team to Belgrade, instead staying behind to attend George Whittaker's funeral. There were thus some spare seats on the plane and Matt thought about asking his closest friend, Paddy McGrath, a keen United supporter, to go along. 'I'm going to invite Big Paddy to Belgrade,' he told his wife Jean, namesake of Paddy's wife. 'You can't ask him to go, Jean's near her time, she won't like it,' said Jean Busby. 'All right, I'll not ask him,' said Matt.

Jimmy Murphy, Busby's wartime friend and United's assistant manager, didn't go either. Instead, as manager of Wales, he was needed at Ninian Park for a vital World Cup qualifying play-off game against Israel. By a curious twist of fate Wales had been given a totally unexpected second chance to reach the finals in Sweden later that year; an Arab country had refused to play Israel and were disqualified, and Israel therefore had to play one of the seven runners-up in the other groups. They drew Wales.

The Welsh reprieve gave Murphy a terrible dilemma. He told Busby his heart was really with United and he'd much rather go to Yugoslavia with the boys. He could apologise to the Welsh FA; he felt sure they'd understand in the circumstances. 'No, Jimmy. Your duty is with Wales on this occasion,' Busby told him. Murphy usually sat beside Busby on journeys and had the room next to his on away trips, but he did what the Boss said and let Busby go without him. Chief coach Bert Whalley would take Murphy's seat on the plane next to Busby.

Frank Swift of the *News of the World* was a big Busby supporter. Swifty had been 'adopted' and coached by Busby as a youngster at Manchester City, where they played together, had travelled 2,000 miles behind enemy lines in Italy with Busby's army team and saved Busby's penalty when England beat Scotland at Hampden in 1945. He was an old friend. When Swift's newspaper wouldn't pay for him to go to Belgrade, Busby invited his old pal to travel with the United party on their chartered Elizabethan aircraft.

Geoffrey Green of *The Times* had booked his tickets for United's flight, but at the eleventh hour the manager of his newspaper refused him permission to go for financial reasons. He was sent instead to report on Wales' World Cup match at Ninian Park.

Daily Mirror correspondent Frank McGhee was also due to fly with United, but at the last minute his editor, Hugh Cudlipp, diverted him to the north of England. Cudlipp had an idea for a five towns contest in the north with darts, snooker, brass bands and angling. The trip to Belgrade clashed with a very important darts fixture. Archie Ledbrooke was sent instead.

Donny 'Old International' Davies, of the *Manchester Guardian*, was also drafted in to replace John Arlott.

Wilf McGuinness's name was on the team sheet pinned up by Busby the previous Friday for the Red Star match because of a slight doubt about Roger Byrne, who had pulled his thigh muscle. McGuinness was due to report on the Monday morning, but on the Saturday he twisted his knee in a reserve match against Wolves. He was carried off, and later his knee locked. McGuinness was told on the Sunday morning by physiotherapist Ted Dalton that he might have a cartilage problem, and would have to pull out of the trip.

McGuinness's injury and the doubt about Byrne earned Geoff Bent a rare trip with the first team, at the expense of Ronnie Cope. Bent, who hailed from Salford, had played a dozen games as Byrne's deputy over the previous two years. He had yet to play a League game in the current campaign, but was widely thought to be good enough to have played regularly in most League sides.

Bent went home to tell his wife Marion. 'I'm going to Belgrade tomorrow,' he said. She was shocked. 'I don't have to go,' he added. Bent was worried his wife wouldn't cope alone. 'You won't be able to manage on your own,' he told her. 'I will be able to manage,' she said. 'You go and enjoy yourself.' Years later Marion recalled how unsettled her husband was at the time. 'It was the first time he'd ever been like that, because he just didn't want to go – not there, behind the Iron Curtain.'

The next morning Cope discovered he wouldn't be going to Belgrade. His bag was packed and he was just waiting for the taxi to come when Jimmy Murphy pulled him to one side. 'Ronnie, the Boss has just rung through; Roger Byrne has been injured and he wants Geoff Bent to go in your place.' Cope didn't take it very well. Murphy tried to placate him. 'Well, look, calm down, it's only a trip out,' he said. Cope wasn't satisfied. 'Ah, well, I'll see the Boss when I come back and see about my future,' he said. He wanted a transfer.

The players would be accompanied to Belgrade, as always, by the backroom staff who'd helped weave their varied talents into a single super-fit team widely thought to be capable of dominating world football for years to come. The skill and experience of the young stars, under Busby's watchful eye, meant there were no heights they couldn't aspire to in the years ahead.

Five

United in Belgrade

Before leaving for Manchester's Ringway Airport on the Monday, some of the players went down to the laundry room at Old Trafford to listen to the FA Cup fifth-round draw on the radio. Irene Ramsden and her sister, who loved the players like their own sons, ran the laundry. They were known as Omo and Daz, after the popular soap powders. Busby called them his 'laundry lassies'.

Eddie Colman brought some towels he wanted washed, while Ray Wood was there to hear the draw; he was upset because Harry Gregg would be in goal against Red Star. The players listened intently as United were picked to play Sheffield Wednesday at Old Trafford. It wouldn't be an easy match, but at least they'd got a home draw.

The north's top football writers joined the party of footballers and officials who assembled at Ringway for their flight into the unknown later that Monday. As well as the two Franks, Taylor and Swift, there was *Daily Mail* photographer Peter Howard, his telegraphist Ted Ellyard and writer Eric Thompson; Alf Clarke of the *Manchester Evening Chronicle*; Don Davies of the *Manchester Guardian*; George Follows of the *Daily Herald*; Tom Jackson of the

Manchester Evening News; Archie Ledbrooke of the *Daily Mirror*; and Henry Rose of the *Daily Express*.

Jimmy Murphy turned up to join in the goodbyes. 'See you Thursday, lads,' he said. 'See you do a good job.' United's players knew they faced a difficult task. After their 2–1 first-leg win they were very much aware that the Yugoslavs had a top quality side with some extremely good players. They could look forward to a terrific battle. Dennis Viollet felt that whoever scored first would probably win.

Captain James Thain may not have known much about football or the United party he was flying to Belgrade, but his co-pilot Kenneth Rayment did. He'd piloted the British European Airways service flight that had taken many of them to Bilbao for the European Cup quarter-final against Atletico Madrid the year before.

When the United party boarded the BEA aircraft they were surprised by the unusual interior. The cabin was elegant, spacious and very comfortable. There were ten rows of seats in each section: the four nearest the cockpit faced the back of the plane and the other six faced forward. The Dakotas and Viscounts the United party was used to from previous trips to Europe only had forward-facing seats.

The plane's layout suited the card school, among them Harry Gregg who loved to play poker. He wasn't short of company, since his deputy Ray Wood, Billy Whelan, Johnny Berry and Jackie Blanchflower were also keen players. Busby kept a close eye on the card school. He didn't like it if the stakes were high, because it affected how the players felt about each other. But cards did relieve the boredom of long journeys.

While the United squad was in the air Wilf McGuinness was seeing a specialist. He was told he'd torn his cartilage and would have to have an operation on the Friday.

United's plane landed at Hamburg to refuel before a similar stop in Munich, where the weather was a bit rough with some cloud, though nothing to unduly worry Captain Thain. The landing in Belgrade was more difficult since there was low cloud and fog. In fact, the weather was close to the limits below which BEA's regulations prohibited a landing attempt. The plane only got down to the snowy ground safely after a skilful performance by Rayment, who handled a complex 'let-down' procedure perfectly while Thain looked intently for the runway. The Elizabethan was very quiet, and the airport's station engineer didn't even know the plane had landed until it taxied into the parking area.

The players' families and landladies had made sure they were well prepared for the trip to Eastern Europe, and they'd packed lots of food for their boys, who were loaded down with hundreds of bags of sweets, chocolates and eggs. One player was so worried about going hungry that he'd even taken a miniature gas stove. It was Bobby Charlton's first trip behind the Iron Curtain, but he'd been well briefed by the other lads who'd played against Dukla in Prague. They told him it was dull and depressing. Bill Foulkes remembered the food queues in the Czech capital and the difficulty in getting anything decent to eat. The players told Charlton the food wasn't fit to eat in Prague and that all Iron Curtain countries were the same. The United players were determined not to go short; they'd taken a large stock of tinned food, soup and fresh fruit.

Charlton wasn't going to be caught out. He'd piled chocolates and sweets into his bag and thrown in four packets of biscuits, just in case he got weak from hunger. The customs officer in Belgrade took a long look at them and grinned. He probably thought Charlton was a secret binger. Charlton grinned back politely. A few minutes later, when the United party was dropped off at one of the brightest and most modern hotels Charlton had ever seen, he grinned again, though more sheepishly this time. The place looked like a skyscraper. Harry Gregg thought it was the most beautiful hotel you could ever wish to see. It was a really fabulous place, run by the State for the benefit of foreigners. The food, service and general standards were absolutely first class.

United's luxurious residence was a deceptive introduction to Belgrade. The city was depressing. Blanchflower's main memories of Yugoslavia would be its bleakness and food queues. It was his first trip to the Eastern bloc and it didn't make a very good impression on him. While food didn't seem to be quite so scarce as before, Foulkes thought the whole place gave a horrible impression of poverty. He hoped the Yugoslavs didn't think they could kid the United party that their people were living a wonderful life under

Communist rule. Nevertheless, the players were well looked after and given the VIP treatment. The food at the hotel was so good that Charlton gave his biscuits and sweets to the cleaner! The players didn't need their store of extra rations after all.

The weather in Belgrade was cold and wet. People were even skating near United's hotel. The army stadium pitch, where the game would be played, was covered in thick snow. The city was gripped by the excitement and tension, which only surrounds really big football matches. There was thus no chance of the game being called off.

The Yugoslavs knew all about the Busby Babes long before they came to Belgrade. They were familiar with the great tradition of English football – it was hard but fair. And to the Yugoslavs Wembley was always the place for the big game. Red Star's match against United was therefore a sell-out. According to one report, 'No international match has ever created . . . such a mad scramble for tickets in Belgrade. Soccer chiefs from all the Balkan countries have gathered here in force, and officials of the European Cup Committee, whose headquarters are in Paris, have also made special journeys to see the game.'

The lines on the pitch had been marked in red so the players could see them in the snow. But, amazingly, on the day of the game the sun came out and melted all but a few patches of snow on the pitch. The soft ground would suit United's play. Don Davies of *The Guardian*, writing under his pseudonym of 'Old International', described the scene at the stadium before the match: 'At Belgrade today in warm sunshine and on a grass pitch where the last remnants of melting snow produced the effect of an English lawn flecked with daisies, Red Star and Manchester United began a battle of wits and courage and rugged tackling . . .'

Roger Byrne had come through an intensive fitness test and was cleared to play – Geoff Bent wouldn't be needed after all. Foulkes thought the tension inside the huge stadium was unbelievable, with thousands of people shouting and cheering, while Gregg had never known such partisan support.

Both sides lined up to be presented to local dignitaries. Byrne glanced along at his team-mates: Scanlon, Gregg, Foulkes, Taylor,

Viollet, Charlton, Morgans, Jones, Colman and Edwards. He was in good company. Photographs were taken of what would become known as The Last Line-Up.

Red Star believed they'd sail through the match and easily claw back the first-leg deficit. After the performance the Yugoslavs had put up at Old Trafford, United also expected trouble. Their defence had hardly made a mistake then and on their own ground United reckoned they'd be even harder. But Red Star's complacency contributed to a lapse in concentration from which United scored after just 90 seconds through Viollet. It stunned the 52,000 crowd and eased the pressure on United who now led 3–1 on aggregate.

Red Star responded in the first five minutes with a tackle on Edwards that left him with an injured ankle. The crowd also did their best to knock United out of their stride. Red Star's goalkeeper Beara, nicknamed the Black Cat, was very confident and claimed nobody could beat him from outside the area. But Charlton took the smile off his face on the half-hour with two glorious goals in two minutes – including a mighty drive from outside the box. United were now 3–0 ahead in the match.

In the first half the Reds were very composed, keeping possession and playing with a great deal of confidence. Just before half time, Viollet felt a little bit of 'needle' beginning to creep into the game. Red Star's little inside forward Sekularac started having a go at Edwards. Despite Red Star's tactics, United's 5–1 half-time aggregate lead was daunting.

The British journalists covering the game thought Busby's side were home and dry. Instead, United relaxed and Red Star staged a comeback. Right-winger Morgans, who'd played well until half time, was treated roughly straight after the restart. As United kicked off Morgans saw Sekularac coming towards him. The Yugoslav ran his studs down Morgans's thigh, ripping it open. Austrian referee Karl Kainer warned Sekularac, but he got away with the awful tackle. Morgans limped off.

United kept their cool and continued to play the better football. The 'needle' increased in the second half, when the crowd started getting at United. It wasn't until the game was nearly lost that Red Star started to show United what a good team they were. The first real sign of trouble for Busby's side came when magical inside-left Kostics, a reserve in the 1951 team which played at Old Trafford, beat Gregg from outside the penalty area just two minutes after half-time. It was backs to the wall for United from then on.

After 55 minutes Foulkes went with an opponent for the ball. They both fell. Foulkes struggled up first, only to be dragged down again. Referee Kainer thought Foulkes was trying to push his opponent down and awarded a dubious penalty. Tasic slotted home the spot-kick and Red Star scented blood. The score was now 3–2 in Belgrade and 5–3 on aggregate. The crowd began to scorch the roof of the stadium, bombarding United's players with anything they could get hold of; one or two United players gave the crowd the Winston Churchill victory sign.

The battle Busby's team expected before the match now began. The players lived on their nerves but still felt fairly confident they could win the game. Morgans limped back onto the pitch with just over 20 minutes left. The match continued to be just as physical, with a succession of fouls committed by both sides. The referee had lost his grip.

With just ten minutes left Gregg came out of his area to narrow the angle, slid beyond the edge of the box and collided with a forward. Red Star were awarded a free kick just outside the 18-yard area. United's players formed a wall as Kostics prepared to shoot. They knew all about his famous swerving free kicks. His shot came off the top of Viollet's head, which took a bit of the pace off the ball, and it spun into the top left-hand corner of the net. Red Star had drawn level at 3–3 on the day.

Now all hell was let loose and United came under tremendous pressure. They showed the true character that made them such a great team, but for the players the minutes to full-time seemed endless as they lived up to the name of the Red Devils by fighting to hang onto the draw. Fortunately for United the equaliser had come too late. They held on to reach the semi-final 5–4 on aggregate.

Byrne had never been so glad to hear a final whistle in all his life. United's players were thrilled but very relieved it was over. They walked off the pitch hugging each other as they went. Sheer guts and hard work had got them through the match. Viollet thought anything less would have seen them go under. 'It was an amazingly tough match and it's to the great credit of a wonderful team that we came through it,' he says.

Despite their late scare, Foulkes felt United were by far the better side and Red Star's most experienced players, right-half Mitic and goalkeeper Beara, agreed. 'Manchester United are the better qualified team for the semi-final,' they said.

United didn't care for Red Star's continental tactics, while the Yugoslav players and their fans didn't like what they considered to be tough tackling by the British. They didn't like the way United's players got stuck in and sorted them out while still playing the ball and coming away with it most of the time. Referee Kainer was also heavily criticised. He'd given 24 free kicks against United and 11 against Red Star. United thought his refereeing had been extraordinary, and his handling of the game was vigorously questioned by the British press. (At the end of his career Kainer couldn't remember another game among his 1,812 matches where he got such a bad press.)

Whatever the post-match arguments, the draw was enough to take United into the semi-finals for the second year running. They now believed 1958 would be their year in Europe. Foulkes felt they were good enough to win the European Cup. So did Busby.

Many miles away, at Ninian Park, Cardiff, Jimmy Murphy had been watching his Welsh team play their World Cup qualifier. But his thoughts were more on United's game in Yugoslavia. When he heard they'd reached the semi-final it was a great load off his mind. He didn't like not being there with Matt and the boys.

The Belgrade crowd showed their frustration at the result and the Reds' uncompromising approach to the game by booing the United coach all the way back to the hotel. The main thought in the minds of United's players wasn't the game they'd just played, but the forthcoming match against Wolves on Saturday. It was a crucial encounter in the race for the Championship.

Later that night, the players and officials of United and Red Star joined journalists and local dignitaries at a banquet in the Majestic Hotel. The early years of the European Cup saw great friendships develop between the teams. Although Red Star were clearly disappointed to be knocked out, it was a pleasant evening. United's players liked the Yugoslavs; when they gave a banquet they wanted everyone to enjoy themselves. In Russia, on the other hand, such events were traditional and since the Russians were the last people to break with tradition their dinners were rather dull, 'about as lively as Sunday morning in Oldham', according to Charlton. In Yugoslavia it was different; the post-match banquets were good fun – not that the United squad enjoyed all the proceedings. The players mocked the dignitaries' self-regarding speeches and could barely conceal their sniggers. But they stayed long enough to pick up their customary gift. The year before in Madrid they'd received a gold watch. In Belgrade they were presented with coffee cups. The consolation was that they were served by beautiful Slav waitresses who had fun teasing them.

There was plenty of wine and excellent Yugoslavian violinists. The meal was rounded off when waiters came into the dining room carrying sweetmeats on trays lit by candles set in ice. The United party stood to applaud the skills of the chef, and Byrne led the singing of 'We'll Meet Again', the song made famous by Vera Lynn during the Second World War. Busby and United Secretary Walter Crickmer told the Red Star party they should visit Manchester, where the doors of Old Trafford would always be open to them.

Charlton teamed up with Red Star's inside forward Sekularac, whom he nicknamed Shecky. Sekularac was easy to get along with. Unlike most acquaintances made after international matches, this one would last. (When Charlton later returned to Belgrade with the England team Shecky came round to the hotel to look him up.)

The United squad were by now very relaxed after securing their semi-final place and were looking forward to unwinding after the formalities. They usually had to turn in by 11 o'clock, but Busby gave them an extra hour or two to have a few beers before going to bed, though he reminded them about the tough game against league leaders Wolves on the Saturday. He made them promise they'd get to bed at a reasonable time. The time extension was welcomed. 'We were so excited that there was no way any of us could have gone to bed and got to sleep at 11 o'clock,' recalls Viollet.

Busby retired to a private room in the hotel for a few drinks with some journalists and non-playing members of the United party. He ordered beers and whisky all round – a tradition of their journeys together in the quest for European glory.

Jimmy Murphy was badly missed. He was at the centre of many of the good nights in Europe, and would play the piano for a singsong. The musically versatile Murphy could play popular music or his own versions of Bach and Chopin. That night, Yorkshiremen Mark Jones and Tommy Taylor led the singing of 'Ilkla Moor Baht 'At'. But Busby's contribution, Harry Lauder's 'I Belong to Glasgow', was the highlight of the evening. The players joined in the chorus, but only Busby knew all the words.

Viollet wanted to sample the local nightlife, but there wasn't really anywhere exciting to go in Belgrade. Instead, he went down to the hotel bar, where he had several beers and an enjoyable conversation with Frank Swift. 'I am sure we re-enacted the entire 90 minutes,' says Viollet. They talked for an hour and a half about the game and then went to bed. Everyone had to be up early the next morning to catch the plane back to Manchester.

Miro Radojcic, a correspondent with *Politika*, was one of Yugoslavia's most respected political and sports reporters. His newspaper was soon to describe United as 'unsportsmanlike and often unscrupulous', but that didn't stop Radojcic taking Tommy Taylor, Edwards and Byrne to a bar called Skadarija, or 'Way of Life', for some Slav hospitality. The Crystal Bar, as it had become known, was one of the few nightspots in Belgrade.

Other players went to a cocktail party at the British Embassy staff club with the BEA pilots, stewardesses and the radio operator. The event underlined United's unofficial status as diplomatic visitors to Belgrade. Later, the Embassy staff, obviously pleased with United's behaviour and performance, took some players to their homes, where they tried to ply them with more drinks. Foulkes and Scanlon were each given a bottle of gin.

The team was in high spirits. They knew they were among the best four clubs in Europe, and that brought its own glow of satisfaction. They reckoned they might even prove they were the best of them all, the greatest achievement of any British club. After the tension of the matches with Real Madrid in the semi-finals the previous year, Manchester was very much aware of the importance of the European Cup.

Late that evening, Eddie Colman got up to his usual antics, swapping the shoes the United party had left outside each of their hotel rooms to be polished. He stopped when a team-mate warned him he was moving Busby's shoes – a definite *faux pas*.

By now, the card players were getting restless. Frank Taylor had gone to the hotel bar, as had Pegg and Charlton; like Viollet they were all disappointed that there was no exotic nightlife in Belgrade. They played poker for dinars (3,000 to the £1) until four or five o'clock in the morning. The weak local currency gave the game an air of fantasy. 'I'll open for 3,000,' 'I'll make it 6,000 to play.' It sounded like big-time gambling and they laughed at the ridiculously high-sounding stakes. Gregg was having all the luck and winning most of the money. Halfway through the night the players tucked into the hard-boiled eggs, biscuits and other food their wives and landladies had packed for them and had a party. It was a great night. They eventually went to bed to get some rest before their early departure the next morning.

It was late into the night when Edwards, Tommy Taylor and Byrne said goodnight to Miro Radojcic. Radojcic sat up half the night alone, thinking about his new friends and the feature he wanted to write on them the next day. Radojcic loved football and was attracted by the flair of United's young team. As dawn broke he suddenly had an idea. Why not fly back to England with the official party and write a story about the country's best team from the Manchester angle? That would give more substance to his article.

Radojcic went back to his apartment and packed an overnight bag. Early in the morning he took a taxi to the airport where, as a well-known local personality, he felt sure he could talk his way onto the flight.

Six

Heading for Munich

The next morning, United were heavily criticised in the Yugoslav press. *Politika* said: 'Manchester were unsportsmanlike and often unscrupulous. In the second half the British players felled opponents in an impermissible manner. Many times we asked ourselves where was the British fair play.'

The British papers saw the match differently. The *Daily Express* thought it was 'almost unbearably exciting in the second half, a rough, tough tale of tempers and crazy decisions'. The *Daily Mail* said the referee '. . . would have been howled off an English ground for his niggling anti-tackling phobia.' United had conceded 36 free kicks, while Red Star were penalised 11 times. It was a question of the interpretation. The Yugoslavs saw it one way, the British another. But the referee had the final say.

That morning United's players were told to get their passports, which would be sent ahead to the airport. Harry Gregg got up to fetch his passport from his room and offered to bring Johnny Berry's as well. It was in Berry's suitcase along with his visa. Gregg collected both passports, but since there had been no mention of visas he'd dropped Berry's back into his case. Gregg had his visa with him.

There were some aching heads on the coach as the United party made their way to the airport. The players were tired and a little sore physically, both from the match and the drinking, but they were also happy about their triumph.

A wintry sun shone on the players and officials as they assembled at Belgrade airport for the trip home. It was a larger gathering than had flown out from Manchester. There was, of course, the team, the United officials and the press, as well as Busby's friend Willie Satinoff – a Manchester businessman, keen United supporter and well-known racehorse owner who'd come along for the ride. But they were now joined by travel agent Mr B.P. Miklos and his wife Eleanor; Mrs Vera Lukic, the wife of the Yugoslav air attaché in London, and her baby daughter Vesna; and Mr N. Tomasevic. The crew was the same: Captains Thain and Rayment, Radio Officer Rodgers and three cabin staff, Tom Cable, Margaret Bellis and Rosemary Cheverton.

The United party was feeling the worse for wear after the night's celebrations. They just wanted to get home to Manchester. Radojcic joined them and was told he'd be welcome on their flight. It was then that he discovered he'd left his passport at home. He asked the airport officials to delay the plane for as long as possible while he took a taxi back through the snow to get the all-important document. The plane was, in any case, delayed because Johnny Berry couldn't find his visa. The efficient-looking Yugoslavian woman in charge at immigration wouldn't budge: no visa, no exit. As Gregg well knew, Berry's visa was still where Gregg had dropped it – in his suitcase. That case had by now been loaded onto the plane with the rest of United's luggage. There was thus a delay of about an hour while all the luggage was unloaded. Eventually, they found Berry's suitcase and he was allowed to board the plane.

While Radojcic was frantically racing against the clock, the passengers were settling into their seats in the plane's cabin. As they boarded through the large door at the back of the plane Frank Swift saw his namesake, Frank Taylor. Swift waved and pointed to the empty seat next to him. 'C'mon, Dad,' he shouted. 'I've kept this seat especially for you. Right back here in the tail – the safest place.'

Swifty always said that because in the Second World War many tail-gunners had been thrown clear and survived when their bombers crashed. But Taylor, who did usually sit with his friends at the back of the plane, shook his head. 'No thanks, Frank. There's a lot of space up front.' 'Be like that, Dad,' said Swift laughing. 'What's the matter, are you too good for the rest of us?'

Taylor didn't know exactly why he refused Swift's offer; in fact, he'd been really looking forward to having a few more laughs with the former Manchester City keeper on the flight home. But he'd once read about a terrible air crash in which the only survivor was in a seat facing the back of the plane, and this swayed him. The bad weather usually encountered in February and a crossing of the French Alps didn't indicate a smooth flight, at least on take-off and landing. So Taylor made his way towards the front of the plane. As he passed Matt Busby and Bert Whalley halfway down on the right side, he noticed how tired and drawn Busby looked. This wasn't surprising. It was less than a month since he'd left hospital after an operation on some veins in his leg. It had sapped his energy. Busby should have gone to the South of France to recuperate, but there was no way he was going to miss the crucial European Cup tie in Belgrade. Unfortunately, the midwinter trip had put him under severe strain. It was an indication of his devotion to United that he'd undertaken the journey at all.

At the front was the flight deck, where William Rodgers sat with his radio equipment. Next, on the left side of the aircraft, came the luggage compartment corresponding to the galley on the right side. Then there were two rows of backward-facing seats in pairs. Frank Taylor found a place on the left side of the plane in the middle of the first full row of backward facing seats. On Taylor's left, in the same row but on the other side of the aisle, was United's Irish keeper Harry Gregg. He was spread out across both seats. In front of Taylor sat Bobby Charlton and to Charlton's right, next to the window, was Dennis Viollet. Most of the other players were in the middle of the plane. Johnny Berry, Roger Byrne and Jackie Blanchflower were all ready for their usual game of cards. Bill Foulkes and David Pegg were close by.

As Taylor put his seatbelt on he hoped that one of the other journalists would come and sit with him, but they all had the same idea as Swift. Taylor could see all eight of them laughing and joking together in the rear seats, where he thought he might join them after take-off. Some were going to the annual Manchester Press Ball that night, where Frank Swift was to be the MC. Others were looking forward to getting home to see their families. Meanwhile, in the cockpit, Captain Thain's final briefing to Rayment was that he should do as he wished; Thain would interfere only if he didn't like something.

The Elizabethan took off from Belgrade on a crisp, cold morning. The sky was blue with a hint of sunshine and there was just enough snow on the ground to provide a Christmas atmosphere. But radio reports from Munich weren't encouraging. The cloud base was very low and, with a lot of aircraft using the airport to refuel, the crew would have another landing with full let-down procedure, as they had on arrival in Belgrade on the outbound leg of the journey. Among the passengers there was the usual air of nervous apprehension about the flight. But Foulkes had no worries about flying. 'They could turn the plane upside down and fly it that way for all I cared. If there was turbulence or the plane hit an air pocket it used to fascinate me. Those things never bothered me, because I had complete faith in the aircraft.'

Back in Belgrade Radojcic had returned to the airport in another taxi, only to find that United's plane had already left. Despite the lengthy delay while officials searched for Berry's suitcase the journalist was too late to join his new friends on their flight back to England.

For most of the journey the Elizabethan flew at about 18,500 feet. The temperature outside was between minus 21–25 degrees centigrade, but inside the insulated pressurised cabin it was warm and cosy. The card games, crosswords and conversation hid any visible signs that anyone was afraid of flying. Viollet, Charlton and Pegg fooled about with Eddie Colman, who was sitting further down the plane towards the back. Some people caught up on lost sleep, others looked out at the snow-covered landscape and chatted over the latest news, read books and magazines and generally passed the time as best they could. Busby and his trainers wondered about the

League match against Wolves on Saturday. The players were in a good mood. They were back in the European Cup semi-final, and thinking about beating Real Madrid and going on to win it this time.

Frank Taylor stared out of the window for a while with the route map in his hand, trying to identify the jagged mountain ranges that appeared briefly between the clouds. About one and a half hours into the flight he got bored and felt a little annoyed with himself: he didn't even have a good book to read. Across the gangway he could see Harry Gregg curled up over three seats having a nap. His eyes then wandered down the plane to the card school, where there was a lot of laughing and talking.

There were two card tables in the midships of the aircraft, a six-seater and a four-seater. There was a poker school and a rummy school in the different parts of the plane as the players carried on the card games begun the previous night. Harry Gregg had intended playing cards with the party of six on the flight from Belgrade, but his lucky streak the night before, when he'd won quite a bit of money, had made him cocky and he'd been taking the mickey. He wanted to use up his spare Yugoslav currency and was getting a lot of ribbing from the rest of the boys. 'Ah, Greggy, you miserable bastard, give us a chance to get our money back.' They decided the stakes would be in English money, but Gregg was having none of it. 'No, I'm having a kip,' he said. Gregg told them he'd play after they'd taken off from Munich, where they were due to stop briefly to refuel. He went to sit near the nose of the plane, two seats from the bulkhead on the four-seater side looking diagonally across at the six-seater one seat behind.

Further back in the tail of the plane sat the journalists, among them Taylor's friends Henry Rose of the *Daily Express*, Eric Thompson of the *Daily Mail* and George Follows of the *Daily Herald*. They were laughing and having a good time. Taylor waved to them and shouted: 'There are plenty of seats up here.' Follows shouted back, 'What's the point? We are sitting comfortably here, and we would have to shift all our hand luggage.'

Tired of his self-imposed exile, Taylor decided to join his friends. He passed United trainer Tom Curry who was smoking a pipe and then hesitated as he came alongside Busby and Whalley. Busby looked as grey and tired as when he'd boarded the aircraft in Manchester. The 2,000-mile round trip was catching up with him. Taylor carried on towards the back of the plane and the other sportswriters. All the seats were taken. 'You are a chump,' Swift told him. 'You wouldn't need to stand if you had taken the seat I offered you.'

The plane was by now flying smoothly at about 180 miles per hour as its twin engines droned their way towards Germany and the refuelling stop at Munich. Taylor and his pals were laughing about old times when the 'FASTEN SEATBELT' sign on the bulkhead lit up. He went back to his seat as stewardess Margaret Bellis made an announcement over the intercom: 'In a few minutes we shall be landing in Munich. Extinguish your cigarettes. No more smoking please, and fasten your safety belts. We will have time only for light refreshments in Munich, but we will be serving a proper meal after we take off for Manchester.'

The cloud over Munich was thick from 18,500 feet down to about 500. As the plane nosed into it Rayment switched on the de-icing equipment. Fuel burners in the wings heated the air up to 170 degrees fahrenheit and circulated it under pressure through special ducting built into the leading edges of the wings, the tailplane and the rudder. It was snowing quite heavily as they circled slowly on their descent towards Reim Airport. Taylor grew concerned about the speed of the approach when he felt the plane plunge. It seemed to be losing height far too rapidly. The plane moved lower and lower, with the high wing keeping it on an even keel. Now there were no bumps.

The plane had cut through the low-lying clouds. Taylor realised it must have been tough for the pilots to keep the aircraft steady and bring her down safely in the snowy conditions. The passengers didn't see the ground until the plane was about to touch down because of the very low cloud. Once it was broken they caught their first glimpse of the airfield. Stretching before them was a plain of fresh white snow, streaked with dark pencil lines. Taylor thought the lines must be runways, while the huddle of buildings were the airport offices and restaurant. He could see hedgerows whizzing past the portholes. They passed over the perimeter fence and, after one final downward thrust, skimmed along the runway.

It was starting to snow again and the ground was slushy. The wheels threw back the snow and the spray soared high above the cabin windows. The snow had looked white from the air, but once the plane was on the ground it was churned into a dirty, dark brown slush. Taylor tensed and leaned closer to an emergency exit in case the aircraft suddenly skidded on the ice. In the cockpit Rayment applied the brakes. The plane was at last cruising down the runway before turning off towards the terminal buildings and the refuelling point. The engines were switched off at 1311.

Those on board were in a relaxed mood when they landed on German soil. Taylor certainly felt much happier now they were safely down. The first part of the journey was over. It wouldn't take long to fill the plane with petrol while they had a warm drink, and then they'd be heading back to their families in Manchester. Taylor was looking forward to seeing his wife Peggy and his two boys, Andrew and Alistair.

It had been raining in Munich from early morning until almost midday, and the rain had then slowly turned to snow. The tarmac was a mixture of water and slush. Foulkes felt they'd skidded pretty badly when the plane landed. The temperature was above freezing but the air outside was still raw and as soon as the cabin door was opened a biting wind blew into the plane.

Duncan Edwards was the first to face the sleet. It lashed across his face as he walked down the steps. Edwards looked huge in his overcoat as his strong arms moved backwards and forwards. 'Get your snowshoes on, lads. Short studs are no use in this stuff,' he called over his shoulder as he trudged through the slush to the airport terminal.

It was a welcome break for the passengers as they trooped into the terminal building. They were glad to have the chance to stretch their legs. It was so cold that the United party scurried towards the terminal as fast as they could to seek out the promised light refreshments. They were looking forward to getting home; it was just a few more hours' flying time from Munich.

As the United party filed into the coffee lounge, Captains Thain and Rayment, and Radio Officer Rodgers, were splashing their way to the Met office for a briefing on the weather conditions for the rest of the journey to Manchester.

The ground staff refuelled the plane, supervised by BEA Station Engineer William Black. The Elizabethan carried 1,000 gallons of fuel, 500 in each wing. It was usually filled with petrol under pressure from below the wing, but since Black was the only licensed Elizabethan engineer available that system couldn't be used. Instead, he supervised refuelling through the emergency filter on top of the wing. Black covered the aperture with tarpaulin to keep out the snow. As he moved along the wing he noticed the snow melting as it hit its surface. None of it was sticking to the top and the shortage of snow on the wing didn't help the refueller; as some of the United players passed by on their way to the airport lounge they pelted him with snowballs, but he couldn't collect enough snow to throw any back.

Edwards was the first to enter the warmth of the coffee lounge. Eventually, Eleanor Miklos, the wife of the travel agent who'd organised the trip, served them all with coffee. Frank Taylor joined his friends in the annexe to the main lounge. Through the window, which ran the full length of the room, he had a clear view of the airfield. He could see the ground crew working on the Elizabethan and wondered whether they were checking for ice on the wings, like in wartime Britain.

In the Met office Thain and Rayment completed the flight plan. Thain took it to the Air Control office while Rayment went to the BEA office. They met up again outside the building and talked about the snow that had fallen on the wings. Rayment said he'd looked at them and they didn't need to be swept. Thain agreed and left to sign the plane's papers in the BEA office while Rayment walked to the Elizabethan. Thain then made his way to the plane and, as he approached it, studied the snowfall on the right wing. A thin film had formed but couldn't easily be seen because it had thawed where it had fallen on the ribs. Thain watched the melting snow running off the trailing edge of the wing. As he stood by the plane, Station Engineer Black asked if he should apply defrosting liquid. Thain replied that, no, it wasn't necessary.

When it landed, the plane had two minor faults: the toilet pump was unserviceable and the water system for the galley needed topping up. Black had arranged for the problems to be fixed. The cold water tank was refilled from a servicing panel aft of the crew door. As Thain neared the aircraft a man struggled to lift a stiff hose to the level of the panel. He slithered about as he tried to get a grip with his rubber boots in the slush. Thain put his foot behind the man's heel and steadied him as he connected the hosepipe and pumped water into the tank.

All the passengers were by now anxious to get home, though some of the players had a last look round for presents and souvenirs as they wandered through the airport shops. The place didn't make much impression on Bobby Charlton, but then airports never did. They were the same the world over. Johnny Berry kept one girl busy winding up mechanical toys he was thinking of buying for his kids. Then the call came over the tannoy: 'Will all passengers with the Manchester United party please board now . . .' 'Thank God for that,' said Henry Rose. 'We don't want any hold-ups. I've got to complete my "Postbag" for the *Express* before going to the press ball tonight.' His sports 'Postbag' was a popular item in the paper and one of the secrets of his success. He carried it everywhere – on planes, trains and even into airport lounges. 'Come on, we're going,' somebody called. There had been a delay of only about ten minutes.

United trainer Tom Curry stood by the door and counted the players to make sure nobody was left behind. The party stood together outside the coffee lounge as they were counted again before squelching across the tarmac to the waiting plane. As they did, Foulkes asked the steward Tommy Cable what time they'd land in Manchester. He looked at his watch. 'It should be about seven o'clock,' he told Foulkes. The passengers, clutching their duty-free goods, trooped back on board. Taylor paused as he entered the plane to see his press colleagues fastening their seatbelts. 'I'll come back and join you as soon as we are airborne,' he told them before pushing his way through the crowded gangway to his own seat and fastening himself in. Charlton strapped himself into his seat next to Dennis Viollet and waited.

Seven

Disaster Strikes

Within half an hour the United party was once again returning to the coffee lounge in the terminal building after two aborted take-off attempts while the crew discussed options. 'It's probably ice on the wing,' Frank Taylor told Frank Swift as the passengers trooped off the plane. 'We might be here for two or three hours.'

It began to snow quite heavily as the party trooped back across the slushy tarmac. Harry Gregg sensed that the atmosphere was one of trepidation, but there was also an air of bravado and some optimism. Frank Taylor looked up at the wing of the Elizabethan monoplane as they passed to see if ice on the wings could have been the problem. He'd been an airframe fitter in the RAF for five and a half years during the Second World War, and it was the first thing a rigger would look for in snowy conditions. Taylor stared hard at the high wing. It was impossible from the ground to get a full view of the upper surface. But why was he concerned? The ground crews would have checked the wings when they refuelled. Besides, it was 13 years since he'd serviced a plane; there were new innovations like heaters in the wings and other gadgets. First-class ground engineers would be servicing the plane; they'd know what they were doing. He removed such thoughts from his mind. On the way to the coffee lounge he told Duncan Edwards and Bobby Charlton there was no danger whatever the problem, because there was a point of no return on the runway where the pilot could still pull up safely if he wasn't happy.

Back in the airport lounge the players were pretty quiet. Most sat around waiting. Some looked round the shops again and got more presents and cigarettes. Coffee was ordered and Eleanor Miklos dashed about once again serving everyone. Gregg told some of the others they probably wouldn't be flying home that afternoon. They all began to talk about the possibility of travelling back to England overland, via the Hook of Holland. They could have a good time with a few beers. But nobody really took the suggestion seriously, and they all had a good laugh despite the tension.

The first two attempts to take off had been quite unnerving. Duncan Edwards was convinced they wouldn't be flying that day. He sent a telegram to his landlady, Mrs Dorman, at Gorse Avenue, Stretford: 'ALL FLIGHTS CANCELLED FLYING TOMORROW = DUNCAN'.

The journalists were livelier than the players. Their apprehension was masked by the usual jokes. Archie Ledbrooke of the *Mirror* was laughing at the antics of the *News of the World*'s Frank Swift and the *Mail*'s Eric Thompson. Swift, over six feet tall, was swapping overcoats with Thompson, who was only just over five feet. Someone asked if there were any good hotels in Munich, just in case the engineers didn't find the problem and the party had to stay overnight. Henry Rose of the *Express* wandered from one group of people to another, trying to find out why the plane had stopped. 'We must get back tonight,' he said. 'It's the press ball in Manchester. I'm going into the office first to finish my "Postbag", although I've mopped up most of it already.'

Meanwhile, Black, the station engineer, had immediately gone to the cockpit to check on the trouble. The pilots explained about the boost surging. Black told them it was quite common at high altitude airports like Munich. Rayment had flown there in the past and was aware of the problem; Thain had also landed at Munich before but only in Vikings. Black described the recommended procedures to overcome the problem, but the pilots explained that they'd already tried these without completely eliminating the noise. The only other course of action Black could propose was retuning the engines, meaning an overnight stop. Thain didn't think that was necessary because the right engine had performed normally. They talked about opening the throttles even more slowly. Finally, after discussing the state of the runway, Thain said they'd attempt to take off again. The pilots didn't leave the cockpit, but they talked about the snow and looked at the wings from the flight deck. They agreed that the plane had lost the film of snow they'd noticed before the first take-off attempt. Once again they decided there was no need to sweep the wings.

It was only then that they discovered they had no passengers. The pilots hadn't realised the United party had returned to the terminal. Black went to tell the Traffic Officer to recall the passengers. Suddenly a voice came over the loudspeakers in the terminal building asking them to board the plane once more. They were astonished. Foulkes had only just got his coffee when the announcement was made. He shivered as a cold feeling swept over him. Frank Taylor was also surprised, as it seemed only a few minutes since they'd got off. Gregg and Blanchflower hadn't even had time to light their cigarettes. Blanchflower stuck a fag Gregg had given him behind his ear and the pair of them made their way to the door.

Vera Lukic, who'd joined the flight in Belgrade so that she and her baby daughter, Vesna, could be with her diplomat husband in Britain, was petrified. She had decided to take a taxi to the train station when Frank Taylor came up to her. 'Mrs Lukic, the plane is ready,' he said. 'We must go to Manchester.' Reluctantly, she joined Taylor and the rest of the passengers making their way to the door of the terminal building.

United trainer Tom Curry again stood by the door to make sure nobody was missing. 'Come on, Geoff . . . come on, Roger . . . Duncan . . . Eddie . . . Billy. We don't want to be kept here all night. All aboard now.' Most of them hadn't had time to drink their coffee before they were herded out to the plane.

Despite the heavy fall, the snow was no more than a footprint deep as the United party squelched back to the plane. Some players joked about crashing. 'Well, this is it, boys,' they said. But Foulkes wasn't worried anymore. He'd got his nerve back and assured himself how much he enjoyed flying. He'd never been worried by it; he could have flown upside down in a thunderstorm and it wouldn't have bothered him at all. But as Frank Taylor trudged through the snow he harboured a nagging doubt: 'They couldn't have de-iced in this short time. Must have done it before we left Belgrade, or maybe when we first landed. It certainly couldn't have been done in these past few minutes.'

Some of the passengers were uneasy after the failed take-off attempts, but they all trooped back on to the plane without any signs of panic or protest. Busby wanted the United party to get back that Thursday so the players could have a good day's rest before playing Wolves on the Saturday. They were anxious to get home. Nobody had the courage to stand up and say, 'This is crazy.' Like most people, they were afraid to lose face in front of their friends. As Gregg would say many years later, 'Sometimes it takes a brave man to be a coward.' Besides, they knew that pilots didn't take risks. Their lives would be as much in danger as those of their passengers if they did.

Nobody heard the pilots talking about the snow on the wings or their decision not to have them swept, but by now the implications were clear. The plane was the centre of attention in the airport and there was much muttering about developments on the tarmac.

Inside the terminal building in his first-floor office the Airport Director was preparing for the arrival later in the day of Chancellor Konrad Adenauer. The director stood by the window and watched. On the floor above a group of young trainees looked down at the plane and discussed the amount of snow they thought they could see on the wings. They wondered why it hadn't been swept. Somebody took a photo of the gloomy scene; through the camera's viewfinder it looked as if there was some snow on the wings. An army officer touring the airport installations had watched the first two take-off attempts from the control tower. He now waited with a colleague near the baggage ramp on the apron.

A Volkswagen carrying two members of the airport staff drove down the runway to check that Chancellor Adenauer would be in no danger when his plane landed. A Convair took off and was almost submerged in waves of spray and slush. It would have been a typical scene for a fairly busy airport on a dark, wet, winter afternoon except for the presence of the Elizabethan aircraft with which all didn't seem to be right.

As the passengers walked up the steps at the back of the plane *Mail* photographer Peter Howard took a picture. 'Another scoop,' said Duncan Edwards as he went inside the cabin. When Frank Taylor reached the door of the plane he saw a reassuringly broad back which he thought must belong to Station Engineer Black. There was obviously a technical discussion going on in the cockpit. Whatever the cause of the failed take-off attempts, they'd have it under control now. Taylor walked into the plane without any lingering doubts as he moved along the gangway.

The card school was just settling down again. The banter among the players continued, but it had an understandably nervous tone. Having endured two aborted take-offs, the passengers were not surprisingly subdued. The first thing Harry Gregg noticed when he entered the cabin was the unusual sight of the steward, Tom Cable, securely strapped into his seat. It took courage to be a coward and if Cable felt like that who were they to complain, thought Gregg. Nevertheless, it was hardly reassuring for the passengers. 'You are now asked to fasten your seatbelts very tightly,' said one journalist. Gregg had decided that when the plane took off he'd give the card players a chance to get their money back. In the meantime, he returned to the makeshift bed he'd arranged before they landed. As he walked up the aisle he noticed Bill Foulkes's head protruding above the top of his seat. 'Hell, if anything goes wrong here he's going to be decapitated,' thought Gregg.

Everybody changed seats. Bobby Charlton moved from the one he'd sat in opposite Gregg on the flight from Belgrade to a place closer to the front. Dennis Viollet did the same. The card school had been set up again but David Pegg, who'd spent the first two take-off attempts sitting on the other side of Charlton, didn't want to play anymore. He also decided to move. 'I don't like it here,' said Pegg, 'it's not safe.' He went to the back of the plane to sit with his best friend, Eddie Colman, who'd also moved from a seat closer to the front, and Tommy Taylor. Frank Swift stood up near the back and said, 'That's right, lads, this is the place to be.'

Gregg decided to get down below the height of the back of the seat. He sat very low, opened the front of his trousers and pulled his tie down. Then he slipped even deeper into the seat and propped his legs up against the one in front of him. Directly across the gangway were Vera Lukic and her daughter Vesna, and in front of them, on facing seats, sat the poker school.

There were five players across the aisle to the right of Foulkes on a six-seater: Roger Byrne, Johnny Berry and Liam 'Billy' Whelan sat on one side, with Ray Wood and Jackie Blanchflower on the other. Byrne was holding a camera. A seat had been left for Gregg who looked up, grinned at Byrne and said, 'I don't want to die in Germany, I don't speak German.' Frank Taylor sat in Charlton's old seat, directly behind the five card players.

Foulkes took his shoes off to make himself more comfortable and slid down in his seat as far as he could. Gregg could still see his head over the top of the seat in front of him. Foulkes was next to a window about halfway down the aircraft, on the right-hand side of the gangway, with his back towards the cockpit. Foulkes had been playing cards on the flight from Belgrade with Kenny Morgans, who sat to his right, and David Pegg and Albert Scanlon, who were both facing him. It wasn't a gambling school; they'd just had a few rounds of Find the Lady, or something similar. This time they didn't play cards and Foulkes put them in their cardboard pack.

On the surface everyone seemed calm as the tables were cleared for the promised meal; in reality, they were all apprehensive as they sat back waiting for take-off. Gregg looked at Foulkes and again thought, 'If this thing belly-flops it'll jack his brains out.' The bulkhead, which held the wings on, was directly above Foulkes's head. Matt Busby and Bert Whalley sat together on the seat behind, while Mark Jones, Tommy Taylor and Duncan Edwards were all at the back of the plane where they'd now been joined by Eddie Colman and David Pegg.

Frank Taylor, who'd been at the back with the other journalists on the flight to Belgrade, came to the front, where he'd sat on the trip from Belgrade, to talk to someone. He was asked to sit down and strap himself in, which he did. Taylor was three seats away from the partition, which separated the passengers from the galley where the stewardesses prepared the food and drinks. Beyond that was the radio officer's place and then the cockpit. The crew were just getting things in order as Station Engineer Black left. Taylor half turned and looked over his left shoulder to speak to Peter Howard of the *Mail*. 'Pretty quick, don't you think, Pete?' he said, referring to how fast the ground crew had solved the technical fault. Howard nodded. Taylor resisted the temptation to change seats. Instead, he discreetly slipped his false teeth out.

Although there was no panic there was a sense of unease, perhaps even more than that, from some people. Charlton fastened his seatbelt and looked at his watch: 2.50 p.m. Nobody was talking much now. 'I am not taking my coat off this time,' Charlton told Dennis Viollet.

The stewardess counted the passengers. 'Everyone here?' she asked, making a last-minute check as the plane moved towards the runway. 'Blimey,' she said, 'we're one short.' There was a call to stop the plane. Tom Curry checked the players as the stewardess looked through the passenger list. Alf Clarke of the *Manchester Evening Chronicle* was missing. The chance of United being stranded in Munich all night had awakened his journalistic instincts. He'd called his office just after 2.30 p.m. to file a short story saying the flight would be held up by the weather. It could have been another scoop. He told the office he'd made arrangements to return the next day. He'd bought tickets for the press ball that night and so he also phoned his wife to tell her that because of the delay at Munich they might be late into Manchester.

Having finished his calls, Clarke hurried breathlessly across the tarmac to the waiting Elizabethan. When he finally got back on board he was greeted by mocking cries of 'Scoop, scoop, scoop'. The players were getting tired and impatient. 'Come on, Alf . . . quick, man . . . ' they said. 'Here comes Alf. Good old Alf . . . come on, we want to get home.' Clarke fastened his seatbelt. He was clearly upset that he'd caused the delay. 'What are you so excited about?' he said. 'Anyone would think we were going somewhere special. I had to tell the office about the delay. After all, we might have had to stay in

Munich all night.' 'Oh blimey, don't say that, Alf,' someone said.

The pilots were informed that the last passenger was aboard. Steward Tom Cable got up from his seat across the aisle from Albert Scanlon and went to the back of the plane to shut the door prior to take-off, and Rayment gave an estimated arrival time. The stewardess told the passengers lunch would be served straight after take-off. On the flight deck, Thain and Rayment stayed in the positions they'd taken up at Belgrade, Rayment flying the aircraft from the left-hand seat, Thain, acting as co-pilot, sitting on the right. Thain made it clear that if boost surging occurred on this run he'd control the throttles.

At 1456 and 30 seconds Rayment was at last able to ask the control tower for permission to taxi out to runway 24/25, and then the pilots conducted a complete power check and routine cockpit checks. At 1500 they sent another message: 'Munich – 609 Zulu Uniform is ready for take-off.' The tower responded: '609 – the wind three zero zero one zero knots – cleared for take-off.'

At 1502 Rayment received an ultimatum. 'Your clearance void if not airborne by zero four. Time now zero two.' The pilots had two minutes to decide if they were ready to take off for Manchester. If not they'd have to delay the return home again, and this time the wait could be much longer. 'Understand valid until zero four,' confirmed Rayment.

It was still snowing outside the air-conditioned cabin and the temperature had fallen further. A sheet of ice and slush covered the runway. Inside the passengers were fidgeting. For most, the desire to get the journey over was tempered by the uneasy feeling that it was tempting fate to try to take off a third time. Some were scared. Roger Byrne was in the seat next to the window. He didn't like flying and looked terrified. Roger joked that it was all or nothing now, a sentiment echoed by Foulkes. Johnny Berry, sitting next to Byrne, also disliked flying at the best of times. Gregg looked across at the six-seater and saw Berry's face contorted with fear. Gregg was also quite worried by this time – indeed, everyone was – but he tried to crack a few jokes. Billy Whelan, a devout Irish Catholic who would have made a good priest, leaned across to Albert Scanlon and said, 'Albert, this is the end but I'm ready for it.'

Frank Taylor, on the other hand, didn't understand why people were alarmed. There were even a few weak jokes about checking whether the pilot had got the elastic fully wound up ready for take-off. 'Had we been in a depressed state after defeat we might have been more apprehensive,' wrote Matt Busby years later. 'As it was we had just won our way into the semi-final of the European Cup, a most cheerful situation.'

Frank Taylor hadn't eaten breakfast and was looking forward to the meal they'd been promised when Rayment and Thain decided to try to take off one more time. Suddenly, there was a thunderous roar as the engines burst into life. Taylor listened intently. Not a cough or a splutter as the motors throbbed louder and louder, until they'd reached their familiar high-pitched whine. Then the plane began to roll away from the terminal buildings to the runway.

At 1503 Radio Officer William Rogers informed the tower that Zulu Uniform was moving again. 'Roger – thank you. Rolling,' he said. 'Munich tower – Roger,' came the reply.

Rayment opened the throttles to 28 inches with the brakes on. The engine revved up and the readings were both steady. He released the brakes and the plane moved forward again. Sprays of slush arched from the wheels, streaming past the cabin windows and blocking the view. Foulkes could see the snow coming down and the slush flying about through the Elizabethan's big windows.

On the trip the players had been passing around a book called *The Whip* by Roger McDonald. It was a piece of titillating pulp fiction regarded as a bit risqué. The book had reached Gregg and he was reading it on the plane. He'd been brought up on hellfire, brimstone and damnation and it crossed his mind that if they crashed while he was reading it and he died, he'd go straight to hell. As the plane moved towards the runway again Gregg, from his vantage point under the wing, put the book down and watched the wheels churning up the slush like a speedboat.

On the flight deck, Rayment continued to open the throttles. Thain again followed with his left hand until the levers were fully open. He tapped Rayment's hand and Rayment moved it. Rayment called 'Full power' and Thain, watching the instrument readings like a hawk, replied 'Full power'. Temperatures and pressures were satisfactory and the warning lights were put out. The speed and roar of the engines built up but not, to the sensitive ear, as fast or as smoothly as they should have done.

Viollet, watching the wheels through the plane's windows, felt a terrific surge. At about 85 knots an hour, however, the old problem started again: Thain noticed a sign of boost surging. He called out 'Port surging slightly' to Rayment above the noise of the engines as he pulled the port throttle lever back until the surging was controlled and the reading was 54 inches. Thain then pushed the throttle back again until it was fully open, indicating 57 inches throughout. He called 'Full power' and looked at the temperatures and the pressures. Thain then glanced at the air speed indicator. It registered 105 knots. The recommended procedure seemed to have worked.

But the solved problem was quickly replaced by a new one. The air speed indicator needle was flickering. The figures flashed before Thain. When they reached 117 knots he called out 'V1'. This was Velocity One, the point on the runway Frank Taylor had mentioned to Charlton and Edwards, after which it wasn't safe to abandon take-off.

Thain waited for a positive indication of more speed so he could call 'V2' – the speed required before taking off. In this case it was 119 knots. Rayment adjusted the trim of the aircraft. Thain hadn't looked out of the cockpit, but didn't feel anything to suggest the plane was losing speed. The needle wavered at 117 knots and then suddenly fell to about 112. He was now aware of the lack of acceleration. What the hell was going wrong this time? The needle dropped further, to about 105 knots, and then wavered. In the cabin, Viollet felt the loss of power, as though they were braking, and saw the wheels locking.

Thain had experienced a failure of the air speed indicator at a similar stage of take-off once before, but had continued and the aircraft took off normally. On that occasion it was later discovered that an engineer working on the instruments had removed the panel and on replacing it had somehow trapped a tube leading to the air speed indicator. This had prevented the instrument from giving a correct reading. This flashed through Thain's mind when he now saw the indicator showing a loss of speed.

Back in the cabin the card-school boys had a go at Gregg again. 'Give us a chance, you miserable swine,' they called out. But Gregg was concentrating on the view out of his window, watching a tree and a house passing by. *Daily Mail* photographer Peter Howard, sitting in the second row of seats on the right side of the aircraft with Ted Ellyard, thought he heard the right engine make a noise like a car changing gear. Gregg also detected a change in the tone of the engine on his side of the plane and sensed that it seemed to be straining, though he couldn't be sure. Others also thought they heard the engine note on the right side drop.

Frank Taylor didn't notice any change in the sound of the engine, but was becoming slightly alarmed at the huge wave of slush being thrown backwards by the port wheel. He wondered why it was taking so long to become airborne. Gregg's eyes were glued to the window, watching the slush spray up as the wing wheel tore through the carpet of snow. The rod connecting the underside of the wing to the wheel was going up and down like a yo-yo, but there was still no sign that the plane was lifting off the ground.

The plane ploughed along the runway, speeding past a red building on the right that it had stopped almost opposite on the two previous runs. They were passing places Gregg hadn't seen before. Frank Taylor was sure they'd already gone past the point of no return, although he couldn't see whether the wheels had left the ground because of the wave of brownish slush. 'Have the wheels gone up yet?' he shouted to Viollet and Charlton. Although they were sitting just in front of him, they couldn't hear above the roar of the engines and gave no reply. Charlton watched the fields slipping past the window. 'We're taking a long time getting off,' he thought. As they sped on and on and on Matt Busby's thoughts sounded just like that: 'On and on and on and on,' until they changed to 'Too long, too long, too long!'

The plane was not going up. Rayment shouted, 'Christ, we can't make it!' Thain looked up from the instrument panel for the first time and realised they were running out of runway.

Beyond the perimeter fence, outside the airfield, stood a house that normally wasn't a hazard. Amid the snow Thain could see the house and a tree in the path of the aircraft. He raised his left hand from behind the throttles and banged furiously on the levers to try to get more power out of the two engines as he fought desperately to avoid disaster. He was trying to give the plane enough lift to get off the ground. But the throttle levers were already in the fully forward position. Meanwhile, Rayment was pulling the control column back.

Foulkes was suddenly hit by the strongest possible feeling of foreboding. Somehow he knew they weren't going to make it. He quickly slipped his pack of cards into his right hip jacket pocket. Then he crouched down in his seat again with his head on his chest. He strapped himself in so tightly his seatbelt was almost cutting him in half; he could hardly breathe. He was extremely uneasy and kept thinking they shouldn't be taking off, they were wrong to take off. How could they take off in all this snow? By now the engines were surging as if they just couldn't get going. Once again Viollet felt the sensation of a surge and then a loss of power. Even then he didn't think anyone was worried; it was just a question of waiting for the plane to leave the ground.

As Gregg listened to the engines straining it was obvious to him that something was going very wrong. He didn't know why, but he loosened his tie and unfastened the top button of his shirt. Then he slid his six-foot frame downwards in his seat, instinctively put his feet against the back of Foulkes's seat in front of him and braced himself. Gregg's mouth was dry; he felt tense. He could hardly see Foulkes's head now Foulkes had slid downwards in his seat. Gregg realised Foulkes was also bracing himself. For what, he thought? Someone began to laugh in an uneasy sort of way. 'What are you laughing at?' said Johnny Berry. 'We're all going to get fucking killed here.'

As the Elizabethan sped past the landing lights it was clear to both pilots that they had to take emergency steps. Rayment hurriedly called 'Undercarriage up' and Thain made a desperate attempt to retract it so the aircraft could slide on its belly to a quick stop. He selected 'up', put his hands out in front of him, gripped the ledge and peered over the edge. The aircraft's passage was smooth, as if it had taken off. Foulkes felt the plane bounce and then go up in the air. Gregg also thought they seemed to be rising and felt the undercarriage going up. Stewardess Rosemary Cheverton believed they were airborne.

In fact, the Elizabethan hadn't left the ground at all. Suddenly, Foulkes noticed a lot of slush flying past the windows and heard a terrible noise, like when a car leaves a smooth road and starts to run over rough ground. The plane had slowly turned to the right and skidded off the runway onto the grass stopway. Jackie Blanchflower also felt as if the plane was going down a cobbled road. Rayment slammed on the brakes, but the aircraft was impossible to control. Gregg was aware that the brakes were being applied. Here we go again, he thought as the plane began to slide.

Frank Taylor leaned over as far as his seatbelt would allow so he could look back through the window to see what was in front of the plane. His feeling that they'd passed the point of no return became a shattering reality when he saw a line of wooden poles making up the perimeter fence. There was 250 yards of grass stopway beyond the concrete runway, and just 50 yards left. As Taylor saw the fence rushing towards them his heart froze. Fear washed over him. He knew in that chilling split second that they would crash. Viollet turned to Charlton and said, 'Hey, Bob, just relax.' But Charlton had also seen the fence coming at them and knew they couldn't clear it. He had no idea what lay beyond.

The control tower heard a howling, whistling noise as Radio Officer William Rogers sent his last message: '15 hours 04 minutes 00 seconds: Munich from B-Line Zulu Unif . . .' The words stopped abruptly. The tower heard a loud background noise as the plane roared on and crashed through the perimeter fence. At the exact moment Bill Foulkes expected the plane to get off the ground he heard the first of a series of sickening bangs. Gregg also heard a terrific smashing sound. Busby and many of the other passengers threw out their hands to shield their faces. But that noise was the last thing Charlton would remember.

As the plane crossed a minor road, Thain knew they couldn't get between the tree and the farmhouse up ahead. Inside the house, mother-of-four Anna Winkler was busy sewing. Her husband was away and her eldest daughter was at a neighbour's. Two other children were asleep. Thain lowered his head and waited for the impact. The plane's wheels struck a small ridge and began bouncing across rough ground. After another 250 yards there was an unmerciful screech and a bang. Frank Taylor, still confused by the sight of the boundary fence, felt a sudden blow behind his left ear and his senses slipping away. 'A playful tap from an overzealous Frank Swift?' he wondered. No, he was sitting yards away. Harry Gregg, perhaps? Taylor fought to stay conscious. In his dazed state he felt a fierce bucking and a tremendous rending of metal, with the plane shaking like a wild thing. Taylor thought he saw the wheel on the left side crashing through the crumpled fuselage towards him. He heard confused noises, a fearful ripping and tearing and grinding of metal like a giant hammering the side of the plane with a sledgehammer. Then he passed out. Gregg also heard tearing, ripping, thumping and banging as the wing on the left side of the plane, only a few feet from Taylor, smashed into the farmhouse. The wing, part of the tail unit and most of the undercarriage were ripped off and the house burst into flames. As the fire spread Anna Winkler threw two of her terrified children into the snow, while four-year-old Anna crawled out through a window.

About 100 yards further on from the house, the right side of the fuselage behind the remaining wing struck a wooden hut containing a truck loaded with fuel and tyres. There was a tremendous noise as it exploded into a pungent fireball. The impact ripped off the rear of the plane just behind the wing, where the card tables were. That rear portion, containing the journalists, careered off on its own for another 70 metres, tearing up snow-covered ground and stripping off one of the engines before hitting a barn. What remained of the undercarriage had been torn away as the plane broke in half leaving the front, with the right wing still attached, slithering and screeching along.

A number of passengers, including Bobby Charlton, Dennis Viollet, Matt Busby and Jackie Blanchflower, were thrown out of the plane into the snow. Blanchflower was catapulted out of the top as the front section clattered and bumped along the ground. He lay in the slush watching the front part of the plane spinning round as it lurched helplessly out of control. The wing sliced through the trees in its path like a giant scythe and the plane turned on its side, almost upside down. A lorry driver watched a wheel come off the undercarriage and shoot towards him.

The passengers inside felt everything going upside down and round and round. *Daily Mail* photographer Peter Howard experienced a rolling-over sensation as he cartwheeled through the air. Foulkes also had a feeling of spinning all over the place. Gregg felt that the whole crazy, bucking aircraft must be spinning round and doing cartwheels. The seat in front of him kept pressing against his outstretched legs and he had to force them forward again. The terrible crashing, grinding noise went on, but Gregg couldn't hear a whimper or a murmur from anyone. He thought about death: stark, ugly death. 'I won't see my wife and little girl again,' he said to himself. He thought about the great life and wonderful family he'd had. And in a dazed, stupid sort of way, he thought of death in a strange land and, ridiculous as it was, the fact that he couldn't even speak German. Finally, he thought about his parents and Ireland.

As the plane twisted it hit another tree just beyond the house and this came through the left side of the flight deck, where Rayment was sitting. The bulkhead behind Frank Taylor was caving in and all sorts of stuff, including the luggage, started coming down on top of the passengers. Some of them were sent hurtling through the air inside the cabin. Howard suddenly felt as if the plane was breaking up. Seats started to crumble. Everything seemed to be falling to pieces. He instinctively put his arm up to prevent a suitcase hitting his face. Howard landed on his hands and knees as the front of the plane span round and round. There wasn't time to think. Busby thought the world was crashing in on them. 'This is it,' thought Foulkes as the passengers were thrown all over the place. Gregg felt something hammer the top of his head. Blood ran down his face and for a split second he thought his head had come off. Foulkes was also hit on the back of the head and was suddenly looking up at the sky. He couldn't believe what was happening. One moment he was looking at the pack of cards in his hand, and the next the tail of the plane seemed to fall away in front of him. Everything seemed to go black all of a sudden for Gregg and Foulkes, as if darkness had fallen. Foulkes lost consciousness for a couple of seconds. Gregg could smell the stench of aircraft fuel. Then more objects hit the front and back of his head and his nose. Small shafts of light appeared, as sparks began to fly, then it was dark again. He alternated between darkness and light, consciousness and unconsciousness.

There was then a hellish noise before, quite suddenly, the plane stopped. Blanchflower saw a little puff of fire coming out of it. Inside the cabin there was no noise at all – just absolute quiet. Everybody seemed to be struck dumb. There was no screaming or shouting, no crying or moaning, just deadly silence. It must only have been quiet for seconds, but it seemed a long time to Howard. Thain thought it was uncanny.

Radio Officer Rogers never did finish his call to the control tower.

The administrative staff in the airfield buildings watched in horror as fire engines and ambulances hurtled down the runway. The vehicles were racing towards a terrible scene. The Elizabethan, now just a mangled heap of metal, lay half-buried in the icy sludge and mud. A pall of murky black smoke billowed up to mark its final resting-place. It was just 54 seconds since the plane had begun rolling down the runway. The once-sleek aircraft was now a smouldering ruin that had left a trail of death and destruction. Less than a minute before, Frank Taylor had been sitting in the company of the 'Young Kings of British Soccer' as they laughed and joked. They were at their peak. Now they lay dead or dying, or brutally injured and shocked.

At the Rechts der Isar Hospital in Munich Professor Georg Maurer, the Chief Surgeon, had been walking briskly along the corridor of Station 1 on the fourth floor of the main building. He was on his afternoon rounds, checking his private patients. Maurer was a short, stocky man with warm brown eyes that sparkled mischievously behind his rimless glasses. He was jolly but radiated authority and confidence in everything he did as he strode purposefully around the wards like a sergeant major.

It was now 1515. His medical teams had been busy since 0730 working in the operating theatres grouped together down the corridor through the frosted glass doors labelled 'OPERATION SALES'. He'd handled his share of the 25 operations that day, but the long hours of concentrated work seemed to have little effect on him and he didn't look tired. He walked quickly among the beds with enough time for a brief word with his patients in a friendly yet efficient manner. Behind him came his entourage of doctors: Opelt, his chief assistant, Gross, a young trainee, and Sister Maria Gilda, a nun and the Chief Nursing Sister.

As they came out of Room 405 Maria Spitzener, a short nursing orderly with black hair, ran frantically out of Sister Gilda's private office: 'Herr Professor, Herr Professor, Telefon!' she shouted. Maurer could tell by her voice that it was serious. He hurried to the phone and as he listened the warm smile left his face. Maurer spoke loudly so his staff could hear: 'Ja . . . ja . . . Flugzeug catastrophe at Reim . . .' Once they heard 'catastrophe' his assistants rushed to their emergency stations. They knew the drill well. Maurer was an efficient organiser and had prepared them for emergencies. The professor had been decorated with an Iron Cross 18 years before, after saving the lives of British and German soldiers on the beaches at Dunkirk in France where the Allies had landed to try to stop Hitler's troops crossing the English Channel. Maurer's wartime experience had taught him the need for a well-planned emergency service to deal with casualties. One of his first tasks after being appointed head of the hospital was to set up medical teams to deal with air crash victims.

The hospital staff raced around preparing for the arrival of the crash victims. The intercom hummed with the names of doctors, nurses and theatre sisters being called to help. 'Achtung! Achtung! Herr Professor Kessel . . . Herr Professor Thysinger . . . Herr Doktor Lechner . . . Frau Doktor Schmidt . . . Frau Doktor Jacques . . .' The blood bank was put on alert. Male nurses and orderlies got trolleys and stretchers ready to deal with the injured.

Back at the scene of the crash, Harry Gregg's world was pitch black though he knew it was daylight when the plane took off. 'I'm dead; I'm in hell,' he thought. He was afraid to touch the top of his head. He felt that the objects that had hit him must have sheared off his scalp. As he plucked up the courage to touch his face, he felt warm, sticky blood. He reached down to unfasten his seatbelt and realised it wasn't there. It had been broken in the crash. Still unsure whether he was alive, Gregg rolled over and saw a small shaft of light. 'Christ, I'm not dead,' he thought as he lay there on his side.

He crawled towards the light and heard a hissing sound all around him. His mind couldn't connect it with the plane and the danger of fire from escaping fuel. By now he was convinced he was the only one alive in all the carnage.

Eight

The Aftermath

Captain Thain broke the silence that followed the noise of the crash. Alarmed by the encroaching flames, he shouted 'Abandon aircraft' before quickly undoing his seatbelt. Radio Officer Rogers turned off the master switch on the battery and tripped a couple of circuit breakers before leaving the plane through the emergency window in the galley door, which had sprung during the crash. There was, in any case, no way out through the door to the passenger cabin: it was blocked with luggage.

Rayment, who was sitting on the wrecked left side of the cockpit, had been hit on the head by a tree. 'Are my passengers all right?' he asked. Thain urged him to try to move. 'Come on, man, get out,' he said. Rayment tried to leave his seat but was trapped. He shouted out that his foot was jammed. In fact, his leg, which was broken in about five places, was stuck in the pedals. Thain suddenly realised Rayment was trapped and shouted, 'Hang on, Ken, we'll get you out.' There was no reply from Rayment, who'd fallen into a deep coma. Thain had no choice but to leave his co-pilot. The drill was to get the passengers who could move away from the aircraft as quickly as possible.

Daily Mail photographer Peter Howard began to stir. He was surprised to be alive and able to move. His first thought was to get away fast. To his right he saw the shocked face of his assistant, Ted Ellyard. 'Are you all right, Ted?' he shouted. 'I think so, mate,' Ellyard replied. Howard was dazed, but he scrambled through the broken spars and twisted metal to find a hole in the wreckage. Fear gave him extra strength as he tore at the debris to get out. The smell of petrol was a frightening reminder that the tanks could explode at any moment. He crawled out on his hands and knees pulling Ellyard with him. Ellyard couldn't see and was drenched in plum brandy, which had been bought as a present in Belgrade. As soon as he got clear Howard's first instinct was to run as fast as he could. He knew he was okay, but he was terrified. He pulled Ellyard out and ran with him until they were 30 yards clear of the plane. Ellyard was still complaining he couldn't see; Howard looked at his eyes and found they were covered in mud.

Meanwhile, Gregg felt knocked about. He discovered his window was on its side and he was partly on the ground. He still couldn't hear anything except a tremendous hissing. He climbed out of his seat and crawled on his hands and knees up a steep incline towards daylight. He kicked at the hole where the light was coming from to make it a bit bigger, looked down and saw United's chief coach Bert Whalley lying in the snow in his airforce blue suit. Whalley didn't have a mark on him and his eyes were wide open, but he was dead. Gregg pushed some bits of broken metal aside and then kicked his way out. He crawled through the hole in the side of the plane and got down to the ground. Suddenly he noticed that his shoes were missing. How they came off without ripping his feet off as well he'd never know. He stood up and looked around. He was in deep snow, though he didn't really notice it. Pieces of aircraft were strewn all around as far as the eye could see. He realised that most of the plane was gone – no wings, no tail end. It had broken off exactly at the wings. The part of the aircraft Gregg had come out of was about 30 or 40 yards away from where the rest of the plane had hit the petrol dump. It looked like a huge dart sticking into the house, and kept exploding. The remains of one wing were nearby and there was an empty socket where the engine had been.

Gregg stood there certain he was the only one left alive. He thought he was dreaming. His nose was bleeding and he had a sore back, but otherwise he was okay. Small fires were starting to flare up nearby as he swayed uncertainly, close to the shell of the plane. Running around barefoot in the snow in his battered dark-blue suit, he found one shoe and picked up another later. They were from different pairs. Then he saw some of the survivors, including Peter Howard. He called to him to come back.

Captain Thain followed Rogers through the emergency exit to inspect the seven or eight small fires. Some were at the end of what remained of the left wing and others were under the right wing, which was full of petrol. The two stewardesses, Margaret Bellis and Rosemary Cheverton, had already left by the crew door and Thain, expecting the plane to go up at any minute, ordered them to get well away. 'Get clear, run for it!' he shouted. But they ignored his instructions and continued to help the injured. The passengers nearest the flight deck heard the pilot's plea and tried to get clear of the plane.

Thain knew the fires had to be put out and had climbed back onto the flight deck with Rogers to collect the two portable fire extinguishers. He told Rayment to hang on until the fires were dealt with, but he was now unconscious. As Thain jumped down from the cockpit, he saw Howard, Ellyard and some of the other survivors. 'Get away . . . go on, run . . . get away!' he shouted. Then Thain and Rogers attacked the flames from four or five small fires burning at the end of the left wing. Suddenly, Thain came round the side of what was left of the nose of the plane. He was trying his best, albeit ineffectively, to douse the spreading flames. Thain was still trying to get people out of the aircraft. He saw Gregg and yelled, 'Run, you stupid bastard, run! This plane is going to explode!'

Bill Foulkes, after being unconscious for a few moments, found himself sitting in his rear-facing seat staring into space. There was nothing beneath his feet except a hole. He'd no idea what had happened. In fact, the plane had split in half on a diagonal under his feet. Foulkes soon realised the back of the aircraft had simply disappeared. Albert Scanlon had gone but Foulkes, still strapped to his seat, seemed to be all right. He realised Ken Morgans had also disappeared from beside him, although Morgans's seat was still intact. Foulkes looked out of the window and saw smoke coming from the engine. Then he watched a man dousing some of the flames with a hand fire extinguisher before tapping on the window beside him. Foulkes thought this was odd because of the gaping hole in front of him where the fuselage had been torn away. He didn't realise the man was Thain. He was close enough to touch him. 'What the hell are you doing in there?' shouted Thain. 'Get out, man, get out. Get clear, run for it.'

Foulkes tried to move but couldn't. He panicked. It was a while before he pulled himself together and suddenly remembered his seat belt was holding him down. He quickly unbuckled the strap and felt his head and knees to see if everything was still there. Wearing only one shoe, he scrambled out through the jagged hole as fast as he could and sprinted across a field. As he ran the snow got deeper. The image of engines blowing up after a crash, which he'd seen so many times in films, passed through his mind. He sensed the plane might explode at any second, but he didn't really have a clear thought in his head. He ran through the thick snow until he was standing, out of breath, some 30 or 40 yards from the plane. His feet were wet and it was very cold.

Foulkes had reached the edge of the airfield. He was on a road where a group of Germans, mainly women, were gathering to watch the confusion. They were talking excitedly, but Foulkes couldn't understand them. They didn't realise Foulkes had been on the plane. He looked down at his stockinged feet; he'd run through the snow and slush without realising he wasn't wearing shoes. That brought him to his senses. He looked round for the first time and couldn't believe his eyes. From about a mile away he saw the plane cut in half. It was a mass of jagged metal. He noticed smoke hanging over the wreckage and realised they'd crashed. He could make out the part of the plane he'd left, but all he saw clearly was the tail fin with the Union Jack on it sticking up in the air as it blazed away in the petrol dump. This part of the plane seemed to Foulkes to have hit a house or a lorry, or both, since it was perched on high above both of them. Burning bushes and drums were scattered everywhere. Bodies were strewn from the plane in a neat line, lying in slush and water where the snow had melted.

Gregg could see five people in the distance running through the snow towards the woods. After Thain's warning Gregg heard other shouts for him to run as the aircraft was about to explode. Gregg thought Thain's sheer cold-blooded courage in trying to combat the fires was remarkable, particularly as the captain knew the danger of an explosion. Gregg could hear hissing and was about to take Thain's advice and join the others when he heard a child crying. It brought him to his senses. He remembered seeing a woman carrying a baby when they boarded the plane and thought about his daughter Lynda, who was about the same age as the infant. He was, by now, furious that people were running away from the plane when they could have been helping to save those still alive. 'Get out, get out, run for it!' they shouted. 'Come back, you bastards, there's people alive in here!' Gregg screamed. At first they carried on running, but eventually they came back.

Ignoring a serious head wound and the fire risk, Gregg bravely went back into the wreckage to search for survivors. He was terrified of what he'd see. He found a suit first. There was nothing in it, which came as a relief in the darkness. He stepped over one or two people who were badly knocked about. Then he found the baby's carrycot. It had been buried, but was empty. He scrambled towards the crying sound until he saw a small white coat. It seemed limp and lifeless. He was afraid to touch it in case the baby had been crushed, but when he picked up the coat it was empty. Again he heard the cry from inside the plane, or what was left of it, nearby this time. He retraced his steps to the hole through which he'd escaped; he pulled frantically at the pile of rubble just inside and found the child. It was 20-month-old Vesna Lukic, daughter of the Yugoslav air attaché in London. Her face was badly swollen and bruised but otherwise there wasn't a mark on her. Gregg had no idea how she'd been protected in the crash. He picked her up and got ready to crawl through the gap again when he heard a woman's voice.

Howard, Ellyard and the others had by now joined Radio Operator William Rogers and the stewardesses in braving the risk of an explosion as they went back into the wreckage to try to free survivors. It was a terrible mess. Howard wanted to shut his eyes. He was conscious of the same deadly silence there had been just before the crash. They all did what they could. It looked to Howard as if those at the front of the plane were the lucky ones who got out. The luckiest were in the rear-facing seats, with their backs to the crew's cabin. Howard looked around for anyone he knew. He saw Rayment trapped in the cockpit, but he couldn't see his friend Eric Thompson of the *Mail*. He began to realise what an awful thing had happened.

Foulkes, recovering from his momentary panic, realised his mates were still by the plane and decided to join the others in their rescue operation. The nearby Germans couldn't believe he was actually a survivor himself. As Foulkes walked back towards the Union Jack on the tail fin and the scene of utter desolation he came across bodies, saw all the debris and the seats thrown about all over the place, many with people still in them. He could see Matt Busby sitting up. Everyone else looked unconscious.

Roger Byrne was still strapped to his seat, leaning over backwards as if his back was broken. Foulkes could see from the way he was sitting that he was beyond help. He also saw Jackie Blanchflower and Dennis Viollet. Bobby Charlton had suffered a slight knock on the back of his head. He was still strapped in his seat, unconscious. Johnny Berry was there too. Apart from Byrne, Foulkes thought the others seemed to be all right. He believed that Byrne was the only one who was dead and that only a few other people were injured.

Suddenly, Foulkes realised he was standing in a crowd of people. He didn't seem to have a mark on him. He walked nearer the plane in a daze. He couldn't really believe he'd been in a crash. He saw Gregg bending down and then coming up and walking round the back of the plane carrying a baby, Vesna. She was crying. Foulkes hadn't even known there was a baby on board. Gregg's face was covered in blood. He looked in a bad way. Foulkes thought he must be badly cut, but he only had a tiny nick on the side of his nose. 'Hey, give us a lift here!' shouted Gregg. 'Give us some help!' Gregg then ran about 50 yards to stewardess Rosemary Cheverton and gave her the child. She took Vesna tenderly in her arms and gave her a cuddle.

Gregg went back inside the plane to find the woman he'd heard earlier. Suddenly, in front of him, another pile of rubble moved. As the woman appeared Gregg helped to free her. It was Vesna's mother, Vera, who was six months pregnant. Gregg pushed her out through the hole in the plane. Her face was black and one of her eyes was badly cut. She had two broken legs and a fractured skull. It was a miracle she'd survived. Vera was crying for her baby. As soon as she saw the child was safe, she gave a cry of relief. Peter Howard helped the sobbing mother across the snow to be reunited with her precious daughter.

Gregg began to look around for anyone he might know. He didn't have to look far. The passengers were now tearing wreckage apart as they desperately sought survivors. Howard and Ellyard went back into the plane repeatedly to help rescue those who were trapped and to reassure the injured. They found Ray Wood, Gregg's understudy, groaning even though he was unconscious. He was trapped under one of the plane's undercarriage wheels. Gregg tried to get him out, but couldn't. Instead, he propped him up against the bags containing some of United's strip.

Albert Scanlon had fallen straight through the bottom of the plane and now lay partly across Wood under the wheels. He had a fractured skull and was badly hurt. His ears, eyes and nose were bleeding and he was starting to burn. Gregg tried to get him out of the wreckage, but his feet were trapped by one of the heavy baskets containing the kit. Gregg couldn't move him. Howard kept Scanlon company as Gregg climbed out of the plane again and ran round to the back of what was left of the front section.

Gregg saw the tail of the plane embedded in the practically demolished building about 100 yards away, the fins pointing towards the sky. Beyond that was another building with its roof gaping. He focused once more on the area around him and the first person he saw was Foulkes. He also found Charlton and Viollet lying limp, half in, half out of the plane. Next to Viollet lay what looked like the circular clutch plate of a car, only it was much bigger. Gregg thought they were dead. He grabbed them by their trouser waistbands and dragged them like rag dolls through the snow some 20 yards from the plane. He then put them into seats which had been thrown from the plane, he didn't really know why. Charlton wasn't cut, but Viollet's head was split open and he was covered in blood. Gregg left them for dead. He saw others he recognised and thought they had also been killed. Later, Foulkes came across Charlton and Viollet. Like Gregg, he thought they were dead.

Jackie Blanchflower was sitting up to his waist in water. Roger Byrne lay across his legs and midriff with his eyes open. Byrne was just in his vest and pants, and didn't have any shoes or socks on. Blanchflower saw the fire where the aircraft had hit the house. He started talking to Byrne but, although United's captain didn't have a single mark on him, he was dead. Blanchflower watched Foulkes and Gregg go in and out of the plane helping people get clear.

Howard and Ellyard gradually cleared the debris inside the plane as they tried to get Wood and Scanlon out, using a crowbar to lever the wheels away. Unfortunately, in their anxiety to get Wood free, they levered his leg as well and broke it. When Wood regained consciousness he asked Howard for a cigarette. Howard gave him one and was about to light it when somebody stopped him, pointing out that they were underneath the ruptured petrol tanks. Wood couldn't remember anything about the crash. He had no idea how he'd got where he was. He thought he must have been very close to the point at which the aircraft split in half.

Howard and Ellyard left Wood and Scanlon with the ambulancemen and nurses who'd by now arrived at the scene and resumed their search for survivors. 'There's one more here,' shouted Ellyard. Howard joined him. 'It's Frank Taylor,' he said. Taylor lay critically injured in slush beneath a metal spar, under the aircraft. They helped recover Tommy Taylor, though they thought he was beyond help. Gently they pulled him out of the plane. Howard tried to comfort him but Taylor just stared at them.

Howard saw Radio Officer Rogers running around, still trying to put out the flames. Thain could see bodies. He did what he could. It was chaos. The fire extinguishers were far too small to tackle such a large blaze. They were soon exhausted and thrown away. Foulkes looked around to see what he could do to help. As he searched he saw that the tail end of the plane was ablaze.

Gregg was trying to find his old friend Jackie Blanchflower. He began calling his name. Eventually he saw Blanchy lying in a pool of water. He was quite badly injured and bleeding a lot. His right arm was gashed and seemed almost severed at the elbow. When Gregg went to him Blanchflower opened his eyes. 'I've broken my back, Harry,' he said. Gregg was relieved to hear him speak but was worried about his injuries. 'Don't be silly; you'll be all right,' he said, trying to reassure him. But Blanchflower looked far from all right. His right arm was bleeding badly and was the most obvious of his serious injuries. With help Blanchflower was made more comfortable. Gregg removed his own tie and wrapped it round the top of Blanchflower's arm like a tourniquet to try to check the bleeding. Foulkes told him repeatedly that he was tying it too tight, but Gregg didn't seem to hear and didn't take any notice. He pulled so tight that the tie snapped in half. He looked up and saw a stewardess who'd returned to the wreckage. She was watching; she didn't know what day it was. 'Get me something to tie his arm with,' Gregg told her. She just stood there looking at him. The plane kept exploding. 'For fuck's sake, will you get me something to tie his arm with?' Gregg shouted. Eventually, he tied Blanchflower's arm with half of his tie and managed to stop the bleeding.

Bobby Charlton, who'd been slumped over in the seat Gregg had put him in, woke up as if he'd just been enjoying a nap. He thought he was still in his own seat. Everywhere there was slush and water, desolation and misery. Charlton thought he'd only blacked out for a few seconds, but he'd been unconscious for at least ten minutes. Then he saw the house. 'We must have hit it,' he thought. Charlton watched people in fire helmets running towards him screaming. He heard a din starting to grow far away, near the airport buildings. The slush was soaking into his skin but it didn't bother him. He could see flames flickering around the front of the plane. Viollet was still in his seat next to Charlton, who could see some of the other lads lying around near him. Nobody moved. Everything was still and stricken. He felt he was in the middle of a painting. Charlton saw Gregg run out of the plane. He thought that was good, and expected some of the others to follow. He didn't realise Gregg had been in and out a couple of times already.

By now, Foulkes had left Gregg with Blanchflower and run across to help Busby, who seemed to be semi-conscious. The Boss lay a little way from Charlton, halfway between the farmhouse and what was left of the plane's nose. Charlton watched as Busby painfully tried to push himself up with one hand. He was in a half-sitting position, propped up on his elbows with his feet straight out in front of him. He was having trouble with his legs. One ankle was turned completely the wrong way and was clearly broken. Otherwise, Busby didn't look too badly hurt; it seemed that he just had a small nick behind his right ear. But his ribs were crushed and he was holding his chest in pain. Foulkes knelt down next to him and asked if he was all right. 'My chest, my legs,' he kept moaning weakly. He was icy cold. Foulkes tried to put a coat under him because the ground was very wet, but Busby gave a terrible groan. 'What have I done?' Foulkes thought. He managed to wrap Busby in his jacket and then sat holding his hand and looking around. At that moment Foulkes thought he and Gregg were the only ones on their feet.

Charlton released his seatbelt and stood up as if he was waking from a deep sleep. Without a word he walked over to where Foulkes was helping Busby. He thought the Boss looked old and pale. 'We're young and fit, but will he be strong enough to make it?' Charlton wondered. It somehow seemed so unfair. Foulkes asked if Charlton was all right. He didn't feel hurt, but just kept staring, in a daze. Then, like Foulkes a few minutes before, Charlton took off his jacket and put it underneath Busby as he lay in the slush. Dennis Viollet also woke up, in much the same way as Charlton. He stretched out and then walked across to join him. Charlton put his arm around Viollet, who asked the dumbest question of his life: 'Have we crashed, Bob?' Viollet saw the carnage around him; it was only then that he understood what had happened. Gregg turned round and got the shock of his life when he saw Charlton and Viollet standing there watching the fire. He'd pulled them out and left them for dead, and there they were looking at him. He was so relieved.

Gregg found Foulkes with Busby. 'My legs, my legs,' Busby moaned softly. Gregg straightened Busby's foot, propped him up and talked to him. Foulkes and Gregg vigorously rubbed Busby's hands and back to try to revive him until help arrived. Everyone able to walk was helping to make the survivors as comfortable as possible.

Great plumes of black smoke climbed into the leaden sky above the wrecked plane, but the Elizabethan had not burst into flames, as

Thain had feared. The airport fire brigade put out the remaining fires under the shattered left wing. A man with a portable extinguisher tackled a fire under the right wing and got it under control fairly quickly. As he moved away, the fire broke out again and Thain dragged him back to put it out once more.

All this time, Rayment sat pinned in his seat in what remained of the cockpit. Attempts to reach him from within the plane had failed. Thain snatched an axe from a fireman's belt, ran to where Rayment was trapped and hacked away to cut a hole where he thought the rescuers might be able to get to him. The fireman seemed to get the message then. Thain signalled to Rayment and gave him a thumbs-up sign. Rayment smiled.

One of the first witnesses on the scene was rescuer Karl-Heinz Seffer. He climbed onto the plane to try to get Rayment out. It was sleeting and Seffer was wearing wellington boots. He had to move about the wing and fuselage; if it had been icy he would have slipped. The surface was wet but there was no ice. Eventually, more rescuers had to climb on the fuselage via the wings and wrench the tangle of machinery away from above to lift Rayment clear.

A man in a long tweed overcoat appeared with a medical bag and a hypodermic syringe. He went to different bodies and then turned to shout, 'He's dead.' Gregg shouted at him to help the injured in the aircraft. Gregg was on his knees trying to comfort Blanchflower, who was moaning. Blanchy watched Charlton as he wandered about. The sight of so many people stirring cheered Foulkes up. He began to believe that most people were all right. 'It's not so bad after all,' he thought. The illusion would soon be devastatingly shattered. All of a sudden there were explosions from the burning half of the plane. The force knocked the doctor backwards off his feet. It was a strange sight as he fell on his backside in the snow with his legs in the air, still holding the syringe.

As one of the stewardesses came towards them, vehicles started pulling up in sheets of spray a couple of hundred yards away. Coal wagons, lorries, Volkswagens. People stood open-mouthed in horror at it all. Some were dazed. Thain got very irritated and angry with them, but they were just trying to come to terms with the devastation after suddenly arriving at the scene. At times Thain just couldn't get people to move to where they were needed. Eventually, he was led away by first-aid men and driven to the airport building. He left the airstrip quite certain that Rayment would be all right.

Soon a man drove up in a Volkswagen minibus. The back seats had been taken out. Stretchers were put down one after another. Vera Lukic and her baby daughter Vesna, Scanlon, Woods and Frank Taylor, who'd all been brought out of the plane, were bruised, shocked and, in some cases, unconscious and gravely injured.

Howard and Radio Officer Rogers had one last look around. They noticed a white shirt in the wreckage. It was 18-year-old Kenny Morgans. He was breathing heavily, trying to gasp in air. The Welsh youngster had been given his big chance in Belgrade after leaving England overjoyed and full of hope that he might become the new Billy Meredith, one of United's all-time greats. He was unconscious and pinned down by a metal pole. Howard and Rogers got a crowbar and levered the wheel away from Morgans.

Periodically, as Gregg had run about trying to help the survivors, he'd prayed and cried unashamedly. Some people thought he'd lost his mind. But his reaction wasn't surprising because he was suffering from shock. He'd never seen death before and never wanted to see it again. Throughout his ordeal Gregg's main concern was the health and safety of others. When the rescuers seemed to have everything under control he sank to his knees and cried again, thanking God that some of the passengers, at least, had been saved.

Suddenly, Howard remembered he'd taken some pictures before take-off. He looked for his camera but couldn't find it in the wreckage. The debris was all over the place and covered more than 150 square yards. Howard wandered aimlessly from the wreckage trying to pull himself together after the shock and horror he'd suffered. The ordeal was beginning to affect him. Then he saw a body lying on the ground. He carefully lifted the head and saw United's young captain, Roger Byrne. He knew instinctively that Byrne was dead even though there were no marks on his face and no traces of injury.

Howard then joined Captain Thain in the airport building to help him prepare a list of the injured and dead. Inside the BEA office

Thain was given coffee. A call was put through to the Air Safety Branch in London so he could officially report the accident. A plaster was put on the knuckles he'd damaged during the first abandoned take-off. The pilot of another BEA flight, which had just landed, brought him some miniature bottles of whisky and brandy. Thain asked him to phone relatives of the crew on arrival in London and give them the news first hand.

Outside, a man came rushing by and flung a stretcher alongside the stricken Busby. Foulkes and Charlton were told to help load Busby into the ambulance, which had just arrived. He was put inside along with Johnny Berry and Jackie Blanchflower. All were badly injured. The driver and his mate motioned to Charlton, Foulkes, Viollet and Gregg to get in. The ambulance, a Volkswagen van, had bumped and bounced only a short distance over the snow-covered fields when someone ran in front to stop it. The back doors were opened again and another stretcher carrying the badly burned Eleanor Miklos, wife of the travel agent, was placed next to Busby. Foulkes thought she seemed to be quite badly hurt. Then they started off again at high speed across the snow and slush onto a road. The driver was anxious to get them to the hospital and was going a bit too fast. The ride, with the van skidding in the snow, was frightening. Foulkes asked Viollet if he was okay. Viollet replied that he was, although he felt he was going to be sick. Charlton said he felt the same way. Then Viollet fell unconscious for a moment.

Foulkes didn't know how far it was to the hospital, but the journey seemed to take ages. The driver's frightening speed threw the passengers all over the place as his van lurched on the icy road. Foulkes couldn't stand it. He thought they were going too fast for safety and that something dreadful was going to happen. He felt that somehow he had to stop the driver. Foulkes told him to slow down. 'What the hell do you think you're doing,' Foulkes shouted, 'trying to kill us all?' The driver took no notice and just kept driving. Foulkes got up and punched him on the back of the head as hard as he could half a dozen times. Just then, as the van swerved about at breakneck speed in the snow, Viollet regained consciousness. He looked up and saw Foulkes with his hands around the driver's neck trying to strangle him. The van was going all over the place, but the driver continued to ignore Foulkes. The big United defender's reaction was due to shock. He shouted for Charlton and Viollet to do something, but they just stared vacantly, as if they were being taken for a pleasant Sunday afternoon outing. Charlton was just relieved to get away from the slush and snow. Eventually things settled down and what could have been a second crash was avoided.

Eventually a police car caught up and then moved ahead with its siren blaring to warn the traffic. More police cleared a path through the streets of Munich for the other ambulances to follow towards the Rechts der Isar Hospital.

Snowflakes were still falling from the grey winter skies. The citizens of Munich watched curiously while the fleet of ambulances and police cars rushed to the hospital.

Nine

The Rechts der Isar Hospital

Within 20 minutes the ambulances had sped through the gates of the Rechts der Isar Hospital and stopped outside the Casualty Department. Professor Frank Kessel's heart sank as he watched them screech to a halt. The short, flushed Austrian was head of the neurosurgical department. His work was about to begin. The ambulance doors were opened and the stretchers were slid out and carried away. He thought how young the victims looked.

Kessel knew a few things about football. When Germany invaded Austria in 1938 he had fled and eventually made his way to Manchester, where he spent ten years as a surgeon at the Royal Infirmary. He played sports and was a keen football fan. He looked down at Frank Taylor and Frank Swift lying together. They were both bleeding from the mouth. Swift had passed away on the stretcher next to Frank Taylor on the way to the hospital. His main aorta artery had been severed, probably by his seat belt. Kessel didn't know Taylor, but he recognised Swift as the former England and Manchester City goalkeeper. Then he saw Matt Busby, the elegant Scottish halfback he'd watched playing for Liverpool and Manchester City before the Second World War. 'Das ist ein

Englischer Fussballspieler,' he shouted to his colleagues.

Busby was fading away. His life's work was in ruins and many of his closest and dearest friends had been killed. They were young men. He'd watched them grow from boys. They were like sons to him. But they were gone. Busby was still clinging on to life. Only his physical strength and tremendous willpower, plus the skill of the doctors, could save him.

The stretcher-bearers began bringing some of the players into the hospital. Viollet saw Swift lying there just before he was stitched up and then he passed out. Those admitted for examination were kept in the ward for a while, and those fit enough were taken to identify people in the corridor while the medical teams worked on them. Less than half an hour after the *Lord Burleigh* had begun its final take-off attempt the seriously injured were all in the hospital. The emergency procedure was certainly efficient as a team of 50 surgeons set about saving lives.

As soon as they reached the hospital the extent of the tragedy started to hit Foulkes. He noticed that everyone was very efficient; they were so calm and organised. He was admitted for examination along with Gregg, Charlton, Howard, Ellyard, Thain, Rogers and the stewardesses, Bellis and Cheverton. The shock was clear in their faces. Gregg and Foulkes wandered down a corridor, not really knowing what they were doing or where they were going. Foulkes was only wearing one shoe. His wet sock made imprints on the floor. Eventually, they met Howard, Ellyard, the crew and a Yugoslav journalist. Charlton had a few scratches on his head and hands. His mind was blank. The blood seemed to have drained from his veins. He felt as if he'd never been warm in his life.

On the surface, though, Foulkes, Gregg and Charlton seemed okay. A nurse took them to a room where they sat around for a while. They wanted to get in touch with the British Embassy to let their families know they had survived the crash, but they couldn't find anyone to help them. After making desperate efforts to indicate what they wanted, the survivors were able to phone the British Consulate and give their home addresses. They asked the Consulate to let their families know they were safe and unhurt; they knew their relatives would hear about the crash on the radio. They had to stop them worrying. Eventually, some people from the Consulate arrived at the hospital and in no time the wires started to travel home to Manchester.

A nurse came out of a room and asked Foulkes to step inside the ward. She wanted him to identify a little man on the bed. Although the man's face was a terrible mess, Foulkes recognised Johnny Berry. His head was tilted and his bottom teeth had cut through his upper mouth and into his nose. Gregg identified Ray Wood who had split his lip and the inside of his eyelid as well as suffering a broken leg being freed from the wreckage. This nightmare of identifying the crash victims went on, with the doctors operating as Foulkes and Gregg identified people. The nurse had given Foulkes a label. He wrote Berry's name on it before returning to the corridor to catch up with the others. Then he remembered he was only wearing one shoe. His wet sock was flapping on his other foot. He pulled the sock up and joined the others. Viollet was taken to a ward while the rest of the survivors were put in a waiting room. They were given some soup to warm them up. It had a disinfected hospital smell.

Since Viollet was obviously not badly hurt, the nurses had put him to bed in the first vacant room they'd found. When he woke up Viollet found himself in a room with four or five Germans. The hospital had lost him for a few hours in the confusion of people being brought in for emergency treatment.

Ray Wood, an obsessive tea drinker who liked a strong brew, asked one of the nurses for some tea as soon as he arrived at the hospital. She brought him cold peppermint tea in a feeding bowl. He lay there drinking his cold tea worrying about his leg, which by then was also very cold, and thinking about the film *All Quiet on the Western Front*, in which people smiled at the patients and made a point of not telling them about their amputated legs. Fortunately, Wood's legs were still there. He was also worried about his wife and whether she knew he was all right.

Busby's first recollection after the crash was a brief, fleeting glance in a snatch of consciousness. He could see a big room with several covered bodies in it. He thought he saw a doctor looking down at one saying, 'This one is dead.' Busby felt it was Frank Swift, though he never knew why. Then he heard Professor Maurer telling the doctor to keep quiet. Gregg heard over the intercom that Swift was dead. Swift was a real hero, everybody's hero. Strangely, although Gregg had seen death earlier on, touched it even, Swift was the first person he *really* knew was dead.

Suddenly a party of nurses appeared brandishing needles. Charlton was still walking around when one of the nurses in a white coat grabbed his arm. 'Are you all right?' he asked. Charlton nodded, but the nurse still got hold of him and gave him a couple of shots with a big needle. He fainted before he knew what had happened and was taken to a ward. Howard, Ellyard and Gregg were also given injections. When they first put Gregg on a table he got off. They gave him the first shot and he said, 'I'm not staying in here.' Foulkes was next. Gregg said, 'You stay, I'm not.' His overpowering instinct was that he must get away from the hospital. The two were walking down a corridor with the Yugoslav journalist, a huge man, when he suddenly collapsed. He decided the doctors had better have a look at his leg. They discovered it was fractured. It was the only time Foulkes and Gregg came near to raising a smile as gallows humour got the better of them.

All the survivors were by now in a kind of trance. The whole atmosphere was so unpleasant. There was nothing Gregg and Foulkes could do. They decided to get out. Gregg's nose was cut but he didn't want any treatment. They left the hospital and stood on the steps outside.

Although Thain was relatively unharmed, he was taken by car to the hospital where he met other survivors. Now that the immediate pressure was off the obvious question arose: why had the plane crashed? After the boost surging was dealt with, and before Rayment's startled cry, the engines were running at full power, yet the aircraft had decelerated. What retarding force had caused the engines to lose speed when the plane should have been accelerating? Only Rayment seemed likely to throw any light on the riddle. Thain was anxious to talk to him. He spoke to a doctor who told him Rayment had been brought in. He was very ill, but would survive. With this assurance Thain decided not to disturb him for now.

As they stood outside the hospital, Foulkes and Gregg were approached by a BEA representative, who arranged for them to be taken to the Starhaus Hotel. Foulkes asked if she could get him some shoes. She took the one he had as a guide to size, went to a store and bought him some high fur-lined boots. When Foulkes and Gregg reached the hotel they were filthy with dirt and grease. Their clothes looked as if they'd been dragged through the gutter. The hotel manager gave them each a warm coat and other clothes, and put them on the top floor, away from the other guests.

Foulkes and Gregg sat in their hotel room in a daze. They didn't know what to do; they just followed each other around. When Foulkes went to the toilet, Gregg went with him. When Gregg went out on the balcony, Foulkes followed. Finally, they sat and gazed out of the window. The snow was piled as high as the cars. Gregg thought about what the snow was burying at the airport. They shared a bottle of whisky someone had given them, though Foulkes didn't usually drink.

Thain eventually left the airport to join the others at the Starhaus Hotel. He checked in and went to his room. On his own for the first time since the crash, a sudden surge of emotion swept over him and he began to cry.

Whilst all this was going on, the chief German accident investigator had flown in from Brunswick. During the flight he thought the most probable cause of the accident was ice on the wings. (In fact, slush on the runway had slowed down the aircraft and caused the crash.) When the investigator arrived he was taken to inspect the wreckage in the dark, amidst a heavy snowstorm.

Halfway through the night the crew called Gregg and Foulkes to say they were going to eat. The two United players decided to join them. Predictably, nobody wanted any food. Thain was desperate to talk to everybody about the accident. They were pretty good listeners. He spoke to Gregg about what had happened. 'Jim, I saw the wheels lock and unlock twice,' said Gregg. 'No, you didn't,' replied Thain. 'Jim, I watched them lock and unlock,' insisted Gregg. Thain told him about the final run, about Velocity One, the point of no return when the pilot has to lift the undercarriage and get off the ground. He told him that point had been reached. When everyone left for bed the crew gathered in Thain's room and the discussion started again. Then BEA's chief pilot appeared. He'd flown out hurriedly from England. Thain went over the details once again.

Almost as agonising as grief for the dead was anxiety for the fate of the injured hovering between life and death. They included: Busby, right ribs broken, collapsed right lung, right foot and knee broken; Duncan Edwards, thigh smashed and kidneys punctured; Johnny Berry, in a deep coma with a fractured skull and severe head injuries; and Frank Taylor and Ken Rayment, both with multiple injuries. Rayment had a complicated fracture of the left leg and injuries to his thigh, stomach, head and possibly kidneys. Jackie Blanchflower had a fractured right forearm, a smashed pelvis, 13 broken ribs and damaged kidneys. He was in such a bad way that he was given the last rites. Eleanor Miklos had a fractured spine and paralysis of the legs. Dennis Viollet, Bobby Charlton, Albert Scanlon, Ken Morgans and Ray Wood all had minor injuries. In those first 24 hours Taylor, Busby, Berry and others could have died.

The main danger to many of the injured was shock. Some were still unconscious, most susceptible to complications, and many were on the survival threshold. When Frank Taylor came round he saw a doctor giving him a painkilling injection. In the first few hours after the crash Taylor felt as though he had a huge hangover. There were fleeting periods when he was conscious and almost euphoric, tangled moments of reality and then a dream-like existence when he seemed to be floating like a disembodied spirit. It was all so disjointed, like the pieces of a puzzle that wouldn't fit together. No matter how hard he tried he couldn't focus properly. He kept looking at Busby in the next bed, wondering why he was there. He remembered leaving Belgrade, where he had his own room in the Hotel Metropol. 'How come Busby is now in the same room?' he thought. 'Why is Ken Rayment with us?'

In the general confusion nobody knew the exact number of casualties. In fact, 20 of the 44 people on the plane were already dead. They'd been killed instantly on impact. The number of deaths caught the airport firemen on the hop without enough blankets for the bodies. A manager told them to strip the covers off all the VIP cars and use them as makeshift shrouds. The firemen felt dreadful, especially when they returned from the mortuary and the same manager ordered them to go back for the car covers.

Ten

Manchester Mourns

The first hint in Manchester that something was wrong came just after 2.30 p.m. on Thursday afternoon, when Alf Clarke called the *Evening Chronicle* to say that the United party might be delayed in Munich overnight. The paper had more or less been put to bed, but the story was squeezed into the stop press column of the early afternoon edition. Clarke had called just in time. By three o'clock the final editions were leaving Withy Grove. Newsboys ran along the streets shouting, 'Manchester United plane held up in Munich blizzard!' It was the sort of story the fans would read.

That weekend's match against Wolves at Old Trafford was approaching and the Reds were once again certain to grab the headlines. Despite the long trek home, United were favourites to win and close the four-point gap at the top of the table. That would leave them just one win behind Billy Wright's team and closer to a third successive Championship. Only Huddersfield and Arsenal had ever captured three titles on the trot. If United didn't return in time to play they'd probably be heavily fined, or worse. It was just the sort of problem critics would use to support their case that the Reds should concentrate on domestic football.

Old Trafford had been a hive of activity all day. The ground staff were busy preparing the stadium for the Wolves game. The office staff were just as occupied with that match and the ticket applications for the FA Cup tie against Sheffield Wednesday. In other parts of Manchester, the daily newspapers were beginning their routines. Reporters were setting off on scheduled stories and sub-editors were casting their eyes over agency copy to see what they might use to fill the Friday morning papers.

Shortly after 3 p.m. a telephone call to Old Trafford brought the news that the plane carrying the players and staff had crashed attempting to take off from Munich airport following a refuelling stop. There were no further details. Everyone at United, including Matt Busby's secretary Alma George, chief scout Joe Armstrong and Fred Owen, hoped the accident wouldn't turn out to be too serious. But soon the news that there were fatalities came through. There were no names yet.

United's assistant manager, Jimmy Murphy, came hurrying off the train from Cardiff just before four o'clock in the afternoon. Murphy walked out of London Road Station in Manchester and shivered. It was cold. Murphy hailed a taxi. 'Old Trafford, son,' he told the driver. Murphy called everyone 'son'.

His mind ran over the events of the past few days and the coming weekend's work. They had to get things moving at the ground before the Wolves match, which would be tough. He wondered if all the players were fit after Belgrade and how Matt had stood up to the journey. What a man! Imagine travelling so soon after coming out of hospital following an operation on his legs. But that was Matt. He went wherever his team went.

Murphy's taxi stopped in the forecourt at Old Trafford. Usually there was a lot of activity at the ground, but everything seemed unusually quiet. Murphy didn't notice that the League Championship flag above the ground was flying at half-mast. He still had no idea anything had happened. He paid the driver and hurried through the door of the main entrance. Murphy carried his briefcase up to the boardroom, taking the stairs two at a time. It had been a long, tiring journey from Cardiff, but he wanted to make sure everything was okay for Matt and the boys when they arrived back from Belgrade.

There were only three or four staff on duty. A strained, unreal atmosphere seemed to hang in the air. Then Alma George called after him: 'Mr Murphy . . .' Murphy was anxious to get to his office and therefore a bit offhand in his reply. 'Yes, dear,' he said. 'Mr Murphy . . . you don't understand,' she said. 'Understand what, dear?' he replied. There was something in her tone that made him pause near the top of the stairs. He turned to see her anguished face. Alma had come to the club as Busby's secretary and had seen all the players arrive as mere boys. She was white, dazed and scarcely able to speak. 'Mr Murphy, please stop,' she said. 'Haven't you heard the news? The United plane has crashed at Munich.'

At first he didn't take it in. 'I don't think you understand,' Alma said again. 'The plane has crashed. A lot of people have died.' She was right, he didn't understand. She told him a third time and now her tears began to fall. Murphy's feet stopped. So did his heart. The hands of the clock on the wall pointed to four o'clock . . . but time meant nothing now. A good few minutes passed before Alma's words began to sink in and he was struck by the enormity of the disaster. He couldn't believe it. The words seemed to ring in his head. Murphy would take the numbing horror of that moment to his grave.

Alma left him and he went into his office, which was sometimes irreverently called Murphy's Bar. Some of United's biggest deals had taken place there. Murphy's head was in a state of confusion. He started to cry, and the tears flowed for 20 minutes. He took a bottle from a cupboard and poured himself a glass of Scotch. Then he phoned the police, the papers and the BBC asking for news. Like everyone else close to the biggest tragedy to hit a British football club, he was too numb to take in the awful grief. Murphy sat devastated by the telephone. Fans queuing for cup tickets at Old Trafford were among the first to hear about the disaster. Ticket sales were immediately stopped and the ticket office was shut. The main office was also closed to everyone except staff.

News of the delay to the United party in the *Evening Chronicle* had only just hit the streets when the full horror of the accident was revealed to the press. Within minutes, the Reuters teleprinter flashed an unbelievable headline: MANCHESTER UNITED PLANE CRASHES IN MUNICH . . . STILL SEARCHING FOR SURVIVORS.

The Manchester evening papers were the first to carry the story. Its impact was devastating. The whole city was simply stunned. A group of fans who'd gathered at Ringway Airport to welcome the team home were in shock. The telephone lines at Old Trafford were now ringing non-stop. People were beginning to gather outside the ground on the forecourt; journalists had to join the growing crowd outside. Police were called to try to disperse the crowd, but few people were keen to move. Workers from nearby factories soon swelled the crowd as the five o'clock hooters blew. They rushed through the Old Trafford gates to hear more about the rumours that had swept through their buildings earlier. Only hours before they'd been talking about the draw with Red Star, and United's chances of beating Wolves.

As the sketchy details chattered across the teleprinters editors called emergency news conferences to remake the front pages. Extra editions were published. At first details were printed in the stop press section. By six o'clock that evening a special edition of the *Manchester Evening Chronicle* hit the streets. Only three hours had passed since the crash, but the paper had a detailed report of how the disaster had happened. The lead story said that about 28 people were feared dead and that it was understood there may be about 16 survivors, including four crew members. The paper also carried Alf Clarke's match report and comments from players and officials after the Red Star game.

The news quickly spread around the country on radio and television as well as the early editions of the evening papers. The BBC interrupted its afternoon programming to broadcast a newsflash. Housewives listening to *Mrs Dale's Diary* on the radio were devastated when they heard the news. Crowds in Manchester and across the country crowded around newspaper sellers, waiting for the latest updates. But the full horror of what had happened wouldn't become apparent until people read their newspapers the following morning. Instant television coverage was a long way off, and BBC radio didn't issue news bulletins around the clock.

The *Daily Mail* had received the earliest first-hand account within an hour of the disaster. The paper's photographer, Peter Howard, exhausted and shattered by the crash and by his rescue work amid the wreckage, phoned to give them the bare facts. He was still in a state of shock.

'I am phoning to tell you the terrible news,' he said. 'Manchester United's plane has crashed at Munich. We were just taking off. We had only just got off the ground. Can you hear me? I'm all right. I feel a bit wobbly. Tell my wife I'm okay. Please let her know. It's all a bit mixed up, but Bobby Charlton, Albert Scanlon and Ray Wood are injured and have gone to hospital. Most of the crew are safe. Harry Gregg looked to be okay when I saw him just after the crash, but I haven't seen him since.'

Bobby Charlton's brother, Jack, was drying himself in the Leeds United dressing room after training when the news came through to Elland Road. Arthur Crowther, the club secretary, walked in and announced, 'The Manchester United plane has crashed and they don't know if there are any survivors.' Then he left. 'Your kid's on that plane,' said one of the lads. 'Yeah,' replied Jack who was standing stark naked. He got dressed as quickly as he could and went up to Crowther's office. Five or six people were sitting talking about the disaster. Jack asked if anyone had any information about the crash. They tried phoning around but nobody knew what had happened.

Jack decided to go back to the family home at Ashington. There wasn't a phone at his parents' house, but his mother knew he'd come. He phoned his wife Pat and arranged to meet her at the station. It was bitterly cold. Thick snow lay on the ground. A man was talking about the crash on the train but Jack couldn't speak to him. The journey went on for ages. From Newcastle Station they took a taxi to the Haymarket where they could catch a bus to Ashington. The taxi dropped them off and as they walked to the bus stop, Jack saw a man selling papers. He could read the stop press in the papers folded over the man's arm: Bobby Charlton's name caught his eye at the top of a list of survivors. 'Bloody hell, he's okay,' shouted Jack. They still didn't know if Bobby was badly injured. The paper just said he'd been taken to hospital.

When they got home Jack's mother had already heard the good news. The local constable had come running up the street smiling and waving a piece of paper. It was a message from the Foreign

Office saying that Bobby was safe. A few minutes later, a neighbour arrived to say the plane was 'a burning inferno' and that there were no survivors. 'If that woman had arrived a few minutes earlier,' Jack's mother said, 'you could have buried me at home.'

United players Johnny Giles and Nobby Stiles had finished their work for the afternoon and were waiting with the ground staff boys for Arthur Powell to let them go. He was keeping them in suspense. Powell came into the dressing room with assistant trainer Bill Inglis. 'Sit down, lads, I've got some bad news for you,' said Inglis. 'The plane has crashed.' They didn't know any more details, but the two old-timers didn't think it was too serious. 'We'll let you know later,' Powell told them. The players sat around joking among themselves. They thought those in Munich might have broken arms or something. 'We might get a game in the "A" team now,' someone said. There was no more news so Powell let them go.

Stiles took a bus into town. He got off at Piccadilly to catch the number 112 up the Rochdale Road to his home. Stiles lived in a rough area of small terraced houses, but everyone always left their front doors open. He bought a paper headlined: MANY DEAD. He'd never forget it. Stiles got off at his stop, Cassidy's pub, and went into the local church. He prayed and cried. Stiles was a punter, a supporter. He wasn't just praying for United. He idolised them. When he got home everyone was devastated. They listened to the radio all night in a state of shock.

The lady next door to Ray Wood's family thought that since Harry Gregg was United's first choice goalkeeper, Ray would still be at home in Manchester. As Ray's wife was hanging out the washing in the garden the lady came out and said, 'Mrs Wood, does Ray know that the plane has crashed and most of them are dead?' Fortunately, the news got through later that Ray Wood was comparatively healthy compared to some of the others.

Johnny Berry's eight-year-old son Neil had returned home from school and was playing marbles in the street in Davyhulme. His mother shouted loudly for him to come in. He thought he was about to be told off for something, because he was usually allowed to play out until teatime and that was still a long way off. Instead, his mother told him she'd just heard on the radio that the plane his father was on had been involved in a crash. Young Neil thought this was tremendously exciting news. He imagined his father and the other players falling from the sky in parachutes wearing their football kit – much more exciting than being a footballer. His mother became more and more concerned and within a few minutes some of the other wives and their friends came round to sit and wait for news. There was no ready source of information. They had to rely totally on the television and radio. Granada television gave regular news flashes about the accident. Nevertheless, communications were slow and they had to wait for hours and hours.

It was a night Neil Berry would never forget. He still hadn't fully taken in what had happened. The thought of any of the young men who had been so good to him having died never occurred to him. He still expected them to fly home on another plane and be ready to play again on Saturday. Then the news started coming through.

In the city crowds of people flocked to the news-stands and grabbed the papers to read about the crash. The *Manchester Evening News* billboards said: UNITED DISASTER – GRIM FIGHT FOR LIFE. The headline read: MATT 50:50. People had assumed until then that the crash wasn't too serious. Even though they knew there had been deaths, they thought that maybe the fatalities were older people, or the crew rather than fit, young footballers. They couldn't be dead. But they were. In the streets of Manchester people cried. In shops, factories and pubs there was a grief-stricken silence.

A young boy came up to Eddie Colman's girlfriend Marjorie English. 'There's been a plane crash,' he told her. 'United's plane's crashed and they're all dead.' She thought he was joking. 'Don't be sick. Don't be silly,' she said, disgusted. 'No, it's true,' he replied. She still thought he was joking. 'I don't believe you,' she told him. David Pegg's sister Irene and the rest of the family turned on the radio as they desperately tried to find out more about what had happened. The reports only confirmed there had been a plane crash. Bill Foulkes's wife Teresa missed the first bulletin about the disaster.

Gordon Clayton had missed the trip to Belgrade through injury. He'd played the first two games the previous season but had just been diagnosed with arthritis, a problem that would eventually force him to retire. Clayton was sitting on the balcony at the Ritz Ballroom, the players' old haunt, having a cup of coffee with Jackie Lynch, the manager, at an afternoon tea dance when someone told them the United plane had crashed. There was always someone saying something like that, but he went out to get a paper just to make sure. He came back and sadly broke the news to Lynch. 'It's true,' he said.

The first person Clayton thought of was Mark Jones's pregnant wife June. He took a taxi from town to their house on Kings Road, Chorlton, but she wasn't in. June had gone to the shops, where she learned about the disaster when someone had said, 'The Manchester United plane's crashed.' The next person Clayton thought of was Jackie Blanchflower's wife Jean. He went round to see her at their place in Ryebank Road, and stayed the night answering the phone and dealing with visitors to the house. It was bedlam. Jean was in a terrible state. They knew Jackie was alive, but had no news on his condition. All they could do was wait for a phone call.

Wilf McGuinness was enjoying a quiet day in the city centre with Joe Witherington, a friend who worked in sales for the *News Chronicle*. They'd had lunch and at around 3.30 in the afternoon were walking down Princess Street going into Whitworth Street when they saw a newspaper placard: UNITED IN PLANE CRASH. McGuinness wasn't immediately alarmed. He thought they'd probably had a bump on the runway and the papers were making something out of nothing. The plane hadn't been in the air, so he thought they were all right. McGuinness and his pal went to the *News Chronicle*'s offices anyway to check out what had happened. Then news of a few survivors came through – Harry Gregg, Dennis Viollet, Bobby Charlton and Bill Foulkes were the first names, but still nothing about the others. McGuinness was by now in a state of shock. He decided to drive home with his friend.

It was about six o'clock when McGuinness got home. His mother and father told him that some of the passengers had been killed. He went with his parents, who were very religious, to Mount Carmel to do a novena and cried and prayed throughout the service. His prayers were mainly for Eddie Colman and Billy Whelan. 'I'll do anything if they're all right,' he said to God.

Matt Busby's son Sandy saw the newspaper placards at Victoria Station as he made his way home from training at Blackburn Rovers. He was reserve wing-half under former United great Johnny Carey. Sandy thought it was just the papers building up a story for publicity, but he phoned home just in case. Two friends of his parents were visiting from Bellshill in Scotland. His aunt, who was a bit of a panicker, answered the phone. 'Is that you, Sandy?' she said. 'Get home straightaway, get home, son, get a taxi.' He jumped into a cab and got home as fast as he could. When he arrived he realised for the first time the seriousness of the situation. His mother Jean was in a state of shock; a semi-coma. She just sat on the sofa staring into the fire. People were talking to her but she wasn't answering them, not even her daughter Sheena, or Sandy. Nobody could get any sense out of her. It wasn't surprising. She faced the prospect of losing her greatest friend, the love of her life and the only man who completely understood her.

The Busbys' house was becoming crowded with friends and relatives when the news started coming through. There was no good news at first. They heard Frank Swift was dead just as his wife walked in the door. She didn't know yet.

Sandy wasn't the most religious person but he ran upstairs to his room, knelt down and prayed by the side of his bed. Shortly afterwards a call came through assuring them Matt was alive. Sandy's uncle Johnny ran up the stairs shouting, 'Sandy, Sandy, he's alive, he's alive!' As soon as Jean heard Matt hadn't been killed she recovered enough to start thinking of others. She immediately sent her children to the houses of those who were known to have died. It was testimony to her indomitable spirit and incredible selflessness. The Busby dynasty was founded on such generous acts. These acts of kindness had never been so important as they were immediately after the Munich disaster. Sheena went straight to the house of first team trainer Tom Curry. He was one of the first confirmed dead.

Matt's great friend, Paddy McGrath, first heard about the accident at home at about four or five o'clock that afternoon when his brother rang him from a reception at The Cromford Club. Frank McGhee of the *Daily Mirror* called later to tell McGrath that Busby had been pulled out of the wreckage. They didn't know if he was alive. McGrath rang Matt's parish priest, Monsignor Sewell. 'What shall we do?' he asked. 'You pick me up and we'll go round to the house,' suggested Sewell.

The city was quiet as they made their way to the Busbys' home in Chorlton. It was strange. Manchester was suffering from a kind of depression McGrath had never seen before, even during the war. Bill Ridding, a former United player from the 1930s, who now managed Bolton, was there when McGrath and Sewell got to the Busbys' house in Kings Road. Ridding answered all the phone calls from the press in London, who were trying to find out who'd survived. Frank Swift's daughter and son-in-law were there, as well as his wife. Ridding called McGrath over and said, 'Can you get Frank's wife away? He's been killed.' McGrath asked his son-in-law to take Swift's wife and daughter home and tell them. Johnny Carey arrived from Blackburn. Henry Rose of the *Daily Express*, a pal of Paddy's, had died instantly. When Henry's girlfriend Elsie Nichols arrived at the Busbys' she didn't know for sure that he was dead, but she kept saying, 'I know my Henry's been killed.' A doctor had to be called to sedate her.

Jimmy Savile had been preparing for that evening's Manchester Press Ball when the news came through that the plane had crashed and many of the players were dead. He put a notice outside. It just said: PRESS BALL CANCELLED. Savile locked his door and turned on the radio. The reception was poor; he had to put it in the middle of the floor before it would work properly. Savile and his staff sat around listening to the reports as they came through. The food prepared for the guests was all around them. Even as they heard the news bulletins it was hard for them to conceive that such a terrible thing had happened. They were to stay there all night. 'It was one of the most shattering experiences ever to confront the city,' says Savile, 'the biggest disaster Manchester had ever known.'

Journalist Geoffrey Green of *The Times* might have been on the United plane that afternoon. Instead, his late change of assignment had taken him to Cardiff for the World Cup qualifier between Wales and Israel. Green returned to London overnight and went to the cinema in the afternoon. When he came out at around tea-time the first thing he saw was an evening paper billposter screaming out the dreadful news in the heaviest type. He ran home like a hare just in time to hear the phone ring. It was the office. They'd been trying to reach him for two hours.

At this stage, precise information on the casualties was scarce and confused. No one knew anything much apart from the chilling fact that United's plane had crashed on take-off at Munich's Reim Airport. Green went to the office, where he wrote two pieces for *The Times* and did four broadcasts for the BBC, all without knowing for sure who was still alive. One of the television broadcasts was with England manager Walter Winterbottom, a former United player whose team would take part in the World Cup in Sweden four months later. Winterbottom didn't know it yet but three of his key players would not be making the trip to Sweden: fullback Roger Byrne, halfback Duncan Edwards and centre forward Tommy Taylor.

Green's colleague David Miller stood numbly by the Reuters teleprinter in the sports department of *The Times* as the appalling roll call of disaster began to chatter in the late afternoon. Years later the memory would still bring a shudder.

Alex Stepney was a schoolboy in Mitcham, Surrey. After school he walked home and heard the news. He worked as a delivery boy for a local corner shop. As he rode around, at every house he came to he asked for the latest news on United.

Pat Crerand was getting a trolley bus up to Glasgow Cross when he saw the headline UNITED IN PLANE CRASH on a big placard outside a paper shop. 'Well, the papers don't always tell the truth,' he thought. 'They'll have just bumped into something, it's probably nothing.' Crerand, a young lad who'd just signed for Celtic the year before, then took a train from Glasgow Cross to Celtic Park. When he arrived the crash was the only topic of conversation among the players. They all knew United and what a great team they had. Everybody knew Matt Busby so well. They didn't know any details and more information was slow coming through. But it was a big shock to everyone in Glasgow.

Denis Law, a young Scottish inside-forward at Huddersfield Town, was in a small café across the road from his club's Leeds Road ground when the news came through that there had been a plane crash and Manchester United were involved. He heard some players had been killed but he didn't know who. Then it became known that Busby was on the danger list. United's manager had kept an eye on Law from the time the youngster had played against the Reds in a Youth Cup match at Heckmondwike, just outside Huddersfield. The pitch was close to a canal and if you kicked the ball too hard over the touchline it ended up in the water. It wasn't a great place to make an impression on anyone, but despite the conditions the young Law impressed Busby. It was just a couple of years before Munich, and United were the biggest name in football. Huddersfield were 2–0 up at half time, but were overrun in the second period and lost 4–2. Some time later Busby offered Town £10,000 for the 16-year-old. Law wasn't told about the bid. It was an awful lot of money for an amateur who'd barely started out in the game and had yet to make his League debut. Indeed, the British transfer record was only about £30,000. Huddersfield's manager Andy Beattie turned Busby down. If he hadn't, Law could have been on the plane at Munich.

The novelist H.E. Bates was driving home from London on that cold February afternoon when, under the first lighted street lamps he passed, he suddenly saw one of the blue-and-yellow news placards usually designed to shock people into buying a paper. It said simply: MANCHESTER UNITED AIR CRASH. His immediate reaction was a mildly cynical one. 'I am getting too old to be caught by newspaper screamers,' he thought. At six o'clock that night, out of pure curiosity, he turned on the TV. As the news came on the screen seemed to go blank. The normally urbane voice of the announcer seemed to Bates to turn into a sledgehammer. He turned deathly cold and sat listening with a frozen brain to that cruel and shocking list of casualties.

Bolton Wanderers' centre-forward Nat Lofthouse, the man they called the Lion of Vienna because of his brilliant two-goal performance in an international match against Austria in 1952, was also listening to that six o'clock news bulletin along with the customers in his pub. The whole place was stunned by the news; Lofthouse simply found it very hard to believe. It stunned the whole of Britain and nearly killed half the north.

The lights from the windows of the back street barber's shop pierced the evening gloom as young United fan Cliff Hague was getting the customary short back-and-sides. Suddenly the door opened with an urgent jangle and a man in a flat cap and cheap, baggy trousers rushed into the shop. 'The United plane has crashed,' he said. Then he banged the door shut and was gone. Hague didn't know who he was. Maybe he knew the barber; maybe he just had to find some way to come to terms with his own horror and dread and had stumbled towards the light. Inside there was a pause. The handful of customers gazed at each other. Nobody spoke. The snipping of the scissors resumed, but Hague was oblivious to it. Cycling home, his legs pumped the pedals as fast as they could so that he could begin the evening's vigil by the radio.

Hague had been going to Old Trafford for five years, during which time the Busby Babes had filtered into the team. He remembered a 1–5 home defeat against Bolton, men against boys, redeemed by a Tommy Taylor header into the net in front of him. But there had been enough magic to hook him for life. He had the autographs, the pictures on the bedroom wall. For Hague, and thousands of Manchester boys like him, life would never be the same again.

When Geoffrey Green of *The Times* got home that night he went to bed and cried. The tragedy was closer to him than to the thousands of United fans like Hague, who also suffered. Green had lost so many good friends.

'Everybody knows where they were the time they heard about the Munich air crash,' says Bill Foulkes. 'It was one of those shocking events that nobody ever forgets.' The disaster touched everyone, whether they were football fans or not. If England was stunned, Manchester was grief-stricken. 'In Manchester the agony was personal,' says former United player Eamon Dunphy in *A Strange Kind of Glory*. 'Some people cried openly in shops and bus shelters, but most were too numb with shock to weep . . . an aching disbelief seeped into the communal soul.' 'In the past,' wrote Vincent Mulchrone, 'the heart of a community may have been the church, or the castle, perhaps the local pub. Today there is no doubt that the heart of this city lies with a football team.'

At Old Trafford agony piled on agony for Jimmy Murphy as the hours ticked by. Then suddenly, after the silence, everything came to life again as the phones began a ceaseless ringing. Murphy answered them and tried to sort out what had happened. One by one the names of the dead were added to the casualty list. At first it was known that some players, officials and journalists had been killed and that Matt Busby was alive. Gradually the death toll mounted. Bert Whalley . . . Geoff Bent . . . Busby's friend Willie Satinoff . . . David Pegg . . . Billy Whelan . . . Mr B.P. Miklos, whose widow Eleanor would never walk again . . . Mark Jones . . . When it was realised the dead included England players Roger Byrne and Tommy Taylor, Murphy's senses went numb.

They were Matt's boys. Murphy's too. United's assistant manager had seen them come to Old Trafford as part of Busby's master plan to build the greatest side in Europe . . . and they were gone. Foulkes's wife Teresa heard the second news bulletin, which named the survivors. In a sense, she had the relief before the shock.

There were tears in newsrooms across the country for the players and those closer to home: colleagues. By eight o'clock that night it was known that eight journalists had also died in the crash. The press had for once sampled tragedy as a felt reality rather than a marketable commodity. The late final edition of the *Evening News* was headlined: UNITED CUP XI: 28 DIE. The final tally was lower, but only slightly.

BBC newsreader Kenneth Kendall had a thankless task, announcing:

> Here is the news. So far we know that there are 23 survivors after Manchester United's air crash at Munich this afternoon. The aircraft was returning from Belgrade where Manchester United had entered the semi-final of the European Cup. It had reached Munich and was just taking off for home in poor weather when the crash came at three o'clock.

First reactions were predictable. By now thousands of people had gathered outside Old Trafford in driving sleet to glean what they could and to see if they could help. There was a greed for news of the wonderful boys who'd died and a public expression of mourning. The police threw a protective cordon around relatives and friends who'd lost their loved ones. Those left at Old Trafford did their best to calm and console the grief-stricken. But what word of sympathy could Murphy find to comfort the bereaved? There was nothing to lift the blanket of despair. He'd always find it hard to describe how difficult things became in those hours after the news of the crash.

A tribute from H.E. Bates referred back to the Second World War and British Prime Minister Neville Chamberlain's attempts to appease German Chancellor Adolf Hitler in the same city of Munich. Bates thought the casualties from the United air disaster were 'now to give the word Munich an even sadder meaning than it had acquired on a day before the war when a British Prime Minister had come home to London waving a pitiful piece of paper and most of us knew that new calamities of war were inevitable'.

Percy M. Young wrote in *Manchester United*:

> There were those who felt that comment of this order, and the incredible national demonstrations of sympathy and sorrow were extravagant; and their case was assisted by the policy of certain newspapers which sought to turn sadness into sensation. Those who made too stringent observations missed the whole significance of the event. Football has become a part of the folk tradition – as such a symbol of life. Munich, which so crudely and so illogically extinguished youth and vigour, showed the spectre of Chesterton's Fate acting 'the same grey farce again'. Tragedy is not of necessity an end in itself. In this case an immense gesture of faith in common human values was stimulated, which became an antidote to earlier griefs.

By now Johnny Berry's family were in a terrible state. Manchester City Hospital had sent round some nurses. They'd given tranquillisers to those who needed them. Six agonising hours after the family first heard about the crash, they were told that Berry was alive.

In Ashington, Jack Charlton and the rest of the family were relieved that Bobby was going to be okay. But there was also sadness as the news came through of those who'd died. Jack knew them all: Tommy Taylor and David Pegg had been at his wedding only a month earlier and Duncan Edwards and Billy Whelan had often driven over the Pennines with Bobby for a drink on Sunday mornings. Bobby's mother wanted to fly straight to Munich, but she was recovering from a recent breast cancer operation. The doctors advised that it wouldn't be safe for her to travel. Meanwhile, Jimmy Murphy suggested that Bobby's mother should come and help out in the offices at Old Trafford, where there was plenty of work for her to do.

Arrangements were made for a party of relatives to fly to Munich to see the survivors. Neither Foulkes nor Gregg liked the idea of their wives coming to see them or the rest of the team, so many of whom were in a far worse state. As soon as they found out about the trip they got on the phone and pleaded with their wives not to come. Foulkes convinced Gregg's wife Mavis there was nothing wrong with him; Gregg did the same with Foulkes's wife Teresa. At first the wives didn't seem to believe their husbands. But Foulkes and Gregg managed to convince them that they wouldn't have been able to phone if they'd been seriously injured. Foulkes was desperately afraid of them coming over on a plane.

At 10.10 p.m. the phone rang at Dick Colman's home. He picked up the receiver. It was Murphy at Old Trafford confirming that his son Eddie was dead. Colman told the family and left the house wearing slippers. It was raining. From that moment he didn't remember anything until he was standing in Manchester Piccadilly sometime after three o'clock in the morning soaked to the skin. He wouldn't be able to sleep or eat for two weeks.

Murphy was like a man living through a nightmare, waiting to wake up. He locked the door to his office, put his head on the desk and wept. The previous Monday he'd waved goodbye to them. 'See you Thursday, lads . . . see you do a good job.' They did. They'd got United through to the European Cup semi-final. Now they were gone at the very moment when they had the world at their feet. Murphy would never remember what happened over the next few hours. The hands on the wall clock had pointed to four o'clock when he first heard of the tragedy and were pointing to four o'clock when he went home the next morning. All he knew was that there was a bottle of Scotch in his cupboard and the following day it was empty, which was extraordinary. Murphy was a beer drinker, yet he'd drunk a bottle of whisky without knowing it. So Jimmy Murphy didn't get any sleep that Thursday night. All he could see were his boys, and he prayed that Busby and the rest would be spared. When he finally got home Murphy realised he'd have to reconcile his grief and carry on alone.

Eleven

The Days After

On Friday morning, at about six o'clock, there was a knock on the door at the home of David Pegg. A policeman was standing there. He'd come to tell the family David was dead.

The scale of the disaster had become clear overnight. The morning papers reported 21 dead, including seven players: left-back Roger Byrne, who didn't know his wife Joy was pregnant, and his stand-in Geoff Bent, who left a wife, Marion, and baby Karen; right-half Eddie 'Swivel-Hips' Colman; centre-half Mark Jones, who had a wife, June, and a young son, Gary; inside-right and devout Catholic Billy Whelan; centre-forward Tommy Taylor, who was planning to marry his fiancée, Carol; and the good-looking outside-left David Pegg. Seven of the greatest players ever assembled in one club had been wiped out, and the greatest of them all, Duncan Edwards, was fighting for his life. Bert Whalley, one of Murphy's closest friends and one of the greatest coaches he'd ever met, was also dead. Tom Curry, the first team trainer, and secretary Walter Crickmer had perished. The journalists who died were Don 'Old International' Davies of the *Manchester Guardian*, Henry Rose of the *Daily Express*, George Follows of the *Daily Herald*, Tom Jackson of the

Manchester Evening News, Alf Clarke of the *Manchester Evening Chronicle*, Eric Thompson of the *Daily Mail* and Archie Ledbrooke, who'd been sent by the *Daily Mirror* in place of Frank McGhee. Frank Swift of the *News of the World* had died from burns. Others who perished included the steward Tommy Cable. Apart from Edwards, those fighting for their lives included Matt Busby, Johnny Berry and Captain Kenneth Rayment.

Charlton's mother managed to get a lift over the Pennines early in the morning from a newspaper delivery driver. She'd followed Murphy's suggestion and was travelling to Old Trafford to work. It would help take her mind off things while she waited for Bobby to come home.

Stanley Williamson put his finger on what it all meant to the people of Manchester in *The Munich Air Disaster*.

> Mingled with the tears shed in the streets of Manchester on Thursday, 6 February 1958, for the brilliant young athletes who would never again grace the turf of Old Trafford, there were tears for the exuberant pride, the shared glory that must surely be things of the past. Manchester was sorry for its dead footballers and their families. It was perhaps, and without recognising it, even sorrier for itself. Before many days were past it was clear that the Lancastrian instinct for display, so sharply contrasted with the Yorkshire affectation of indifference, had taken charge.

Manchester hadn't been hit this badly since the Blitz. 'The awful day of the Munich disaster was something which none of us had ever lived through before,' says Jimmy Savile. 'It was like a day that never happened in your head.' As reports seeped through, men, women and children wept unashamedly on the streets. Amid the horror of the news many factories, offices and pubs fell silent in disbelief. By the end of the day it was, according to one newspaper, 'a stunned city of tears and silence'.

The leader column in the *News Chronicle* on the morning of 7 February said:

Cutting out all the cant about sportsmen being ambassadors, it remains true that a team at this level of achievement plays a definite part in national prestige. It may be loved or castigated at home: abroad its triumphs and humiliations are looked upon nationally. Even those who have no interest in football must recognise that hundreds of millions of people, whose pleasure cuts right across the more formal frontiers of diplomacy, are today united in a sense of loss.

'Silchester' of the *Manchester Guardian* wrote of Busby, in what all feared might be an obituary:

Above all, he recognised, in hitherto unparalleled numbers, fine players very early in their footballing lives. He wanted them so to think about the game that when a movement broke down, they spun a fresh one out of its fragments. Because he had no time for drilled footballers, the genius he discovered remained genius. His players were men in their own right, so that even youths such as Colman, Edwards and Whelan stood out as characters as well as fine players . . . Even under strain they invested the playing of the game with something near indeed to glory in the imagination of hundreds of thousands who had never come within miles of Manchester. If their triumph has become a wreath it is one which will not fade in many memories.

Williamson described how the people of Manchester felt:

The community had suffered, without a shadow of warning, the drastic excision of part of its living organism, and the shock was truly traumatic, a numbed sense of loss, reinforced by the appalled recognition of finality which is the essence of despair. We weep not only for the dead, but for ourselves, or our own broken hopes, for the sudden void in our own lives. The future momentarily ceases to exist, and we are adrift and desolate.

David Lacey of *The Guardian* put the aftermath of the Munich disaster in context 40 years later.

> The reaction to the Munich tragedy was one of shock followed by sadness and then something else: anger, deep and irrational feelings of anger that so much should have been lost through a whim of circumstance. English football felt cheated, and in a way it was.

In Munich, Foulkes and Gregg didn't sleep a wink all night. Gregg just lay on his bed trying to think. By the morning he felt very stiff. He couldn't move his back. It was so painful he couldn't get out of bed. Eventually, he rolled off the side. His nostrils had been split in the crash and Foulkes said he should go back to the hospital for stitches. Foulkes wanted to see how all the lads were getting on and returned to the hospital himself, leaving Gregg in the room alone. When he got there, though, the staff wouldn't let him onto the wards. Captain Thain was there, too, with one of the stewardesses. They were trying to find out who was in the United party and how many there should have been. They found a list of passengers who were in the hospital.

It wasn't until Friday morning that Viollet was able to think at all clearly. His main worry was that his feet and ankles both hurt like hell. He'd lost his shoes in the crash and had hurt his feet walking about afterwards – although he was pleased to see they were still there. Suddenly things started to come back to him and he remembered seeing many of the lads lying on the ground among the debris of the plane. He tried to dismiss the memory from his mind for he was sure it wasn't really true, or at worse that they had, like him, merely been unconscious for a while. Foulkes came to visit and Viollet asked whether Colman was all right. It was then that Viollet realised the pictures flashing through his mind were real and not just a nightmare. It had actually happened.

Gregg wasn't too keen to go to the hospital, but the hotel manager lent him an overcoat and he was eventually taken back. His head and face were X-rayed, his back was massaged and he was given injections. After each spell of massage and injections the doctors asked in sign language if he felt better. After the fourth time he felt anything was better than the agony he was undergoing. When the chance came he nodded his head firmly to indicate his back was easier. Enough was enough.

In Manchester people couldn't believe what had happened. The city was in mourning. Children wearing United scarves walked silently to school, their heads bowed. Men weren't ashamed to be seen weeping. A black tie was hard to get as shops ran out of supplies. Like the previous afternoon and evening, Old Trafford was swarming with people desperate for any snippets of news from Munich.

Busby's family – his wife Jean, son Sandy, daughter Sheena and her husband Don Gibson – joined Murphy and other friends and relatives of the survivors at Manchester's Ringway airport. BEA had arranged a mercy flight for them to see their loved ones. Murphy's job had suddenly become overwhelming. He was trying to run the club and get a team together at the same time as travelling to Munich.

The Viscount plane took off at nine o'clock in the morning bound for Munich via Paris. Murphy, usually very talkative, sat in silence during the flight, brooding. The heartache was locked up inside him. Like the others on board he was close to tears. Wives, mothers and girlfriends tried desperately hard to keep their spirits up, but they were living in agony, dreading what was waiting for them at the Rechts der Isar Hospital.

Jimmy McGuire, President of the United States Football Association, came to see Matt Busby. Although very ill, Busby recognised his old friend, and nodded when McGuire spoke to him. It was a start.

When Charlton woke up after his injections he found himself in a room with a German patient who was reading a newspaper. Charlton watched him for a few seconds before he remembered the events of the previous day. He wondered how the others were getting on. 'What has happened to my friends?' Charlton asked the man. 'Is everyone okay?' The German understood English but he looked at Charlton uncomfortably. He was a nice man and didn't know what to say. Charlton asked if the newspaper had published any names. 'Some are dead,' the man said hesitantly. 'They are named here. So are those who are ill.' Charlton asked for the names. The German read them out in a sad, monotone voice. Later, Charlton spoke to his mother on the phone. She wanted to come out to see him. He told her not to come. He wasn't hurt. He wasn't even deeply troubled psychologically. He just couldn't take in what had happened and so it washed over him; he was in denial. Soon afterwards Charlton was moved into a room with co-pilot Ken Rayment and his team-mates Wood, Scanlon, Morgans, Blanch-flower and Berry. Viollet joined them shortly afterwards, but Berry was soon moved to another room because of his critical injuries.

Like the others, Wood didn't know who'd survived and who hadn't. People kept reassuring him that some of his friends were in other hospitals and that was why he couldn't see them. They all talked about their friends, wondering who was alive, who had a chance of recovering. Charlton was the only one who'd heard the list but he said nothing because he couldn't remember clearly. He could hear the German's voice but not the names he'd reeled off. All he had was a jumble of names that nagged at him.

Apart from his other injuries, Wood had suffered a hefty bang on the head. He had a constant screaming noise in his ears and asked people to turn the radio off even though there wasn't one on. He also began to develop double vision. Every time the nurse put out two tablets for him to take he could see four; when he tried to pick them up he kept missing. It was like something from a Charlie Chaplin film.

When Wilf McGuinness turned up at Old Trafford, he went to the dressing room with some of the other lads. Freddie Goodwin and Ian Greaves were there, but no other first-team players. Trainer Bill Inglis came in and they all sat staring at each other. They didn't talk, not even to say how terrible it was. The players were told to come in on the Monday. After that the weekend was a blur for McGuinness.

As friends and relatives flew out to Munich, the United board met at director Alan Gibson's house in Bowden, Cheshire. The minutes scarcely told in their cold, black-and-white terms of all the drama and heartache surrounding the club. It was recorded that Mr

Harold Hardman, the chairman, and Mr William Petherbridge had attended the funeral of fellow director Mr George Whittaker. His death had left United with only three directors. Condolences were extended to the families of the dead and injured. Mr Louis Edwards was appointed as a director and Busby, who'd originally introduced Edwards to Hardman, thereby gained another great ally. He wanted to bring Edwards on to the board because he was the right sort of material. Edwards was a strong character. As a successful businessman he'd bring new ideas into the club. Finally, Walter Crickmer's assistant Les Olive was appointed acting secretary, a position that would soon be made permanent. The minutes also revealed that Murphy, standing in as temporary manager for Busby, was about to interview Blackpool's Ernie Taylor with a view to his transfer to United. It was also agreed that Jack Crompton, United's former goalkeeper, should be appointed the new team trainer if available; Johnny Carey and Jack Rowley had offered their services to the club in any capacity; £150 would be forwarded to the visiting relatives detained in Munich; and Professor Maurer, his wife and some members of his staff at the Rechts der Isar Hospital in Munich would visit Old Trafford for the League match against West Bromwich Albion on 8 March.

By the time the meeting ended the mercy flight to Munich had landed. None of the passengers knew quite what they'd find when they got there. They had nothing to cling to but hope and prayers. As the plane touched down they saw the broken remains of the Elizabethan beyond the perimeter fence. 'So this was where the team died,' thought Murphy.

Busby, Edwards, Berry, Rayment and Frank Taylor were the most critically injured. All the relatives could do was put on a brave face and live in hope; it was like torture. For some there was a feeling of nothingness, as hope alternated with despair. They could only wait and pray. The destiny of their loved ones rested in God's hands.

Twenty-four hours after *The Manchester Evening Chronicle*'s special edition had first detailed the horrific news, and just as the whole of Europe was reacting to the tragedy, the paper listed the 21 dead on its front page under the headline: MATT FIGHTS FOR LIFE: A 50-50 CHANCE NOW. The paper reported that 15 others were injured and, of these, four players and Busby were in serious condition. *The Chronicle* also carried a picture of Gregg and Foulkes at Morgans's bedside and details of how the other patients were responding to treatment.

In Munich, Busby's family took the lift up to the intensive care unit. Sandy walked anxiously ahead of the group with a nurse, looking in each room to see if he could recognise anybody. As he walked past one room he saw a poor old man in a plastic oxygen tent. He was three yards past when he realised it was his dad. He looked a strange green colour. Sandy ran back to warn his mother what to expect. Busby lay in a bed near journalist Frank Taylor. His chest had been crushed, and he'd suffered massive internal and external injuries including a punctured left lung. He was hovering between sleep and consciousness. His wife Jean held his hand. He seemed to acknowledge his family's presence. Sandy and Sheena begged him not to leave them. Jean was told that the injuries were so severe he'd been given a tracheotomy operation to help him breathe. Matt's life was in the balance, and he seemed to be slipping away. Only his courage and the sound physique built up in his days as a footballer kept him going.

After Busby slipped back to sleep his family went to comfort the others. Berry and Rayment lay silently in deep comas; Rayment had a huge scar across his shaved head. But Edwards was the most serious case. He had critical kidney injuries and his right thigh was smashed. A kidney machine was being flown from Freiburg, near Stuttgart, to Munich in a desperate attempt to save his life. As with Busby, his injuries would have killed other men instantly, but both of them were physically very strong with unusual spirit. In Edwards's case, that was the only thing keeping him alive. His parents and fiancée flew to Munich. Thousands of people felt sympathy for them. The plane crash had sparked an extraordinary emotional response all over the country; even allowing for the drama of the accident and saturation media coverage, that emotion was genuine enough.

Murphy, by now checked into the Starhaus Hotel, met up with Gregg and Foulkes. They could see he was terribly upset, but he put on a brave face and joked for their benefit. He told them it might be better if they stayed on in Munich over the weekend in case any of the boys asked for them. He wanted those in hospital to know that some people had survived. They agreed, although neither relished the prospect of visiting the hospital again.

Murphy took Foulkes and Gregg back to visit the injured. Everyone was very nice to them. The same lady doctor Foulkes had spoken to before took them in to see everyone. The mess had been cleared up by now, and everything was highly organised. Small wards of about six beds led off a main corridor. Murphy, Foulkes, Gregg and Professor Maurer went to every bed. 'Strong man, fifty-fifty,' said Maurer as he took them to see Busby. 'Duncan Edwards, fifty-fifty; Frank Taylor, fifty-fifty; Jackie Blanchflower, fifty-fifty.' Maurer and his team had hardly slept as they battled to save the critically injured, but not even he could forecast who would live.

Busby was in his oxygen tent breathing through a tube. He looked terrible. Foulkes thought Frank Taylor, who was in the same ward as Busby, was in good form considering. Taylor had a broken arm and leg. He seemed to be asleep. Edwards called for help. 'Let's have some bloody attention,' he shouted. The nurse looked at him admiringly. 'A very strong boy, very strong,' she said.

Murphy told Charlton, whose head was bandaged, to go home to Newcastle for a couple of weeks when he got out of hospital. Murphy said he should only return to Manchester when he felt like it. Blanchflower, who was quite a good golfer, was nursing his injured arm. He was worried it might affect his swing. Blanchflower, who thought only Byrne had died, was thankful for Tom Curry's fitness training. He was sure he'd never have survived if he hadn't been so fit. Viollet had been hit on the jaw and also had a gashed head. He still looked very groggy. Viollet was always fussy about his hairstyle and was fretting that the gash might affect his parting. Scanlon had a fractured skull, but otherwise wasn't badly hurt. Gregg couldn't believe that Scanlon had recovered so quickly. He'd last seen him lying on the ground at the airstrip with his skull split open and blood gushing from the wound. Scanlon was now covered in bandages. He was still ill, but at least he looked human again. Wood's face was gashed and he was suffering from concussion. Morgans and Berry were also there.

Foulkes spoke to a nurse about Berry and Edwards. 'How's Duncan?' he asked. 'Fifty-fifty,' she replied. The nurse thought Edwards's prospects were better than 'Digger' Berry's. Berry was wired from every finger and toe. When Murphy saw him lying in the hospital he didn't think he'd survive. But he should have remembered that as a player Berry was full of guts, fast and determined, afraid of nothing. Maurer gave the odds on Berry: 'Twenty-five–seventy-five, maybe better. But I'm not God,' he said.

'Don't you speak to the poor, Foulksey?' Frank Taylor shouted as Foulkes and Gregg made their way back through the ward. Foulkes went over and sat on the end of his bed. Taylor asked if they wanted a beer. He said a nurse would get some. His leg was strung up high but he told them he was having a smashing time. He didn't know what had happened to the other players either. 'Where's the rest?' he said. Foulkes asked a nurse which hospital they should go to next to see the other lads. She looked puzzled. He asked again where the rest of the team had been taken. 'This is it. This is it,' she said. 'Aren't they at the other hospital?' Foulkes wondered. 'There is no other hospital,' she replied. Suddenly everything became clear. The truth dawned on Foulkes for the first time. He asked a lady doctor where Bert Whalley and Tom Curry were. She just shook her head. Foulkes was sickened and shattered. He began to realise just how lucky he'd been and just wanted to get out, to get away. He couldn't believe it. But he stayed with Gregg – they followed each other everywhere, because both hated the idea of being alone with their thoughts. While they were relieved that so many of the lads were alive, they still couldn't stop thinking about those who had died.

The second day after the crash Busby spoke to his wife Jean. He seemed to be trying to cheer her up. Nurse Greta Thiel was impressed by the fact that the first thoughts of the injured were for their colleagues. She was amazed by their team spirit.

As relatives and friends began to arrive reporters soon surrounded Foulkes and Gregg. British press photographers wandered around the wards taking pictures of everyone regardless of how ill they were. Professor Maurer and the players' relatives complained bitterly. Eventually all the wives gathered in Foulkes's and Gregg's bedroom. It was a terrible ordeal and they comforted each other. Gregg couldn't praise them too highly. Jean Busby and her daughter Sheena and Johnny Berry's wife impressed Foulkes with the absolute calm with which they approached the situation. Duncan Edwards's pal, Jimmy, and his girlfriend Molly were there along with Jackie Blanchflower's wife Jean, Dennis Viollet's wife Barbara and Albert Scanlon's wife, who was expecting a baby. They were all very upset and trying not to show it. Foulkes went to the toilet and saw Murphy sitting hunched up on the stairs. Murphy had his head in his hands and looked as if his world had fallen apart.

The press were desperate to know the full story of the crash. Eventually Foulkes and Gregg went to their hotel and tried to tell them exactly what they thought had happened. Nevertheless, the insensitive behaviour of the British photographers forced Professor Maurer to issue a statement. 'On Saturday morning, Mr Busby, who is seriously ill, asked me to save him from the photographers. He said, "The flashes are hurting my eyes".'

Busby wasn't expected to live. His wife Jean and children, Sheena and Sandy, watched as a Roman Catholic priest administered the last rites – twice. The hospital issued a statement: 'We do not have much hope of saving him.' Busby lay comatose in his oxygen tent, barely alive. But at least he had a chance. He was tough and had always been a fighter prepared for a challenge. Now, at 49, he faced the biggest battle of his life. Jean was fantastic. It was harder for her than most. She'd known many of the dead players almost as well as Matt. Not long before he'd written: 'With Jean I have had the two most priceless assets any man can hope to possess – a good wife and a happy home life.' She comforted and cared for everyone despite her obvious worries about Matt. There was little hope left for him. Professor Maurer banished everyone from Busby's bedside. He didn't want anything to knock him back. All Busby could feel and all he knew was pain.

Foulkes, Gregg and Edwards's friend, Jimmy, were taken to the scene of the crash. BEA's Anthony Millward was at the airport. A German official asked Foulkes and Gregg to explain exactly what happened. Then they looked around the wreckage to help identify the luggage. Foulkes got back into the part of the plane where he'd been sitting. His bag was missing, but jammed up against the roof in the rack above his seat he found his briefcase full of magazines and his overcoat. Neither was damaged. He was even more amazed to find that the bottle of gin given to him at the British Embassy in Belgrade was intact in one of the pockets of his coat. As he climbed out of the plane clutching the gin someone took a photograph.

While rummaging around, Foulkes found a cap with Colman's name on it. The players used to go to a place called The Continental in Manchester where, as a gimmick, the owner would present flat caps with the person's name inscribed inside to mark a certain number of visits. Colman used to wear his cap and Foulkes had found it along with his red and white scarf. There was also a paper bag containing an apple, an orange, some tea and sugar. His mother had packed it for Colman. Finding the cap upset Foulkes so much he felt he could stand it no longer. Suddenly, Edwards's friend Jimmy started shouting. He'd found a very valuable diamond ring, and a lot more jewellery. The German official sent for an armed policeman who was left to guard the wreckage. The jewellery belonged to Eleanor Miklos.

Another official took them back into the airport building and gave them a stiff drink before they went to look through the salvaged luggage. Ironically, the baggage belonging to those who'd died seemed to be okay. Foulkes got very upset reading all the labels. He found a briefcase belonging to United's secretary Walter Crickmer; it was filled with cash, traveller's cheques and his silver hip flask.

Back at the hotel Foulkes searched his jacket. The pack of cards was still in his hip pocket. He took them out and gasped. Although his pocket hadn't been ripped, a quarter of an inch had been sliced cleanly off the top of the pack. The cut looked as if a razor had made it, and it could have sliced Foulkes in half as well if it had hit him. That's how close he'd come to death.

That night in Munich, Foulkes, Gregg and Charlton couldn't stop talking about anything and everything that had happened. What they were saying had no impact on Murphy. At any moment, he half expected to see Tommy Taylor's beaming face coming through the door; or Big Dunc creeping up behind him to give him a whack on the back with a 'Hiya Jimmy . . .'

On the Saturday morning there were photographs in the papers of Foulkes and Gregg standing among the debris. They were living through a nightmare.

Morgans woke for the first time in 48 hours. He'd been in a deep coma for two days, during which time he had been given lots of blood. When he opened his eyes he saw two German reporters at his bedside. Professor Maurer told Morgans who'd lived and who'd died. The reporters told him they'd been to the crash scene and he was the last to come out.

When Scanlon woke up, the last thing he could remember was Whelan saying he was ready to die just before the crash. Scanlon had a telephone in one hand and was holding a nurse's hand with the other. He was shouting something down the phone. He looked around and saw he was sharing a room with Rayment, Viollet and Wood, who were close to him, while Charlton and Morgans were at the other end. But Scanlon soon lost consciousness again. When he woke up he heard a voice saying 'Albert Scanlon will never play football again'. Just then Murphy walked in and came to the end of his bed. Scanlon was crying and told him what he'd heard. 'That's not true,' Murphy told him. 'Albert, you're all right. The doctors say you will be playing again soon. Take my word for it.' That was good enough for Scanlon; he trusted Murphy completely.

Twelve

The World Reacts

The impact of the disaster seemed to affect almost everyone. People wanted to do something to acknowledge the loss of so many fine young players and journalists. The Lord Mayor of Manchester, Leslie Lever, cancelled all social engagements except those concerned with charity. He also opened a Disaster Fund. Among the first contributions were a thousand guineas each from Great Universal Stores and *The Manchester Evening Chronicle*. A Manchester United Supporters Fund was opened. The BBC postponed a programme called *Match Abandoned* and showed a film instead. A chain of shoe shops paid its tribute to the team by filling all its windows with pictures of the players flanked by red carnations and white lilacs. The Queen sent condolences. Six hundred people stood silent at a by-election in Rochdale. The Hallé Orchestra saluted the dead in Sheffield with Elgar's *Nimrod* variation. Even a City supporter said, 'I'll go and cheer them when I can.'

The weekend after the crash the players who'd died were remembered at sporting events across the world. On the Saturday snow lay on pitches across the country. The symbolic significance wasn't lost on the crowds huddled together at football and rugby grounds in Britain and Ireland. Fans of every club stood, heads bowed, as referees blew their whistles for a two-minute silence. At many grounds *Abide With Me* was sung before the kick-off. The players wore black armbands. Many believed they shouldn't have been asked to play at all. At Twickenham a 60,000 crowd stood in silence before a rugby international between England and Ireland.

Europe also mourned the loss. At the European Skiing Championships at Bad Gastein in Austria 10,000 fans stood in silence as the floodlights were dimmed. On Sunday football crowds all over the continent did the same. Germany's Eintracht Frankfurt flew their players in two separate planes for a friendly against Arsenal.

Messages of sympathy poured in from many countries, including Spain and Hungary, and were sent by royalty, heads of state, religious leaders, dignitaries and government officials. Queen Elizabeth, German Chancellor Konrad Adenauer, President Tito of Yugoslavia, the King of Sweden, the Pope, the Bishop of Chester, the Rector of the University of Bordeaux, the French and Italian Ambassadors, the Apostolic Delegate and Lord Derby, the Lord Lieutenant of Lancashire, all sent messages of sympathy. They also came from municipalities and sporting organisations, such as the South African and Australian cricket teams playing their fourth test in Johannesburg and the Russian State Committee for Physical Culture and Sport.

Others joined the official tributes, which reflected the great sense of personal loss felt by so many and a general appreciation of the integrity for which United stood. These condolences included those from private and public schools, both primary and secondary, ships at sea, works and offices, inmates in Her Majesty's prisons, the D'Oyly Carte and Lirica Italiana Opera companies, the London County Council Tenants' Association, the Salvation Army, the Sikh Community of Manchester, the Soroptimists International Association and the Society of West End Theatre Managers (SWET).

There was international support for a suggestion from Red Star's president that United should be named Honorary Champions of the European Cup for 1958. 'It is impossible to believe that such a team excellent sportsmen have been struck by such a terrible accident,' he said. 'The news will cause deep sorrow to all sportsmen of Britain, whose sorrow we fully share.' The battle on the pitch in Belgrade just a few days before was now all but forgotten. The Yugoslav newspaper *Sport* even proposed renaming the European Cup the *Manchester United Cup*.

For many people, not only in Britain but all over the world, this was the moment they began to take an interest in United. They heard about the crash and were moved by the team that had lost half its players. They began to follow the Reds to see how the club would pick itself up and carry on. The fact that many of the players who died were so young seemed to be an important part of the fascination. United became everyone's second-favourite team and every neutral wanted them to win.

People were very generous. At Jimmy Savile's Plaza ballroom in Manchester people threw money on to the dance floor. Money had poured into the appeal fund set up by the Lord Mayor. At Stamford Boys' Secondary School in Ashton, two lads gave their headmaster £7 10s (£7.50) in pennies and the inmates at Strangeways Prison raised 12 guineas (£12.60).

In Munich, Frank Taylor eventually returned to reality for the first time after hovering on the brink of eternity. He was very happy to be back. Slowly and methodically he let his eyes wander curiously around the dimly lit room. He could see the figure of a man in the next bed with a kind of plastic tent around him. 'Is that really Matt Busby?' he thought. Taylor looked hard. Yes, it was. So he hadn't been dreaming. 'That's Matt, isn't it?' he asked his wife Peggy. 'How is he doing?' 'He's doing fine too,' she replied. 'The doctors have just told Mrs Busby that he is going to get well. You are both going to be moved out of here. Now stop worrying. Everything is going to be all right.'

Taylor and Busby were in an intensive care unit. Although both had severe injuries, they were now well enough to be moved down the corridor to a normal private room. As Taylor lay there trying to piece things together he realised he couldn't see any of his press colleagues. 'Why aren't they in this room with me?' he thought. Whenever they travelled to European Cup ties they either shared a room or had one close by. 'Where's George Follows, Henry Rose,

Eric Thompson and the rest of the lads?' he asked. This was the question his wife and brother were afraid he'd ask. In his present weak state the shock of being told they'd been killed might be too much for him. Peggy looked at her husband and said, 'I'm afraid they couldn't take them all here. They are safe in another place.'

Before Taylor could ask any more questions he heard a voice he knew very well. It was the best player United had ever had at Old Trafford, Duncan Edwards. The big fellow opened his eyes briefly and turned his head as Murphy approached his bed. 'Oh, it's you, Jimmy,' Edwards mumbled. 'What time is the kick-off on Saturday? Is it three o'clock? I can't miss the Wolves match,' he added, by now speaking loud and clear. As if by telepathy, Murphy, Foulkes and Gregg all came up with the same answer: 'Usual time, three o'clock.' Taylor lay in his bed listening as Murphy patted Edwards, choking back tears. Taylor couldn't see the lump in his throat, but he could hear it in his quick reply. 'Okay, son . . . don't worry,' said Murphy. 'We're resting you, Duncan. We don't need you to beat Wolves.' That's all he could think of saying. 'Get stuck in,' Edwards murmured sleepily. Then he called for a nurse, turned his head and drifted back to semi-consciousness.

Taylor would never forget that moment. Edwards was lying there almost helpless with terrible injuries, kept alive by a kidney machine, and yet all he could think about was playing for United again. It seemed nothing could extinguish his great spirit.

Murphy stood comforting Edwards as the Busby family arrived at Big Dunc's bedside. The horror of the scene was magnified for Sandy Busby by his memories of the happy, carefree times he'd spent with his friend Duncan training and playing around on dark evenings at United's Cliff training ground. Taylor watched Murphy as he came over to speak to him. He was the same old Murphy – flashing eyes, big broad smile and the ready joke. 'That's the big fellow,' said Taylor. 'How is he?' 'Oh, fine, fine' said Murphy, 'You know Duncan. He says he's all raring to go.' Taylor accepted that. But Murphy and the others knew Edwards was desperately ill. Even if he lived, his right thigh was smashed and he'd never play football again.

Taylor knew Murphy was a good friend of George Follows. Murphy would know better than anyone where Follows and the rest of Taylor's press colleagues were. Taylor wanted his brother Bill to meet Henry Rose, who'd been his idol when he was a schoolboy. 'Jimmy, where are Henry, Eric, George and the rest of the lads?' asked Taylor. 'When they are well enough, I want you to take my brother to meet them. Where are they?' Murphy had to think quickly. He didn't want to break the sad news to Taylor at this stage. He pointed upwards, as if towards the floor above. 'They are all up there, son,' he said. 'Quite safe. They're in good hands, don't worry about that.' There was a slight break in Murphy's voice, so he changed the subject. 'You're a careless fellow,' he went on, pointing to Taylor's right leg, which was in plaster. 'Fancy giving your leg a knock like that. How's it feeling?' 'I'm all right, Jimmy,' replied Taylor. 'I'm fit enough to play on Saturday if selected.' Murphy liked to tease journalists like Follows and Taylor by telling them how out of shape they were. This time he forced a smile. 'I know you are, son,' he said and walked away. He saw Busby in his oxygen tent but didn't speak to him on that first visit because he was sleeping. As he left the room Murphy brushed away a tear with his handkerchief. It was a terrible time.

Although the surgeons now felt Busby might live, no one except those close to him thought he'd be a force in football again. But Murphy knew. In one of his conscious moments the Boss waved a feeble hand to beckon him to his side. Murphy had to bend low over the bed to catch his words as Busby gripped his hand: 'Keep the flag flying, Jimmy,' he whispered. 'Keep things going till I get back.' Busby didn't yet know how many of his boys had been killed. But Murphy did. As he stumbled out of the hospital into the snow, which still lay like a thick carpet over Munich, Murphy was close to tears. 'Yes, I'll keep things going, Matt,' he thought. 'But where am I going to find the players? Where am I going to find the players?'

On the Sunday night the Busby and Taylor families had their prayers answered. Seventy-two hours after being taken to hospital Professor Maurer announced that both men were off the danger list.

By now, Maurer and his team were completely exhausted as they battled to save the lives of Berry, Edwards and Rayment. Blanchflower also needed constant attention now, even though at first he wasn't among the critically injured. Ominously there were signs that he might have suffered the same severe kidney damage as Edwards.

Thirteen

Heroes' Welcome

The days dragged by for Foulkes and Gregg. After another visit to the hospital things looked blacker than ever for some of the badly injured. As the weekend approached Murphy wisely decided Foulkes and Gregg would be better off at home. He kept telling them not to bother about football, but they all knew they had to start thinking about the club's future sometime soon. It would be best if they returned to Manchester as quickly as possible to help get things moving again. The weekend match against Wolves had been cancelled, but United still had lots of games to play in both the League and the FA Cup.

The airline officials offered to fly them back at BEA's expense. Foulkes couldn't believe they were stupid enough to even suggest flying. He said they'd never get him in 'a stinking plane' again. Gregg felt the same. Instead, they arranged to travel back with Murphy by train and then boat via the Hook of Holland before taking another train to London.

Ten years of work and planning had been wiped out in a flash at Munich. Murphy's heart and prayers were with those cruelly injured and left behind clinging to life in the hospital, yet he had to try to shut these thoughts out of his mind and concentrate on salvaging what was left of Manchester United. The club had to complete its League programme and its FA and European Cup ties.

Gregg and Murphy stepped from the train at London's Liverpool Street Station into a barrage of arc lights and cameras. It was the biggest collection of photographers Foulkes had ever seen, and he'd seen some gatherings in his time. He managed to walk out behind the crush of people without being noticed.

They were the first of the Busby Babes to reach England alive since the Munich disaster. Crowds packed the station. The many people who wanted to speak to them made Foulkes and Gregg uncomfortable. Foulkes asked a policeman the way and hurried from the platform. He had a knack of making himself scarce. Foulkes and Gregg hid behind a lorry while they waited for their car. It was an unwelcome climax to what had been a difficult journey.

A sleek Daimler limousine took Foulkes and Gregg to see their wives, Teresa and Mavis, who were waiting for them at a hotel. The two men were really glad to see them. The players didn't want to take the train to Manchester, so Murphy hired a Rolls Royce. As they were driven through the English countryside Foulkes and Gregg reflected on their luck in having a future again. They tried to blot out the awful memories of Munich by concentrating on football. Gregg began to consider what the future would mean for United. He realised what a task Murphy had on his hands.

There was little relief for Foulkes and Gregg on their return to Manchester. Everyone wanted to offer his or her sympathies. Foulkes was too upset and shocked to think about it all. Once Murphy had seen them safely back to their families the reaction set in. He couldn't sleep that night as he wrestled with the problems of trying to raise a team, any sort of team, to represent United. Foulkes and Gregg had returned to a heroes' welcome.

Vesna Lukic had good reason to look upon Gregg as a saviour. 'In our family he's always been treated as a hero,' she'd say years later. 'If it hadn't been for Harry Gregg our family wouldn't have been here at all.' Gregg views the incident modestly. 'Life's not about heroes,' he says. 'You help where you can. Sometimes you wished you'd bloody helped when you didn't do it. But you can't make those decisions consciously.'

Nothing good could come out of such a horrific crash, but it did have one significant effect on Foulkes and his wife. They'd been married for four years, but had no children. Realising how desperately lucky he was to be alive, they decided to have a family as soon as possible.

By now the atmosphere in Manchester was almost hysterical. The question was no longer who'd died, but why. Geoff Bent's wife Marion was very angry. She couldn't understand why the passengers were allowed to get back on the plane after two take-off attempts. 'I mean they were all grown men,' she says, 'they could all speak up, and nobody said anything.' Gregg knew that if someone had objected the disaster could have been averted. He has developed his own theory to explain why nobody did. 'If anyone had had the courage to stand up and say "This is crazy" it wouldn't have happened. But it takes a very brave man to be a coward.'

Fourteen

The Coffins Come Home

After the weekend the melancholy task of bringing home the bodies began. Munich was suddenly transformed by a freak heatwave which surprised even the locals.

On the Monday morning the flag-draped coffins were brought through the streets of Munich before dawn and loaded onto a BEA Viscount. Later, through a guard of honour formed by the Munich City Police, representatives of the civic authorities and West German football clubs took wreaths into the cabin. In the afternoon, following a service attended by the British Consul, the aircraft took off for England, flying low over the wreckage of Zulu Uniform.

After a stop in London, where four coffins, including those of David Pegg and Liam Whelan, were unloaded, the plane continued to Manchester where the Lord Mayor was waiting with relatives of the dead and United directors at Ringway Airport. Wilf McGuinness had taken Eddie Colman's girlfriend Marjorie to the airport. The League Championship flag flew at half-mast above the terminal building.

The BEA Viscount landed at 9.35 p.m. It was just over an hour late. One by one the coffins and 58 wreaths were carried from the plane to the 17 waiting hearses. 'We watched them bring them in,' recalls Marjorie English, 'which seems a bit morbid, but you just felt you had to be there. We watched them bringing the bodies off. Then you realised that they were dead.'

At 11.15 p.m. the coffins were ready to begin the solemn journey to their various destinations. Those of Roger Byrne, Eddie Colman, Geoff Bent, Mark Jones and Tommy Taylor were taken to Old Trafford. The bodies of the journalists and local businessman Willie Satinoff were taken to private addresses.

If he'd returned to Manchester alive Roger Byrne would have learned that his wife Joy was expecting a child. Other players already had families who'd never know their fathers. Geoff Bent's wife Marion was left alone with their baby daughter Karen. Ex-bricklayer Mark Jones, 24, left a young wife June and a baby son Gary. Jones also loved his black Labrador, Rick. The dog pined away and died shortly after the disaster. David Pegg, 22, had got into the England side at a time when Tom Finney and Stanley Matthews were coming to the end of their international careers. Like Duncan Edwards, Tommy Taylor was planning to marry. He'd told his fiancée Carol that he was looking forward to getting home from Belgrade for a pint of Guinness and to listen to his records with her. Eddie Colman, the 'cheekie chappie' from Salford, was just 21 and single, but as one of the Busby Babes he had, like all the others, been part of one of the closest families of them all.

When the coffins arrived the city of Manchester was for the first time brought into direct contact with the tragedy. Despite the late hour, and ignoring the rain that had begun to fall, people waited in their thousands at the kerbside to pay their respects to the players and journalists. The city that had cheered their young stars off now wept as they came back in coffins. They were the men and women of the terraces: businessmen in their new cars, Teddy Boys (a fashion craze followed by lads with crepe-soled shoes, quiffed hair and a love of rock and roll music), housewives carrying young children, cloth-capped men with bicycles, schoolboys and office girls in headscarves. They stood along the roads from Manchester airport to Old Trafford and cried quietly or knelt in prayer. Hundreds more who'd never seen United play just wanted to be there. The largest crowd in United's history had turned out to pay their respects. As the cortège passed by the crowds of people, the only sounds that could be heard were the wheels of the hearses on the road and people crying.

The ten-mile route to the ground was lined for miles with cars standing nose to tail; every roundabout was crowded with mourners. One estimate put the numbers at 100,000. By the time Old Trafford was reached the crowds had increased. The biggest concentration was outside the entrance to the stadium, the nearest point to the small gymnasium under the main grandstand that had been turned into a chapel of rest. Mrs Betty Clarke of Addison Crescent, Old Trafford was one of the first people to arrive at the ground. 'I stood in the rain for hours to see them last night,' she told reporters the next day. 'I never knew them personally, but they were to me every mother's ideal of a son.'

Slowly the crowd dispersed as the now empty hearses turned away from the ground. But all night long people came to the doors of Old Trafford laying flowers and crying and praying. Eventually, after everyone had left, Constable Tom Potter and a colleague were locked inside the gymnasium with the coffins. The policemen glanced at each other with tears in their eyes. By 2.00 a.m. all was silent around the shadowed stadium. A dim light sneaked out from under the gymnasium door where the bodies had been laid out to rest before being passed on to the families for the funerals.

It was a very long night for the two policemen. Constable Potter could smell the varnish on the coffins. It was something he'd never forget. Years later he'd say, 'Whenever I smell new varnish I think of those coffins in that gymnasium, and seeing them there with tears in my eyes, and morning couldn't come quick enough so I could go home and try to forget it. But I never have.'

As a new dawn broke over Manchester the first streaks of daylight filtered through the gymnasium windows overlooking the railway line. The coffins lay on black cloth-topped tables. Numerous wreaths and flowers were placed along the wall-bars. Outside, supporters began to reappear on the forecourt. Manchester mourned as the bodies of its famous footballing heroes lay in their spiritual home. The players now departed knew the gymnasium well from the endless games of head tennis they'd played there over the years. United's long-serving laundry ladies, Mrs Irene Ramsden and her sister, Mrs Taylor, polished all the coffins. It was the saddest day of their lives dusting the caskets of lads who such a short time ago had played hide-and-seek in their laundry. But they wanted them to look as they should before the parents came.

Later that dismal morning players and officials arrived at the ground. They gathered in the gym. For several silent moments they stood with heads bowed and their thoughts elsewhere. As the morning passed the relatives arrived to take the coffins to various destinations for their final journey. The coffin of Marjorie English's boyfriend Eddie Colman, the youngster from up the road, was the first to leave.

Fifteen

Murphy Takes Control

Jimmy Murphy returned from Munich to take control of the team's affairs and ensure the club's survival. He concealed his grief just as in the past he'd hidden his warm, sensitive nature so he could do a better job. 'Life must go on' was Murphy's slogan as he used his powerful personality to awaken those left at Old Trafford from their nightmare.

For United to carry on they had to get away from Manchester and its shattering atmosphere of hysteria. The city was still grieving, occupied by the voices and faces of men whose loss was almost unbearably shocking. During the week, in the dressing-room, at the training ground and in matches 'out the back', the ghosts of Curry and Whalley, Colman and Byrne lingered tormentingly – especially for Murphy. Chairman Harold Hardman told him to take the players out of the atmosphere of sorrow that hung over Manchester. Hardman wanted them to be kept away from the crowds and the feverish anxiety in the city for long periods.

Murphy took the squad to the Norbreck Hydro in Blackpool. They'd started going up there during the European Cup runs of the previous two seasons. Gordon Clayton and Wilf McGuinness were injured so they stayed behind to represent the players at the funerals. It was a week of funerals: Henry Rose and Willie Satinoff on Tuesday; Roger Byrne, Archie Ledbrooke, Frank Swift and Eric Thompson on Wednesday; Geoff Bent, Alf Clarke, Tom Curry, Tommy Taylor and Bert Whalley on Thursday; and Eddie Colman, Walter Crickmer and Tom Jackson on Friday.

Colman's girlfriend Marjorie couldn't believe how many people turned up. 'The funeral was unreal. There were thousands and thousands of people on each side of the road standing there in respect. That really blew my mind, it was so awesome.' The epitaph on Colman's gravestone read: 'In Loving Memory of a dear son Edward Colman who died in the Munich air disaster on 6 February 1958. Aged 21 years.'

Busby's laundry lassies, known at the club as Omo and Daz, went to a different funeral each day to say goodbye to their friends. Thousands of fans turned out to pay homage. Where families requested that funerals should be private, the supporters stayed away from the gravesides. Instead, they lined the route to look on in tearful silence as the cortèges passed.

Desmond Hackett of the *Daily Express* wrote a moving epitaph to Henry Rose, whose funeral was the biggest of them all. A thousand taxi drivers offered their services free to anyone who was going. There was a six-mile queue to Manchester's Southern Cemetery. The cortège stopped for a moment outside the *Daily Express* offices in Great Ancoats Street, where Hackett wrote in the style of Rose: 'Even the skies wept for Henry Rose today . . .'

Besides his Labrador, Mark Jones's other love was his aviary birds. His wife June appealed for good homes for the 50-odd birds. People with cages arrived at the house in ones and twos to take them away. June also looked after the interests of the other players' wives. 'What about these girls; they've got no wages?' she told the club. June saw that they got some money and took them all out to Munich.

Meanwhile, the world held its breath in the hope that Duncan Edwards would somehow pull through. People followed every scrap of news about his fight to stay alive. Edwards, who'd now been joined by Blanchflower, was one of the most seriously injured. As well as severe shock his body had been cruelly battered. He'd suffered irreparable kidney damage, broken ribs, a pneumothorax, a broken pelvis and a smashed right thigh. On 12 February, six days after the crash, Edwards's condition deteriorated. His life was slipping away. In a desperate bid to save him the doctors performed a six-hour emergency operation. It was the day AC Milan were playing Borussia Dortmund in one of the other European Cup quarter-finals. While Edwards battled against the odds the other players watched the match on television in the hospital.

Although Edwards's condition was gradually getting worse some of the other players were responding to the care and attention lavished on them by the dedicated hospital staff. Nurse Sister Almunder was helping to look after Albert Scanlon. 'Ah, Mr Scanlon,' she said when he regained consciousness, 'it's nice to see you awake. It's the first time I've seen you conscious in the six days you've been here.'

Edwards briefly awoke the day after his operation murmuring 'Where am I?' and yelling 'Goal, goal!' It was very distressing.

A South African woman with four kidneys offered to donate two to Edwards. She was turned down because it was thought that kidney grafts didn't take successfully. Big Dunc, by now hooked up to a kidney machine, had to battle on with the same superhuman strength that made him such a force as a player. Murphy was sure a lesser man would have died in the first few hours after the accident, so severe were his injuries. He hoped and prayed that this boy's unconquerable spirit would pull him through. The surgeons said it might be five years before Edwards could use his right leg again even if he recovered from his much more devastating internal injuries.

Charlton, Viollet and Scanlon were in the best shape, just a few stitches here and there. They were allowed visitors. Some Irish girls from a local village brought them cases of cigarettes and drink, a present from the American forces stationed there. Some of the other players' families started to come over as well. Scanlon was confined to bed and not allowed to see the players in other wards. One day little Kenny Morgans was wheeled in to see them. Charlton looked at him. He'd remembered that Morgans's name had been in the paper, but he hadn't known until now on which list. At least that was one doubt out of their minds. It would be a few more days before they'd know the full extent of the disaster.

By 15 February the Lord Mayor's Disaster Fund had passed the £8,000 mark. Dartmoor prisoners donated £5 10s (£5.50); Mrs Eunice Launsbach raised money by writing a pantomime in which 12 of the 22 bridesmaids at her wedding took part; and the Manchester United Supporters Club launched its own fund to raise a memorial to the dead and assist their dependants. United had personal accident insurance of £10,000 each for the 21 players and officials. The British European Airways plane was insured for £750,000 and the total cost to Lloyds was estimated at close to half a million pounds. A week after the accident BEAs' Chief Insurance Officer opened preliminary talks with relatives of the dead and injured. Claims were expected to reach almost £100,000. The airline's liability for compensation for death was limited by international convention to £3,000 per person.

Amid all the sorrow a memorial service was held at St Martin's-in-the-Fields, London on 17 February. The Bishop of Chester, Sir Thomas Beecham, gave a moving oration. It included these words:

> We are here today to express on behalf of a great company the sympathy which we feel at so sudden and grievous a blow. We may well ask why this particular accident has called for such widely spread expression of sympathy. It is, I think, due not solely to the drama of the setting or the fact that skilful players, officials and writers, well known and admired, have been killed, though of course these factors are present in our minds. It is rather due, so I believe, to the character of the team to which those players belonged and the fine sport which they have created and upheld. Those well fitted to express an opinion have spoken of the quite outstanding quality which Manchester United has displayed and, during the last ten years under the genius of Matt Busby, young men have not only been trained to a high standard of technical efficiency but they have also been inspired with a loyalty to the club and to the game which has been a pattern for the best that man can achieve. This character has brought the team to the highest places in

the game in this country. It has made the name of Manchester United a household word. It has also given the team an opportunity of travelling to many foreign countries and there, in addition to playing football, they have proved themselves fine ambassadors on the football ground and off it.

When we remember that during the season a million people each week in this country watch professional football, we can appreciate the responsibility which is laid upon these young players. They are admired, idolised, glamorised, imitated. They set a standard which, unseen perhaps, certainly leaves its mark upon the moral standards of our society. They have a responsibility not only to play efficiently but to play well, and it is because Manchester United have acquitted themselves so splendidly in the discharge of their duty that the team has become a byword for those who play a good game wherever football is played.

Sixteen

Starting Again

For Manchester United, Munich was the end of an era. But life had to go on despite the tragedy. 'Even if it means being heavily defeated, we will carry on with the season's programme,' said Chairman Harold Hardman. 'We have a duty to the public and a duty to football to carry out.'

As Murphy and Hardman dried their tears together the chairman offered words of encouragement: 'You have got to keep it going, Jimmy. Manchester United is bigger than you . . . bigger than me . . . bigger than Matt Busby. It is bigger than anybody. The club must go on.' It was an example of the spirit that burned within Manchester United.

Bill Foulkes had been told by his doctor to take a long holiday away from it all. But how could he? He couldn't stop thinking of poor Murphy on his own at Old Trafford. Foulkes remembered Murphy saying they had to have a trainer before anything else, now Tom Curry had gone. Foulkes suggested former United goalkeeper Jack Crompton, whom he knew was doing a very good job for Luton. Foulkes doubted Crompton would come, but in fact he jumped at the chance to return to Old Trafford as trainer-coach. One of his first tasks was to oversee the unpacking of the skip containing the playing kit from the Red Star match. Nobby Stiles was on the ground staff. His job was to clean the boots. The pitch in Belgrade had been heavy and the boots were caked in mud. Second team trainer Bill Inglis told Stiles to clean the boots of the lads who'd survived. Stiles was allowed to take Tommy Taylor's boots as a memento if he cleaned the others. (Stiles later gave the boots to an old school friend who became a United scout, and he eventually gave them to the club. They're now in the United museum.)

United's fifth-round FA Cup tie against Sheffield Wednesday was rearranged for Wednesday, 19 February – 13 days after the accident at Munich. Most people had expected United to pull out since everything at Old Trafford seemed to be moving at half-pace. But the sense of urgency grew as the game with the Owls drew closer.

A United team could be pulled together from the reserves, but without some experienced players it wouldn't be worth putting on the pitch. Ferenc Puskas and Zoltan Czibor were two of the more prestigious players who offered to play for the Reds. It was a noble gesture from Puskas whom Busby had tried to buy in 1956 during the Hungarian uprising. He would obviously be a big attraction at Old Trafford and Murphy seriously considered signing the great striker. United wrote to the Hungarian Football Association in Budapest about the possible transfer of Puskas, Czibor and another player called Kocsis. But while Puskas was earning £800 a week playing for Real Madrid, the maximum wage in England was £20 a week during the season and £17 in the summer. United would have to find him a job outside football to make it worth his while getting around the FA ban on foreign players by becoming a British citizen. On top of that, Puskas was also an international celebrity used to VIP treatment. The more Murphy thought about the idea the more he realised it would be wrong to try to buy this great player. Apart from being impractical it seemed to Murphy that signing Puskas would undermine Busby's whole philosophy towards football. The Boss had always aimed to develop a team of dedicated youngsters who saw the Reds as their club. He wanted United to be something they'd grown up with so they'd feel as much a part of Old Trafford as the bricks and mortar. This was the ideal Busby and Murphy had set out to achieve before Munich destroyed their work. Murphy therefore rejected the idea of bringing Puskas to Old Trafford and confined his search to England.

A week after the crash, Murphy reported to the directors on his search for new players. 'The following team was chosen provisionally for the match v Sheffield Wednesday: Gregg or Gaskell, Foulkes, Greaves or P. Jones, Goodwin, Cope, _____, Webster, Taylor, Dawson, Pearson, _____.' Murphy was hoping players from other clubs, who United would watch in the coming Saturday's League programme, would cover the unfilled positions.

Meanwhile, the families who'd suffered such personal tragedy at Munich tried to get on with their lives. Johnny Berry's son Neil and his brothers were eventually picked up by their grandmother and aunt and taken to their home in Folkestone. For Neil the true extent of the Munich crash only struck home when he persuaded his aunt to take him to the cinema the following Wednesday. They showed the Pathé newsreel of the crash in a report called 'The Tragedy of Manchester'. It began:

> On the fringe of a Munich airport lies the wreckage of an airliner, still smouldering from a crash in which 21 people were killed. Tragedy enough at any time. But in that plane were a group of young men who were almost the personal friends of millions. Manchester United – the finest soccer team Britain has produced since the war.

Neil saw pictures of the United party in hospital, including Busby in an oxygen tent. He heard the reporter say his father was in a coma. He asked his aunt what this meant and she told him his father was asleep. He had thought this meant it was night-time in Germany. But he now realised that many of the young men who'd given him chocolate bars, played football with him and had always been kind – the likes of Taylor, Edwards, Whelan, Byrne and Jones – were now dead.

Back in Munich, Albert Scanlon was eventually allowed to use a wheelchair. Sister Almunder wheeled him round to see the other players but some of them, like Berry, were too ill. He was taken to see Blanchflower but he was too ill to talk. Scanlon also saw Busby. It was then that the tragedy really hit Scanlon.

Jean Busby visited twice a day. Though she was desperately concerned about Matt, she did her best to take everyone's minds off the pain, both mental and physical, that they were going through.

Charlton left the hospital and travelled to London. His brother Jack came down to Liverpool Street Station and drove him back to the family home in Ashington, where he was to spend a week or two. Neither of them said much in the car and there were long silences, but Bobby felt very close to his brother. Suddenly, he turned to Jack and said, 'I know you want to know what happened and I will tell you, but I don't want you to ask me again.' Bobby told Jack about the plane's attempts to take off. He explained how he'd been taken to hospital and fainted before coming round to hear the terrible news about those who'd died. 'Now I want to forget all about it,' he told Jack firmly.

When Bobby got home he could feel the tragedy. It was awful. The atmosphere was worse than in Munich, where he hadn't been able to take in what had happened. He felt drained. Most of the time he just sat around to while away the hours. So many of his friends and team-mates had been killed and he couldn't understand why he was still alive. He felt as if he was about to cry all the time. 'Why me?' he kept asking himself. He found it unbearable when he met people he'd known through the players who'd died. The press kept hounding him, which made it worse. For a while he insisted he wouldn't have anything to do with football again.

His mother's doctor said he was all right physically, although Bobby already knew that. The doctor gave him a short and kindly lecture on knuckling down to living again. He suggested that Bobby take a ball to the park and have a kick about for old times' sake. He followed the advice. It helped.

By now, Jimmy Murphy was spending 16 to 18 hours a day at Old Trafford. When he went home he couldn't sleep. He kept seeing Busby, Edwards and Berry in the operating theatre at the hospital in Munich. The faces of the club's lost players kept passing across his tired eyes.

United's first game since Munich was now just a few hours away.

Murphy gazed at a blank team sheet. Later, when he finally sat down to pick the team Murphy burst into tears.

After following the sound advice of his mother's doctor, Charlton decided to go back to Old Trafford. He'd watch the cup game to test himself out. Before the match he went into a hotel in the city for a meal. The atmosphere caught in his throat. The people had taken Busby's young United side into their hearts, built their lives around the team's success. The city was shocked. It was all so very sad. But Charlton had to come to terms with what had happened so that he could pick up the threads of his own life and his football career.

One by one he checked off his reactions. He was fine on the way to the ground. He wondered how he'd cope when he went into the dressing room to see the lads before the game. Somewhat surprisingly, that went okay as well. Murphy persuaded Charlton to sit next to him during the game hoping the atmosphere would rekindle his enthusiasm for football and speed up his recovery from the crash.

An emotionally overwrought crowd, every nerve-end jangling, was crammed inside Old Trafford when the gates were closed on that cold Wednesday night. The attendance was officially 59,848, some 7,000 below capacity, but many of those with tickets couldn't get in because of the thousands of mourning fans packing the streets all around the stadium. The supporters outside stood in silence. Inside, the atmosphere was eerie. It was an occasion dominated by memories and ghosts of the past. Some fans wept, others called out the names of those who'd died, most waited in a hushed silence for the teams to come out. Old Trafford was more like a shrine than a football ground. The people of Manchester hid their wounded hearts behind a surge of pride. The stakes were suddenly far higher than just winning a game of football; the occasion had taken on almost religious overtures. Nothing like it had ever been seen before.

Huddersfield's Denis Law had travelled over the Pennines with a friend for the match. He'd never played at Old Trafford; he hadn't even visited Manchester before. They paid £1 for a 2s 6d (12.5p) ticket – eight times face value – to see if United could raise themselves from the ashes of Munich. It was to be worth every penny. Law was drawn by the drama of the occasion. He felt he just had to be there that night as he stood among the crowd on the terraces at the Scoreboard End.

The original match programme was printed before the disaster and had to be scrapped. The reprinted programme carried a message from chairman Harold Hardman on the cover as an article of faith in the future of the club. Under the heading UNITED WILL GO ON Hardman wrote:

> On 6 February 1958, an aircraft returning from Belgrade crashed at Munich Airport. Of the 21 passengers who died, 12 were players or officials of the Manchester United Football Club. Many others lie injured. It is the sad duty of us who serve Manchester United to offer our heartfelt sympathy and condolences. Here is a tragedy which will sadden us for years to come. But in this we are not alone. An unprecedented blow to British football has touched the hearts of millions and we express our deep gratitude to many who have sent messages of sympathy and floral tributes. Wherever football is played United is mourned, but we rejoice that many of our party have been spared and wish them a speedy and complete recovery. Words are inadequate to describe our thanks and appreciation of the truly magnificent work of the surgeons and nurses of the Rechts der Isar Hospital at Munich. But for their superb skill and deep compassion our casualties would have been greater. To Professor Georg Maurer we offer our eternal gratitude. Although we mourn our dead and grieve for our wounded we believe that our great days are not done for us. The sympathy and encouragement of the football world, and particularly our supporters, will justify and inspire us. The road back may be long and hard but with the memory of those who died at Munich, of their stirring achievements and wonderful sportsmanship ever with us . . . MANCHESTER UNITED WILL RISE AGAIN.

H.P. Hardman

The most fitting epitaph for the players who'd died were the words of Laurence Binyon, reproduced in the programme:

> They shall not grow old
> As we that are left grow old,
> Age shall not weary them
> Nor the years condemn.
> At the going down of the sun,
> And in the morning,
> We will remember them.

Since Murphy couldn't give a team to the programme editor earlier that day there were dotted lines on the page where the United players should have been. It highlighted the poignancy of what was a unique occasion and marked the first time an English club had played an FA Cup tie without being able to name one definite player. The fans were told to write the players' names in the programme. Few did. Most just listened in silence as the team was announced on the Tannoy system just before kick-off. United's line-up was: Gregg, Foulkes, Greaves, Goodwin, Cope, Crowther, Webster, Taylor, Dawson, Pearson and Brennan.

Up in the packed press box a new batch of reporters had been assigned to follow United. They were scarcely more recognisable than the team.

Gregg in goal and Foulkes at right back bridged the gap Munich had opened up between the triumphant past and the uncertain future. They were the only two players in the last line-up against Red Star in Belgrade. The others weren't so familiar. Ernie Taylor and Stan Crowther, brought in by Murphy from Blackpool and Aston Villa, made their debuts. The rest of the side had only made 91 League appearances between them. Gregg didn't even know some of the other United players. Crowther had the toughest job of all trying to take the place of the legendary Edwards at left half.

Foulkes's responsibilities as captain certainly hadn't helped his nerves. He worried so much about it after his Munich ordeal that he lost over a stone in weight. People kept coming up to talk to him when all he wanted was peace and rest; he really needed to get away.

Gregg had also lost a lot of weight. They looked almost like a couple of walking skeletons. While Foulkes came to terms with being skipper, Greaves couldn't get Byrne out of his mind. He was changing where Byrne would have sat. He was wearing Byrne's shirt. It was such a terrible, guilt-ridden experience.

As the players came on to the pitch the crowd erupted at the sight of the two Munich survivors, Foulkes and Gregg, their presence underlining Hardman's words in the programme.

The *Daily Express* had arranged to relay commentary on the match by telephone to the hospital in Munich. Viollet was visiting the injured lads as they all huddled around to listen. There was a minute's silence before the kick-off.

The events of the next two hours were a profound, intense act of mass affirmation and rededication. The noise and passion of the crowd carried along Murphy's young side. The Reds weren't just playing a game of football; they were playing for the very soul of Manchester United.

United's youth player Shay Brennan scored twice, one direct from a corner, and Dawson scored the third to secure United's place in the Sixth Round. At the Scoreboard End Denis Law was especially pleased for Dawson. They'd played together for the Aberdeen Schoolboys under-15 team. He was the only United player Law knew personally.

It was an unforgettable night. The team that perished at Munich had struggled to beat the Owls 2–1 a couple of months before. Murphy's scratch side won 3–0. Wednesday were simply overwhelmed by the emotion of the occasion. *The Guardian* reported that at the final whistle 'the crowd exploded into a near delirium of cheers and upstretched hands'.The victory brought life back into the club and gave everyone a lift. Charlton had come through the match okay. He knew then that he could have played. 'But that game against Sheffield Wednesday was more important for what it did for the people of Manchester than for what it did for me,' he wrote years later. 'It gave [them] something to shout for again.' It was clearly no ordinary match and Charlton felt sorry for Wednesday. He wouldn't have enjoyed playing for them that night. 'Had we lost,' he wrote, 'I think Manchester would have died of a broken heart.'

Afterwards, in the dressing room, Foulkes and Gregg sat together, quietly. They were filled with emotion and drained by the experience. They'd carried the hopes of a city on their shoulders – a heavy burden. 'It was an electrifying night but there was no cheering in the dressing-room afterwards – we were all very sad,' recalls Greaves. 'I felt in a way that I shouldn't have been there, that I was stepping into someone else's shoes.'

After the match, David Meek of the *Manchester Evening News*, who'd taken over the United beat the day after the crash from the sadly departed Tom Jackson, wrote: 'The crowd turned for home, their heads full of memories of that remarkable game, their hearts full of sadness as they realised the full extent of Munich. The new team had carried on where the Babes had left off . . . but they would never see their heroes again.'

The tension was felt far beyond Old Trafford. In Munich, Viollet was delighted United had won but listening to the commentary made him homesick. Unfortunately, Busby, the man who might usually have greeted the result with the most joy and satisfaction, couldn't be told about it yet. The extraordinary team selected by Murphy would have triggered too many questions, which couldn't yet be answered.

The *Manchester Guardian* reported: 'As the triumphant crowds swept homeward, whole families stood in the sombre little streets . . . stood on their doorsteps (including sleepless children in their pyjamas, mothers with their hair in curling pins) asking, "Who won? Who scored? What were they like?" Over and over again, until they were convinced that Old Trafford was back in the business it knows so well.'

Although Foulkes was completely exhausted, he couldn't sleep or eat for days after the game; it was as if he had flu. He was drained. Foulkes knew Murphy believed he shouldn't continue playing, and he was certainly playing very badly, but Murphy also had the sense to leave the decision to Foulkes. Murphy didn't think he could face being dropped at this very emotional time. It was then that Foulkes really began to miss all the lads. There seemed to be an empty space where they'd been.

Seventeen

Edwards Loses His Battle

Duncan Edwards, still only 21, fought on with the courage that had brought him so far in football. But eventually the mighty heart of the greatest British footballer of his generation failed. It was 1.12 a.m. on the morning of 21 February, a little more than two weeks since he had played his last match. Admired even as he lay dying, the most brilliant Babe had been beaten by kidney failure.

He was the youngest player capped by England and had been a professional for only four years. His promise would be tragically unfulfilled. Nobody would know how good he could have been. Busby felt he would have been the greatest. Few doubted that view.

In the early hours of the morning Murphy was given the news he'd expected but prayed wouldn't come. He sobbed his heart out. The fact it was almost inevitable didn't lessen the heartbreak. Geoffrey Green of *The Times* penned a fitting rationale for Edwards's departure in *There's Only One United*: 'In the end the gods loved him too much.' Edwards's last coherent words were those whispered to Murphy about the kick-off time for the Wolves match. Professor Maurer insisted Busby must not be told Edwards had died.

BULLDOZER WITH A HEART OF GOLD was the headline the next day. 'He played with tremendous joy and his spirit stimulated the whole England team,' said England manager Walter Winterbottom the day Edwards died. 'It was in the character and the spirit of Duncan Edwards that I saw the true revival of British football.' Maurice Edelston and Terence Delaney in *Masters of Soccer* spoke for many when they wrote: 'Everyone who had watched him could remember some instance of a winter afternoon that he had illuminated with a flash of pleasure and astonishment.'

Edwards's death sent a great sigh around the sports fields of England and plunged Old Trafford into even blacker despair. He more than anyone had been the symbol of indestructible youth, the most awesomely vigorous of the Busby Babes. It was as though a young Colossus had been taken from the country's midst. Most people at Old Trafford believed Edwards would come home. His death was another shattering blow and deepened the sense of loss. Winterbottom was not the only one who cried that day.

One morning, a few days after Gregg got home, he couldn't find the newspapers. He looked everywhere. 'That's strange,' he thought, 'where have the papers gone?' And then he discovered why. People were hiding them to protect him from the news that Edwards had died. The brave boy he'd spoken to only a few days before was gone. As it sunk in, Gregg couldn't accept it. He was so angry.

The day after Edwards's death, Nottingham Forest visited Old Trafford. The match was to be preceded by a memorial service attended by three Red Star representatives. They'd made the long journey overland from Belgrade especially to pay their respects. They also brought gifts to replace those destroyed in the Munich crash.

The Dean of Manchester, the Very Reverend Herbert A. Jones, conducted the service. Originally planned as a tribute to those who'd died, the service had now become more poignant because of the loss of Edwards. Relatives of some of the dead players were among the silent crowd. It was too much for Edwards's fiancée, Molly Leach. She left the ground in tears.

During the prayers the ground was silent as snowflakes flickered through the afternoon air. Both teams stayed in their dressing rooms during the emotional service. When it ended the players finally emerged from the tunnel to a tremendous reception from a post-war record crowd of 66,123. Forest, like Wednesday, were on a hiding to nothing. Once again the survivors of the crash crowded around the telephone in Munich to listen to the commentary.

Forest scored first, but Dawson equalised with 15 minutes left. United had performed another miracle. Viollet, listening to the game in Munich, was reminded again just how homesick he was.

The next day there were services at Manchester Cathedral, the South Manchester Synagogue, the Albert Hall and Belle Vue speedway stadium conducted by the Bishop of Salford.

Unlike United, there had been no miracle for Edwards. His body was flown home so he could be buried in Dudley, where he was born. The whole town was on the streets to watch the funeral procession. The staff and children of Wolverhampton Street Secondary Modern, where Edwards had been a pupil such a short time ago, lined the road outside the school. His England team-mates were his pallbearers.

The world wept for Manchester United. At least Busby's life had been spared. He was slowly improving. The question of how to tell Busby about the deaths hung around the hospital like a black cloud. The doctors wanted him to get stronger first in case depression set in. One of them asked Jean what they should do. 'When the time comes, I'll tell him,' she said. Matt drifted in and out of consciousness for days. He lived in a half-world. As the days slowly passed, Busby began instinctively to feel something terrible had happened. The nuns and doctors said nothing.

Viollet had been confined to bed for just over a fortnight. He hadn't been allowed to walk about and couldn't take a bath or shower. He therefore didn't get the chance to see the lads upstairs. They'd all been together in one room – Berry, Edwards, Busby, Morgans, Scanlon, Wood and Charlton. When Viollet finally got upstairs the first person he saw was Busby. 'How are the rest of the boys?' the Boss asked. Viollet didn't know who'd died and couldn't give him any news; he just wished they were all as well as him.

For three weeks the dreadful facts were withheld from Busby. He was protected by an iron curtain of silence. Jean was constantly at his side. When he asked what had happened she changed the subject. 'Don't worry,' she told him. 'Don't talk. I'm supposed to do the talking.' His repeated questions were answered with the same white lies: Edwards was ill but making progress. Jean, Sheena, Sandy and the hospital staff were constantly tense and nervous in case they slipped up and said something that might raise his suspicions. One careless slip of the tongue could plunge him back into despair. Frank Taylor understood what the Busbys were going through. 'They lived in dread, in a state of forced high spirits, while Busby husbanded his strength, calling on the reserves of that athlete's body to pull him round.'

The news of Busby's fight for survival was passed on to Taylor and Blanchflower by their wives and by a doctor who spoke good English. The updates weren't enough for Taylor. One Friday morning, he asked Sister Gilda if she could wheel him in to see Busby. She wheeled Taylor down the corridor and into Busby's room. It was a shattering sight. He lay silent, stretched full length as though asleep. The plaster on his right leg was bulging the blankets. His bushy hair was now grey and tinged with streaks of white. His eyes opened and recognised Taylor. Busby's pale, waxy face, which could have belonged to a man of 70, lit up. He stretched his emaciated hand unsteadily towards Taylor and held his hand weakly. 'Hello, my old pal,' said Busby in a slow, broken voice. 'How are you, Frank, lad? Looks as if you're not fit for the first team yet.' Although Busby was physically in a bad way there was clearly nothing wrong with his spirit. Taylor knew then that, come what may, Busby would get well and return to football.

The Busbys were a God-fearing family. When Matt was just six, a German sniper's bullet killed his father on the Somme. Now the wheel had come full circle. The Germans were repaying their debt to the Busby family by fighting round the clock to save Matt.

Six days after Edwards's death, Busby overheard a German Catholic priest saying: 'Duncan Edwards is dead.' Professor Maurer had planned to keep the sad news from him for at least another month. Now, for the first time, the grim reality of what had happened really dawned on Busby. He was very weak but his powerful instincts still functioned. He knew deep down that something even more terrible than he could imagine had struck and was being kept from him. He had no idea what. Then, gradually, he became aware that some of his boys must have been killed. He didn't know for sure that they were dead, but he knew something dreadful had happened. He wanted to stay in his oxygen tent and die rather than come out and learn the truth. He prayed for the end to come quickly. Deep down he was afraid to know the truth. Finally, he could stand it no longer. He woke up one evening and Jean was leaning over him. She said nothing. 'What happened?' he asked. She stayed silent. 'Jean, I know about Duncan. I want to know the worst. I want to know everything, for my peace of mind.'

A doctor was called. They tried to change the subject, but Busby wouldn't be put off. Eventually the doctor agreed that Jean could tell him what had happened. A new torture began. Sheena and Sandy listened as Busby spoke to Jean and held her hand. Busby remembered everyone who'd boarded the plane. As he named each one, without saying a word, without looking at her husband, Jean nodded or shook her head and squeezed his hand. Words seemed somehow inappropriate. She thought it would never end. When he learned the full extent of the disaster in which eight of his Babes had perished, he lay back and wept.

Only those close to Busby knew what a struggle the doctors had with him over the next few days. He hardly spoke or ate for almost three days. It was because he'd feared the awful truth he now knew that he'd prayed to die. This new constant mental torture knocked him back and he was as near the brink as ever. He wanted to die. It wasn't just the physical pain. Busby felt he was also going insane: he was raving and creating hell with everyone. 'Why us?' he thought. 'Was it some kind of human error or was this decreed from above? If so, why didn't I die with them? What was so special about me that I survived?' It was well over a month before Berry came out of his coma, but he survived. Unfortunately, he'd never play professional football again.One day, Berry came to Busby's bedside complaining that his best friend Tommy Taylor hadn't been to see him yet. Berry didn't know Taylor was dead. It was Busby's lowest point.

On top of the mental anguish Busby was also suffering physically. He couldn't be given any anaesthetic because of the damage to his chest. Only unconsciousness relieved the agony of the appalling injuries to his right leg and foot. He was spared, but even if he survived how could he face the loved ones of the lads who hadn't? Memories kept crowding in on him. His inner voice kept saying: 'If I had not taken them into Europe, those eight Busby Babes and the other victims would be with us still.' And this was not all. The voice admonished: 'I should not have allowed the pilot to make that third attempt at a take-off.'

The physical agony remained without let-up. Coughing was painful even to think about, but when, inevitably, he did cough, the pain was awful. Lung punctures, broken-bone manipulation and torn-flesh repairs without anaesthetic were a regular drill of undiminishing horror.

The hospital staff, under the direction of Maurer, were magnificent. The twist of fate that meant Germans had saved him wasn't lost on Busby. 'Ironic, wasn't it, that until then Germans to me were Germans – the enemy, if you like. I'd joined up to fight them before the war began, I was called up the moment it started and was in it right through to 1945. And yet there they were saving my life and others; there was nothing they could have done that they didn't do. You learn as you grow older.'

When Sandy next returned to Munich he thought his father still looked like an old, grey man. This was hardly surprising since one side of his body, including his ribs and foot, had been smashed. But some colour had returned to his cheeks. He was moved out of intensive care into a room with a balcony. Not long afterwards Sandy sensed his father had got the football bug again. He would say things like, 'They got a draw, you know.' Nevertheless, his passion for the game he loved was hard to re-ignite at first. He wanted nothing to do with football ever again. 'I will never go back into football again,' he'd say. This went on for weeks.

As soon as he was well enough Busby phoned each player's partner and family. When he called Eddie Colman's girlfriend, Marjorie English, he was really upset. 'I'm so sorry, Marjorie, I'm so sorry,' he told her. She sensed Busby felt the disaster was somehow his fault. Busby told Geoff Bent's wife Marion that he blamed himself because he should have said something. But, in his defence, he added, 'How would I have felt if that captain had been telling me to tell my lads how to play football? That's how I would have felt telling him how to fly his plane.'

As Busby's physical agony gradually eased his more rational mind put up an unanswerable defence: 'A football life is a travelling life. Tragedy could have struck us in a train, in a coach, or even walking across a road. And, after all, effects on human beings are from a million small causes dating from the year dot. Who am I, who was I, to presume to tell an expert pilot how to do his job?' One thing was certain, Busby knew less about aeroplanes than he knew about football. Busby also thought about his young team's enthusiasm for the challenge of European football. They were hungry for a new experience. They wanted to reach their potential, beyond the restrictive nature of the English game. They could have been the best club side in the world. Busby and his players shared the same dream.

But even when he'd talked himself out of his self-condemnation and self-blame, his mental state was worse than the physical pain. Eventually he listened to Jean's wise words. 'I don't think you are being fair to the people who have lost their loved ones,' she told him. 'And I am sure those who have gone, too, would have wanted you to carry on.' Her plea went straight to the heart of the matter. Jean's wisdom, common sense and logic won. Besides, Busby had more foster sons to look after. He mustn't let them, or their parents, down. From that moment he wanted to live.

Eighteen

United Fight On

A week or so after the official memorial service at St Martin's-in-the-Fields in London, another one was held at St Bride's church in Fleet Street for the journalists who'd died. Geoffrey Green of *The Times* gave the lesson before a packed congregation. As he spoke, Green looked up at the tall church windows. Snow had begun to fall. It was highly symbolic. England manager Walter Winterbottom read the second address. St Bride's, known as the 'Wedding Cake Church' because of its tiered steeple, was filled with sadness.

Eventually, Viollet was released from hospital but had to return every day for treatment. His daily visits to the hospital gave him the opportunity to see Blanchflower and the rest of the lads but all he really wanted was to go home.

In the FA Cup sixth round, United were drawn against West Bromwich Albion away on 1 March. Charlton was picked to play outside-left in his first game since the disaster. He wasn't very fit and had lost a yard of pace, but United were desperate.

The programme carried a tribute to Duncan Edwards. It talked about his 'awe-inspiring demonstration of seeming invincibility, coupled with a joy of living that infected his comrades whenever and wherever the going was tough'.

United led 1–0 and then 2–1 with goals from Taylor and Pearson. Four minutes from time Albion equalised. They hung on to earn a replay at Old Trafford. It was a good result.

Viollet was finally allowed to leave Munich. He refused to fly back. Like Foulkes and Gregg he took the train from Munich to the Hook of Holland and then the boat to Harwich. While Viollet was travelling, United were preparing to face West Brom in the replay at Old Trafford on the night of 5 March.

The game seemed to be heading for extra time when young Welshman Colin Webster scored in the 90th minute. United were through to the semi-finals for the second year running. It was one of the highlights of Murphy's career. 'If only the full side had been there,' reflected Foulkes. 'We would have won everything that year, including the European Cup.'

The following morning Viollet arrived back in England on the boat from the Hook of Holland. There was a knock on his cabin door. It was one of the waiters with a cup of tea and some biscuits and the wonderful news that United had beaten West Brom the previous evening. It was a tremendous welcome home.

It wasn't until Viollet returned to Manchester that he realised what an impact the tragedy had had on everyone. 'The feeling in the town was unbelievable,' he says. Although there was an amazing feeling of sympathy in Manchester, Viollet felt an awful emptiness. He went to Old Trafford. It was terrible. The place gave him a strange feeling; there was an eerie vacuum. It was hard to believe what had happened. For Viollet and many others Old Trafford could never be the same again.

Viollet had been at United since the age of 16, playing with lads like Byrne, Colman, Pegg and Edwards. They were all kids together and had a great relationship. 'The camaraderie had gone, never to return, and that was the thing I missed more than anything else. It was more than just team spirit. We would have run through a brick wall for United. You could almost say we had a love for one another. Without that wonderful feeling it was terrible to walk into Old Trafford . . .' But Viollet knew life had to go on. He really wanted to get back into the team and started training again. Although he was warned that any blow to his head could be dangerous, he wanted to get back in the team as soon as possible.

Every match at Old Trafford now seemed to inspire a memorable occasion. On 8 March, Professor Maurer, his wife and some of his staff were guests of both the city of Manchester and United for Albion's second visit in a matter of days, this time in the League. It was arranged so that Maurer might see the club whose injured he'd so skilfully treated. He brought with him a tape-recorded message from Busby for the crowd. The Boss had also written on a slip of paper, in painfully weak handwriting, the names and addresses of the bereaved. He'd asked Maurer to visit them on his behalf.

The 60,000 crowd gave the doctors and nurses a warm reception. United Chairman Harold Hardman told the crowd, 'Words are inadequate to describe our thanks and appreciation of the truly magnificent work of the surgeons and nurses of the Rechts der Isar Hospital at Munich. But for their superb skill and deep compassion our casualties might have been greater. To Professor Georg Maurer, Chief Surgeon, we offer our eternal gratitude.'

The crowd fell silent as Busby's words echoed around the ground in the message he'd recorded at his hospital bedside. It began:

> Ladies and gentlemen, I am speaking from my bed in the Isar Hospital, Munich, where I have been since the tragic accident of just over a month ago.
>
> You will be glad, I am sure, that the remaining players here, and myself, are now considered out of danger, and this can be attributed to the wonderful treatment and attention given to us by Professor Maurer and his wonderful staff, who are with you today as guests of the club.
>
> I am obliged to the *Empire News* for giving me this opportunity to speak to you, for it is only in these last two or three days that I have been able to be told anything about football, and I am delighted to hear of the success and united effort made by all at Old Trafford. Again it is wonderful to hear

that the club have reached the semi-final of the FA Cup, and I
extend my best wishes to everyone.

Finally, may I just say God bless you all.

Many supporters cried as Busby's soft Scottish accent echoed
around the ground, but as the message ended loud cheering took
over. The cheering continued as the Lord Mayor of Manchester and
the Mayor of Stretford led Professor Maurer and his party onto the
pitch to be shown the gratitude of the United fans. Unfortunately,
United lost 4–0. Their amazing run of post-Munich success had
come to an end. The defeat confirmed that it was the FA Cup that
was drawing a special spirit out of the players.

Busby was now fit enough to get up for a few minutes each day,
although he remained weak and in great pain. Others rallied
sufficiently to give hope of recovery only to sink back. Their fate was
in the balance for days and sometimes weeks before the issue of life
or death was decided.

In the period following the disaster those who'd returned from
Munich felt at times as if they were living in a world inhabited by the
ghosts of those who'd vanished.

Morgans came home on the Thursday before the FA Cup semi-
final in which United would play second division Fulham. On the
day itself Morgans played for the reserves – just six weeks after the
crash.

Charlton scored twice against Fulham in a 2–2 draw. The result
staggered the football world. But Charlton and Murphy felt United
were lucky to get a second chance. A replay was just about the last
thing the players wanted, but at least they were still in the Cup. The
lifeline that was keeping everyone going remained.

The replay would be at Highbury. There was so much interest
that it was to be shown live on TV. Blanchflower left Munich on the
day of the match with his wife Jean, but he wouldn't be going to the
game. He couldn't stand the thought of being jostled by the crowd.
They travelled on the *Belgrade Express* and took a ship from Dover.
United sent a taxi to take them to Manchester and the driver had the
semi-final on the radio. Blanchflower didn't want to listen. It wasn't
Manchester United to him. United were the friends he'd left behind.

The loss of his close pal Tommy Taylor was the hardest to bear. He'd never have another relationship like that again. It was a once-in-a-lifetime friendship.

Twice United went ahead, and twice Fulham pulled them back. In the second half the Reds took control. Brennan got their third and Dawson the fourth for his hat-trick. Fulham pulled one back, but it was all over when Charlton struck a scorching last-minute volley to make it 5–3.

Murphy was building enough memories to last a lifetime. In Munich, Busby was boosted by the news that United had reached the Cup final for the second year running. 'Tell Jimmy I am delighted,' he told his wife Jean. 'Tell him to keep it up.' Jean phoned Murphy to say Matt was recovering slowly from his injuries. His crushed chest was a little better and he no longer needed an oxygen tent. She also passed on the heartening message from the Boss that he was 'delighted'. Murphy had certainly kept the flag flying.

But United only won one League match after Munich, when they beat Sunderland on 7 April. Of the others, five were drawn and eight were lost. Their final League placing of ninth was nevertheless remarkable.

Nineteen

Busby Goes Home

Matt Busby eventually made a staggering recovery from the shell of a man who'd been found at Munich Airport. His progress led the doctors to agree he could return to England to see his team play Bolton Wanderers in the Cup final at Wembley.

On Thursday, 18 April 1958, Busby was ready to go home. The TV cameras, journalists and photographers left with the Busby party. In the big hallway Busby said goodbye to Professors Maurer, Kessel and all the other doctors and nurses who'd looked after him before boarding the *Rheingold Express* for the overland journey home with Des Hackett and cameraman Bill Gregory of the *Daily Express*.

Matt and Jean arrived home in a black Humber car in the afternoon. Thirty neighbours and children surrounded the sleek vehicle as it pulled up in King's Road. Four workmen had left a bunch of flowers propped up against the green garage door and a United fan from nearby Sale had delivered two bunches of grapes. As courteous as ever, Matt got out of the car, acknowledged the well-wishers and spoke to the journalists and photographers. 'Are you all right, lads?' he said. 'How have you been while I've been away?' His daughter Sheena ran out to meet her father as he walked unsteadily up the front path on his crutches. A row of flowers lined the hallway and spilled over into the living room. They'd been brought personally by many people, including Ray Wood and his wife Betty.

Busby's convalescence was painful both physically and psychologically. For a while he had to stay at home in bed, with daily visits from the doctor, and couldn't dress and undress without help from Jean and Sandy.

Paddy McGrath, Busby's close friend of over 40 years, went to his house to see how he was one afternoon. It was a pleasant spring day and Busby was sitting in the garden. He was still in a bad way, still a sick man. His nervous system had gone. Busby saw his old pal and, despite his injuries, got up as McGrath came across to him. Busby put his arms around McGrath and they hugged each other. He broke down in tears, but said nothing. 'Never did talk about the crash,' says McGrath. 'But it was always there. In his eyes. Always.'

Twenty

United Reach Wembley

It was said that United had been carried to Wembley on a flood of emotion. Bobby Charlton's impression was that Jimmy Murphy had dragged them there.

Dennis Viollet's determination to get fit again brought its rewards. Finally, he felt ready to play again. He approached Murphy. 'Jimmy, would you like me to play again?' he asked. 'Dennis, that's the best news I've had for a long time,' said Murphy. 'I'd love you to play.' Viollet was in the team for the match against Wolves. United lost 4–0, but Viollet thoroughly enjoyed the game. It was great to be part of the team again.

Busby was terrified at the thought of returning to Old Trafford. He forced himself to go the week before the Cup final. The staff gathered in Ted Dalton's medical room. Busby walked in on crutches. Wilf McGuinness thought he looked old, as if he'd been through hell, and remembered how strong Busby had looked before the crash. It was now clear for all to see how much he had suffered after Munich.

His 'laundry lassies' were there to welcome him back. He gave them a hug and a kiss. Busby wanted to say a few words to mark the occasion. He planned to echo chairman Harold Hardman's sentiment that United would go on. Jimmy Murphy and Jack Crompton stood on either side of Busby as he began to speak. A few words came out; then he broke down. It was all too much. Murphy and Crompton helped him, sobbing, from the room. Looking out at the Old Trafford pitch, Busby saw the empty field and in all his life had never felt such a terrible emptiness. Afterwards he felt better for the tears and was glad he'd forced himself to go back. It was a challenge he had to face. Now, at least, he'd done it.

Harry Gregg had begun to wonder if he'd play in the final. Ever since the crash he'd suffered from violent, blinding headaches. No amount of sedatives could stop the terrible buzzing in his head. In desperation, when he went to bed at night he bound a tie as tightly as possible around his forehead hoping this would deaden the pain. It helped, but not a lot. Finally, he went for an X-ray. There were fears that the blows he'd received in the crash had fractured his skull, but fortunately the X-rays proved these fears were groundless. As Cup final day drew nearer the headaches became less intense.

Kenny Morgans had played in most of the games leading up to the Cup final and expected to to be part of the line-up. But Murphy thought the atmosphere might be too much for him. The day before the final he told Morgans he was going to play Viollet instead. Morgans was devastated. 'I was very disappointed, very disappointed,' he says.

There was talk in the papers of Busby being able to lead the team out from the tunnel at Wembley, but there was never any real prospect of that happening. The Boss was still walking only with great pain. Besides, he felt the honour belonged to the man who'd breathed faith and willpower into the players so that they could astonishingly achieve the impossible – Jimmy Murphy. But at least Busby was well enough to go to the match, albeit against Professor Maurer's advice.

The United line-up was: Gregg, Foulkes, Greaves, Goodwin, Cope, Crowther, Dawson, E. Taylor, Charlton, Viollet and Webster. Many of the United players who'd recovered from the crash felt guilty because the lads who'd battled to get the team to the final weren't picked.

At the tactical discussion before the match Busby came into the dressing room to congratulate the young team and give them a pep talk. He looked around at the youthful faces he'd known as boys, who now carried the responsibility of men. 'Just go out and follow Jimmy's instructions,' he told the team. Busby tried to say more but once again broke down and, tailing off, had to leave the room. The fact that Busby looked grey and very old upset Foulkes, and he wasn't the only one.

Murphy led out the team. The United shirts were embroidered with badges showing the phoenix rising from the ashes. It was a symbol of the club's determination to realise the words of Chairman Harold Hardman in the Sheffield Wednesday programme: 'Manchester United will rise again'. Busby, looking debonair in his customary trilby hat, had taken up a position behind Murphy on the bench down by the touchline.

Foulkes's mum and dad and his wife Teresa sat up in the stands. For the other Munich survivor in the team, goalkeeper Harry Gregg, everything after Munich was an anticlimax. Before the match he shook hands with His Royal Highness the Duke of Edinburgh. It should have been an honour and a delight, but Munich had put life into perspective. Even meeting royalty was now a let-down for Harry Gregg.

After just three minutes Nat Lofthouse swept the ball home. After half-time United's fate was sealed. Gregg was in the process of catching the ball when Lofthouse charged him in the back. The impact jolted the ball out of his hand and into the net, with the shaken keeper following it in. Gregg lay writhing on the ground. He didn't know what he was doing. Lofthouse expected the referee to give a free kick since it was clearly an illegal charge. Instead, the goal was given. Lofthouse wasn't going to argue.

To their credit the United players didn't argue with the referee's decision. 'Nat scored some great goals in his time,' Busby would write years later. 'That was not one of them.'

For the second year running a controversial goal had settled the Cup final. The previous year a sixth minute challenge by Aston Villa's Peter McParland on Ray Wood had smashed the keeper's cheekbone. Wood had to go off, Blanchflower went in goal and

United played with ten men. McParland scored twice; the Reds lost 2–1. They seemed fated not to win the Cup.

To put things in perspective Bolton had played United in the League at Old Trafford in mid-January just a few weeks before the Munich disaster, and were thrashed 7–2.

Foulkes was glad to get off the pitch. The crowd was very sympathetic. Busby walked slowly around the pitch, as the fans streamed away from the stadium, to congratulate Bolton in their dressing room. It said a lot about his sportsmanship.

'There was a lot of pain around Wembley after that match,' says Charlton. 'For the fans, who had seen as poor a Cup final as they will ever see. For Harry Gregg, who had been hurt in the back in the charge. For me, who was beginning to think that the Milburn family had used up their share of Cup final luck when Jackie Milburn (Charlton's Uncle) had pocketed three Cup winners' medals in three appearances.' Charlton felt for Murphy. He'd coaxed and cursed but United didn't have enough to give. Charlton collected his losers' medal and headed slowly towards the tunnel, thinking about another place and those who'd perished there.

'There need be no recriminations about the performance of Manchester United,' wrote Busby later. 'Surely their greatest performance was in reaching Wembley at all in view of the circumstances. Could any other club have done as much?'

After the game, United held a banquet at the Savoy Hotel in London. The atmosphere was great; it was as if they'd won the Cup. In contrast, the atmosphere among the Bolton players was almost as though they'd lost. A few of the doctors who'd treated the injured in Munich had been invited to the banquet and the players spent some time talking to them. The doctor who'd warned Viollet about the dangers of playing again blew him a kiss and wagged her finger at him as if to say, 'You naughty boy!' Some of the families of the players who'd died at Munich also attended. Viollet felt a bit guilty that he was there, while their sons or brothers weren't.

The team returned to Manchester without the Cup. Instead, they had something more precious – a strange kind of glory. The players boarded the traditional open-top bus and were driven towards the Town Hall from the station. There were thousands of well-wishers lining the route. Foulkes had never seen so many people. In Albert Square there seemed to be a million people just standing in silence. They were hardly moving. A lot of people had brought their children. They all seemed to be crying. Foulkes felt terrible that he had no Cup to show these people who'd become so emotionally involved with the team after Munich. 'I can't stand any more of this,' he thought. As captain he had to get up and say a few words. Afterwards he sat down with Busby and Murphy in the Town Hall. The delayed shock flowed and Foulkes cried like a baby. After that he just had to get away. It was too distressing after all he'd been through already.

Manchester United had one final commitment to fulfil after the disappointment of their FA Cup final defeat. They still had to play a European Cup semi-final against AC Milan. The Reds put up a fight in the first leg at Old Trafford on 8 May and came back from a goal down to win 2-1 with a goal from Dennis Viollet and an Ernie Taylor penalty. There was a glimmer of hope that they could reach their first European Cup final. Unfortunately, United's season caught up with them in the return on 14 May in Milan. The Reds had the support of every neutral in world football, but it was too much to ask their patched-up team to overcome such experienced opponents. United lost 4-0. Their brave effort to keep the flag flying in Europe had failed and their traumatic season was over. Busby's quest to win the European Cup in memory of those who'd lost their lives had, however, just begun.

Twenty-One

Munich – The Legend

On the afternoon of 6 February 1958, Manchester United stopped being just another football club. The tragedy spread the club's name around the globe in the hours following the accident. 'Before Munich it was just Manchester's club,' says Bobby Charlton. 'Afterwards everyone owned a little bit of it.'

Bill Foulkes agrees.

> I think the crash started the legend of Manchester United. It brought United's name to the attention of the world. It made a massive impact on the footballing world and it certainly helped to build the aura that surrounds the club . . .
>
> United were a local club before the tragedy. Manchester people followed us and some fans in the rest of England had latched onto the Busby Babes, but we weren't really known worldwide. In fact, generally we didn't command great attendances in the early days.
>
> We had bonus clauses in our salary which meant we got extra if our crowds were over a certain figure, which I think was around 28,000. We always used to be looking at the crowd

before kick-off to see if we could expect anything extra. But I know from my wage packets that we weren't getting those kinds of gates too often!

At that stage I could never have anticipated it growing into a world-renowned club the way it has. It all changed after the crash, though. Suddenly everybody wanted to come and watch Manchester United.

In the immediate aftermath I actually found it very stressful. It was almost like hysteria. It wasn't actually a pleasant thing to have to deal with, but you just had to get through it. On a personal level it changed and gradually died down, but for the club it all took off on a worldwide basis.

Without doubt the crash built up United's following around England, Europe and the world. It's fantastic how that support has swelled. Before we were just footballers; afterwards United players were treated like film stars and celebrities.

Harry Gregg would never forget Munich: 'I will always remember standing on that snow-swept airfield feeling helpless and alone.' But his memories also harboured more satisfying feelings: 'I will always feel part of something great; the greatest club in the world.'

Gregg remains grateful that he had the opportunity to play with the Busby Babes. 'They carried the passions of the people; they carried every schoolboy's dream of belonging to them . . . they were all great players – gifted giants. They were all great to play with. I can always say that I was part of that greatness; part of the Manchester United family, and proud of it. There are not many who can say that.'

Gregg had his own ideas on what set the Babes apart from other football teams. 'The most important thing about the Busby Babes, the Red Devils, call them what you want . . . they say they might have been the greatest team, but one thing's very sure – they were the best loved team.'

The task now was to rebuild for the future. United simply had to win the European Cup in memory of the lost Babes and to exorcise the guilt that Busby would carry with him for the next ten years.

Book Two
DESTINY

Prologue

Quest for Glory

Manchester United's quest to win the European Cup was forged amidst the charred remains of the Elizabethan airliner that crashed on take-off at Munich's Reim Airport on 6 February 1958. From that moment Matt Busby's goal of conquering Europe was to became an obsession, which permeated the whole club. It was the only thing in football he really cared about. The goal of becoming the first English team to win the European Cup was paramount.

Players arriving at Old Trafford in the early 1960s felt the powerful, overriding importance that winning the trophy had taken on at United. David Sadler, who joined the club in 1962, had no doubts that victory in the European Cup was Busby's dream. 'Almost from when I joined everything was geared towards winning that cup,' he says.

Pat Crerand, who arrived at United a few months after Sadler, also knew how important the trophy was to Busby and his team. 'When I came in 1963 there was this great underlying wish to win the European Cup. I think that was the aim all the time I was there.'

George Best was very much aware of the importance of the European Cup. In his autobiography *The Good, the Bad and the*

Bubbly, he outlined the feeling at the club towards winning the elusive trophy.

> All great clubs have ambition. At United it was more than that. It was a mission, a crusade underwritten by the blood of the players who died in the Munich air crash . . . We didn't sit around talking about it. Yet there was an aura about Old Trafford. It was as if the ghosts of the Busby Babes were still around the place and we all knew what was expected of us. It was even more pressing for players like Charlton and Foulkes who had been aboard the airliner when it crashed. They had seen their colleagues die in the pursuit of the Cup, the greatest club prize in football. They wanted to win it desperately – for their own satisfaction, obviously, but also for the men who had died.
>
> For Sir Matt Busby it was nothing less than his life's ambition. He had been badly hurt in the crash and at one time it looked as if he wouldn't be able to continue as manager. But he did, and it was the search for the Holy Grail of victory in Europe that kept him going . . .
>
> Playing in Europe was always special. It was the icing on the cake of your work. The atmosphere was different: tenser and more exciting. I also happen to like travelling, which added to my enjoyment. It was different for Charlton and Foulkes. They had been aboard the plane that had crashed in Munich and it took courage to get into an aircraft again after that. They never said anything when we flew off somewhere. They didn't have to. You could see what they were thinking: it was written large on their faces, on Bill's especially. But they were not going to give up or back out. They had a job to complete and they knew, we all knew, that this was the side that was going to do it.'

New players with no experience of European competition were coming into the United side. Charlton, a player who such a short time ago was one of the youngest of Busby's Babes, had quickly become one of the team's elder statesmen. 'He was now 30 and looked older still,' wrote Norman Harris in *The Charlton Brothers*.

'Just a long whiff of hair covered his balding head, and on the field his features were taut with visible concern and involvement. He was now truly a senior statesman among a team of increasingly assorted individuals. There was something of the appearance of Matt Busby himself. Bobby knew how badly Busby wanted to win the European Cup and he felt quite sure that the Boss would retire if he failed to win it this time.'

After their attempts to win the European Cup in the late 1950s, United had to wait until 1966 for another crack at lifting the trophy following their league title the previous year. They once again reached the semi-finals but with George Best carrying an injury they were beaten 2–1 on aggregate, ironically by a team from Belgrade, this time Partizar. It was with an uncertain team that United, having won the League in 1967, prepared for their fourth assault on the European Cup. They were supported by a wave of patriotic enthusiasm created by England's World Cup victory the year before and were now practically an international side, supported by the public.

One

Welcome in Malta

It was like Beatlemania. The scene at Malta's Luqa Airport was unbelievable. Thousands of cheering locals dressed in red and white to enthusiastically welcome their favourite team: Manchester United. Flags and banners were draped everywhere. The players' names were painted on separate red and white sheets. It was certainly a more staggering welcome than George Best could ever have dreamed about. It was as if the Maltese fans were celebrating the return of their own team.

It was a phenomenal sight. Every camera on the island from cines to modest box models seemed to have been brought out. 'This is what Manchester United means to these people,' thought the 22-year-old Best as he looked in wonder at the amazing sight that greeted United on their arrival. The whole island seemed to have turned out. Best thought it was like one of the old-style welcomes the Beatles used to get on returning to London from an American tour. Even the Queen wouldn't get as big a reception when she visited the island a few weeks later.

United had flown to George Cross Island for the second leg of a first-round European Cup tie against Hibernians Valletta after comfortably winning the first game at Old Trafford 4–0. Anticipation was running high. The locals were looking forward to watching United's star players – and especially the famous Holy Trinity of Best, Denis Law and Bobby Charlton – take on Hibernians' modest team of part-timers. For many of the home fans it was a dream come true to see United play in Malta. They'd followed the Reds for years without ever thinking that one day their team would face the men from Old Trafford in the European Cup.

The Maltese were pro-British and they loved United. For years the Reds had enjoyed a great following on the island. The place seemed to be populated entirely by United fans so great was the club's support. The locals even had their own United Supporters Club. The Manchester players were their idols. The Maltese thronged the route to United's elegant new Phoenicia Hilton Hotel. A cavalcade of about 100 cars, motorbikes and buses, their horns and hooters blaring, escorted the coach from the airport. The players were pelted with flowers and the coach driver got so caught up in the excitement that he seemed to make the journey in record time.

When the players arrived at the hotel they had to fight their way through the crowds. The United party thought the hotel was fantastic and the service was excellent. The locals showered the players with kindness. The United Supporters Club organised a big cocktail party for the officials, the players and the press. They made presentations to Busby and the club. In fact, there was nothing the Maltese wouldn't do for them.

The one drawback was that the locals followed the players everywhere. When they went to their rooms they found a dozen or so Maltese already there. If any of the United party left the restaurant to go to the toilet, five or six locals followed them. A guard of supporters was constantly stationed around the hotel. This meant the players were virtually imprisoned because if any of them went outside they were mobbed, albeit in the nicest possible way. It wasn't the most relaxing build-up to the match but it was so hot outside that, fortunately, very few of the players actually wanted to go out.

When United were first drawn against the Maltese champions there was a mix-up and it was announced they'd be playing a team called Floriana. But the mistake was eventually sorted out and in some ways it didn't matter which Maltese club United were paired with; the main thing was they'd got an easy draw and would almost certainly reach the next round.

Not that the players were complacent. They were determined from the start to win the match. Pat Crerand felt United were under pressure from the moment they kicked off against Hibernians. Before the first leg at Old Trafford nerves were on edge and it was certainly tense inside their dressing room. Every ground staging a European Cup tie had this special atmosphere.

The part-timers of Hibernians were not up to English First (now Premier) Division standard, so United were expected to win easily. A multi-talented priest called Father Hilary Tagliaferro, who was also a sports writer, coached the Maltese. During games he sat on the touchline dressed in his full habit. Unfortunately, he lost one of his players before the game at Old Trafford. To break the journey the Hibernians party stopped in London to watch Arsenal. But 17-year-old winger Francis Mifsud got lost after going to buy an ice cream. He was missing for two days and Scotland Yard had to be called in to find him. Mifsud couldn't remember the name of his hotel in London, so he travelled north on his own. A girl he met on the train to Manchester took him to Piccadilly Station to meet the rest of his worried team-mates. There was a happy reunion when he turned up, and Scotland Yard was able to call off its search.

It was a warm autumn evening when 43,000 fans packed into Old Trafford to watch United play Hibernians. The Maltese team were an unknown quantity. Goalkeeper Alfred Mizzi had played in trials for Portsmouth and Arsenal and had also turned down a move to Atletico Madrid. He did very well against United, but couldn't prevent his side going behind after just 12 minutes. Eighteen-year-old Brian Kidd, playing his first European match, crossed for inside right David Sadler to head home. Then, two minutes before half-time, Law fired home an unstoppable right-foot shot from fully 30 yards. It was his first goal in an injury-plagued season – tonight he was playing with a bruised toe. His strike was important because it confirmed there would be no Maltese miracle. Psychologically, it was the worst possible time for Hibernians to concede a goal.

In the second half Law kept the pressure up with a couple of jack-knife headers. By now the Maltese had been gradually worn down until they were resigned to a siege of their penalty area. Sadler made it three in the 58th minute with a firm, accurate shot after Best had sidestepped a couple of defenders. Then, just three minutes later, Sadler turned provider when he laid the ball off for Law to score his second and United's fourth. Sadler played so well he might have scored four or five goals.

United keeper Alex Stepney had handled the ball only five times in the whole game and got an ironic cheer from the crowd when he made his first proper save in the 85th minute. Hibernians had managed just one shot in the entire match.

Although it was a comfortable victory, the general view was that the result was a bad one for United. David Meek, of the *Manchester Evening News*, summed up the mood among the press: 'Manchester United are launched into the European Cup with an overwhelming display of superior talents but, like that other majestic launching earlier in the day, with a few misgivings.'

The other launch was the one presided over by Queen Elizabeth at Clydebank in Scotland, when the £29 million ship named after her, and forever known as the QE2, set sail to the cheers of 100,000 people mingled with bellowing sirens.

The match gave little indication of how far United might proceed in the European Cup, although they were now virtually assured of getting through the first round. At least the Maltese were happy. 'We are delighted,' said Father Tagliaferro. 'This is the kind of scoreline we hardly dared to hope for. We got the result we set out for and, but for the goal just before half-time, which was a bad time psychologically, the score might have been even closer.'

Hibernians were now looking forward to an entertaining second leg and promised United a pleasant time. But Father Tagliaferro had a warning: 'The heat will affect Manchester United more than they realise in Malta and this score means we shall certainly draw a record crowd of about 20,000.' The part-timers clearly felt they were still in with a chance. 'Although United know about the conditions in Malta, I think they will still come as a shock to some of the players,' said Father Tagliaferro.

United had ordered specially designed ultra-light shirts with a deep V-neck and short sleeves especially for the match. The players had heard all about the Maltese pitches before they arrived, but the surface at the Empire Stadium was still hard to believe. The Gzira pitch was made of a peculiar mixture of rolled sand, gravel and lime. It was stony and uneven. In fact, it was terrible. Not surprisingly, Law was apprehensive when he saw the surface he later described as 'rather like an unmade road'. He'd been suffering with an injury all season and playing on the bone-hard pitch wouldn't help his dodgy knee.

Father Tagliaferro had underestimated the attendance – more than 25,000 fanatics crowded into the Empire Stadium to cheer on both teams. But the match posed problems for the press. There were no telephones at the small ground so David Meek of the *Manchester Evening News* had to watch the match from the roof of a block of flats overlooking the pitch. The owner's young son ran the copy downstairs every time the phone rang with a call from Manchester. Unfortunately, Meek didn't have a whole lot to write home about.

United showed little desire to exert themselves in the steaming conditions created by the blazing hot sunshine. Tony Dunne hit the post on 16 minutes with a free kick, but Hibernians packed their defence and kept the game, if not the tie, alive. The crowd was woken up by Nobby Stiles who had a scuffle with defender Privitera in the second half; Best also hit the post; then Charlton almost broke the crossbar with a close-range shot. But with their goalkeeper Alfred Mizzi again in superb form, Hibernians held out. Law struggled throughout the match, repeatedly jarring his knee on the rock-hard ground. The conditions were a lottery and when the ball went up in the air nobody knew what it would do when it landed. Hibernians' best chance came to Zerri on 68 minutes but Stepney acrobatically saved his shot. It was the last bit of excitement in what was a pretty dull game.

When the United players ran off the pitch at the end to escape the autograph hunters instead of lining up to salute the crowd from the centre circle, the locals took it as a symbolic retreat after a very poor performance.

The rather undignified goalless draw was an embarrassment for the Reds. The Maltese had played their hearts out; United had been too apprehensive to produce anything special. Although they'd put on a very efficient defensive display, the Reds had let down the crowd, who'd hoped to see attacking brilliance. It was especially disappointing for the hundreds of United fans in the crowd. But a more realistic view of the two legs was that a 4–0 win wasn't a bad way to begin a European Cup campaign.

'The Maltese held us to a goalless draw thanks to the magnificent tactics and coaching of Father Tagliaferro,' said United's assistant manager Jimmy Murphy. Murphy was enchanted by the cleric's great love of football and the two became firm friends. Father Tagliaferro was to play an important part in United's European Cup campaign – and it wasn't the last they'd see of the Maltese fans either.

Two

The Tough Guys of Sarajevo

The next round, in the middle of November, brought a much tougher draw. United's opponents were FK Sarajevo, Yugoslav champions and losing Cup finalists, kinsmen of the Partizan Belgrade team that had ended United's European ambitions at the semi-final stage in 1966 when they beat the Reds 2–1 on aggregate.

Everyone knew the Yugoslavs were among the best teams in Europe, fanatically dedicated to the game. But Sarajevo hadn't had a good start to the season and were near the relegation zone. They'd also lost half their championship-winning team to rival clubs during the close season. Therefore, players like fullback Mirsad Fazlagic, Yugoslavia's captain, looked to the European Cup to give the club a boost.

By contrast, United were in confident mood and topped the League after beating Liverpool 2–1 at Anfield the previous Saturday. Best had grabbed both goals in a scintillating performance. 'We shall try to play like that on Wednesday,' said Busby, looking forward to the Sarajevo match.

But after the way United had been beaten by Partizan in 1966, when they were favourites to win the European Cup, everyone at Old

Trafford viewed the game with some concern. It was justified. Before the tie nobody in England knew much about Sarajevo, but they'd certainly know all about them by the time the two games had been played.

The journey to Yugoslavia was long and difficult. For some time before the match United's officials pondered how to get to Sarajevo. It was a very remote, ancient city with a large Muslim population, a quiet little place tucked away at the far end of a long, tortuously winding road through high mountains. It was famous as the site where Archduke Franz Ferdinand, heir to the Austro–Hungarian throne, was assassinated – an incident that led to the outbreak of the First World War.

Sarajevo was many miles from Belgrade and impossible to reach by scheduled flight. Apart from the risk of fog, the airport only had a grass runway and couldn't accommodate anything larger than a twin-engined plane. Busby and United chairman Louis Edwards tried a 'dummy run' on an advance-spying mission to watch Sarajevo play, but after two uncomfortable nights on a sleeper train from Belgrade, they vowed such transport simply wouldn't do for United's players.

Eventually, Busby put the memories of the Munich disaster to the back of his mind and ordered a special charter plane for the first time since the fateful return trip to Belgrade in 1958. For almost a decade United had travelled to Europe by train. This time they'd fly to the Adriatic resort of Dubrovnik and then journey by coach to Sarajevo. It was expensive, at more than £3,000 for the 3,000-mile return trip, but, though still not the most relaxing of journeys, it was well worth the cost. The BAC 111 bus-stop jet was fast and made what would have been a difficult journey much easier.

After they'd arrived safely at Dubrovnik airport, the United party faced an arduous six-hour, 200-mile coach trip to Sarajevo. The route was a succession of bends, first along the coast and then into the mountains. 'It was a tedious journey,' recalls Best. 'Never have I felt so uncomfortable. Life can be miserable cooped up in a coach for an hour, but on this [occasion] we virtually put in a full working day. Often we were on tricky, winding roads that curled up and down the mountains with a sheer drop to one side.' It was dark before they reached Sarajevo. Stepney thought the moon shining on the barren, stark rocks made the city look like a setting for Dracula's castle. Crerand had his own thoughts on Sarajevo's history. 'I know why Ferdinand got himself shot here,' he told the others, 'he couldn't stand the thought of the journey home.'

In Sarajevo the United party got a terrific reception, which lasted throughout their visit (apart from during the match). The Reds had 48 hours to recover from the strains of the journey so it was unlikely to affect their preparations. They were in far better shape than if they'd followed normal travel routes. They even had time to visit one of the bazaars in the Turkish quarter of the city to pick up souvenirs and also saw the place where an 18-year-old Serbian student gunned down the Archduke as he crossed what became known as the Gavrilo Princip bridge. A pair of footprints sunk into the path marked the exact spot. Crerand couldn't resist trying them for size. 'I can't think what he [the assassin] was doing standing up to his ankles in concrete!' he said. 'I don't know if he could play but he could certainly shoot a bit.'

On the football front, United's main concern was the players who, for various reasons, were unavailable. Law had played 13 consecutive matches between the middle of September and the end of October, including one for Scotland. It was to be his longest unbroken run of the season. But he'd turned out a number of times when he wasn't really up to it. On several occasions he had ducked out of treatment because he was tired of being on the physio's table all the time, and there were certain days when he knew the training wasn't going to be particularly strenuous for his knee, so he trained and put up with the pain.

In the evenings Law would put hot kaolin poultices on his leg, prescribed by the club. At first he'd only used them when he was injured, but during the 1967–68 season, he put the poultices on his leg every night. That was also painful, because the poultices had to be hot and after a while his leg became very tender around the knee. Another treatment Law used at home, one he'd learned from Roy Goodall in his days at Huddersfield, was to run alternately very hot and ice-cold water on his leg. This had a sort of flushing effect on the injury and gave some relief. One way or another, he had turned the family bathroom into something resembling a hospital casualty ward.

Law doubted if he could have played on without a break for much longer. Yet it wasn't his injury that ended the 13-match sequence. Instead, he was suspended for six weeks after being sent off against Arsenal in a League match at Old Trafford on 7 October.

The rest ought to have done his knee good, but Law was reporting for treatment again within a week of starting his suspension. He was still in training and the first sign of trouble came when he had pain behind his knee after sprinting. He seemed to spend more time having treatment while he was suspended than at any stage of the season.

Busby's efforts to persuade the FA to release Law from suspension for the European Cup tie against Sarajevo failed. Stiles was also missing after failing to respond to three weeks of treatment on a knee injury he'd picked up against Sheffield United. Stiles was advised by doctors to have his cartilage removed and had the operation a few days before the Sarajevo match. He'd be out of action for another six weeks. Forward David Herd was also still recovering from a broken leg.

In his hour of need, Busby turned to two more of his youth squad. The inexperienced Scottish youth international Francis Burns replaced an out-of-form Brennan, and fellow Scot John Fitzpatrick, who sported even longer hair than Best, filled in for Stiles. Winger John Aston came into the side in place of Law, with Kidd having already stepped into Herd's shoes with astonishing maturity. The changes made barely a ripple on the surface of United's performances although the lack of big-match experience among the youngsters inevitably resulted in desperation creeping into their game at times, and Fitzpatrick fell into the over-exuberant ways of Stiles.

Though United were playing a team with no previous experience in the European Cup, Sarajevo had a strong line-up with four internationals including Fazlagic. Yugoslavian teams were known to be disciplined and Sarajevo were no exception. They were a fairly ruthless outfit, but the Reds were determined to contain them with their own well-drilled teamwork.

Sarajevo saw United as the great enemy from England and Busby warned his players to expect a very physical game. When the match at the Kosovo Stadium began, it was clear there would be no love lost on United. Sarajevo's tactics were to kick the Reds out of the game. The 40,000 crowd, another record inspired by the visit of United, watched as Best was repeatedly hacked down and battered black and blue. He'd never been so tightly marked in his life, with two and sometimes three players having a go at him every time he got the ball. Kidd was also heavily marked and Burns was so violently chopped down by a scything tackle that Fazlagic was booked. Crerand would later call Sarajevo 'as vicious a team as I ever want to meet'. He couldn't understand why they wanted to play it that way because they had plenty of ability; Best thought they weren't very interested in playing real football.

The Reds began the game playing very deep, with only Kidd up front, and Sarajevo did their best to take advantage of the space available. Sarajevo were quick thinkers, especially on the counter-attack, but they couldn't break down United's disciplined defence. On 22 minutes Prlyaca slipped the ball through to centre forward Musemic. The young local hero, playing his first match after an appendix operation a month earlier, swayed to his right leaving Foulkes groping thin air. Musemic shot wide of Stepney, who didn't move fast enough and could only slow the shot. The ball seemed to trickle over the line before Stepney recovered and dived on the ball as Dunne tried to rescue him. The journalists high above the halfway line knew straightaway it was a goal, but fortunately for United the referee was unsighted and the linesman didn't flag. It wasn't given. Sarajevo's outside right Prodanovic, one of three front men, repeatedly protested and was warned by the referee. It was his last significant contribution. After 35 minutes he was hurt in a tackle and hobbled off with a leg injury. There were no substitutes allowed at that time and Sarajevo were down to ten men.

Just before half-time Fitzpatrick was booked for dissent. It was a dismal end to a first half in which United hadn't made a single chance. They came out for the second half in a more positive frame of mind, but the match continued to simmer and the referee struggled to keep control. Fists and boots flew as both sides battled for their lives. United trainer Jack Crompton was on the pitch so often that Crerand reckoned half the crowd must have thought that he was playing! Busby understandably lost his temper. 'I can't remember Matt ever being quite so angry,' said *Daily Mirror* correspondent Frank McGhee. 'It was the most disgraceful exhibition of vicious tackling I have ever known.' David Meek of the *Manchester Evening News* drew a comparison with history: 'Archduke Ferdinand . . . died a quick death compared to some of the assassin-type tackles the Yugoslavs dished out.'

Busby's players had been spat on, kicked and hounded. The referee saw it all but took very little action. Despite the provocation there was too much at stake for United to retaliate. Their great restraint prevented the match from becoming a full-scale war. As the temperature rose, they turned the other cheek, with the defence taking the greatest credit. Stepney was superb, Fitzpatrick played with dogged determination and Dunne, Crerand and Foulkes were outstanding. Kidd was also very brave as he took on the Sarajevo defence almost single-handed.

The strain of playing with ten men began to tell on Sarajevo late in the second half. Prlyaca, who worked the ball well and had a fierce shot, eventually faded. Without his promptings the attack lost its cutting edge. Indeed, it was the Sarajevo defence, superbly marshalled by Vujovic, which proved to be the best part of their team. With 15 minutes left, United decided they could afford to attack. Kidd came closest to scoring for the Reds with a 25-yard shot that was heading for the top corner until Mustic deflected it over the bar at full stretch with his fingertips. United were looking for a late winner and the home crowd seemed to sense that their team's brave attempt had failed. 'United finished the game playing proud football, passing the ball about at last in lordly style, leisurely but recognisable as that of a team who, luck or no luck, had everything under control,' wrote R.H. Williams of the *Daily Telegraph* in his match report headlined MANCHESTER UNITED FAVOURED BY FORTUNE – INJURY-HIT SARAJEVO ALMOST CAUSE UPSET.

David Meek had paid £10 to have a phone installed nearby so he could get his match report back home as quickly as possible. Unfortunately, his phone didn't ring with his connection to

Manchester until it was too late for the paper's special late-night edition! If the report had got through it would have told the story of a match in which United had unashamedly played for a goalless draw. Despite some outrageous treatment by Sarajevo, they'd succeeded. 'I was pleased with the result and even more so with the way the team behaved under extreme provocation,' said Busby. Meek believed the performance was a sign of how much United's players had grown up. 'The composure they showed was an early indication that the team had matured considerably . . .' he wrote. 'Matt Busby has always preached the maxim . . . lose your heads and you lose the match. In the past not every player has been able to put this lesson into practice, but in this match they were exemplary in the face of killing tackles from three or four of the Sarajevo players.'

United had not only controlled their anger, they'd also directed most of the game and played at their own pace. 'They gave a masterly interpretation of their own free-style version of the 4–3–3 set-up in which they defended safely and frequently menaced their opponents' goal,' wrote Meek. Foulkes, who'd played more European football than any other British player, rated Sarajevo as the toughest team he'd encountered. He thought their tackles were disgraceful. Stepney would later describe the match as one of the hardest of United's European campaign. Sarajevo had, in truth, been a bit unlucky. But Stepney's thoughts on Sarajevo were hardly an advert for tourism – he decided he wouldn't like to send his worst enemy into exile there.

United flew home confident about the second leg, but Sarajevo were also optimistic about their chances. There was enough skill in the Yugoslav team to ensure they'd be treated with respect in the return on 29 November. But they had not been quite good enough to indicate that their prospects of reaching the next round were bright. Their manager said it was a privilege to play at Old Trafford and that he expected United to score six goals. With this build-up, the Reds knew he quietly fancied his team's chances. Indeed, Sarajevo had promised to attack in the return game in a bid to win the tie. The papers were helping the Yugoslavs' efforts to lull United into a false sense of security by forecasting a big score as revenge for the humiliation Partizan had put United through two years earlier.

But the Reds were older and wiser now; they wouldn't underestimate their opponents.

Fitzpatrick was suspended for the return leg, so Burns moved into midfeld while Brennan regained his place at full-back. Sarajevo were missing Prodanovic, whose injury in the first leg proved serious enough to keep him out for at least six months.

There were 62,801 inside Old Trafford when the gates were shut. It was the first full house of the season. Tensions were running high after the reports sent back home of Sarajevo's tough style. But Busby had a pre-game message for the players and fans: 'Keep cool and stay steady, both on and off the field.' Before the match Meek asked Fazlagic, who'd captained a Yugoslav under-23 team at Old Trafford three years earlier, about Sarajevo's rough play. 'I have a big heart,' he said, opening his jacket for Meek to take a look. A Yugoslav journalist laughingly added that Fazlagic also had big feet.

Sarajevo played as tough a game at Old Trafford as they had in Yugoslavia. But when United took the ball to them it was obvious who was the better team. Best had no doubts the Reds would win. United dictated the early stages, with Crerand in great form setting up repeated attacks. Kidd almost uprooted Mustic's left-hand post from 25 yards. Then, on 11 minutes Brennan and Crerand again broke out of defence to start another fine build-up. Kidd produced a measured cross for Best who managed to avoid the flying boots to reach the centre with his head. Mustic could only palm the ball out at full stretch to the alert Aston who stormed in to score just inside the near post. By half-time all the action had taken place in front of the Sarajevo goal as three attempts by Best and others by Burns and Kidd nearly found the target.

The crowd was buzzing as they anticipated the second half. Sarajevo might have been trailing, but with men like the hard little Silijkut, Bajic and Antic in attack and Fazlagic in defence, United had to remain focused. 'Yet always Best remained the centrepiece of the chessboard,' wrote Geoffrey Green of *The Times*. 'He was the knight and the bishop as he slanted on varying angles . . .'

Best responded to Sarajevo's attempts at a comeback by rattling the post twice. His last effort after 58 minutes was deflected on to the post by Vujovic before spinning along the line into the arms of

Mustic. Green described Best as 'a player full of fantasy; a player who lent magic to what might have been whimsy. He may have been provocative as he goaded some of the Yugoslav players with gesture. But Best now lives the life of a marked man, and these days has to suffer much.'

The tension could have been cut with a knife when minutes later Best indulged in more than gesture and was very lucky not to be sent off. After all the abuse he'd taken in the first leg and again in the return, it wasn't surprising when he took a swing at Mustic. Fortunately, although his punch whistled under Mustic's nose it failed to connect and the referee didn't see the attempt. The Sarajevo keeper put on a great act of being hurt and complained to his team-mates that he'd been struck in the face. It was a great mistake. From then on Sarajevo lost their heads and the match. An incensed Prlyaca hunted Best down, as he went looking for revenge. At the first opportunity, less than half an hour from the end, he kicked the elusive Best so blatantly that referee Roger Machin had no choice but to send him off.

It was Sarajevo's undoing. Best got his revenge in sweeter fashion by scoring from the resulting free kick. Crerand passed to Aston, who pulled the ball back from the left after it looked as if it had gone over the by-line, out of play. Foulkes headed the reverse pass against the bar and the irrepressible Best volleyed home United's second goal on 65 minutes. The Sarajevo players, incensed at the original decision, surrounded the linesman who had to be given police protection before order was restored.

To their credit, ten-man Sarajevo put the incident behind them and concentrated on trying to get back into the match. Stepney made a brilliant save from Antic before outside-right Salih Delalic headed home a cross from Blazevic three minutes from the end after Fazlagic had broken out of defence. Another goal for Sarajevo and United would be out of the cup on the away-goals rule. Stiles, watching from the stands with the suspended Law, felt as weak as a kitten during the last couple of minutes, knowing an equaliser would be worth two goals. But, try as they might, Sarajevo were frustrated to the finish. They'd left it too late to make a comeback.

The Yugoslavs' tough tackling had left a bitter taste among the

United players. As the teams left the pitch there was some jostling in the tunnel and suddenly a fight broke out between Crerand and Mustic. Busby, one of the first to try to break it up, was whacked on the face. Thankfully tempers cooled behind the dressing-room doors. Afterwards Crerand was man enough to pay tribute to Sarajevo. 'They were one of the best sides we have played,' he said. 'They play it physically strong as well as being a great footballing side.' Green had his own views on the battle: 'If the Slavs now think that much of the United tackling was too forthright, Manchester themselves could point out a good deal of body checking and other irregularities. This is what happens when the two ideologies of how to play football come face-to-face.'

Three

Gornik Zabrze

United were through to the quarter-finals of the European Cup. Old ambitions began to burn fiercely. The first note of caution came when they were drawn to play Gornik Zabrze. The Reds would once again have to travel across Eastern Europe – this time to meet the Polish champions.

Worryingly, Denis Law was still struggling with his injured knee and was having more cortisone injections. Law played seven consecutive matches after his suspension, but by early January he was in a worse state than ever. On the 11 January his consultant Mr Glass said there might be a piece of cartilage left in his knee from the operation he'd had while playing for Huddersfield nine years earlier. Glass suggested Law continued playing, but said he should only train on soft ground. At the end of the season he could have an operation to remove the posterior horn of cartilage.

Law played throughout January in constant pain. On the 27th United drew 2–2 with Tottenham at Old Trafford in the third round of the FA Cup. After the match, Busby decided that while the squad were in London for the replay Law should visit a Harley Street specialist. So, as his team-mates prepared to face Spurs, Law visited Mr Osmond-Clarke, an orthopaedic surgeon (who later treated the Queen and eventually received a knighthood). His report (which Law didn't see until years later) offered a startling opinion. 'There may indeed be a tag of the external semilunar cartilage still in the joint and it might help to remove it . . . But the fact will remain that this is a degenerating joint and that nothing and nobody can prevent further deterioration, be it slow or fast. My own view is that this knee has reached a stage when it will handicap Mr Law in top-flight play and I very much doubt if it will stand up to it for more than another season or two. Even then I would suspect that the knee would give rise to many complaints and periods of unfitness . . . My conclusion is that if Mr Law and the club are agreeable to take a chance on a further exploration of the knee . . . I feel it would be reasonable to take that chance, but I cannot confess to be optimistic myself about the possibilities of a successful outcome . . .'

While Law was being examined in Harley Street, United's other injured forward, David Herd, made his comeback in the FA Cup replay against holders Tottenham after being sidelined for a year with his broken leg. United lost 1–0.

But the Reds began to turn it on in the League. After beating Sarajevo they won eight, drew two and lost only one of 11 League games. Best scored in five successive matches. Bristling with confidence, they were more than ready to play Gornik.

The last time most of United's players had heard of the Polish side was when they played the double-winning Tottenham team of 1961. Spurs thrashed them 8–1 in the return leg of a first-round European Cup tie at White Hart Lane for an aggregate score of 10–3. But while the current Gornik side contained some of the players who'd lost to Spurs, such as goalkeeper Kostka and left-winger Musialek, they were now far more experienced.

In the previous round, Gornik had beaten the fancied Russian side Dynamo Kiev, who'd earlier knocked out the holders Celtic in the fastest-ever dismissal of European champions. Gornik had now emerged as the dark horses and were considered among the best of the last eight teams in the cup. They were a fast, intelligent side with several outstanding players. Their skills were supplemented by the toughness expected in players who had been raised in the Polish coalfields.

Everyone had a healthy respect for teams from behind the Iron Curtain. Gornik weren't a super side, but United respected the Poles. They knew no team reached the quarter-finals of the European Cup without a lot of skill and technique. Busby, his assistant Jimmy Murphy and United chairman Louis Edwards travelled to Poland to watch Gornik play. Murphy lost count of the number of hours he and Busby spent flying to Europe to watch Gornik or making detailed plans for the game. After the Boss had briefed United's players they approached the first leg with some trepidation.

The day before the Reds played their first-leg tie against Gornik on 28 February, Law felt excruciating pain in his knee at training. On the morning of the match he went to see Glass at the Jewish Hospital to have another painkilling injection. This time he was given Protocain for the first time. Since Law would be playing late that evening, his wife Di had taken the children to her sister's, so after his visit to the hospital Law went home to an empty house to get a couple of hours' sleep before meeting the rest of the team at 4.30.

Unbeknown to him, he was allergic to Protocain. His leg came up like a balloon. Law woke in a state of agonised delirium. He couldn't walk but there was no one else in the house; he crawled head first down the stairs to get to the hall so he could phone United and tell them what had happened. Somehow, in his fevered condition, he managed it.

The following day Gornik selected the side that had beaten Kiev in the Soviet Union. It would soon be clear why the hard, strong and extremely clever team had confounded the Russians.

Not surprisingly, Law failed a fitness test just a few hours before the match. His knee was so bad that he couldn't even go to Old Trafford and had to stay in bed. He was already doubtful for the second leg. Jim Ryan, who could go forward and beat opponents, especially down the wing, was brought in to deputise.

A crowd of 64,000 – another full house – crammed into Old Trafford. All the tension of a quarter-final was there but, unlike

Sarajevo, Gornik wanted to play football and were met on those terms by United. The Poles had come straight to Manchester from their mid-winter break and didn't really seem match-fit. They were immediately forced back. Many clubs had gone to Old Trafford determined to play it tight defensively, but few had faced such tremendous pressure and power as Gornik.

United threw everything at the Poles but Gornik held out. Their resistance was as stubborn as Sarajevo's – except that they usually played within the rules. The Poles put on a remarkable exhibition of defensive football. Goalkeeper Hubert Kostka was brilliant and saved Gornik repeatedly. Whatever the angle or distance, he seemed unbeatable.

The Poles showed how to play against Best and hold him without resorting to unscrupulous tactics. Henryk Latocha stuck close to the Irishman but played him mostly fairly, and well. Nevertheless, Best's sleight of foot still resulted in some harsh treatment, even from Latocha. This was, however, no rough-and-tumble match but rather a game full of fast, skilful and sporting football.

There were very few gaps for United to exploit. When they did prise open the Gornik defence they were overeager and their shooting was off-target. A goal just wouldn't come. The crowd wondered how long the intense pressure could last before United scored. They'd forced 16 corners in the first half but were still without a goal. But Busby's team didn't worry. The players had learned that they could score two goals just as easily in the last ten minutes as in the first ten. They knew that if they'd opened up like madmen, trying to win the game with the first kick, they couldn't have hoped to find a rhythm that would prove successful.

Charlton and Crerand worked like troopers in midfield as United tried to score, but there seemed no way round or over the Gornik defence. Busby's side had most of the play, but Kostka made some superb saves. Time was running out and United were committed to all-out attack, even though their relentless pressure exposed them to the swift counter-attacks that were Gornik's speciality.

For the first hour it looked as if Latocha had succeeded against Best where Sarajevo had failed. The Irishman was by now receiving exceptionally tough and unlawful treatment from his markers. But on 61 minutes United at last gained reward for their almost constant attacks. The move was started by Dunne who found Crerand. The Scot, in turn, saw a gap and fed Best along the edge of the penalty area. United's winger took the ball wide to the right of goal, swept past Latocha, lost then regained the ball, and finally managed to escape. He cut inside and let fly with a rocket shot from an acute angle that the despairing Florenski tried to intercept but instead deflected past Kostka into the net. Best, the man with the brave heart and the flying feet, had produced a flash of brilliance. Jimmy Ryan led the applause. It was a goal United had threatened from the start when Crerand took control of the game with a brilliant display of accurate creative passing. The crowd cascaded down the terraces behind the goal. They'd waited so long for their team to score and how they celebrated.

The goal took some of the apprehension out of United's play but they continued to suffer a sense of foreboding. United's bombardment continued but still Gornik's defence wouldn't give an inch. The Reds' efforts to score became increasingly frantic, yet it looked as though they'd have to settle for a 1–0 win. 'Corner kicks were lobbed like howitzers but all failed to explode into another goal until the last minute,' wrote Albert Barham in *The Guardian*. 'Header followed header, shot followed shot, and always there was Kostka there at the last.'

There was just a minute left when Crerand took the last of his many free kicks. Kostka punched the ball out and it landed at the feet of Ryan, who drove a mis-hit shot towards goal. Kidd, standing on the extreme right of the penalty area, stepped across the path of the ball and cutely back-heeled it slowly through a crowd of players wrongfooting Kostka. 'It rolled remorselessly on past one outstretched leg, then another, then a third until it crept away from the unsighted Kostka and over the line,' recalled Roger Macdonald in *Manchester United in Europe*. 'Kidd could not have chosen a better moment for an almost impossible goal, for threading the elephant through the eye of a needle.'

At the end the relieved United players lined the route to the tunnel in a guard of honour to applaud the visitors off the pitch. The loudest roar from the crowd was reserved for Kostka, the last Polish player to leave the field. The fans and the United players knew just how hard it had been to score against him. After the bitterness of the Sarajevo tie the Gornik match was a refreshing reminder that football could be a very sporting affair. 'Both English and Polish champions played superbly skilful football that was forceful but immaculately clean and sporting,' wrote David Meek of the *Manchester Evening News.* Busby agreed. 'It was a fine sporting game . . . something that hasn't always happened to us in the European Cup,' he said.

Kidd's soft goal had given United a real chance of reaching the semi-finals in the second leg in two weeks' time. They could now go to Poland with an advantage that might prove decisive. The 2–0 win was a fair result, especially with Law missing again. The Poles were sporting enough to pay Busby's team some handsome tributes. Gornik had created too few chances to test United's defence, but they warned they'd be no pushovers in the return match.

The following day Law was admitted to St Joseph's Hospital, Whalley Range, on Moss Side. It was run by nuns. He was in agony, his leg bursting. Glass drained the fluid from his knee, an experience Law compared to having a large stone block lifted off his head. The relief as the syringe did its work was tremendous. He didn't know how much fluid came out but it felt like a bucketful. When it was over, Law was put in a splint; he felt he was in heaven.

United slumped to a surprising 3–1 home defeat against Chelsea on 2 March, just ten days before facing Gornik again. After a month of pain and trouble in February, March would be little better for Law. He came out of hospital a couple of days after United's loss to Chelsea to say goodbye to his wife who was off to Scotland to await the arrival of their third child and spent a miserable few weeks living alone at home and travelling each day to the ground for treatment.

Meanwhile, Busby went to watch Gornik and was shocked at the bad weather and dreadful winter playing conditions. The state of the pitch and the weather his players would have to deal with were among his greatest fears as he prepared his squad for another trip behind the Iron Curtain. Since the Poles had looked so useful at Old Trafford, some people began to say two goals might not be enough.

United knew that only a solid, sensible performance, without mistakes, would see them progress to the next round.

Before leaving for the return leg Busby, knowing that without a fit Law United's chances of winning the European Cup were slim, made a secret bid for West Ham's England striker Geoff Hurst, the only man to score a hat-trick in a World Cup final, when England beat West Germany 4–2 in 1966. The day United left for Poland Busby phoned West Ham. Manager Ron Greenwood was out so Busby left a message with the secretary: '£200,000 for Geoff Hurst: yes or no? Please telephone or telegram your answer to Katowice. Busby.' When Greenwood was given the message he was shocked. He cabled his answer to Busby immediately. It was short and to the point: 'No. Greenwood.' He resented Busby's impersonal approach, but in any case nothing would have persuaded him to part with Hurst. The Reds would have to pray that Law regained full fitness quickly.

United's players were upbeat. They had belief in their ability to make progress even without Law. 'We went to Poland heartened by the knowledge that we could and should do a Partizan act of our own,' recalls Stepney, referring to the 1966 semi-final.

Four

Be Prepared

The match against Gornik, to be played on 13 March, was switched from the Gornik Stadium to the massive Slaski Stadium in Chorzow, halfway between Zabrze and the county town of Katowice deep in the heart of the coal-mining area of Upper Silesia. It was difficult to reach by scheduled flight so United hired another special 'bus-stop' charter plane at a cost of £3,000 for four days. There was certainly no air of false optimism when United flew out to Poland. Murphy and Busby had already made the nightmare journey in the heart of winter. They knew what to expect. It was clear the return leg was going to be tough, but United's players didn't realise just how bad the conditions would be until they arrived.

The flight to Krakow gave the first hint of what was in store. Their plane droned into Eastern Europe. On arrival the players crammed into a small coach. The two-hour journey from the airport to Katowice confirmed their worst fears. The weather was below freezing and brief flurries of snow whistled about their ears. It was like driving through a blizzard. The earth looked barren and white and the small farms on the road seemed poor and dark. Best believed it was bad for morale.

Katowice was a desolate place – bleak, snowswept and bitterly cold. There were no controls on industrial emissions and the pollution had turned the snow black. The football season had just restarted after the mid-winter break, when conditions were so bad that playing was impossible. 'Deep snow lay everywhere, crisp but not very even,' wrote Geoffrey Green in *The Times*. 'A blizzard was blowing and bent figures in the streets fought against the clawing elements.' Before he'd even seen the pitch Busby told the reporters travelling with United that he'd fly the team home and return every week, if necessary, until the conditions were right.

At least United were looked after superbly at the Katowice Hotel. Despite warnings from Paddy Crerand, who'd been to Poland three years before with Scotland, even the food was surprisingly good. The chef came out beaming during meals to make sure everything was satisfactory. Shay Brennan gave the thumbs-up sign over his steak with a cup of Polish-brewed tea at his elbow. 'Little things like this make a tremendous difference to the spirit of a touring team,' says Stiles, 'and we felt happier when we had settled into the hotel and found we were going to be comfortable.'

But Busby wasn't happy with what he saw 48 hours before the kick-off. He was shocked by the amount of snow. Since travelling to watch Gornik play two weeks before he'd been dreading such weather. 'If conditions are bad I shall make representations to the referee, Mr Lo Bello,' he told reporters. 'This is too important a game for United. We have come here to play football and after the first great game at Old Trafford we do not want a shambles of a ground to spoil it here.'

Snow fell for two days before the match. It was so cold that the only time the players left the stuffy atmosphere of the centrally heated hotel was for an hour's training at the Slaski Stadium and to buy fur hats to keep their heads and ears warm.

Autograph hunters besieged the hotel despite the freezing temperatures. They hung around outside for almost the whole of United's stay. Mingling with the fans were the local 'spivs' offering black market exchange rates of almost three times the official zloty rate for pounds and dollars. And it wasn't just foreign currency that was in short supply. The locals also stopped United fans to see if they could buy polo-neck jumpers and razor blades. But while some goods were scarce, the shops and conditions had improved a lot since Crerand had played there in 1965.

The day before the match the pitch was covered in three inches of snow. United trained once more at the Slaski Stadium but the session was farcical. The ball picked up snow as it rolled along and there were patches of ice underneath. It was dangerous. Unless the snow was removed the game couldn't be played. Busby was seriously concerned about the risk of injury and the fact that it would be almost impossible to play entertaining football before thousands of fans who'd paid good money. He sensed his pursuit of a lifetime's dream was about to be tossed into a lottery.

The players were divided about the conditions. The fresh snow had given the pitch a cushion on which to play. Charlton didn't want the match called off. 'They are all so important these days and there is obviously a build-up for a big match like this,' he said. 'The players are keyed up. I feel two goals are enough . . . the conditions are difficult. It is the fierce cold as much as anything that worries us. You have almost to run with your eyes shut.' Crerand thought the conditions would be more of a handicap to a team trying to attack, but United were going out to defend.

Nevertheless, all the United players, except Best, thought the pitch would be too dangerous. He saw it as a challenge to his skill and balance. But he had another reason for wanting the game to be played: he didn't like being behind the Iron Curtain and just wanted to leave. But even Best could see Busby's point. To throw everything away on an ice-bound pitch would be ludicrous.

As well as his fear of possible injuries to his key players, Busby thought the pitch could lead to freak goals. He decided to find Concetto Lo Bello, Italy's top referee, to get the match postponed. 'We don't want to come this far and then go out on a farce of a pitch,' Busby told David Meek. 'We've come here to play a game of football. And we've travelled a long way. We haven't come all this distance to stake everything on a game of chance at such a vital stage, in such an important competition.'

The Poles, who were used to such pitches, wanted to play. They promised to bring in labourers who'd work all night sweeping the playing surface, stamping down the snow and adding salt so it would be a firm, white carpet that would take a full stud. The pitch might not be perfect, but it would be playable, they argued.

United weren't convinced and went in search of the referee. But he was travelling on the overnight sleeper train from Vienna and didn't arrive until the morning of the match. He saw the pitch and declared it playable. The decision went against Busby's better judgement and his wishes but United now had to play. The Boss shrugged his shoulders and gave in to the inevitable. There were no complaints from the players who accepted the decision.

The players were offered a distraction from the weather conditions with the chance to visit the prisoner of war camp at Auschwitz. The trip was arranged by the travel agent who organised the flight, not Busby, and there was no pressure to go. Some people decided to visit the camp; others, including Busby, chose not to. 'In those days you went because you thought you would never get the chance again,' says Stepney.

BBC commentator David Coleman had been unable to fly with the team because of a speaking engagement on the Monday at an Olympic fundraising dinner. He eventually reached Gornik at six o'clock on the morning of the match and bumped into United chairman Louis Edwards getting out of a taxi. Edwards told Coleman he should have explained why he couldn't travel with the team and maybe United could have helped in some way. As Edwards went off to bed he turned to Coleman and said, 'Don't tell Matt,' as if he was one of the players who didn't want the Boss to know he'd been out late.

Busby made some late changes to his side. Foulkes was still recovering from torn cruciate ligaments in his knee and refused to play. Busby was very annoyed. David Sadler would have to deputise again. Jimmy Ryan had performed well as Law's replacement in the first leg, but was sacrificed for the sake of the team. Wing-half John Fitzpatrick, a more defensive player, was brought in to harass in midfield and help protect United's two-goal lead. David Herd was recalled to reinforce the forward line in place of Aston. The Reds had only three players up front and needed experience and scoring power to benefit from any counter-attacks. Herd would add physical strength and long-range shooting to their armoury. Herd had scored many goals for United, but he was worried because he'd had little first-team action for a long time. The other players felt sorry for him. 'What a game to come back to,' he told Stiles. 'I'm scared stiff. I hope my stamina is better than last time.'

The three players brought into the team were all given special instructions: Fitzpatrick was to harry Gornik in midfield; Ryan and Herd were to hold the ball as long as possible whenever United got it up front to them. They would aim to play a defensive 4–3–3 formation. 'Given no alternative by the conditions, a modest lead, and a team which leaned too heavily on the fantasies of Best, Busby decided, for the first time in 28 European Cup ties, that this would have to be a rearguard action,' wrote David Miller in *Father of Football*. 'It was not that he was swallowing his principles; he was ruled by circumstance.'

Most of the Polish fans were inside the Slaski Stadium by 4.30 p.m. even though the game was an evening kick-off. There were no stands. The ground was just a huge bowl. The temperature was 20 degrees below freezing. Eventually 105,000 gathered to watch the match. They were the lucky ones. Another 100,000 who'd applied for tickets were disappointed. Gornik had to make radio announcements telling ticketless fans to stay away. Crerand thought the crowd's enthusiasm was fantastic. Everyone seemed to have brought a horn, and they blew them like mad. The supporters may have just been trying to keep warm but they created an unbelievable noise, complete with wailing sirens.

The surface was covered in snow and white flakes were still falling. So much snow was piled up between the goalposts that it made the goals appear smaller. It would be a test of endurance for United, even though they were experienced in Europe. 'There is a job of work to do here,' said Busby. 'So let's do it properly.'

Just before kick-off Stepney looked across at the Polish players and was staggered to see them wearing polo-neck shirts, gloves and tights as protection against the weather, while United were just in their normal nylon shirts. Charlton's mind went back two years to the day when, giving notice of things to come, England had beaten Poland on the same ground in Katowice and thought how different the conditions were on this winter's night.

The Poles had to attack and threw everything at United. The game was being played in near-blizzard conditions. The red lines marking out the pitch were almost invisible after the first ten minutes. Undaunted, referee Lo Bello insisted the match should continue. Geoffrey Green of *The Times* described the scene: 'Later, the driving snowflakes, swirling like a necklace in the lights, fled to leave us in the grip of a dark, bitter night. It was so cold that even these hardy Poles, the miners of Gornik, turned to lighting bonfires on the open terraces.' Years later Jimmy Murphy would still shiver when he thought about this match: '. . . the ground was dusted with snow and icy blasts of wind cut through clothing so that conditions were aptly described as borrowed from a Siberian horror film,' he recalled.

The press wore pyjamas beneath their jumpers and coats for extra insulation. Although that helped keep them warm, they still struggled to report at the press tables, which were out in the open. They couldn't make notes on the snowy, soggy paper. But they did have telephones and could at least get their reports back to their papers on time. BBC commentator David Coleman took the extra precaution of wearing a balaclava to keep his head warm.

The Poles had to make the most of their rare opportunities since United were playing well. The Reds showed remarkable speed and balance, given the difficulties posed by the pitch.

Dunne took a knock just before half-time and hobbled off at the interval. In the dressing room his left ankle was heavily strapped. United also had a visit from referee Lo Bello, who warned the players he wouldn't allow tactics such as time wasting. In particular, he warned Stepney that he timed goalkeepers and if they didn't release the ball after four seconds, he penalised them by awarding an indirect free kick.

In the second half, Dunne's injury left him a virtual passenger. United had to carry him and Gornik often threatened to score. But somehow United held out; they dug in and battled. Fitzpatrick, Ryan and Herd made a truly Herculean effort.

Charlton played a fine captain's role in directing operations as he slowed down and changed the tempo of the game using his great control. Alongside him Crerand also had a good second half, while

Best was a constant threat. Green of *The Times* thought Best often seemed to be in two places at once, while suggesting a nerve-wracking influence in still another. The Irishman's movement was almost balletic as he danced his way through the snow in a bid to keep the pressure off United's overworked defence.

With 20 minutes left Stepney dribbled out to the edge of his area and was looking to throw the ball clear when, true to his word, Lo Bello penalised him for wasting time. Stepney couldn't possibly have cleared the ball in time, hampered as he was by Polish forwards. But Gornik were given an indirect free kick almost on the penalty spot. All United's players stood virtually along the goal line. Kuchta's shot was blocked but the Reds were now disorganised. A minute later he found 'Wlodek' Lubanski with a diagonal pass from the right and the young forward struck a scorching shot on the run that flew in off the bar.

It was the first goal United had conceded in almost three and a half hours of European football on the Continent – proof that until that moment they'd mastered both the conditions and the Polish attack. But the Reds would now need all their experience to keep out Gornik, whose attacks became frenetic after they'd taken the lead. The Polish champions still had just enough time to save themselves by scoring again and forcing a play-off.

Late in the game Lepner struck a well-hit shot which Stiles got across to but could only half stop. The ball was heading for goal when out of the corner of his eye Stiles saw the flash of a red boot scything past his ear to hook the ball clear. Only as he moved upfield did he realise it was Herd. The forward had justified his place with a solid defensive performance, even though he was playing as a striker.

In the past, United might have buckled, but Stiles and Fitzpatrick were everywhere and made sure the defence would not be breached again. The last few minutes seemed like an eternity to Stepney but Lubanski's effort was the only goal of the match. United had won 2–1 on aggregate and Gornik were out of the European Cup. 'By the end a grey sadness for the Poles had surged over the white setting; the sky took on a more leaden hue and a chill wind blew through the eastern world,' wrote Green of *The Times*.

Stepney would later describe the match as probably the most difficult of United's European campaign, Best rated it as their best performance of the tournament and Stiles said the two legs were the most sporting international games he'd experienced at club level. Jimmy Murphy was also impressed. 'Certainly of all the brave performances Manchester United have put up in the European Cup – one thinks automatically of that magnificent fightback against Bilbao in 1957 when we had to get three goals to win the tie and succeeded in so doing, or the great display of pulling back two goals against Real Madrid in the same year when the Spanish masters had coolly snatched a two-goal lead at Old Trafford – that night in Poland when Manchester held Gornik to a single goal must rate highly among the club's great performances.'

Busby was satisfied with his team's ability to carry out orders and keep to a pattern. 'We played to certain tactics and they succeeded. Away from home you have to try to contain the opposition.' They hadn't looked like Manchester United, the team that was supposed to thrive on flair. Busby conceded as much, recognising, perhaps for the first time in his life, that grim defence, however out of character, was sometimes necessary.

The Boss was especially pleased with the experience younger players like Sadler, Fitzpatrick and Kidd were getting in Europe. 'I've a feeling this is our year,' said Busby. 'I think things are running for us this time and I feel happier than on previous occasions when we have got so far. We were the first [English] club to enter the European Cup, because we felt it was a world game. It is the one thing the club wants to win and the one thing I want to win. It's good to be back and feel the warmth of a dream still living on . . . that the Reds will win the European Cup.'

Gornik, who'd played fair in a sporting but hard-fought game, were very upset at the end of the match. Their Hungarian manager Geza Kalocsai was disappointed at the way United had packed their defence. But he had no doubt about the major difference between the teams. 'If there is a better winger than George Best I haven't seen him,' he said. 'He could have got into any of the world's greatest teams.'

As there was nowhere to celebrate in Katowice the United party went back to the hotel and, for a change, had a glass of wine with their meal. There was then an impromptu party. It was clear that they wanted to stay together. They sang and drank and Busby was called upon to give his version of 'I Belong to Glasgow'. He once again confirmed the players' suspicions that he'd never have made the grade as a singer. United's joy was partly explained by the fact that they had so much to look forward to – they learned that the other semi-finalists were Juventus, Benfica and Real Madrid.

None of the players fancied playing an Italian team. 'The Italians had become masters of boring the pants off the rest of Europe with their defensive play,' was how Stepney described their thoughts on Italian football. Benfica had an impressive reputation because several of their players, including the brilliant striker Eusebio, had starred in the superb Portuguese team that had reached the World Cup semi-final against England in 1966. That left Real Madrid. Most people would have preferred United to play Madrid in the final since the clubs had built up a special relationship over the years, after the Spaniards' sympathetic response to the Munich disaster.

After travelling some 14,000 miles through Malta, Yugoslavia and Poland, United hadn't scored a single goal, but they'd also only conceded one. Busby's team had overcome Hibernians, Sarajevo and now Gornik to reach the semi-finals of the European Cup for the fourth time since 1957. They'd fought a step nearer a ten-year-old dream to conquer their last football Everest. Stepney felt Busby's team were playing almost perfectly. 'The right formula had been adopted, and we had contrived to make it work – tight controlled defence away, with every man tackling, covering, marking and intercepting. But at home, we gave ourselves more freedom of expression in attack, and scored the goals that mattered.'

United's semi-final opponents turned out to be the mighty Spanish Champions Real Madrid. It was a mouthwatering prospect. If United could survive the semi-final in the spring they'd surely start as favourites in the Wembley final on 29 May.

That night in the freezing coal-mining city of Katowice, many miles from home, United's players went to bed early. As they lay there most of them thought about the possibility that this could, finally, be their year.

Five

Real Madrid

The whole country had become captivated by the prospect of United winning the European Cup. With Jock Stein's Celtic having become the first British team to lift the trophy the previous season, the Reds knew they were playing an important role in the renaissance of British club football at European level.

But United had gone off the boil. They lost 2–0 at Coventry in their first match after returning from Gornik and were beaten in two successive home games against Manchester City (3–1) and Liverpool (2–1). Another worry was Law's continuing injury saga; his only match towards the end of March was the loss to City at Old Trafford. At one stage Busby's team had topped the League by five points, but the succession of bad results, especially the home defeats, had seen their lead chipped away.

By now, though, Law's thoughts weren't really on championships. He was so fed up with always being injured that he decided to see an osteopath. Whatever the pros and cons of his various treatments it was rest that really made Law feel better. He also had the distraction of his new son Robert, born on 14 April, to take his mind off his injured knee. Law's family would be in

Scotland when United played Real Madrid ten days later.

Just four days before the semi-final the Reds had a crucial home game against relegation-threatened Sheffield United. The experienced Foulkes was missing; there were rumours he wouldn't get the chance, after all, to claim a European Cup winner's medal. Best and Charlton both had fitness tests but were given the all-clear. It was a terrible game, but despite playing poorly United picked up two vital points with a goal from Law in the first five minutes. It had been the final test for his troubled knee before the semi-final. The question now was whether United could afford to play him when his fitness and form were in doubt.

The League table showed just how tight the championship race was. United were top with 54 points from 39 games followed by Leeds, a point behind with a game in hand, and Manchester City, four points back but also with a game in hand. 'Success for us against Real Madrid . . . and the League didn't really matter too much, for we would be in the final of the European Cup,' said Stepney. 'But if we failed against Real and lost the championship . . . it was a thought which didn't bear thinking . . .'

After the Sheffield match United's players all agreed they'd have to play much better the following Wednesday against Real. Crerand tried to put a brave face on things. 'Och,' he said, 'everything will be a'reet on the neet. Ye'll see . . .' As Stepney drove home that evening he thought about the task facing Busby over the next few days. 'The Boss is going to have to solve a few problems this weekend,' he thought. 'I'm glad I haven't his job to do.'

Of all the teams who'd fought for the European Cup, none had done more to glamorise the competition than Real Madrid. They'd won the tournament six times, including the first five in a row from 1956 to 1960. They'd reached the final on two other occasions after competing in every European Cup since it began. They, more than any other club, had captured the imagination of the people of Europe, showing that skill and entertainment were a potent cocktail that would lead to success.

Although Real were United's rivals, they were as close to the heart of Old Trafford as any other club. After the Munich air crash in 1958, the people of Madrid had been wonderful friends to

Manchester. They offered free holidays in Spain for the survivors. Some of United's players accepted and had a marvellous time in the sun. The teams had therefore developed a friendship unusual in football. There was a special relationship between Madrid and United. 'Matt and all the people at Madrid were very close,' says Sadler. 'And Madrid, of course, had been the great European side, the team to aim at ... Madrid had a special place up there for Matt and United.'

Real's president, Santiago Bernabeu, had tried to lure Busby to Madrid as manager. Busby would always remember the offer: 'Their actual words were: "We'll make it heaven and earth for you", and I knew they would.' Busby could have probably won the European Cup not once but several times with the Spanish champions. He thought about it for a week and then decided his heaven and earth were in Manchester. Busby knew the boys who'd died in the air crash could only be commemorated by the team they'd once played for.

During the post-Munich years Busby had tried to prepare his players for an eventual return to European competition with a series of friendlies against the very best sides Europe had to offer. In 1959 he flew to Madrid to persuade Real to come to Old Trafford. At that time the Spanish champions could command the enormous sum of £12,000 to play a friendly. Busby told them the Munich air crash had ruined United financially as well as physically and he'd be grateful if they'd take that into consideration. Santiago Bernabeu turned to the club's business manager and said, 'We must treat Matt and Manchester United generously.' They did. Madrid came at less than half price.

Real visited Old Trafford three years running from 1959. They were guaranteed a share of the gate receipts, worth about £10,000, after the first trip. The games were grand occasions followed by hotel banquets and exchanges of gifts. When United visited Madrid in 1959 Secretary Les Olive was given £40 to spend on fishing tackle as a present for Santiago Bernabeu.

Given their friendship it was fitting that the Reds should play Madrid in 1968 as they battled to deliver Busby's El Dorado – the fictitious Spanish land that according to legend was filled with gold.

Busby could happily live without the gold; he wanted silver in the form of the elusive European Cup that Real knew so well.

The momentous semi-final encounter was the first time the teams had met in European competition for 11 years. United's fourth semi-final appearance provided a long-awaited chance to take revenge on behalf of the Busby Babes. Real had beaten the pre-Munich United 5–3 on aggregate in the 1957 European Cup semi-final. That great Real side had such superb ability that every other club team had been judged by their achievement. They had become the yardstick by which other clubs were measured.

In the build-up to the match, United heard varying reports about their opponents. Real came to Manchester with a tremendous reputation. Their manager was Miguel Munoz, who'd captained Real to their first two European Cup wins. He'd retained Real's captain, the great but ageing Francisco Gento, on the left wing. Gento had played a record 82 European Cup matches for Real. He was a little tubbier and perhaps not as fast as he had been, but he was still captain. Some people in Madrid believed his time had run out and that he should make way for someone younger. But Munoz was standing by the swarthy, chunky Gento and refused to drop him.

Munoz had largely rebuilt Real from the team of all talents that had taken Europe by storm. The club was in a period of change in which their youth policy was playing an important role. Munoz had to pin his hopes on Spanish-born players because of restrictions on foreign imports. He'd moulded a team that had won the Spanish league title six times in seven seasons and the European Cup in 1966. They tackled quickly, worked hard, had an outstanding midfield player in right-half Pirri and were known for their counter-attacks, which brought unexpected goals. In defence they had a great player in Zoco, who was the perfect sweeper.

Nevertheless, some said they weren't fit to be compared to the Madrid of Di Stefano, Puskas, Santamaria, Kopa and company; that they lacked the stars whose individual ability and flair for the unorthodox had made them masters of Europe. Stiles thought that perhaps they were overrated because in this phase of their development they couldn't hope to be as good as the old team. It seemed an illogical argument to Best. After all, he reasoned, they'd reached the semi-final of the European Cup. While they were no longer the Real of old they still ranked as one of the world's most famous and powerful clubs and a great tradition still ran strong in their blood. The United–Real match was deemed by many to be the tougher of the two semi-finals. And according to Real's left-back Sanchis, 'The team which wins this tie could win the European Cup.'

In fact, United couldn't have faced a bigger challenge. Although Madrid weren't the great side they'd been when they won the first five European Cups, they could still beat anyone in the world on their day. Busby had shed any illusions his players might have had as soon as the semi-final draw was made. 'They're still a top-class team, comparable with any side in Europe – or the world,' he warned. Busby went out of his way to stress that although the legend may have faded in the eyes of some people, there was no doubt Real were well organised. They were strong all round, had skill allied to a tremendous workrate and could win a game even when they seemed beaten. As if to emphasise their pedigree they'd just won the Spanish championship again the previous weekend. Some felt United had also passed their peak in 1966. Whatever the shortcomings of both teams, there was no doubt the semi-final had brought together two sides of high reputation and regard.

The Reds had the slight disadvantage of playing the first leg at home. Most of their players realised that the semi-final was likely to be the toughest game they'd yet played. It was a view shared by Real's manager Munoz who also felt it would be the hardest test his side had faced all season.

As Real boarded their plane on the Sunday for the flight to Manchester's Ringway Airport they were unaware that two of United's best players were having treatment at Old Trafford. Best had taken a knock on the ankle and Charlton, the more doubtful of the two, had ricked his back – the price the Reds had paid for two precious points against Sheffield United. For Charlton especially it was a battle against the clock to get fit. Meanwhile, Real would arrive without their star forward Amancio Amaro Varela, who was suspended after being sent off against Sparta Prague.

Gento believed that even if they lost the match at Old Trafford it wouldn't spell the end of Real's dreams. United would have to win by a handsome margin to kill the Spaniards' hopes in the return. Gento thought Charlton could guide United to victory in the first leg, but that prospect didn't worry him unduly. 'I will be delighted if it's United winning – by only 1–0,' he said. 'We can then win through in the return game – I hope.' Munoz rated Best, Charlton, Crerand and Law as world-class. He conceded that any of them could do damage, but it was Charlton he feared most. The Spaniards had christened Charlton 'El Monstruo del Futbol Ingles' or 'The Monster of English Football'. United were told it was meant to be a compliment to the man who'd tormented Spain's national team at Wembley the previous month. Real feared he'd do damage to them at Old Trafford. But Munoz didn't know that Charlton and Best were fighting to be match-fit, or that Law wasn't certain to start either. Fortunately for United, Real also had problems. Besides missing Amancio, De Felipe had fitness problems. The centre-half, who'd succeeded the famous Santamaria, had already missed several European Cup games. Zunzunegui had been a capable replacement but Real really wanted De Felipe to anchor their back four.

Charlton knew how badly Busby wanted to win the European Cup; he felt quite sure the Boss would retire if United failed to win it this time. If they were to lift the trophy, Charlton knew it would have to be mainly through grit. If they could get past the semi-final surely nothing could stop them. But would grit be enough against a Real side which had outclassed them a decade before? Charlton remembered how in 1957 Busby had returned from watching the Spanish champions full of glowing phrases about Gento and Kopa, saying their centre-forward Di Stefano was the greatest player he'd ever seen. This time he came back from Madrid saying they only had one real danger, Amancio. Busby spoke of one or two other players of promise but not in extravagant terms. Charlton realised this was no act to bolster confidence; the Boss loved football too much not to find joy in watching great players and say so if that was the case.

On the morning of the match, Stepney woke up and realised straight away that this was the day. There were just a few hours to go before the most vital game in his life so far. It hit him like a bomb.

Usually when United played at home he'd wake up, turn over lazily and then go straight back to sleep until around 11 a.m. He rarely had trouble relaxing – pre-match nerves didn't bother him. But this time it was different. The moment he woke up his mind was on the game. However hard he tried he just couldn't relax and drop off to sleep again. Eventually he gave up at which point he fell asleep. Soon after his wife Pam brought him a cup of tea and said it was almost lunchtime. By now he felt relaxed and quite confident everything would be all right. He knew, somehow, that the 63,000 fans who'd pack Old Trafford wouldn't see United lose.

Before Stepney knew it the time had come to say goodbye and drive off to meet his team-mates. There were still almost four hours to go before the kick-off . . . hours in which they'd be given their final briefing by Busby, have a meal and give themselves the chance to wind down and yet, at the same time, build themselves up to a peak attitude of mind which would see them eager and confident as they went out to meet Real Madrid.

Law was still struggling with his dodgy knee. The osteopath had been strapping it up in an attempt to hold the joint together, so Law turned up for the match heavily bandaged. It was solid, like a ballbearing with no movement. This raised suspicions at United. When they found out about his private treatment the club wasn't pleased and quite a row ensued. 'It's my life and my leg, and I'll do it my way,' insisted Law. He hadn't done a lot of training and wasn't feeling that good. He certainly wasn't 100 per cent fit and shouldn't have played, but the season was nearly over. Busby decided to gamble on Law's fitness. He was told to stay up front.

The teams for the match on 24 April were:

UNITED: Stepney, Dunne, Burns, Crerand, Sadler, Stiles, Best, Kidd, Charlton, Law, Aston. Sub: Rimmer.

REAL MADRID: Betancort, Gonzales, Sanchis, Pirri, Zunzunegui, Zocco, Peruz, Luis, Grosso, Velazquez, Gento. Sub: Araquistain.

The only survivors from the '57 semi-final were Charlton and Real's captain Gento, since Sadler was preferred at centre-half to Foulkes. Real had many great players but after watching them Busby told his team that number four, Pirri, was 'head and shoulders above the lot', with the exception of the missing Amancio. Good in the air, solid in defence and looking for goals, Pirri was Charlton's idea of the perfect player.

A full house of 63,200 packed Old Trafford to the rafters. An audience of several million watched on television. Geoffrey Green of *The Times* soaked up the atmosphere from the press box. 'It was a golden evening; the merest whisper of a breeze touched the flags on the rim of Old Trafford and there was a lovely glow in a cloudless sky as the evening sun went down.'

When United ran out the stadium was buzzing with an air of excitement. It was impossible to avoid getting caught up in the atmosphere of expectancy. 'All around the ground there was this tension, hidden and unseen – yet you felt you could have severed it with one swift stroke of a sharp knife,' says Stepney.

Real were known as an attacking side, but they came to Old Trafford to defend. It was left to United to go for goals and they poured forward. Their best chances were carved out by Best in the opening minutes but it was Crerand who went closest to scoring when he hit the base of the post after just three minutes.

United were dominating the game, with Charlton an absolute master in midfield. But the massed Real defence was tough to break down. The Reds' cutting edge was blunted because Law was a shadow of his usual self. He lacked the vital spark that made him such a formidable player as he struggled with his injured knee. In David Miller's words, 'the reflexes slowed, the snap near goal no longer a thing of wonder and fury'. United had to look instead to a fighting-fit Best for a breakthrough.

On the half-hour mark Aston collected a fine long pass from Kidd and went on a mazy run down the left wing. He lost the ball to Gonzalez but, with a doggedness that deserved reward, went past him at the second attempt. Aston pulled a perfect ball back diagonally from the byline to carve open a chance for Best who'd ambled into space just inside the area. The Irishman thundered an instant, explosive left-foot half volley into the roof of the net from 15 yards. Real's keeper Betancort didn't even see it and turned, dejectedly, to pick the ball from the back of the net. (Years later Stepney would rate it as one of the greatest goals Best ever scored.)

As 63,000 cheering fans split the air a scared cat ran from one end of the pitch to the other. 'One felt that here at last . . . the cat had really been set amongst the Spanish pigeons,' wrote Green. Best felt on top of the world. United were ahead and looking to add to their lead. The crowd saw them hit the kind of form that had been missing for weeks. The occasion and the pursuit of the trophy they cherished above all others lifted them.

The Spaniards undoubtedly missed Amancio. Despite showing once or twice that they could still be dangerous given half a chance, for most of the match Stepney was an untroubled spectator. Betancort was constantly called into action, making defiant saves and brilliant interceptions. But, while United created lots of chances in the remaining hour of the game, they couldn't increase their lead. In fact, they lost some of their sharpness in the second half. Best in particular was unable to repeat his rapier strike as the stubborn Sanchis subdued him with a marvellous combination of concentration and intensive marking.

The Real defence was particularly impressive, with Zunzunegui, Sanchis and Zocco a solid barrier in front of the penalty area backed by the tremendous Betancort.

United had played their hearts out but despite toiling all night against an experienced defence they'd little to show for their efforts. It had been virtually one-way traffic for 80 of the 90 minutes and it seemed that Real had indeed come to play for a draw. They'd broken away and shown they could be dangerous, but on the whole seemed content to contain the Reds.

After the match United's dressing room was rather subdued. The players were filled with a sense of disappointment. They talked about being optimistic for the second leg, but deep down they all felt a one-goal lead was a pretty tenuous advantage. Busby came in and smiled a 'Well done, lads' at them, insisting that a win was a win. But they sensed he'd have been far happier with at least two goals. And so would they. Crerand, of course, wouldn't hear of a United defeat in the second leg. 'Och, they'll be tough, a' reet,' he conceded, 'but we'll get through.'

Real had made it clear they still knew what the European challenge was all about. The Spaniards had surprised United with their flair and control. Still, Law knew this wasn't the Real Madrid of old. 'If we had been at our best we would have slaughtered them,' he said. 'They were a poor side compared to what they had been . . .' Stiles felt United had been so much on top, even in the second half, that Real hadn't been as much of a challenge as Gornik.

It had been a fine, sporting game controlled with the minimum of fuss by the Russian referee who later said: 'The number one footballer and gentleman on the field for me was Bobby Charlton, and I have never had more pleasure in taking such a match.'

But while Charlton enhanced his already famed reputation, one of United's unsung heroes had given one of the best displays of his career: John Aston. The speedy United winger had laid on Best's goal and continued to create chances throughout the match.

Green summed up the tension that had built up inside Old Trafford during the match. 'So we lived through a night of exposed nerves. It was like biting on a sensitive tooth as the roar rose and fell like a solid wall across the stadium. The action was compelling enough to dispense with the lighting of a slow fuse. The promise of an explosion was implicit from the start, and its effect was hardly helped by being forecast. But this, in effect, was but a preamble to the tightrope that must be walked between victory and defeat some three weeks hence [in the second leg].'

It had been a marvellous spectacle, a game that had enhanced the reputations of two of the world's greatest clubs. United's players finished the game happy that they'd done well. 'We've made it,' Stiles told Stepney. 'A clean sheet tonight, and a clean sheet in Madrid. Now for Benfica in the final.' However, the players were fully aware that Real's star striker Amancio would be back for the second leg and that Madrid would come out and attack.

The United fans went home pondering whether their team's lead was too fragile to withstand the rigid test it would undergo in front of Real's fanatical supporters at the Bernabeu Stadium in Madrid. Green put the question nobody at United wanted to hear: 'One wondered whether the sun had also gone down once more on their effort to scale the Everest of European club football.' But optimistically he added, 'Those who think Manchester United's chance has gone, should be reminded of two years ago when they led Benfica only by 3–2 from Old Trafford and then destroyed the Portuguese on a magical night by 5–1.'

The players and supporters also remembered the European Cup semi-final against Partizan Belgrade that year when United had the same 1–0 lead from the home leg but lost 2–0 away to crash out of the competition. Had they blown it again? Would one goal be enough?

Between the first and second legs of the semi-final United had to play their last three League games. Their form now became increasingly erratic. Just five days after their slender win over Madrid they lost 6–3 away to FA Cup finalists West Bromwich Albion. By the end of the match their defence was in shreds. It was a major setback to their title hopes. On top of that Law was back on the treatment table again. Meanwhile, Manchester City's 2–0 home win against Everton moved them above United on goal average. It was the first time City had been top all season.

United hit back in their next match. Without Law they thrashed Newcastle 6–0 at Old Trafford on the penultimate Saturday of the season. Best grabbed a hat-trick in an outstanding display, Kidd struck twice and Sadler also scored. United remained level with City on 56 points but, despite the size of their win, were still in second place on goal average with just one game to play.

During the week Busby went to Madrid to watch Spain play England in a European Nations Cup match. There were six Real players on view. Stepney was in the England squad and got a preview of the magnificent Bernabeu Stadium. He gasped in amazement at the atmosphere generated by 125,000 people in the great oval drum of a ground. England won 2–0.

Before the second leg, Busby also flew to Lisbon with United chairman Louis Edwards and several journalists, including David Miller, to see the other semi-final first leg between Benfica and Juventus. Benfica won 2–0 but it was clear they'd slipped even farther than Busby and the rest had heard. 'They can still turn on the magic occasionally,' said Busby, 'but I don't think they are as good as when we beat them two years ago. They looked slow in midfield in the first half. Obviously the big one for us is next week. If only we can survive that I feel we have a good chance at Wembley.' Busby decided the winners of the United–Real tie would lift the European Cup and added, 'I think we will win because I am convinced we are the better side.'

In the championship race United could only hold on to their title on the final, dramatic day of the season if they got a better result versus Sunderland at Old Trafford than City achieved against Newcastle at St James's Park. United's match seemed easier than City's. 'City were in superlative form at the time,' remembers Stepney, 'responding with every nerve and sinew to the outrageous propaganda of their assistant manager Malcolm Allison. Big Mal loved to beat the drum, and there can be no doubt he inspired that team to play with speed and aggression. In many ways there was an old-fashioned directness about their five-man forward line of Mike Sumerbee, Colin Bell, Francis Lee, Neil Young and Tony Coleman. They thrilled people wherever they played, and never more so than on this last day of the season when they took an invasion force of 20,000 people up the Great North Road . . .'

Busby gave Foulkes a test in a practice match before the Sunderland game. He put reserve striker Alan Gowling against him. Gowling knocked Foulkes around a bit. The veteran defender came through it but his knee blew up afterwards. He had the fluid aspirated off and was selected to play against Sunderland. Although Foulkes wasn't really tested, which was just as well since he could hardly walk, United still lost 2–1. City won 4–3 against a Newcastle side that the Reds had ironically softened up just a week before. The championship was over. Busby was quick to congratulate City. Worryingly, Foulkes's knee swelled up again after the match. Busby now had the task of lifting his players. There were just four days before United faced Real in Madrid.

Six

Santiago Bernabeu

As the United players boarded the plane for Madrid Bill Foulkes knew it was his last chance of European glory. He'd been in at the start of Busby's pursuit of European success. He was United's rock, a typical centre-half, durable, focused and effective. Busby encouraged creativity in his teams but he knew all about strength as well. Others came and went, Foulkes seemed to go on forever. He'd linked the Johnny Carey era of the early '50's with the famous Busby Babes and survived the Munich crash.

After United arrived in the grand city of Madrid, Real's 72-year-old president Santiago Bernabeu spoke with dignity about his old friends and rivals. 'I want Manchester United greeted and treated and respected as the greatest club in the world,' he said in a speech to celebrate another League title success for Spain's most famous club. 'And as our friends for many years nothing must go wrong. If we are beaten in the European Cup by Manchester United on Wednesday then we shall have lost to a great team. We have met them on many occasions and it is about time their luck changed.'

Bernabeu, a lawyer, had been with Madrid for 56 years and had seen the club rise from nothing. The 'father' of Real had joined them as a centre-forward in 1912. He was a first team player for 14 years and had also been captain. He was still playing when he was elected to the managing board and later became team manager, club secretary and, in 1942, president. The magnificent Estadio Santiago Bernabeu, which had begun life as the Nuevo Chamartin Stadium in 1944, was renamed in his honour in January 1955 as he helped build the club up to the glorious peak that saw them win five European Cups in a row.

The trophy room underneath the stadium, a massive glittering hall of silver and gold, was home to 1,500 cups, trophies and shields. It took two cleaners a whole year to dust and polish all the silverware and then when they'd finished they had to start all over again. Pride of place went to the six replicas of the European Cup. Real also possessed the original cup that was given to the club in honour of their tremendous achievements. But they reckoned there was still space for another – the new European Cup that was being presented for the first time.

United's fans were filled with anticipation as the return match with Real Madrid loomed. Cliff Butler, a lifelong United fanatic, was preparing to travel to Madrid. It was his first journey abroad and his first time on a plane. The trip cost £20, 'a lot of money in those days', he said. (Butler, the club's statistician and then photographer, went on to edit the programme *United Review*.) Busby's pal Paddy McGrath had organised a flight through the Irish Club in Manchester and four or five of the players' wives and girlfriends travelled to Madrid for the match.

The festive atmosphere in the Spanish capital wasn't only due to the arrival of United and their fans. The game was being played during the festival of San Isidro, Madrid's patron saint. The players were quickly whisked away from the celebrations to the Fenix Hotel, a mountain retreat 13 miles outside the city.

Busby put a positive spin on United's failure to win the League. Far from being bad, he said, it had actually done them good. 'That slip in the League could be the spur,' he told reporters. The players had agreed with him, both in training and afterwards when they discussed the semi-final. 'This cup, Manchester United wants to win most of all,' added Busby. 'It is and has been uppermost in our minds.'

On the morning of the match, United's players began to feel the butterflies fluttering in the pit of their stomachs. Once again Best, the man with nerves of steel, was the exception. As he enjoyed a lie-in his mind kept going back to the game against Benfica two years earlier when United took a 1–0 lead to Lisbon and scored five. If they could do it once, reasoned Best, they could do it again.

For the rest of the team the tension was by now almost unbearable. Stiles, Crerand and the other Catholics in the squad decided to visit the local church for Mass. It would help take their minds off the match. When the collection plate was passed around Stiles didn't have any loose change so he put down a 100-peseta note. Crerand glanced at him in amazement. 'Hey, Nobby, that's bribery,' he whispered.

Both Manchester and Madrid were ablaze with red and white on the day of the match. United's hotel was almost as packed as the one they'd stayed at in Malta, only this time the supporters were true Mancunians. Nevertheless, United's followers inside the Bernabeu included a large group from their supporters' club in Malta.

Although United had played at the Bernabeu before it was still a shock for them to be reminded of the fabulous facilities. The players had individual baths, showers and changing rooms. Everything was top class. British players were embarrassed when they saw the facilities at some of the top European clubs and realised foreign teams had to visit their grounds and use shabby dressing rooms.

The second leg on the night of Wednesday, 15 May was billed as the most important match in United's history. Stiles saw it as a kind of haunting dream gradually moving towards reality. Charlton felt responsible for every player; responsible for the success Busby wanted for the club. He was anxious that United should do justice to the occasion with the whole of Europe watching. He wanted them to express themselves in their play. The pressure was extreme. Busby looked nervous. So many players appeared young and vulnerable. Suddenly this seemed the most critical, the only critical match Charlton had ever known.

By now Law was feeling pain in his knee every time he kicked a ball. He'd had a fitness test in the morning, but it was hopeless. He clearly wasn't fit and the game was far too important for United to start taking chances. Busby couldn't take the risk so Law was replaced once more by Kidd, who'd play up front next to Best.

In their ties so far United had switched the team around depending on the conditions, the opposition and Busby's tactical plans. Against Real he wanted to keep it tight, especially early on, but he also knew a breakaway goal would be priceless. For the second away leg in a row Busby decided to play defensively despite United's slender one-goal lead. The performance in Katowice had helped persuade him that if the Reds could win through playing defensively then, however much he disliked the system, it was in United's interests to try to hold what they had. He opted for their customary away tactic, a 5–3–2 formation. The Boss asked the versatile Sadler to play a dual role in an inside forward's number 10 shirt. He'd provide cover as an extra defender just in front of the back four, but had the freedom to break forward when United had the ball. A more straightforward change saw Brennan come in at left back for Burns, who'd played the first seven European Cup ties.

Foulkes was recalled for his 29th of United's 32 European Cup ties. He'd missed the first leg because of torn cruciate ligaments in his knee and despite struggling through the Sunderland match he still couldn't stop or turn. Busby didn't explain why he was in the team. He just told Foulkes he was playing. The Boss wanted his experience but Foulkes thought it was a big gamble – he didn't feel anywhere near 100 percent fit. His knee was aspirated again and then strapped up tightly but he could still only hobble around. Eleven years earlier he'd played in United's first European Cup semi-final. That was the last time they'd met Real in European competition. Tonight he was the only survivor from the Busby Babes who'd lost at the Bernabau to that mighty team of the late '50s.

In Busby's game plan Aston had the toughest job. He was expected to be on the left wing when United attacked but he also had to drop back to stop the dangerous Pirri when Real had the ball.

United's team was: Stepney, Brennan, Foulkes, Stiles, Dunne, Crerand, Charlton, Sadler, Best, Kidd and Aston.

As for Madrid, they could now bring back their dangerous inside right Amancio after his suspension. A player of marvellous technique and thrilling skill, he was regarded as the successor to Alfredo di Stefano. Amancio would do much to ensure that the match was another sublime example of European competition, the kind of game visionaries like Busby and Gabriel Hanot, the man behind the drive to set up the European Cup, had hoped for at the birth of the tournament in the mid-1950s. Stiles was given the difficult job of man-marking Real's top scorer. Amancio, like so many of Stiles's other victims, wouldn't forget the United defender in a hurry after their battle on the pitch.

Chairman Louis Edwards and the other United directors were entertained in the guest-room by Santiago Bernabeu as the players prepared for the match. During the evening, Edwards was introduced to a man who spoke very good English. Edwards praised him on his use of the language, to which the man replied that he also spoke a little Spanish. It was hardly surprising. 'I am the British Ambassador here,' he told a rather embarrassed Edwards.

Before the match Busby gave his players a warning: 'If they do get an early goal to equalise on aggregate watch yourselves because for a spell you will think they have gone mad.' He knew how much more Real depended on inspiration to raise their game to great heights than his own team. He also knew that if the Spaniards didn't score they'd probably become frustrated quicker than United would.

The hot sun had been shining all day and the night was humid. The sticky weather favoured Real. The teams walked onto the pitch to be greeted by 120,000 predominantly Spanish fans who'd grown anything but complacent with success. The atmosphere, complete with firecrackers, was tense. The Bernabeu was like an inferno. Among the crowd were 30,000 die-hard United followers, including the large contingent from their supporters' club in Malta, but you couldn't really hear them above the din being made by the Real fans. 'The Bernabeu was an awesome sight,' says Cliff Butler. 'It was all concrete – concrete tiers, concrete terraces and concrete seats. But it was a fantastic atmosphere when the Spanish chanted, it was just an incredible, amazing scene.'

The rest of Spain held its breath. 'Only those who have played in these conditions know just how hard it is to keep calm and composed when it seems that thousands of fans are about to spill over the terraces onto the pitch,' thought Murphy. He wondered at the torment in the players' minds as they tried to keep ice-cool in the fiery atmosphere. It was Brian Kidd's first taste of the real electric thrill of European football and as he walked out into the stadium he felt full of nerves.

When Amancio stepped on to the pitch he made sure, as always, that his right foot touched the grass first. As a religious man he was not very superstitious but he did believe that a broken mirror brought bad luck and that touching the grass first with his right foot brought good luck. Once, in a friendly against United, someone broke a hand mirror and he was convinced it was a bad omen. He was right. Just after the kick-off he was carried off injured and United won 2–0 to become the first club ever to beat Real in Madrid. He hoped this time would be different.

This was the climax to all Busby had ever dreamed of. His team were just one step away from the final and the Cup he wanted to win so badly. Amid emotional scenes United walked once more into the famous stadium with its crowds towering terrifyingly up the steep-banked terraces. For Charlton there were few more glamorous settings for football than the Bernabeu. He thought its shape on the inside gave the impression of sheer cliffs reaching up towards some mysterious lost world in the night sky.

The injured Law joined Busby and Murphy in the dugout. It was a hot and humid May night, very different from the icy blasts of the Gornik game, thought Murphy. Charlton knew that if Gento attacked with pace along Real's left flank, Pirri and Amancio could do damage elsewhere and the Spaniards would be encouraged to believe they were more than capable of putting United out. 'Concentrate, keep your head, don't give the ball away,' were the thoughts Busby's players took onto the pitch.

Back in England, United fans around the country were either glued to their television sets or listening to the match on the radio. In Cambridge, Roger Hennell and his brother sat excitedly under the sheets in their pyjamas. They weren't supposed to be up so late listening to the match. Robin Murray had gone to bed at his boarding school at about 9 p.m. Like so many young boys he also had a radio under his bed so he could listen to the big match.

As always, the Reds would try to contain Real in the first 20 or 30 minutes – the settling-in approach. 'Our policy was quite clear,' said Murphy. 'We had to be coolly professional and contain them in the first half hour when obviously they would mount attack after attack to try and hammer us into the ground.'

At first it seemed that even Stiles's little 'bribe' wouldn't save United. They walked into a whirlwind. Real were the exact opposite of the team that had played at Old Trafford. They attacked from the first whistle and whipped the ball around as if it were tied to their boots. It soon became clear United would have their work cut out to hold them. The Reds seemed to be chasing shadows.

After only two minutes, Stiles was in trouble with the referee for a crunching tackle on Amancio. The Spaniard soon sought revenge. Stiles had just passed the ball when Amancio suddenly came up behind him and threw a punch. Stiles struck back and Amancio fell to the ground. There were howls of protest from the crowd. The *Daily Mail*'s Ronald Crowther thought Amancio was acting, given the theatrical way he'd slumped down. The game was held up for three minutes while the Spaniard lay on the pitch surrounded by photographers and angry Real officials. Abuse was shouted at United from all around the stadium.

When the match restarted, both sides created chances. On ten minutes Amancio met Perez's corner with his head and Stepney turned the ball onto the bar. Then Crerand swerved a free kick just wide of the post. But the game remained goalless as the Reds put up a stubborn and highly disciplined defensive fight. Busby's plan to contain Real for the first 20 minutes had worked. In fact, United thought things had gone well.

After half an hour Real still hadn't scored. The Reds could see their opponents' shoulders starting to sag. They were slowing down. 'They've gone,' somebody said. And they had. Stiles, who'd snapped angrily all the time at Amancio's heels, could see that the spark had gone out of them. Real were starting to run as though their legs had turned to jelly. United had, indeed, defended well. Although it was a rearguard action in which they had five men in defence and only two – Best and Kidd – up front, they stayed cool and calm. From their touchline seats Busby and Murphy congratulated their boys on a magnificent job in holding the rampaging Spaniards.

But if United thought Real were finished they were deluding themselves. Brooding disaster hung in the air. Suddenly the storm broke; on the half-hour the ball went over United's goal line. The Italian referee gave a goal kick but then noticed the linesman had flagged. After consulting him the referee awarded a free kick for a foul by Aston on Pirri. It was a controversial decision. Amancio floated a bending ball towards Pirri, who timed his run and leap beautifully and then measured the distance perfectly to head past Stepney. United were still incensed by the foul, which they thought was unjustified, and on the bench they weren't happy with the defence that should have cut out the cross. Real were in front on the night and the aggregate score was level. Seconds before they were ready to be taken, but miraculously now the spring came back into their stride and they pounded at United.

Ten minutes later the veteran Gento, nicknamed the Flying Bicycle by Foulkes, broke loose on the left. Pirri slipped an optimistic ball towards him. Brennan got there first but couldn't decide whether to pass to Crerand's side or kick the ball up the line. He misread the ball, stuck out a foot and missed. Brennan turned to see his uncharacteristic error punished as Gento took the ball in his stride and dramatically sped away from him. The Spaniard cut in and flashed a ferocious low drive through the advancing Stepney's legs from an almost impossible angle. Understandably, Brennan didn't feel too great at that moment. If he could have had a bet at that point in the match he'd have put his money on Real.

At 2–0 United were under pressure and a little rattled, but they still felt they could turn the game round. Proof that Real's defence sometimes panicked came when Dunne hit a 40-yard lob into the area. Zoco, under pressure from the persistent Kidd, hacked out wildly and sliced it into his own goal. United were back in the match. The goal hushed the stadium but Real still seemed in no danger.

Three minutes before half-time Stiles was booked for another foul on Amancio. The striker responded in the best way possible. A minute before the break he fought his way clear of Stiles. Showing exquisite balance he received a pass and, without pausing, turned and somehow struck the ball on the half volley. It screwed around several United defenders and past Stepney into the corner of the net. An impossible shot had put Real 3–1 ahead.

'The vast crowd was in a symphony of sound,' wrote Geoffrey Green of *The Times*. 'They resembled a man who has two bottles of wine inside him, pleasantly intoxicated and feeling that there is nothing much wrong with life. This was fiesta time for the hot-blooded crowd, whose wrath flamed out as Stiles stabbed at the fleeting Amancio. Flags and banners waved: the air was full of fireworks and rockets and there was a hot juicy feeling of expectant victory in the air. The stadium at half-time must have seemed to Manchester United like a sheer, granite cliff of sound that was falling about their ears.'

An amazing four goals had been scored in less than a quarter of an hour before half-time. 'I never want to live through another 13 minutes like that again,' said Murphy a year later. 'It is easy now to say that this sort of thing is part of the glorious uncertainty of football; but this was a night of emotion when everyone connected with the club was willing the lads to victory.' The reality was that once again Real were in the driving seat as the whistle blew to end the half.

It was a first period in which emotions had spilled over in the electric atmosphere. Best was double marked and heavily tackled. Secretly, he didn't give United a chance. 'The guy marking me, Sanchis, was a great defender,' says Best. 'I could beat him but he always got back goalside. I was having a stinker really. Sanchis was only a kid but he was one of the best defenders I've ever played against.' Charlton and Crerand, who normally ran games for United, hadn't featured at all. 'We hadn't really seen George or Bobby,' recalls Foulkes, 'we weren't really in the game . . .'

Busby, Murphy and the rest of the United staff were, like the players, stunned. The slender one-goal lead the Reds brought with them, believing it might be enough, was fool's gold. Real were by far the better team, quicker to the ball, more skilful in possession, attacking repeatedly, shooting on sight. 'The great Amancio, like a matador, had teased the Manchester United defence with masterly footwork and passes of the cape . . .' wrote Green. 'At his side, too, there were Grosso and Velazquez and Perez, building up an almost non-stop barrage.' Three times Real had found the back of the net; more often they'd missed or been denied by United's defence. It looked as if they'd simply build on their lead in the second half. With this start and their increased confidence it could be at least six by the end.

As the teams went back to their dressing rooms the Reds were once more tottering on the verge of defeat. 'Not many in the 120,000 crowd would have given a peseta for their chances of pulling back into the match at that time,' reckoned journalist David Meek. United were physically distressed and mentally defeated, down and almost out. They were cornered in Real's backyard. Everyone else thought they were dead. Real certainly did.

Busby had spent the first half chain-smoking cigarettes, hoping his team wouldn't make mistakes. He was sick and despondent as he sensed the European albatross would forever hang round his neck. As he left the pitch Busby turned to Murphy and said dejectedly, 'We've had it, Jimmy.' But he had to keep his feelings to himself and put on a brave face as he found his way to the dressing room.

Back in boarding school in England, young Robin Murray was upset. 'That's it, we're out,' he thought as he turned his radio off and went to sleep – much like United's defence in the first half.

The players trailed into their dressing room, which before long resembled a morgue. Nobody said anything. They were all very quiet, despondent. The players slumped wearily, waiting, sweating and breathing heavily, knowing they'd worked hard and still failed to keep Real out. Charlton thought United were clearly done for. He'd never felt so dejected at half-time; he wasn't used to defeat so obviously staring him in the face. Despite Charlton's disappointment there was a touching example of his team spirit and Brennan's honesty as they slumped down on the benches. 'That goal was bad luck, Shay, I saw it hit a bump as you tried to go for the pass,' said Charlton. Brennan would have none of it. 'There was no bump there,' he said. 'I just made a mess of it.'

Brennan was sick about what had happened. In fact, all of them felt thoroughly fed-up. They sat there expecting Busby to give them 'a right bollocking' in the words of Best, '. . . and we deserved it because we were awful,' he says. United hadn't played half as well as they could. They just didn't get going. But Foulkes took a different view. He thought they'd actually played very well; it was just that they'd been completely outclassed by a brilliant team. Sadler was also aware of the pressure they'd had to face. 'It felt as if we'd really been hammered,' he says, 'under the cosh all the 45 minutes.' Everybody was shattered. Kidd thought they were the most dejected bunch of players he'd ever seen. As a former player Murphy knew how they felt. 'Goals given away like these had been can make even the most aggressive spirit feel a bit sick,' he said later.

The players knew that outside in the Bernabeu the crowd was jubilantly expecting Real to complete a massacre in the second half. United were set up for the kill. 'Amancio had murdered us and it seemed we were in for a real pasting, not just a defeat,' recalls Stepney. United could see themselves losing 6–1. 'We're not getting a kick at all here,' thought Crerand. The players believed they were going out of the European Cup again. 'All our hopes had gone,' says Stepney. They racked their brains trying to think of a way of outsmarting Real. But still hardly anyone spoke. 'There must be something, someone must talk,' thought Charlton. Nobody did. There seemed nothing worth saying. The minutes dragged by as they breathed hard and mopped their faces with towels. They were waiting for Busby or Murphy, but they were very down. Charlton tried to convince himself it wasn't the end of the world – all the things you try to think about when you know you're finished.

After ten minutes of saddened silence, Busby walked in looking quite calm. The players had their heads between their legs. They were gutted. They didn't need telling how desperate the situation was. One or two who hated being blamed started to shout the odds, searching for excuses; the 'rubber dinghy men', Best called them. Someone had to inject new courage into them and the Boss was the man to do it.They all knew that however bad they felt, Busby must have been feeling ten times worse.

At first he said nothing. Charlton had never known him to be speechless before. Even Murphy was quiet. But Busby had never lost his cool in the dressing room. He never swore. There was an impressive serenity about him. He wasn't panicking, so why should they? He looked at his dispirited players: 'Come on, keep going,' said Busby. At first his words had no impact, there was still no real conviction among the players. They knew they'd been getting slaughtered. They sat there, all of them, shamed and dejected.

Busby and Murphy walked round and round the table in the middle of the huge dressing room. They were still silent but Stepney knew they were thinking plenty. Four times United had reached the semi-final. 'Are we to be denied an appearance in the final yet again?' thought Murphy. What could he tell the lads after this series of misfortunes? The procedure at half-time was usually the same. Busby would run through the tactics crisply and quietly. When he was finished Murphy would often enlarge on a point with an individual player, pointing out what was expected of him. No voices were raised in anger because that often provoked tempers and produced tantrums just when they didn't need them. Murphy believed the time to tell players bluntly when they'd fallen down on a job was about 48 hours after a match when they'd be more receptive to criticism.

Suddenly, the referee's whistle blew outside the dressing-room door. It was time for United to go out and face what they thought would be the final curtain. But Busby hadn't given up. He was nothing if not a shrewd motivator. It was then that he showed his genius as a manager wasn't limited to finding or buying players. He'd so often told the team before a game to go out and enjoy themselves that people overlooked his ability as a tactician. It was true that United rarely played the numbers game, but Busby now set about not only rebuilding their morale but also making significant tactical changes.

He reached the door first and turned. 'Hold it,' he said with an acute sense of occasion as the players got ready to go out for the second half. Hiding his true feelings Busby tried hard to force a warm smile as he told them how tired Real looked. Admittedly, things had not gone well, he said, but there were 45 minutes left. He spoke calmly, slowly, clearly, deliberately and unemotionally, as though dealing with children who'd lost their way. Busby chose this moment to pull a masterstroke and revive the dream. 'Don't give up hope. Above all remember the score is not 3–1 for Madrid, because

George scored at Old Trafford. Remember you are only 3–2 down overall at the moment, just a single goal in it and anything can still happen.' Busby reminded them that if they pulled back a goal it would mean a replay in Lisbon. United had beaten Benfica 5–1 there and would stay at Estoril again.

The players were so dejected that most of them had forgotten their 1–0 win three weeks earlier. It was typical, simple Busby logic. He told them just what had to be done – they must be venturesome. 'Well, lads, we've been playing a defensive game and we don't play it very well, do we? The thing now is to attack from the re-start and we should be all right. Don't get panicky and try to be too quick. Keep calm and composed and come at them. Challenge them for the ball; come out to meet it instead of waiting for it. You've done well to get so far, so don't worry. It won't make any difference if we lose by more goals than the one we are behind. If we are going to lose it might as well be by six goals. We must not fear defeat. We must go at them.' Busby also had a few words for Sadler: 'David, I want you to move upfield in an aggressive way. That might surprise them,' he told him. 'I don't think he's ever really heard of the word defend,' Best wrote years later.

The players could hardly believe their ears. Real had dominated the game so much, especially in the last 15 minutes, that to go out and attack seemed to be inviting disaster. 'Here was a man asking us to attack when we had been struggling to get a kick at the ball,' said Crerand. But suddenly they all felt better. They'd been roused and put at ease at the same time. Why not have a go? Why not throw everything at them? Crerand knew that they'd all go out and do exactly as Busby said. Just before the players left Busby added, 'It's a funny old game this. Anything can happen.' He emphasised that a replay, at the very least, wasn't beyond them. 'One more goal and we are level on aggregate. One goal is not a lot to ask in 45 minutes. You're the better side. Go out there and prove it, lads.' They must keep running, working, striving. Above all, they must not give up, even if they did feel a little downhearted. Best laughed. 'I mean there's this old bugger who'd give his left arm to win the sodding cup and we're screwing it up for him and he tells us to keep on playing football.' He thought Busby's team talk was a little bit special.

While Busby was talking Murphy had been wandering around chatting to the players, giving them a slap on the back. 'Come on, boys . . . one final effort, get in for that ball and make them chase.'

The teams left their dressing rooms for the second half. As they walked up the tunnel referee Shardella pulled Stiles and Amancio together. He smashed his fist down into the palm of his hand and said to Amancio, 'Stiles no hit you.' Like a boxing referee before a big fight he told them to get on with the game. As Charlton followed Real's players down the tunnel he noticed they were strutting as if to say, 'Only another 45 minutes and we're in the final.'

There was a new bounce in the step of United's players as they went back onto the pitch for the second half to face the wildly enthusiastic Madrid crowd. Busby's reasoning had made an impression. It had helped change their outlook. United were a footballing side and a defensive game was alien to them. Deep down they'd never lost heart and they went out again believing they could do it. Best was certainly confident that United would go through. Stepney also felt all might not be lost. 'What Mr Busby had said was absolutely right – one goal would give us a lift,' he thought. 'And it would be a jolt for Real.'

As Busby's half-time pep talk began to sink in, it looked as if he might have done the trick. The Reds were given even more encouragement to fight on when they saw Real coming back for the start of the second half. United were amazed. Some of their opponents seemed to be struggling to drag one leg after the other. Busby's team looked at themselves and, compared with Real, they were as fresh as daisies. It seemed obvious to Aston that Real had been told to come out in the first half and run the legs off United. To an extent, that had worked. But now the score was only 3–2 on aggregate and they had shot their bolt.

As the second half began Real came at United again. The Reds weren't playing much better than in the first period and were unable to create chances, but the Spaniards seemed slow to find their first-half tempo. By now, United were committed to attack and the more Madrid came at them the more chance they had of scoring on a breakaway. With new enthusiasm the Reds abandoned their fatally fallible massed defence and hurled themselves into attack with

Sadler pushing forward. It was true they had to risk giving away another goal, but Real were now more open to United's attacks. They sat back a little and gave the Reds more room to play. The Spanish side were playing a containing game, which took the pressure off United. The Reds started to create, to come out. Best and Kidd had struggled largely on their own in the first half, but now they got more into the game.

After a few minutes Crerand started thinking, 'This [Real] team isn't bothered. They think the game is over.' Five minutes into the half Law noticed the same thing. 'It looks to me as if they think they've won it,' he told Busby in the dugout. 'They've gone into second gear. I think we've got a chance if we can get a goal back.' Charlton also sensed the spark had gone out of Real. There was a chance. The Spaniards obviously didn't train like United – they played in bursts, and they'd used up their energy. Real simply weren't the same team as in the first half. It wasn't that United began playing well or created chances; Real just weren't dangerous anymore. The pace had slackened and for the first time in the match the Reds looked tidy.

United just kept plugging away and Betancort was eventually forced to produce save after save. Stiles started shaking a few people up. The fans reacted; a ripe tomato hit him and then a shoe whistled just past his left ear. The Reds didn't feel their goal was under threat and started pushing forward again. United threw everything into attack, but still the vital goal wouldn't come. Since they found themselves without any reward Stiles began to edge forward. He was quickly brought back into line. 'Eh, you! Get back here,' Foulkes growled. 'We've got to keep them out as well.'

As United searched for that elusive second goal a message was passed from their bench. 'Tell Bobby to move up front.' Fortunately, there wasn't time to get it through before Real, feeling the match was already won, suddenly found it slipping away. Charlton, playing deep, engineered a move that led to United winning a free kick. There were just 15 minutes left as Crerand chipped the ball towards the edge of the area. Best just managed to head it up in the air and on to Sadler, who he knew was alongside him, before being dumped on the ground by a defender. The ball bounced between Betancort and his defenders. The keeper left it for them, and they left it for him. As they hesitated Sadler stole in behind them and, although he didn't catch the ball properly, managed to side-foot it from the edge of the six-yard box just inside the post. A stunned Betancort sat on the ground dejectedly. The Bernabeu fell silent. Sadler thought he'd missed, as did Crerand. Then they heard the United fans going potty. It wasn't a classic goal, but the Reds didn't care – it was still in the back of Real's net. The first Best knew of it was when the other players picked him up. The fairy tale had begun.

The goal was the result of the change of tactics that had seen Sadler at last move up into attack and United reverting to 4–3–3, and even 4–2–4, as they risked almost everything. Sadler's strike put the match in an entirely different light. United were back in the game, just one goal behind on the night and level on aggregate. That unlikely goal, from their first real chance of the half, gave them something to try to hang on to. Stiles and Dunne were absolutely brilliant. They covered Foulkes so well that he virtually only had to stand there. 'Right, Bill, we'll keep it tight,' they said. Foulkes appreciated the help. 'I couldn't give Nobby enough credit for the way he covered for me that night in front of me and behind me. I just got on the end of everything in the air . . .' But he still wasn't happy. His knee was getting bigger and bigger.

It looked as if United were at least going to secure a play-off against Real in Lisbon. But, in fact, the stage was set for one of the most memorable, emotional moments in their European history.

The atmosphere after the goal was strange. It seemed to Foulkes that both sides had stopped playing, perhaps because they were too frightened of losing. United were holding on to what they'd got, while Real continued to sit back and not come at them. 'This team's knackered,' thought Crerand. 'They've gone.' Charlton and Foulkes could also tell Real were finished. 'They became a little cagey,' says Foulkes. 'They stopped playing . . . they became very worried and started making mistakes.' The Spaniards began arguing and fighting amongst themselves. Charlton could sense from experience that their supporters were growing anxious. United began running more and working harder for each other. 'We came into the game, you know, it was incredible,' says Foulkes.

The adrenaline was racing through the Reds. 'Who will the Lisbon crowd support if it goes to a replay there?' thought Charlton. Soon another message came from the bench: 'Tell Bobby to stay deep.' The ball went into touch and Charlton wanted it back quickly since time was running out. A Real fan in the front row reached out, grabbed the ball and then shaped as if to throw it down the line. 'Keep calm,' thought Charlton, 'don't panic.' He sauntered over and put his hand out. The supporter meekly put the ball in his hand, as though accepting United would go through. Charlton couldn't believe it. It was an incident he'd never forget.

Real realised they had a fight on their hands. They began to panic and that gave United heart. The Spaniards started arguing with the referee and appealing for everything. Charlton's view of the character of Real's players had changed. 'You wouldn't get into our side,' he thought, 'not with that attitude.'

'Morale decided this game,' considered Eamon Dunphy in *A Strange Kind of Glory*. 'United simply wanted it more . . . The *esprit de corps* of the car park (at the back of Old Trafford where United often trained), the deep unarticulated sense of values and experience shared, bonds first formed in the "A" and "B" teams, the FA Youth Cup and similarly daunting moments in Zurich where the "bottle" factor often saw them through against European opponents who wilted at a certain temperature, these were the resources which in the end proved decisive on this historic night. The commodity now brought into play could not be bought.'

United had their tails up and were determined to at least force a play-off. The Spaniards threw the lot at them in a desperate bid to get back on top. But United's confidence had come flooding back. They summoned reserves of strength for a final effort. The adrenaline worked overtime, pumping energy into their tired legs. They harried and ran, battled and schemed.

The clock ticked agonisingly away until there were just 12 minutes left. United got a throw-in on the right. They were more or less assured of their replay in Lisbon, but it was no longer enough. Real, a different breed, had thrown in the towel. Crerand prepared to take it but nobody seemed to want the ball. Best was marked very tightly and nobody made a move. Then Foulkes took a chance and went forward. The idea was to pull a defender off Best. Everybody, including Madrid's players, seemed to have frozen. On the bench Law, who usually couldn't sit still and watch a game because he got so excited, was suffering. Out of the corner of his eye he saw Foulkes dashing out of defence. The big defender shouted for the ball, even though he knew he shouldn't have. Two Real players went with him, taking the cover off Best. Foulkes's plan had worked. He could see the shock on Crerand's face when the Scot saw it was him calling for the ball. Stiles was also amazed. 'Where the hell are you going?' he shouted.

By now United trainer Jack Crompton and Law were worried. 'Get back . . . get back, Foulksey . . .' Law screamed from the touchline. Crerand, gripping the ball tightly, ignored Foulkes and hurled a long throw up the right touchline to Best. Sanchis, for once, had given him far too much room. This time the Irishman thought he could sort out the Real fullback 'good and proper'.

Best leaned against the tackle as he took possession on the run. In a marvellous snake-like motion he left Sanchis and Zoco kicking fresh air. Charlton was 50 yards behind the play and couldn't support him. Others were trying, among them Foulkes who'd got caught up in the thrill of it all and continued his jog up the field. 'Just what got into him no one will ever know,' says Aston. Charlton thought Foulkes was 'inspired by some inner conviction'. The big defender isn't entirely sure what possessed him. 'Perhaps it was moving slightly forward to call for the throw-in which prompted me to keep running,' he says. The coaches on the bench and his team-mates were screaming 'come back, come back'; they wanted him in defence where he belonged in case Real counter-attacked. Foulkes ignored everyone. He kept driving on and wasn't picked up.

By now Best was free on the right near the byline. 'What's he going to do?' thought Charlton who'd stayed back to cover for Foulkes. Best looked up and out of the corner of his eye saw a red shirt running into the area. Foulkes was the only United player in the box and shouted for the ball. The veteran thought he was going to be ignored again – he expected Best to shoot. Zoco and the other Real defenders went to cover the near post as Best cut in from the right. The Irishman feinted to drive the ball to the near post, and

Betancort left Foulkes to try to block it. In that instant Best had cleverly made an opening that enabled him to pull back a perfect low centre. As he did so he looked up, saw 'Big Foulksey' and thought 'Oh, no. Here we go.' Foulkes was the last person Best expected to see in the box. United's stopper was never famous for his attacking skills. He loved to get among the goals in the five-a-sides, but usually blasted the ball over the bar. Best was sure this one was going into the stand. Charlton could see a red shirt coming on to the ball. When he realised it was Foulkes he couldn't believe it, he was really depressed. Aston had similar misgivings. 'Oh, God, this is going to go over the stand,' he thought. Foulkes never crossed the halfway line unless there was a corner. He was the most disciplined of professionals and rarely left his defensive position, where he was a constant source of strength.

What happened next amazed them all. Foulkes arrived just inside the area with the perfect timing of a natural inside forward. The ball fell right into his path and everyone on United's bench held their breath. 'He had a lot of choices,' says Best. 'He could have stopped it, he could have walloped it.' But Foulkes knew the risks of trying to blast the ball home. 'If I drive it, I'll miss it,' he thought. So, rolling back the years to Munich and before, he calmly took it in his stride and sweetly side-footed the perfect pass into the bottom far corner of the net with all the fluency of an accomplished master goalscorer. 'He didn't half stick it away,' says Best. 'It was brilliant. It was unbelievable.' Best would admit years later that he couldn't have done better himself.

'I couldn't have missed,' says Foulkes. 'The fact that I shouldn't have been playing in the first place made it all the more incredible.' The veteran's team-mates might say it was no more remarkable than Foulkes's assertion that he couldn't have missed. 'Depending on how you read that, he is either extremely modest or revealing delusions of goalscoring grandeur,' says Derick Allsop in *Reliving the Dream*. 'Since the latter option is totally out of character, we should accept the former.' The *Daily Mail*'s Ronald Crowther thought Foulkes had 'made sure of his moment of triumph like a man who had waited so long'. The experience of years lay in that goal. It seemed to have been conceived by a higher authority.

'Foulkes 3–3,' announced BBC commentator David Coleman, who then thought, 'Oh, my God, I've got the wrong player.' As the ball rippled along the netting Law did his renowned jack-knife leap from the trainer's bench, clenched fist raised, and shouted 'Oh, you beaut . . . Bill . . .You beaut.' He smashed his hand into a metal roof support but didn't feel a thing and anyway he didn't care. United now had a great chance to win the European Cup. Murphy and Busby hugged on the touchline like schoolboys, but that was excusable because they were now in sight of the match they believed would help make up for all the hopes and heartbreaks of the years – the European Cup final.

It was only then that Charlton really believed they would be saved and that Real, incredible though it was, had let them off the hook. United had come back from the dead. Aston didn't know who was more surprised about the goalscorer, Foulkes or the rest of them. His appearance in Real's penalty area had certainly staggered the ragged home defence. 'It [the goal] hit the Spaniards with the killing finality of a dagger through their hearts,' wrote Stepney later. Out of nothing a magical recovery had been born. Busby later wrote: 'The sight of Big Bill tearing down the pitch and then connecting with George Best's cross will be a memory I shall cherish to the end of my days. That, indeed, was going at them!'

There wasn't a sound from the 120,000 Spaniards. Amid the deadly silence Foulkes thought it couldn't be a goal. But Brian Kidd raised his arm and turned in triumph and the next thing Foulkes knew was Aston grabbing him around the neck in celebration. The big defender tried to get bodies off him as his team-mates piled in to offer their congratulations. He was the hero of the hour. Foulkes waved them away, turned and ran back towards United's half. He could have done without the adulation because he was worried about his knee. He didn't want his own team-mates to cause him further injury even though he understood how they felt. The United supporters in their thousands, plane-loads of them, suddenly came to life. As a beaming Foulkes trotted back towards United's goal he looked at Stiles and grinned, 'When you've got to go, you've got to go.'

Stepney saw something otherworldly in the fact that Foulkes had put a European Cup final within their grasp. 'It seemed uncanny that Foulkes, the man who saw so many of his early team-mates perish in the snow at Munich airport ten years earlier, should score the goal that rekindled the flames of hope in his wise, old manager.' Former United player Eamon Dunphy also believed there was some outside force at work. 'The goal created from the disparate gifts, and spirits, of George Best and Bill Foulkes in the Bernabeu Stadium can be regarded as good fortune or a mystical fusion of all the instincts and experiences of Matt Busby's life. For a few extraordinary seconds when he was "gone", Best, the genius imp, and Foulkes, the dour coalminer Busby had plucked from the pits of St Helens, came together to rescue United. Popular Bill, the quintessential loner didn't have a pal, much less a friend, at Old Trafford. Bill was not one of the lads, too dour, too bluntly honest, no glib sense of humour. He'd seen too much of the coalface to laugh easily. George was less obviously but more profoundly alone. He was the magic of Busby's childhood dreams. Two outsiders, beauty and filth, George and Bill: Busby's life in microcosm. It was a strange, glorious night.'

Charlton had never been in a match where the players had gone from such absolute depression to perfect happiness. 'That's when reality hit us,' says Stepney, 'and we thought, "This could be our year".' Hugh McIlvanney of the *Observer* was inside the stadium reporting that night. 'The last people to imagine United could come back were Real Madrid,' he says. 'United had been thinking the best they could hope for was a replay in Lisbon.'

There were still ten tense minutes left, but United were now in control. 'At 3–3 we knew it was ours,' says Best. Crerand felt that if United had gone for more goals they'd have got them because Real were demoralised. Instead, the Reds held back and played out time. Their late comeback had shattered the Spaniards. They were helpless, unable to raise their game, showing frustration, appealing for fouls. This only encouraged United. Real sensed they would need something extra-special to win the match. Now they were striving for a play-off. Real came desperately surging into action during the hectic, closing minutes, but with United ahead they had little or no chance.

Stiles organised the resistance. The Reds snuffed out trouble at the first flicker and moved the ball away again to set up their own attacks. David Meek of the *Manchester Evening News*, like Crerand, felt that if the game had gone on any longer United would have won on the night. But they didn't need to score again; it was quite clear Real wouldn't get another goal, even if they played all night. The tide was flowing one way and getting stronger all the time. The Reds had the scent of victory. Charlton couldn't believe it. They'd all but been knocked out of the European Cup and then reprieved. He thought of the old man; of how low he must have been at half-time, how tough it was for him in that gloomy dressing-room, how hard to face the second half.

The closing seconds seemed an eternity with 21 players in United's half and Real battering their heads against a red wall to save themselves. 'But not even Amancio, supple, alert, industrious, and brilliant in footwork, could rescue the monarchs, and in the end the sleek, self-assured football of Real, which they unfurled in the first half, died in the dark,' wrote Green of *The Times*. United's tactical turnaround was the crucial difference to the outcome of the match. 'It brought justice because in the end it was English temperament, fibre, and morale that won through,' Green wrote.

At the final whistle Charlton sank to the ground. He'd felt the same at the World Cup final. He believed United had now won the European Cup. How could they fail after all they'd been through that night? Foulkes felt the same way. He told his team-mates, 'That's it. We're going to win the final now.'

Within seconds jubilant United fans were on the pitch. Charlton was in anguish. It was very emotional. Busby embraced his players in a scene of tears and joy. Charlton broke down because it had been such a hard slog, and it meant so much to win the European Cup for all sorts of reasons, all that had gone before. Stiles sensed that Charlton didn't know what day it was and didn't care. He was so pent up. United had snatched a tremendous 3–3 draw from the jaws of defeat. It was enough for a 4–3 aggregate victory. What made it so much better for Charlton was that they'd done it in Real's stadium, possibly his favourite ground.

The Reds had reached the European Cup final for the first time. It was one of the most incredible turnarounds Murphy had seen in a lifetime of watching the game. 'It was like seeing the Derby favourite coming first round Tattenham Corner leading by five lengths and then being beaten in the last furlong,' he said. 'Only a great side could have fought their way out of the desperate situation Manchester United found themselves in that night . . .'

Foulkes's improbable strike had proved to be just enough. Britain's most experienced player in European football was also the most unlikely goal-scoring hero of all time. 'Bobby, where were you when Bill stuck that one in?' Murphy asked afterwards. 'I was back covering for him, Jimmy, playing centre-half,' said Charlton without the hint of a smile! But Foulkes had more than justified Busby's faith in recalling him by booking United a place in the final with his only European Cup goal. 'After so many games with no thought of scoring, it seems almost unbelievable,' says Foulkes. 'Scoring that goal remains probably my most precious moment in football.' It was almost too good to be true.

United chairman Louis Edwards made the long walk around the stadium to the dressing rooms. As the teams left the pitch United officials crowded around the players, tears of joy running down their faces. 'When the match was over and they knew they were in the final the effect on the players was dramatic, but the effect on Matt was most noticeable,' says Hugh McIlvanney. Busby was certainly more emotional than Stepney had ever seen him before. Others not usually known for showing their feelings were almost delirious with joy. It was truly a great night. Amidst the United celebrations the compassionate Stepney spared a thought for Real. He knew how he'd have felt if victory had been snatched from United. Zoco must have been ready to crawl away and die. An own goal, then two out of the blue and United were home and dry; all that was left for Real was a host of regrets.

The match had been as good as a final. But United already knew the opposition for the real final. In the press box the journalists were writing their reports. Under the headline THERE AT LAST. UNITED V BENFICA IN BUSBY'S FINAL, the *Daily Mail*'s Crowther wrote: 'With a great and glorious fighting comeback that will rank among the all-time epics of football, Manchester United stormed their way through here tonight to the European Cup final before an angry and astonished crowd in the vast Bernabeu Stadium . . . If anyone had told me as the dejected-looking United side walked off at half-time that they would be the winners I would not have believed them . . . No transformation I have ever seen could rival this breathtaking drama . . .' David Meek's report in the *Manchester Evening News* was headlined: REAL REDS REIGN IN SPAIN. He wrote: 'In Yugoslavia it was a trial of temperament, in Poland a trial of tactics, and now here in Spain it was the fighting comeback of all time.'

Under the headline MANCHESTER UNITED IN FINAL AT LAST, Geoffrey Green rejoiced in their success at becoming the first English team to reach the pinnacle of the European Cup. He wrote in *The Times*: 'Manchester United now stand as the heroes of England, having suffered and survived the scar of losing the league title at the last stride only a few days ago, and they must take the field at Wembley as the favourites. Seldom could there have been a more hazardous or remarkable journey than Manchester United made tonight as they recovered from the depths of despair at half-time to beat Real Madrid, the champions of Spain and the symbols of Spanish football power, on aggregate by 4–3. To the end, their goal by Best at Old Trafford was worth its weight in gold after all. This, indeed, was a fairy story. As I sit here, with 125,000 people pouring dumbfounded and stunned out of the stadium, I can hardly believe it . . . All day the sun had beaten down like a hammer, and the night, exquisitely still, was humid. It should have favoured the Spaniards, but it was they who withered, leaving Manchester United to pass into history in a blaze of splendour on a night of enchantment.' Green searched his memory to recall such a night, but he couldn't find one.

There was a fantastic scene when the players returned to the dressing room. The place was in turmoil. Busby and Charlton hugged each other as they unashamedly and understandably cried their eyes out. It was a moving sight for Edwards. Busby kept saying over and over again, 'I can't help it, I can't help it,' as he hugged his players one by one. It was as if the tension and heartache of striving for the trophy over the years had finally been released. Aston felt much the same, as though Real and not Benfica were all that stood between Busby and the realisation of his dream.

'Matt was very moved because he clearly realised that time was against him as far as winning the European Cup was concerned,' remembers Hugh McIlvanney of *The Observer*, the only journalist allowed inside the United dressing room that night. 'There was nothing very profound or sensible being said. It was just an outburst of happiness and everyone was joining in. I was in the dressing room in Lisbon after Celtic had won the European Cup [in 1967] and there was something of the same atmosphere. It was a great place to be.'

Some players, including Best and Sadler, walked straight off the field, through the dressing room and under the showers without even taking their kit off. Then they started singing. Four years earlier Best and Sadler had shared their first taste of success by bringing the FA Youth Cup back to Old Trafford. Now Sadler, with his goal, and Best, with his mazy run up the right wing, had taken United to the last stage in achieving the club's long-standing dream. Perhaps it was because they'd been so steeped in the club's traditions that United were able to summon up the determination and effort needed to make the comeback possible.

Sadler and Best sat on the floor in their kit letting the water from the showers pour over them. Crerand didn't think anyone knew what they were doing. It just wouldn't sink in. The players had dazed looks in their eyes. Best lay flat out like a starfish, shouting and singing. (He'd later say that he took it all calmly.) Trainer Jack Crompton and Bill Foulkes, two of the least emotional men in football, gave each other a French-style kiss on the cheek. The battle cry was 'She's there' as Charlton laughed and cried, and everybody rolled around in a heap like a bunch of schoolboys. Busby looked ten years younger. Minutes afterwards he was still speechless. Someone produced a bottle of Scotch and men who'd never touched a drop before all had a swig. Nobody wanted to get changed and leave the ground. Later when Crerand couldn't see Busby anywhere he thought they'd probably find him lying somewhere. When the Boss finally returned to the dressing room the players broke into a spontaneous round of clapping. Law, who hated watching games, had suffered so much that he said he was applying for the next heart transplant.

Aston had played superbly. Crerand just didn't know where

United's winger had found his energy and strength. He wished more of the Old Trafford crowd who barracked Aston every week had been there to see his brilliant performance. 'After that game in Madrid I really believed that we were somehow fated to win the European Cup,' says Aston. 'The way Real ran out of steam, the way Bill Foulkes scored his goal . . . it was as if it had all been decided beforehand.' It was all a mystery to Crerand: 'I don't know what happened to the Spanish side that night, but I'm sure if we played them every week for a year they would never let us off the hook again as they did in that tie.'

Amancio sat in Real's dressing room looking at his bruises. He was very depressed. Stiles was definitely not his best friend in football. The Spanish newspapers were already setting up their headlines for the next day's early editions: STILES: THE ASSASSIN OF MADRID. When Stiles heard what the papers had written about him he took it as a compliment. 'They could call me what they liked,' he wrote later. 'I had been booked for a minor infringement, had taken more kicks from Amancio than I'd given him, and knew I'd done my job of subduing his threat.' Unfortunately, much of the goodwill that had so long existed between United and Real had been destroyed by ugly incidents on the pitch that night.

United had become only the fifth team in 13 years to stop Real reaching the European Cup final. The Reds were clearly more comfortable attacking so the question arose as to whether they should have steered clear of the defensive approach which rebounded on them in that fatal first half. When Busby had composed himself he praised his team and defended his decision to defend. 'This team proved it had heart in the way it came back, as only great teams can, to win what seemed a lost cause. I think that this heart can win the European Cup. To defend, as we did at the start, was the right thing, even if it looked as if the tactics had gone wrong. I would play it exactly the same way if we turned back the clock. You just cannot leave yourself wide open. We had to play it tight while we were in front.'

In *Father of Football*, David Miller tried to rationalise Busby's decision to defend. 'This, clearly, contradicts what Busby had previously held – that defence was not only bad tactics but poor entertainment. Even though he reversed his battle orders at half-time, what brought him to the point where he was prepared to compromise? In retrospect I feel it must be that, in his fourth semi-final, the instinct to win at all costs overruled the grand conception of football as competitive, artistic entertainment. The football world, which for 23 years had admired his unfaltering loyalty to attack, could hardly complain if he now temporarily took refuge in defence. Besides, the attacking, gambling flourish reasserted itself.'

Busby, like Brennan, had always been a gambler, even though he went about his hobby more discreetly than some. 'If there were two beetles crossing the carpet, he'd bet on them,' someone once said of him. In the Rechts der Isar Hospital in Munich, where they nursed him back to life from the very edge of death, the surgeons remembered that 'he was always very interested in the horses'. Now his courage to take a calculated gamble at half-time in Madrid had brought him to the brink of his greatest ambition.

Crerand knew how important the change of tactics had been. 'Talk about twin centre-forward plans,' he said, 'we beat them with our twin centre-half plan. As soon as we moved Foulkesy and Sadler from our penalty area to theirs they won the match for us.' Charlton thought fate had intervened. 'Having been 3–1 down and overrun for 45 minutes . . . there was no way we should have got back, but we did.' To Crerand it was United's finest hour. 'Our 3–3 draw with Real Madrid after being 3–1 down replaces our 5–1 win at Benfica two years ago as United's greatest performance,' he said. Busby would later describe the night as the greatest in the club's history.

After the match the Real supporters turned nasty. Outside the ground they were venting their frustrations and anger at United's fans. The Mancunians were obvious targets in their red-and-white scarves. The locals were spitting at them and throwing stones. They threatened the United fans and wanted to fight. When the players eventually walked towards their coach a mob was waiting for them and they got a horrendous reception. As Stiles walked around the front of the coach he was punched by a Spaniard and had to push the man away. Another Real fan, high above on one of the tiers of the Bernabeu, was draining off the last dregs of a bottle of wine and looking questioningly at the bottle. When Stiles turned to get into the coach his glasses fell off. As he bent down to pick them up the man dropped the wine bottle, which came flying through the air and hit Stiles on the back of the head. The BBC's David Coleman was sitting next to Crerand on the team bus when they heard the crash of glass. Stiles felt as if somebody had put the lights out. 'It's a good job it's only his head,' said Crerand. 'It might have done some serious damage.' Stiles was lifted onto the bus unconscious. When he came to a few seconds later he was struggling and shouting, 'Let me get at him.' Several players held him back. With blood streaming down his face Stiles remembered Sir Alf Ramsey's words: 'It is enough to beat them.' Suddenly he calmed down. He heard the doctor say, 'That shirt is ruined now. The club will buy you a new one.' Quickly the businessman in Stiles took over. 'It cost £6,' he said. But Stiles was soon put in his place. 'He didn't pay £6 for his suit,' shouted Brennan from the back. By now they were all laughing and Stiles was somehow happy he'd been hit with a bottle. 'If we'd lost they'd have thrown flowers at me,' he thought. The bottle, a shoe and a tomato had all been thrown at United. They were proof of victory.

As the coach was driven away from the stadium the Spanish fans spat and screamed at the players. Nobody flinched and as Best sat there he tried to fathom out one of United's least publicised qualities – their guts. Crerand, the worldly-wise professional, did it for him. 'This team of ours just doesn't know when it's beaten,' he said. Crerand looked at his team-mates one by one and shook his head as if he couldn't quite believe what they'd done.

Stiles had to have stitches in his head before joining the celebrations. It all added to his reputation as the most accident-prone person any of the players had ever met.

Later, there were scenes of joy and celebration as hundreds of supporters who'd made the trip from Manchester crowded in on the players at the Fenix Hotel. In the dark Madrid night 100,000 or so subdued Spaniards found their way to bars, cafes and eventually to bed. Their noisy celebrations had been brought to a premature end at half-time although they weren't aware of it then.

Charlton intended to go out that night with his wife Norma and other friends, but while the players hit the town to celebrate,

Charlton was left behind. After two cold beers he'd started to tremble violently and talk non-stop, as if instantly drunk. He went to lie down but felt no better. His head ached and he felt drained. The others were amazed he was so ill. He'd been so involved in the story of United's European Cup that he couldn't celebrate – he was too exhausted both physically and emotionally. 'After the big games the players are so drained,' says Hugh McIlvanney. 'It's like fighters who say when they win that they're going to drink up the town.' Charlton stayed in his hotel room to recover while his team-mates enjoyed a champagne night of celebration.

After the game some of the players went to their hotel to meet their wives and girlfriends. Busby's son Sandy was there. He was very happy, although a little the worse for wear following the celebrations. The city was packed with fans. Everywhere the players went they found hoarse-voiced, bleary-eyed supporters whose elation at their team's success was heightened by alcohol. Crerand was having a wonderful night out because by then he was convinced that the cup would be United's. He felt sure they'd knocked out the best team in the competition. After meeting up with their other halves for dinner some players, including Best, Crerand, Law and Stepney, went to a nightclub called Stone's. It was packed with United fans. The lead singer of the group was an English lad called Carl Douglas (later to find fame with his record 'Kung-Fu Fighting'). 'To say we celebrated that night is a gross understatement,' says Stepney. Crerand agrees. 'We drank and ate and whooped it up with the enthusiasm of demented dervishes. It was a wild night.'

Eventually, after more drinks, the players got a taxi home. It was late when Stepney flopped into bed. Although he felt tired it took him a while to drop off, and even then he didn't sleep properly. His mind was still whirling from the excitement of the night. He doubted if any of United's players slept well, though Crerand couldn't even recall going to bed!

When United's players woke up the next morning it was to the realisation that there remained only one more hurdle between them and total victory. Each and every one of them was determined that, having got so far, Benfica wouldn't stop them savouring the final, the golden moment of glory. They would make the European Cup theirs come what may. When young Robin Murray discovered United had drawn 3–3 and gone through to the European Cup final he was a very happy lad.

Law woke up to find that his right hand had swollen to twice its normal size after the collision with the dugout roof. He'd actually broken a bone and would be in agony for a week, but it was worth it.

By now, Amancio's bitterness had gone. Real had been knocked out by a great team in which Charlton was the master player. 'One could not help but feel pleased for Señor Busby's sake,' said Amancio graciously. The *Daily Mail*'s Crowther knew what it all meant to the Boss. 'For Matt Busby, the man who has striven so long and so hard for success in Europe and who has never lost faith in his club's ability to achieve it, this was the night on which a dream came true. Now he will proudly lead his men out at Wembley on 29 May as the first English team to play in the final.' In Busby's words: 'We were on the last rung of the staircase to the sky.'

When the United party got to Madrid airport, Louis Edwards was standing at the bottom of the gangplank. 'If you're sober when we get back to Manchester,' he told the reporters, 'you're not getting off.' When Busby left the plane in Manchester he told reporters and waiting fans: 'Like Satchmo [Louis Armstrong] says, "It's a wonderful world".' Some of the United party flew on to London for the Professional Footballers' Association (PFA) Player of the Year award that night. Best was the winner.

Seven

The Final

Benfica, or Sport Lisboa e Benfica as they are officially known, were a national institution in Portugal. They were managed by 48-year-old Brazilian Otto Gloria. Gloria had a healthy regard for Manchester United and Busby, saying, 'I know him well and respect him. He knows so much.' Of the United players he added, 'The one I specially admire is Best. He is what we say "Muito Bon".' In fact, like Real Madrid and United, the two clubs considered each other good friends.

Born in Rio de Janeiro, Gloria exuded bonhomie and sunshine, much like his star striker, Eusebio Ferreira da Silva. Eusebio, 26, was born in Mozambique, a Portuguese colony in East Africa. After 25 games for Benfica, he was selected to play for Portugal. Mozambique hadn't bothered to pick him. He was the finest player produced by Africa and the first from that continent to earn a worldwide reputation. Known as the Black Pearl, Eusebio was always smiling, always ready to applaud his opponents. As European Footballer of the Year in 1965 and runner-up in 1962 and 1966, the Black Pearl inspired a generation of players from the Third World.

In 1962 Benfica defended the European Cup and upset the odds by squeezing past English double winners Tottenham Hotspur 4–3 on aggregate. In the final in Amsterdam they met Real Madrid – the only other team to win the European Cup after their success in the first five tournaments. Puskas scored a hat-trick for Real but Benfica still won 5–3 with Eusebio, one of two changes from the previous year, scoring twice with the sort of cannonball strikes that were to become his trademark.

If Real's memorable 7–3 victory against Eintracht Frankfurt in the 1960 final was the best club match of all time, then the '62 final is considered a close second. Eusebio, the new star, was the difference between the two sides during a year in which Benfica also won the Portuguese Cup and were runners-up in the World Club Championship.

Eusebio had since played in two more European Cup finals and was on the losing side both times to the two Milan clubs, AC and Inter, in 1963 and 1965 respectively. He came to England for the 1966 World Cup finals as European Footballer of the Year. He'd been top scorer in the Portuguese League for the previous three seasons and his club's successes were filtering through to the improving national side.

Portugal reached the quarter-finals with Eusebio having scored three goals, including two against Pele's Brazil. He grabbed four goals, including two penalties, against North Korea and made another as Portugal came from behind to win 5–3. That performance helped to make him the World Cup's leading scorer with nine goals and brought him a cheque for £1,000 from the Knightsbridge Sporting Club in London. Eusebio scored from the penalty spot against England in the semi-final but Portugal lost 2–1, courtesy of two Charlton rockets. The world was left with the abiding memory of a distraught Eusebio in tears as he wandered around the Wembley turf in a daze. If Best's performance against Benfica in Lisbon had made him a superstar in Europe earlier in the year, then Eusebio's impact on the World Cup had made him a household name around the globe.

After his extraordinary feats for Portugal, it had become fashionable to look upon Eusebio as the new Pele. He was to Europe what Pele was to South America. The lithe Benfica forward probably generated more power than his contemporaries. He was also murderously quick. But according to Charlton, he wasn't in Pele's class. 'Given adequate support, Pele was almost impossible to mark,' says Charlton. 'He invented ways of playing the game, gymnastically defying the restraints opponents tried to impose upon him. Eusebio, much more of an individualist, was easier to contain and his temperament was suspect.' Charlton worried a bit about Eusebio before the final, but Pele would have been the source of sleepless nights. Eusebio was bound to threaten United and that meant giving him to Stiles, who'd done such a marvellous job in the World Cup semi-final. Charlton was confident that 'the little man' would be just as successful for United. During the World Cup, Alan Ball had also shown great confidence in Stiles's ability to contain the man known as the Black Pearl. 'That Eusebio is a PR [public relations] player,' said Ball. 'He's always shaking hands, always clapping the other team. It's a con. He wants to be everybody's friend. Sort him out, wee man.'

But while Eusebio, who'd just broken the Portuguese scoring record with 42 goals, was clearly Benfica's world star they were far from a one-man team. Mario Coluna, a very experienced and cunning wing-half, was a great influence in midfield. Jose Augusto was still an exceptional forward. The aptly named Jose Torres (tower) was a very tall man who wreaked havoc on defences from the dizzy height of 6 ft 4 in. He used his height to full advantage both when heading for goal and when sending the ball to the feet of others. The slippery left-winger Simoes, scurryingly quick and combative, was also a handful.

Benfica were a good star-studded team who'd produced some of the most artistic club football in the world. In the early 1960s, inspired by Eusebio, they'd overtaken Real Madrid as the dominant force in European club football. They had reached four European Cup finals in five years but by 1968 were past their best. In fact, they'd been scared out of their lives in an earlier round when the gallant little Irish League club Glentoran held them to two draws: 1–1 in Belfast and then 0–0 in Lisbon. After that they'd scraped through 2–1 on aggregate against French champions St Etienne, with goals from Augusto and Eusebio in a 2–0 first-leg win being just enough, beaten Vasas of Hungary by a more convincing 3–0 in Lisbon after a 0–0 draw away, and followed up the 2–0 victory against Juventus in Lisbon, the match watched by Busby and Edwards, with an impressive 1–0 away win in Turin.

Meanwhile, the press, who'd been pessimistic about United's chances after the first leg of their semi-final clash with Real Madrid, had changed their minds. Opinion had now tilted crazily and the Reds were being shouted home as certain winners. As Stiles nursed a leg injury, meaning he'd have to play the final without a full day's training for a fortnight, he felt United's greatest problem was complacency.

Everyone knew the Reds had slaughtered Benfica 5–1 in the European Cup quarter-final in Lisbon in 1966 (they'd earlier won the home leg 3–2). They said there was no reason there should not be a repeat. Crerand was certainly convinced United were going to win because of those earlier victories. He felt United had always been better than Benfica, and had the 'Indian sign' on them after 1966. But Stiles knew there was no possible link with the Wembley game. 'We had to forget about that [victory in Lisbon], realise that a blade of grass could decide the final, that we had the fight of our lives on against mighty Benfica.'

'The sides were better matched than many United supporters realised,' wrote Derek Hodgson in *The Manchester United Story*. 'Law's absence through injury was a heavy blow and, compared to the 1967 team, United could be said to be stronger in only two positions, those of Alex Stepney and George Best – and at best untried, if not definitely weaker, in others. Benfica, too, had been rebuilding and were a more resilient side than the team that had collapsed before United in Lisbon.'

Many of United's players also remembered playing Benfica on a post-season tour of America and Australia in the summer of 1967 after the Reds had won the title, when they met the Portuguese side in Los Angeles and lost 3–1. Benfica took the game much more seriously than United because they remembered that 5–1 drubbing the last time the teams met. But Benfica were a good side who'd played well and deserved their win. That was the game on Best's mind as he prepared for the Wembley showdown.

All 100,000 tickets for the final had been sold even before the finalists were known. United's allocation of 30,000 were fully taken up and the club expected at least 40,000 supporters.

Ahead of the final Best was named Footballer of the Year by the football writers to complete his own personal 'double' after having already received the PFA award. At 21 he was the youngest-ever to receive the award. Busby was also recognised for his achievements that season as Manager of the Year.

By now it had been decided that Law should have an exploratory knee operation. On the Monday before the final, Law was admitted to St Joseph's Hospital in Manchester. His consultant opened up the knee and took out about an inch-and-a-half of loose cartilage. It was the residue of an operation he'd undergone at Huddersfield ten years earlier. Law would keep the piece of cartilage at home in a jar as a memento.

Before he went to London, Busby visited Law. The striker was still a bit sleepy because of the anaesthetic but recognised the Boss and smiled. He was just relieved that the problem had at last been discovered.

Busby then set off for London and the sixteenth-century country hotel at Egham in Surrey where the team were to prepare for the final. On the way he spoke to David Meek of the *Manchester Evening News* about the mood among his players. In Busby's view they had the one key characteristic that would see them through to victory: 'Their hearts are right and this is the important thing,' he said.

Great Fosters was United's secluded hideaway in the run-up to the final. It had become a hotel in 1930 and for almost 40 years had entertained guests from the world of films, high society and big business. Charlie Chaplin, Vivien Leigh, Orson Welles and Emperor Haile Selassie of Ethiopia had all stayed there. 'It was 400 years old and it looked to me as if they hadn't changed the furniture since the day it opened,' says Crerand. 'You kept expecting to see blokes with swords fighting their way across the lounge carpet.'

By a strange twist of fate Father Hilary Tagliaferro, the manager of Hibernians Malta, the team United had knocked out in the first round, played his part in United's build-up. His knowledge of

Benfica's players and the detailed dossier he provided were invaluable.

Best had it in the back of his mind all season that United would win the European Cup. 'We had been so close and we weren't going to miss out again,' he says. 'There was a feeling that it was now or never. A few of the players were coming towards the end of their careers, and Sir Matt certainly was. We felt this was probably our last chance to win it for him.' It was announced that the players would receive a taxable bonus of £1,000 a man if they won the European Cup. This had been written into their contracts at the beginning of the season.

Martin Edwards, the son of United chairman Louis, and the man who would succeed his father, was in the official party going to the final. They travelled to London by train and stayed at the hotel.

A special train chartered by United left Manchester filled with just about everyone who could claim a connection with the club. The backroom staff, young players, relatives, Busby's 'laundry lassies' and some very special people who had links with United going back more than 10 years to Munich. For the United players who were around in 1958 and the relatives of those who did not return from Belgrade it was a poignant journey.

It was Derby Day at Epsom. The previous year some of the players had met racehorse owner Robert Sangster in Bermuda. He had asked a few players round to his house in the afternoon to watch the big race since a few of them were into gambling. Stiles and Brennan liked a bet. They went down to the TV lounge and watched Lestor Piggott ride Sir Ivor to victory. Brennan had backed him at 5–4.

The race helped take their minds off the final. 'All played it cool outwardly no matter that their inner heart strings must have twanged like guitars,' said Geoffrey Green of *The Times*. After the race the players left Sangster's and went back to the hotel to join the rest of the squad for some rest before the game.

The United party had a light meal and then boarded the coach for Wembley. The police had to work hard to clear a path so the driver could start out on the road to the stadium. As they travelled north through the London suburbs towards Wembley an indefinable ache began to grow in the pit of the players' stomachs.

Twenty-four parents, wives and players affected by the Munich disaster were at Wembley including Jackie Blanchflower and his wife, Harry Gregg, Johnny Berry, Bert Whalley's widow and Albert Scanlon. A group from Orbiston, including Busby's proud mother Nellie, also made the trip.

The players stood together on the threshold of the achievement their grand old manager wanted more than anything. 'The European Cup had become like a holy grail for Manchester United,' says Charlton, 'and I think the older players felt as if we had been pursuing a sort of football golden fleece.'

Best was looking forward to the game. He imagined 90 minutes of pure magic. He decided he was going to score a hat trick, take Wembley by storm. United would hammer Benfica. He had it all worked out before a ball had been kicked. That was George, upbeat, confident, sure of success.

United's greatest danger was the daunting burden of expectation. After Munich Busby had silently vowed to win the trophy for those who'd died. The current team had similarly pledged to do it for the Boss. Such dedication, although private, was taking a heavy toll. The whole football world outside Portugal was willing United to win. Such hopes were a millstone even for those with the broadest shoulders. 'Without being disrespectful to the players involved, the 1968 team was not our best,' says Charlton. 'Manchester City won the league and we had faded. A lot of us were past our peak. I knew I wasn't going to get another chance and about half the team were in the same boat.'

By this time a frustrated Denis Law was getting ready to watch the match on television from hospital. The nuns who ran St Joseph's had cleared the beds on either side of him because they knew Law wanted to watch the game with a few friends. 'I was dying for the lads to do it for Matt,' says Law.

Busby faced a difficult task picking the team. In the end he decided to keep faith with those who played in Madrid. Dunne would again switch from right-back, the position he'd occupied for most of the season, to left-back. Young Burns, who'd been almost ever-present at left-back, was unfortunate to be left out. The experienced Brennan was slotted into Dunne's right-back position. Sadler, who'd played well in five different positions, would deputise for Law at inside-left.

There was no real tension in the squad about the line-up before the final because the Boss had already told the players who beat Real that they'd play at Wembley. This simple but vital action helped put them at ease. It was one more example of why Busby had been such a good manager for more than 21 years.

United did not know that Eusebio was suffering with a fractured knee. But despite the injury there was no question that he would play in the final. Only the great Alfredo di Stefano of Real Madrid had scored more goals (49) in the Champions Cup than Eusebio. 'We played with injuries like that,' says Eusebio.

The line-ups were:

MANCHESTER UNITED: Stepney, Brennan, Dunne, Foulkes, Stiles, Crerand, Best, Kidd, Charlton (capt.), Sadler, Aston. Sub: Rimmer.

BENFICA: Henrique, Adolfo, Humberto, Jacinto, Cruz, Graca, Coluna (capt.), Augusto, Torres, Eusebio, Simoes. Sub: Nascimento.

Six of Benfica's side had played in the World Cup semi-final against England. United only had Charlton and Stiles from that encounter but eight of the side had played at Wembley, the exceptions being Aston, Brennan and Kidd. Aston owed his place to the absence of Law because Kidd was almost certain to play. Charlton would proudly captain United in the absence of the injured Law and in memory of Munich.

Foulkes had been told by Busby straight after the semi-final against Real to get himself ready for the final. 'I don't think it was an emotional thing,' says Foulkes. 'I think he thought I could do the job and had the experience for the occasion. I don't think he would have taken that sort of risk. Munich and everything else didn't come into it because this was his ambition, to win the European Cup. He wouldn't take chances. I couldn't stop, I couldn't turn, but I worked at it to get myself fit enough and played in the final.'

In the build-up Foulkes was a little nervous he'd let the team down. 'Come the final we're talking Torres,' he says, 'and, of course, when you've got a cruciate ligament injury you can't leap, and here's a guy of six foot four, brilliant in the air.' Still, Foulkes wasn't as nervous as he'd been in the semi-final. He didn't really want to play against Real Madrid, but once United got to Wembley he was hoping Busby would pick him.

In the dressing-room Stepney hung his clothes on the same peg he'd used for his first England appearance against Sweden the week before. He followed a pre-set routine before matches and was upset if anything disturbed it. He liked to get ready exactly 30 minutes before kick-off. Long before it was time to get changed Stepney and Kidd strolled out to get a feel of the pitch. Wembley was already almost full. The crowd spotted Kidd and in an instant thousands of voices were singing 'Happy Birthday' to Kidd. Kidd turned to Stepney and said, 'You know, we cannot lose tonight for their sake.' Foulkes felt pretty relaxed. He hadn't been able to get to the ground fast enough. Aston and Kidd were Manchester lads so they knew what was expected of them. Kidd was going on ten years old at the time of the Munich disaster. Best couldn't wait to get out onto the Wembley turf. Charlton looked solemn. Stiles, of the toothless grin, wasn't in a smiling mood as he got changed. Crerand assured the others of his confidence, but somehow Stepney felt even he was trying to put a brave face on things. They hadn't lost and they believed they could win, but nobody could really be certain of victory.

Stepney's thoughts turned to Law, a master at controlling his nerves. He could often be found lying down asleep in the dressing-room, wearing only his jock strap, 30 minutes before the start of some very important games. This match would be torture for the injured striker because he hated watching. Wilf McGuinness, a good talker, was geeing everybody up. But basically the players were left to do their own thing.

Busby wanted his team to dominate the middle of the park. He told the players to concentrate and make sure they did not give the ball away. He knew the chasing that Wembley's big pitch caused on sapped energy. Busby moved around quietly and studiously. It was his job to build up the players. 'You're brilliant; you must be, you're playing for Manchester United.' Busby always concealed any sign of nerves. 'Nobby, you keep tabs on Eusebio. Bill, stick with Torres on the crosses. Now just go out and play your football, all of you, and enjoy yourselves because that is why we are here. All the best . . . '

'Enjoy yourselves . . . enjoy yourselves . . . ' Busby's words were always the same. They disappeared during the long, heart-thumping walk down the tunnel but nevertheless something registered in the subconscious.

As the teams walked onto the Wembley turf side-by-side – United in all blue and Benfica in all white – the stadium reverberated to the thunderous reception. Never had eleven players been so burdened or so motivated as the men Charlton led on to the lush turf on a humid, electrically charged evening. But Foulkes knew United were going to win. They had to. It was their last chance and it was Busby's last chance.

After what seemed like an eternity referee Cancetto Lo Bello beckoned the captains, Charlton and Coluna, to the centre circle. They exchanged pennants. Charlton lost the toss. Coluna chose ends. United would start the match.

At home in Scotland, a 26-year-old Rangers player called Alex Ferguson settled down to watch the match on television. He was disappointed that Law wasn't playing, since the striker was a Scot and one of his heroes. Ferguson's ambition was to get his coaching badges and stay in the game when his playing days were over. Tonight, though, thoughts of his own destiny were put to one side as he prepared to cheer on United.

Charlton kicked off and directed the opening move that established the pattern of the game. Aston accelerated and was fouled. It was to be the first of many attempts to stop the United winger. Nevertheless, the match began slowly, hardly surprising given the acute tension and what was at stake. But once the game was underway Stepney's nerves vanished. Suddenly, he had enough to do just concentrating and ensuring he didn't make any mistakes. After three minutes Crerand floated over a free kick that Sadler could only claw down with his boot and push straight to Henrique. Neither team could really get going and too many free kicks were given away. The tackling reflected the size of the reward.

Benfica knew they had to stop Best. Cruz was chief hatchet man, aided and abetted by Humberto. Early in the game Best was repeatedly battered and bruised, tripped and harried by the two defenders, restricting his impact. Cruz, sensing the referee's patience was running out, let Humberto take over the restraining job. But it wasn't long before Humberto was booked after yet another foul on Best. Indeed, the game was quite nasty at times. Charlton mouthed his disapproval when Eusebio, coming in late on Crerand, wickedly thrust a boot over the ball.

Once the first nervous tension was relieved the match began to blossom. Aston, wearing United's unfamiliar strip of royal blue – the colours his father wore in the FA Cup final 20 years earlier – was showing some exquisite touches on the left wing. Aston quickly worked out that Benfica's fullback Adolfo was a bit square, and if the ball was pushed past him he'd give him trouble. 'They knew all about Bestie and watched him closely,' recalls Brennan, 'but nothing about Johnny, and he revelled in the space.' At this stage, the ease with which Aston sped past Adolfo was the only encouraging feature of United's performance. Dunne was playing behind Aston, who was having a field day. 'The more I could get it to John the better,' says Dunne. 'He was brilliant. Exciting for people to watch.' Brennan agrees. 'I wouldn't have liked to have played against him that night,' he said.

After 11 minutes Eusebio, 'constantly prowling like a caged, hungry animal', according to Geoffrey Green of *The Times*, dropped off to the inside-right channel. One of Benfica's best moves began to develop between Graca and Torres who swept the ball out to Eusebio lurking on the right wing. Eluding Stiles and Foulkes, the Black Pearl took the ball in his stride and unleashed a venomous right-foot shot from the edge of the penalty area. Stepney thought it was going over but it dipped wickedly at the last minute. By then he didn't have time to move and was beaten. All he could do was stand and hope. The ball rapped the crossbar making it 'twang like a bow string' in the words of *The Guardian*'s Albert Barham. Stepney felt very relieved when the ball rebounded to safety. Eusebio had almost made a goal out of nothing. It was a desperately unlucky moment for Benfica, a fantastic escape for United. Eusebio swung his arm in exasperation. It was the fifth time he'd hit the woodwork at Wembley. In fact, he only had one goal to show for his efforts at the stadium.

After that close call United slightly revised their tactics by challenging Eusebio at long range. Stiles played him as he had during the World Cup by leaving the first tackle to someone else, keeping his powder dry for when Eusebio was wriggling clear. 'The thing you couldn't do with Eusebio was let him get set,' says Stiles. 'You had to keep pushing him, pushing him on. He had only a short back lift and he could whack 'em, so you had to keep him going, keep him going; pushing him, pushing him.'

United's best chance came just before the half-hour mark when Aston and Charlton combined to set up a Kidd–Sadler one-two that put Sadler clean through with the goal at his mercy. As Henrique came out Sadler couldn't decide whether to shoot or move the ball past the advancing keeper. Eventually, he scuffed his left-foot shot wide from ten yards. Sadler banged the turf with the palms of his hands. The crowd seethed in frustration. Roger MacDonald thought Sadler's indecision might have come from the pressure of playing a free role. 'Perhaps the strain of his schizophrenic role was too great, for Wembley is a long pitch, and Sadler ran up and down like a yo-yo.' Busby, sitting on the bench alongside Murphy and Crompton, lit a cigarette. So did Wilf McGuinness, who sat behind with Francis Burns and substitute keeper Jimmy Rimmer.

Rimmer watched the game almost anonymously in his plain green goalkeeper's shirt. He was just as emotionally caught up in the drama as the rest of the squad. He shared the anxieties and the tensions. If United won he'd get the same winner's medal as everyone else, and yet he felt a bit of an outsider, as he told Derick Allsop in *Reliving the Dream*. 'I've got to be honest: I would have given anything to have gone on. Just for a minute. Even 30 seconds. So I could have said I actually played in United's European Cup-winning side. I didn't want to wish Alex [Stepney] any harm but I would have loved to have been on the pitch, especially as it was at Wembley.'

Occasionally, when United pushed four men forward in attack, Stiles was left exposed and was forced to commit himself; he seemed exasperated when Eusebio dived theatrically even though he hadn't been fouled. After one tackle Stiles was so convinced Eusebio was acting that he protested with a little fall and feint to expose what he saw as diving. Eusebio angered Stiles after tumbling under his challenge and was booed. But referee Concetto Lo Bello gave Benfica a free kick just outside the area. A frustrated Stiles reacted with a flash of his notorious fangs. The antics amused the referee and Coluna. Eusebio's low shot got past the wall, but not Stepney's safe hands. The save settled United's keeper.

Lo Bello, the Sicilian police chief from Syracuse, must have been impressed with Stiles's mock fall in his efforts to persuade the referee he'd been conned by Eusebio. The United defender's next tackle – his worst of the night – brought Eusebio down again but went unpunished. The reprieve was short-lived though and Stiles was to be continually penalised throughout the match.

But United's tactics seemed to be working. 'Each time Eusebio paced out a run like a fast bowler trying to intimidate a suspect batsman,' wrote Roger MacDonald in *Manchester United in Europe*, 'but United organised their defensive line with such fastidiousness that usually he gave up the search for gaps.'

Despite Stiles's aggression, most free kicks were given against Foulkes. He was penalised several times for challenges on Torres as he climbed on the big striker's shoulders to try to reduce the alarming height advantage. From one free kick, just outside the area, a fierce Eusebio shot was deflected off United's six-man wall to 'an accompanying sound uncannily like crumbling mortar' according to MacDonald. Fortunately, the ball slowed enough for Stepney to scramble it against his body. He had to work hard to get to it and did well to gather the ball. Another time Eusebio failed narrowly to be the first man, so far as *The Guardian*'s Eric Todd knew, to blast the ball over the high Wembley stands. There were times when Charlton felt United were going to miss out again, times when his mouth was as dry as a desert as the tension stabbed into his nerves.

Best was brought down at least half a dozen times in the first half. 'It was crude, perhaps,' wrote Barham in *The Guardian*, 'it certainly was effective.' Benfica's four-man defence – who'd only conceded two goals in the competition – combined so well that

United couldn't convert any free kicks just outside their penalty area. The elusive Best was having a frustrating evening. He was chopped, harried and bruised as he tried to bring his artistry to full flower. Green of *The Times* sympathised with United's 'will-o'-the-wisp', though he could see that Best was trying to compensate by doing too much on the ball. 'Trying to dominate his ruthless opponents, he began to play with a kind of fury which over-stretched itself as he attempted to beat the hordes of Benfica off his own bat.'

Best had more room to work after Humberto's booking. But he taunted too many opponents, sacrificing teamwork for the sake of some individual vendetta. 'I think the game was disappointing from his [Best's] point of view,' says Charlton. 'George loved the big stage, and you could hardly get a bigger stage than the European Cup final. I could see in everything he did that he wanted to use it as a platform for a great virtuoso performance, but it didn't quite happen. There were reasons for that. Benfica defended well, and it was a hot, humid night. The conditions weren't right for individualist stuff, you had to pass the ball around and share the load because the heat sapped your energy, and that didn't really work for George.' The heat was a problem. 'It was a hot night,' recalls Crerand. 'You couldn't breathe in the stadium.'

For a long time it seemed that the match would be a stalemate. The sides knew so much about each other from previous encounters. Indeed, United fielded six of the team that had triumphed 5–1 in Lisbon two years before. With both sides wary of the potency of each other's forwards much of the first half was played in a cagey, careful manner. Aston was United's best hope. Benfica eventually moved Humberto out of the middle to help Adolfo stifle Aston's repeated runs and dangerous crosses.

Aston was so involved in the match that it was passing very quickly for him. The atmosphere was tremendous and when the half-time whistle went he thought they'd only been playing for 15 minutes. Despite the young winger's domination of Adolfo, there was still no score. The drone from United's fans reflected their frustration that the Reds had not taken advantage of their early hold on the game. But Charlton felt that if Aston could maintain his superiority in the second half United would really get amongst Benfica.

Charlton thought that perhaps there weren't enough mistakes in the first half. Most of the players seemed scared of making any. 'It was a case of both teams being afraid to lose, rather than trying to win,' says Charlton. There were more than 30 fouls in the first half, an exhibition of all the worst trends in football, which were reaching a climax. Football was getting out of control, not least in this match.

In a vague sort of way Stepney hoped and imagined that the final would be a glittering replica of the World Cup semi-final between Portugal and England with all that was best in football to entertain the millions watching on television and the 100,000 who'd paid a staggering amount for tickets. But the first half hardly seemed a classic from his view in goal. He was disappointed with both teams. 'Probably the truth is that the tension had taken its toll on every player on the field before the game began,' says Stepney. 'There was too much of the rough stuff, as men went into the tackle chased by the fear of letting an opponent slip past and score a goal which could spell finish. The first half was no soccer spectacular . . .' As Stepney walked off the pitch he shuddered to think what might have happened had Eusebio's vicious shot been a fraction of an inch lower.

The general impression was that the entertainment was distinctly limited. As he did so often, Green of *The Times* found the appropriate imagery to convey the discordant nature of the standoff. 'The first half was episodic and a busy dullness as a spate of ruthless tackling by the Portuguese defence and a symphony of whistling by the Italian referee broke the match into a thousand pieces. A waiter might well have dropped a tray of glasses, such was the clatter, the crash and the bang of it all, with football secondary and both teams clearly out of humour with each other and with officialdom.' Roger MacDonald was also unimpressed with the match. 'The ruthless tackling and the jarring note of the referee's whistle reduced the first half to a staccato movement, artwork with jagged edges.'

But to Charlton the first 45 minutes had been fascinating. Everything either side had tried to do was broken down very quickly. Everybody was running, working. Just because it had been hard to get through didn't make it a bad game, at least for the players. 'We'd had some chances in the first half – David Sadler missed a couple – and I think their defence panicked. They weren't very big and the Latins were used to getting plenty of notice when people went at them. They didn't like people coming at them too quickly – and coming again. We pressurised them, they left a few spaces at the back, but we didn't take advantage.'

At half-time United's dressing room was as solemn as a courtroom. During the vital ten-minute break, when so many games are won or lost, Busby was still preaching softly and persuasively, giving the players quiet words of advice. A reminder here, a pat on the back there, an overall note of caution and a hint of hope that United could and would win. The players looked critically in the mirror and told each other that as the home team they should be making the chances. Then suddenly it was time to go out again.

Busby's gospel worked. United flew at Benfica. Best was not impressed when he was fouled early in the second half. He pointed a finger at his head indicating that his marker had a mental problem. But the rough treatment handed out to Best failed to stop United's momentum. Aston, playing the game of his life, twice went close with two fine shots. Aston's devastating running unbalanced the Portuguese, pulling their defence wide and giving other players more room. 'When the untidy, often ugly, baggage of that first half had been brushed out of the way, the match at last began to find its stature as the blue shirts of Manchester United finally found rhythm, pattern and purpose,' wrote Green.

After 53 minutes the game boiled over. Dunne worked the ball down to Sadler on the left wing. When Charlton saw him on the edge of the penalty area he made for the near post, hoping to drag a defender out of position to create space for someone else to connect with the cross. 'I went to the near post as a decoy as much as anything else,' says Charlton. 'You go to the near post, as you are taught, to take a player away.' At worst Charlton hoped to receive the ball on the ground. But Sadler, anticipating Charlton's break into space, checked onto his right foot and chipped the ball into the centre with almost geometric precision.

Charlton didn't like heading. It wasn't exactly the strongest element of his play and he left it to others, especially Law and Best, who for comparatively short men were quite sensational in the air. But on such a night, in such a situation heading the ball was his only option. Still on the move when the ball dropped short, he soared with more optimism than timing and met the ball perfectly, giving it the gentlest of glances off his thinning hair without even breaking his stride. 'I literally just helped it on its way,' he says. 'It didn't need much of a touch, but it was quite wide out and if the goalkeeper was positioned properly it was going to be difficult to beat him.' But just at that moment, although Charlton hadn't noticed, Henrique came off his line to intercept the ball. He was committed and therefore helpless as the ball looped over him. Charlton thought it had gone wide, but instead the ball went just inside the far post into the bottom corner. It was almost impossible to stop. Charlton was surprised, but also delighted. No goal had ever given him greater pleasure.

It was a wonderful finish and one that the players, including Charlton, never expected. 'It must have come as a shock to my family, my friends, my team-mates, Matt Busby, Jimmy Murphy, Benfica and the world at large when I headed David Sadler's cross past Henrique,' says Charlton. Eamon Dunphy in *A Strange Kind of Glory* thought it was indeed strange. 'Charlton's glancing header was beautifully judged, though he could never remember scoring with his head before. It was weird. The night was weird.' It was Charlton's first headed goal for about ten years and the first time he'd scored in the European Cup since the '66 win over Benfica.

The players danced for joy, swung each other round in delight and generally tried to smother Charlton and Sadler with their congratulations. The area around the pitch became a sea of red as deliriously happy United fans sang, danced and threw scarves, rosettes and caps into the air. For a few moments it was sheer pandemonium. 'Now surely we must win,' thought Stepney.

The goal set the match alight and opened up the play. Now both sides could create chances. The crowd was almost hysterical with delight. 'We shall not be moved,' they sang. The goal gave United the platform to begin to play with some confidence. 'Having got the one [goal] we were on our way,' says Charlton, 'but physically it was still a slog because we were drained and we had to keep forcing ourselves.' The weather didn't help. 'What we didn't expect was that it would be so hot. It was so humid . . . And they didn't throw water bottles on in those days. Players suffered.'

The ball was now definitely in Benfica's court. They had to come forward with all the considerable attacking power at their command. Every one of their forwards had played against England in the World Cup semi-final. Benfica cast caution aside as they searched for an equaliser. Simoes and Jose Augusto were turned back into orthodox wingers, while Coluna and the admirable Graca were flung into a reckless offensive. In focusing on attack, Benfica left their defence precariously stretched. United took advantage. Best popped the ball into the net but was offside. Afterwards Aston was given a lot of the ball – he was on top form and continued to get past Adolfo. Best almost made it two when he broke clear again, but Henrique dashed from his goal and slid the ball away from well outside the area. Best responded with something special from his amazing repertoire, twisting past three defenders to bring an excellent save from Henrique. 'Best, with a shrug of the hips and a twinkle of the toes, made a mockery of any preconceived plans to mark him,' wrote Barham of *The Guardian*.

United's dominance lulled them into a false sense of security. Now it was Eusebio's turn, with Coluna's support, to try to punish them, but Aston came back to thwart him. Stiles scolded his team-mates in typical fashion. Benfica began to seem a little jaded as their attempts to equalise were snuffed out.

The game was going United's way but Benfica, playing in their fifth final, drew on all their experience of European football to produce a valiant effort in the last quarter of an hour. United began to get jittery. 'We knew they were a good team,' says Dunne, 'and a good team can come back. We were uptight all the time.'

United forgot about attacking and setting the seal on victory with another goal. Instead, they became jerky, out of rhythm, and Benfica sensed that all was not lost. Coluna began to draw them together. They went on the attack and kept coming at United.

With only ten minutes left the extent of Benfica's knowledge showed. Augusto, Torres and Graca were involved in a move that melted away the left side of United's defence. Augusto eventually crossed from the right towards the lanky Torres, who at last found Foulkes out of range. Torres rose 'like some Eiffel Tower', in the words of Green, to head the ball carefully down across the face of the goal towards Eusebio who was covered by Stiles. Eusebio, full of guile, deceived United by moving away and taking players with him. As the defence watched Eusebio a gap opened up for the unmarked Graca, who'd stolen forward from midfield to the edge of the six-yard box. Graca had only a narrow angle to aim at the goal. With masterful balance and control he steered a low cross-shot from right to left, wide of Stepney into the net.

The goal was curiously predictable. Stiles thumped the ground in anguish; Graca, in his excitement, leapt to hug a photographer behind United's goal. For Stiles it was like the World Cup all over again, when Germany equalised just before the end. 'It knocked the heart out of us,' he says. 'We suddenly realised how tired we were.' United were shattered and visibly tottered at this reversal of fortune. From the press box David Meek could see disappointment ooze through the Reds. They seemed to lose their pace and zip. Benfica were the team moving forward with confidence as United sought to regroup. The Portuguese sensed victory against the odds. But while United might have been down they weren't out. They still had enough strength to test Benfica's resolve again.

In the last ten minutes Henrique made a tremendous double save. A series of glittering runs by Aston had Benfica on the ropes. After one Aston-inspired attack, Best cut the Portuguese defence to ribbons with a mesmeric dribble only to see his shot blocked by Henrique. The ball rebounded to Sadler who had the goal at his mercy with Henrique out of position, but his shot hit the keeper's outstretched foot and bounced exasperatingly over the bar. Then Best again danced past a couple of defenders before trying, extravagantly and this time unsuccessfully, to dribble around Henrique.

The equaliser had also put the fire back into Eusebio and United's defence, which had held the twin threat of Eusebio and Torres so well, began to crack. Eusebio was the man to exploit it with his support play. He launched himself forward for a shot that Stepney stopped marvellously, low to his right. The 1966 World Cup final and those tormenting last minutes of normal time during which the Germans drew level had made Charlton more aware of the clock. He was already preparing himself for a further punishing half-hour when the critical moment of the match, the grain of sand that tilted the fine balance, arrived.

With three minutes left United were on the attack again. ' . . . that's Manchester United and Matt, still attacking so close to the end . . .' says Stiles. The ball was headed clear by the Benfica defence to Charlton. Meanwhile, Brennan had gone forward and was out of position. Charlton couldn't get a shot in and was muscled off the ball on the edge of the penalty area. Simoes's swift counter exposed United as he motored to the halfway line with Charlton and Kidd chasing back. He had Stiles, Eusebio, Torres and Foulkes in front of him, while Dunne was out wide with Augusto. 'We're in trouble here,' thought Stiles.

Simoes was very fast and Stiles thought, 'If he pushes in too far I've got him.' He was instinctively lured towards Simoes. As he went for him Torres ran out and Foulkes had to follow. But Stiles didn't know that Foulkes had moved; as Simoes swept the ball forward, he thought Foulkes was still behind him. Stiles, Foulkes and Eusebio all went for the loose ball. Eusebio got there first and poked it past Stiles. He'd broken free of his shadow in a way he'd been unable to do in the World Cup semi-final. It was the worst moment of Stiles's footballing career. Eusebio had a clear path between Foulkes and Dunne. Both defenders converged on him, but he burst through them like a matador delivering the killer thrust.

Eusebio advanced on Stepney. He was clear of United's defence and just had to sidestep the keeper. Eusebio had acres of room and seemed certain to score. His pace and accuracy of shot were legendary. Many in the 100,000 crowd closed their eyes and had their hearts in their mouths as Eusebio bore down on Stepney. Wembley went dead silent for a split second as the crowd held its breath. It seemed certain that the European Cup would be lost again, this time by seconds. 'This is it,' thought Kidd as he put his head between his knees in frustration. Crerand and Charlton were bursting with the thought that in the next few seconds the dream of victory would be blown again. 'We hadn't done anything wrong but it was a good pass, a good run, and there's not much you can do about it,' he says. In St Joseph's Hospital a nerve-wracked Law thought, 'That's it, we're never going to win this thing.' Surprisingly, Foulkes wasn't worried. 'It's incredible and it's happened to me very rarely in my life, perhaps only a couple of times, but I knew we would be all right,' he says. Foulkes knew Eusebio was going to miss.

United's place in history was in their keeper's hands. Stepney knew from watching Eusebio on film and during the 1966 World Cup that he scored spectacular goals. He liked to batter the ball with all the power at his disposal. He was a very strong, well-balanced forward. Stepney was full of doubt as Eusebio raced towards him. United's keeper thought the ball was moving fast, but the Wembley grass was quite long and it slowed on the thick and heavy turf. Stepney had come off his line a bit too early. He was in no-man's land when he suddenly realised that he might be too far out. 'If I keep going he'll chip me,' he thought instinctively. After checking for a couple of paces he began to move back. That may have unsettled Eusebio, who gave the ball another nudge with his right foot, slightly too far ahead of him. Stepney realised Eusebio was teeing himself up to blast a shot and it gave him time to come forward again.

If Eusebio had hit the ball accurately, low down to the left or right, Stepney wouldn't have had a chance. 'If he'd played it or taken it a bit further he would have scored,' says Charlton, 'but I don't think he knew who was behind him . . .' In any case, the Portuguese star always wanted to score great, rather than simple, goals. He loved to make the net bulge. Stepney attacked again in the split-second that Eusebio shot. He made himself as tall as possible by standing right up so that in the striker's eyes he must have filled the goal.

Somewhat predictably, instead of taking his time Eusebio went for power rather than precision. He unloaded one of the fiercest shots ever struck with his left, rather than his stronger right, foot on the run from the edge of the area. Foulkes knew it would go straight into Stepney's arms. The ball was a blur as it was whipped like a bullet from a high-powered rifle. Stepney, seven yards off his line, twisted to his left and checked its flight. 'The ball was within my reach, just to my left,' he recalls. Stepney somehow got to it and was thrown back three yards and on to the ground by the force of the shot. But the ball stuck in his hands. 'Unbelievable, really,' says Charlton, 'but the thing about Alex was he had good hands. We thought then that if we got to extra time we would be okay.'

Stepney climbed back to his feet still clutching the ball, thinking 'Thank you'. 'To my amazement, I found the ball was softer than earlier in the match,' he says. It had either burst when Eusebio hit it or when it hit Stepney – either way, it took away some of the sting. 'If it had been as hard as at the start, it might have travelled faster and beaten me,' he says. Years later Stepney added, 'But the mark's still there on my chest. I've had "Mitre" imprinted there ever since.'

Eusebio's three split-second errors had saved United. A relieved Kidd looked up to see his keeper holding the ball. 'If he'd scored,' says Stepney, 'it was all over.' Eusebio graciously ran up to Stepney, said something in Portuguese, patted him on the back and applauded in a lavish gesture of appreciation. Stepney wasn't sure if Eusebio was paying him a compliment and told the Portuguese striker to get on with the game instead of yapping. All the time Stepney kept his eye on the target for his throw-out.

His apparent cool indifference to Eusebio's gracious acknowledgement could be explained by his early days at Millwall. 'I was taught, when I got the ball, to concentrate on what I had to do, my next move. I was told not to worry about anyone around me, to get on with my game, because they can cheat you. I'm not saying he was trying to cheat me, knock it out of my hand or whatever, but my concern was "Come on, let's get it away". I knew there was very little time left and we had to hold out.'

United should have been beaten. If Eusebio had scored it would surely have buried Busby's long-cherished ambition. Instead, the Black Pearl had missed one of the most important chances of his career. By contrast, Stepney had performed heroically. 'With that one save alone,' wrote Derek Hodgson in *The Manchester United Story*, 'the Londoner Stepney . . . became one of the great sons of Manchester.' Busby later called it one of the greatest saves he'd ever seen. Crerand has a slightly different perspective. 'Frankly, I blame Eusebio more than I give credit to Alex,' he says. 'George Best or Jimmy Greaves would have side-footed the ball, but Eusebio drove it at Alex, thank God.' Law agrees. 'I think Eusebio saw the headlines, because he tried to blast it. If he could have his day again I'm sure he would side-foot it in. If Jimmy Greaves had been on the end of that chance we would have lost.' But Crerand still thought the save was 'quite fantastic, certainly the turning point'. 'It was a remarkable save,' agrees Charlton, 'but one that was only possible because Eusebio went for the spectacular goal instead of settling for the simple thing. Pele would have scored.'

United could sense the game slipping away. Stiles felt that if there had been more than ten minutes left Benfica would probably have won. Best wriggled through once more, but the match was destined for extra time. The football had been a complete anticlimax, even though the second half was a great improvement on the first. Fear of the opposition played a more important part than the skills that caused the fear.

At the end of 90 minutes the game was level at 1–1. It was only the second time that the final had gone to extra time. United were the more relieved to be in the contest. They were shattered. It was the World Cup final all over again, thought Charlton, though the equaliser hadn't come quite so late. How United had survived the last ten minutes of normal time only he knew. The interval would at least give the Reds the chance to pull themselves together and briefly rest their tired and aching limbs for the final battle.

The scene before the start of the extra period resembled a battlefield as both sets of players collapsed onto the lush Wembley turf, their strained and aching legs wracked with cramp, every last ounce of strength almost gone. It had been a punishing 90 minutes and extra time was sure to be draining. But they knew Benfica must be tired as well. Charlton thought United's stamina training would stand them in good stead.

All the United staff – Busby, Murphy, Crompton and John Aston Senior – raced onto the pitch to talk to the players for five precious minutes and to dish out massages and faith. The players were exhorted to further effort, and were told Benfica were finished.

'They're tired, you've got them. You've just got to keep going. Keep going.' 'Come on, come on, we can do it now. We've got 30 minutes.' The players lay on the pitch, exhausted. Aston Snr and Crompton came round giving their calves and thighs a rub down as the precious minutes of rest ticked away. Dunne was knackered. He had cramp and his legs felt 'absolutely tied up'. Stepney pulled his feet. He was in terrible pain. But Busby rubbed his legs and said, 'You're ready now. Let's get it together. We've had no luck.' Dunne recalls the impact Busby had. 'There was no pain that could hurt you as much as seeing him if you'd lost. Because he was miserable. He had this face, like a dog. He'd put on his hat and say, "All right, lads, it didn't happen for us tonight. See you. Enjoy yourselves." And you felt like cutting your throat. You didn't want that to happen.'

As Busby busied himself, he was understandably angry. United had started to give the ball away with careless passing. They were hitting it anywhere instead of continuing their confident play. Busby said exactly the same things as Sir Alf Ramsey had during extra time in the World Cup final. The Boss told them they'd been playing not to lose the game instead of playing to win it, that they were throwing the game away. 'You've won it once, go out and win it again,' he said. And that meant 'Keep the ball, don't be trying to hook it into the stands'. He told Charlton and Crerand it was their job to keep possession in midfield. 'You're giving the ball away too much,' he said. 'It's a warm night and it's not a pitch to give the ball away. Get hold of the ball again . . .' He urged them all to start playing confident football again. 'Benfica are shattered. Look at them. We are in much better shape. We've got this far, now let's finish it.' Busby didn't change tactics, he just urged them on. This was the Busby inspiration that could rouse the players and bring 'heart' back into their play. Stiles was amazed that Busby could be so cool in such a situation.

Wembley was a great pitch to play on – Crerand loved the bouncy, spring surface – but it took its toll on the legs. Best, however, still felt fresh, with plenty of running left in him. He looked at his team-mates. Crerand and Stiles, real competitors, were shaking clenched fists to get the others going. 'They were like that in practice matches, so you can imagine how fired up they were with 30 minutes left to win the European Cup,' says Best. As Crerand was fond of saying, 'Nobby could have persuaded the dead to get up and play.' Best then glanced across at Benfica's players. They were in a much worst state than United. Stiles could also see that the Portuguese didn't want to get up and start again, just like the Germans in the World Cup final. Best knew then that United had the game won. Charlton also thought Benfica seemed to be in a bad way, as if Eusebio's miss had demoralised them. It crossed his mind that United were better equipped for this sort of thing.

Perhaps the Reds would at last be able to show the world what they could do. 'We could easily have lost it, and we all knew it,' says Best. 'Now we had a chance to go and win it.' Green of *The Times* captured the moment: 'So out of the gathering darkness, as Benfica seemed to gather new strength and a new poise, United rose. Once more, as in Spain in their return leg with Real Madrid, they fell back on their morale and unconquerable spirit.' Roger MacDonald wrote, 'The teasing of Matthew Busby, who had gone through agonies on the trainer's bench, was over; now came the reward.'

Charlton had his socks rolled down; Best and Stiles followed suit. 'They also rolled up their sleeves, literally and metaphorically, as darkness at last descended,' wrote Derick Allsop. 'It now seems strange that they wore long sleeves on such a warm evening.'

The extra period couldn't have started more dramatically. United's coaching staff had been right, Benfica were tiring. 'With a matador's instincts, George Best sensed it, and within a minute of the restart he had them on their knees, ripe for the kill,' wrote Joe Lovejoy in *Bestie – A Portrait of a Legend*. Gloriously, Best took Busby at his word and began to play football. It took him less than three minutes to come into his own. Stepney gathered a throw-in from Dunne and rolled the ball to Brennan who knocked it back to him. Brennan would later mischievously claim to have started the move! Stepney now opted for the direct approach. He punted a long ball forward, which was flicked on by Kidd for Best to chase. Cruz seemed to have it under control but he was tiring. He tried to intercept the ball but his legs lagged his thoughts. Best took it off him with lightning reflexes 25 yards from goal. The Irish genius sensed blood as he tore away on a magical run with the defence trailing at his heels. 'George was off,' recalls Charlton, 'giving a fair impersonation of Wembley's electric hare, supremely confident, doing ultimately what he always expected of himself in such situations. When George got away like that goalkeepers were inclined to feel that they had chosen the wrong career, and I'm sure Henrique was no exception.'

The whole stadium was already on its feet in a unified roar as Best got to the ball a vital split second ahead of Jacinto and put it through the defender's legs. Henrique saw the danger and came out towards the edge of his area to narrow the angle. Best sent him the wrong way with a dummy to the right, before dragging the ball with his right foot to the left and rounding the keeper with a delicate, elusive diagonal swerve. Stepney, standing on his goal line, watched as Best's shoulders twitched and he flicked his hips as he shimmied this way and that. For one sickening moment it seemed that the Irishman would catch his own pass too late.

Best had always dreamt that if he was in a position to do it he'd stop the ball on the line and head it in. But Henrique was a bit too quick, so he thought better of it. Best timed his final shot to the second as he clipped the ball towards the beckoning goal with the inside of his left foot. Time seemed to stand still as it rolled agonisingly slowly. For a moment it seemed Humberto might track back in time, or Henrique, diving backwards desperately, would make a dramatic stop on the line, or the ball might go wide. Crerand was sure it wasn't going in. From where he stood it looked as if Henrique was going to keep the ball out. But the combined efforts of Humberto and Henrique weren't enough. Instead, the ball found its way into the inviting, empty net. 'Although Henrique arrived at his intended objective, the ball was nestling in the back of the netting with Wembley repeating its Niagara roar,' wrote Roger MacDonald. Best wheeled away, a single arm held high in triumph as Charlton sank to his knees and Stiles did a cartwheel. It was an image that would become famous thanks to the photographers who captured the moment for eternity. The United fans' red-and-white banners and flags were waving again.

Best had taken his goal so coolly that he could have been on the training ground instead of inside the national stadium. 'It was like something from *Roy of the Rovers*,' he said later, a smile of wonder lighting up his face. Best had slipped the defensive net and thrown open the gates to victory. It was perhaps the most famous goal in English club history. Eamon Dunphy described it as a 'classic street-game goal'. With a flash of brilliance Eusebio had been shown how it was done. United knew they'd won. 'There was no way they [Benfica] were going to score again,' says Charlton, 'and they collapsed psychologically.'

The Portuguese were on their knees as the Reds came in for the kill. Charlton found it baffling that they didn't try to alter their tactics. They did nothing to attempt to solve the problems presented by Aston, who continued to carry the ball past them, running on to the corner, putting the length of the pitch between himself and United's goal. It was the best possible way to waste time. Charlton needn't have worried. The cheers hadn't yet died down when Kidd celebrated his 19th birthday in style.

A minute after Best's glorious goal Aston's pace won another of the many corners he'd forced as he cut Benfica's right flank to pieces with a tremendous extra time display. His performance shamed the United fans who'd booed him earlier in the season. Charlton curled over a right-foot cross from the left. It swirled in the lights inside the penalty area. Sadler won the ball in the air and Kidd headed powerfully towards the goal. His first attempt was turned onto the bar by the flailing Henrique, a player Charlton considered too small to be a keeper. But Kidd noticed he was now off his line. As the ball rebounded Kidd, having kept his balance, rose again like a jack-in-the-box. This time he nodded the ball up and over Henrique into the net, off the underside of the bar. 'It was a soft head, really,' says Kidd.

The millions of fans listening to the radio heard the BBC commentator say '... and it's there ... and Brian Kidd celebrates his nineteenth birthday in the grand manner, by scoring the third goal for Manchester United in the fourth minute of extra time.' Kidd was away and running like a greyhound around Wembley. Nobody could catch him. Kidd couldn't believe it. A dream had come true. Aston, having used up so much energy destroying Benfica, couldn't muster enough strength to join the celebrations surrounding Kidd on the other wing.

It really was all over now. Kidd would never forget seeing the ball in the back of Benfica's net. Although he'd scored 15 League goals, this was only his second in the European Cup. 'Now even United could hear the crowd,' wrote Roger MacDonald, 'a torrent of noise, that re-echoed around the girders in an awe-inspiring crescendo.'

United were rampant, Benfica in disarray. The Reds almost scored again when Best's deflected cross bounced on top of the bar. The United fans were in good voice, singing 'We'll be running round Wembley with the Cup'. Kenneth Wolstenholme told BBC television viewers: 'Undoubtedly the Manchester United fans are outshouting and outsinging the England fans in the World Cup final.' The unusual nature of the match was evident when Charlton was penalised for a foul on Eusebio. Like Stiles before him, Charlton suggested his old rival had dived. Not surprisingly, Stiles gave his captain full backing. Eusebio fired the long-range free kick straight into United's wall.

In the tenth minute of extra time Brennan played the ball up to Kidd. The young striker laid it off to Charlton before instantly spinning out to the right to receive the return pass. Then Charlton, remembering Murphy's coaching, darted towards the near post once again as a decoy. Kidd's right leg was for standing on but as he sucked in Cruz he could see that the Benfica defender was coming to kick him. Kidd knocked the ball past him with his right foot, hurdled his desperate tackle and raced down the wing. Using his weaker right foot again he delivered a precise cross into the stride of the advancing Charlton. Kidd didn't hit it well, but United's captain met the ball at speed. Instantly in control, he unhesitatingly and unerringly spun a dazzling flick high over Henrique's head with his natural right foot. It curled beautifully into the far corner. 'It wasn't really a shot,' says Charlton modestly, 'but he wasn't a very big goalkeeper and it just looped over him.' Kidd saw it differently. 'Hell of a strike,' he says. 'Rifled it in.' Radio listeners had missed a treat and could only imagine what the goal was like. 'Bobby Charlton makes it four for Manchester United and does that characteristic little throw salute of the arm, a little jump in the air, and a battery of photographers come on,' said the BBC radio commentator while Charlton celebrated with Best.

It was a goal that only one of the supreme exponents of the game could have scored. Everyone knew the contest was over now. Benfica certainly did. They'd gone from a team in control to a defeated one in ten minutes. After United's sudden attacking burst they didn't quite know what had hit them. 'In those moments the world shifted on its axis and Wembley all at once became a place for men with steady limbs and firm hearts,' wrote Green of *The Times*.

'We might as well have come off then,' says Best. 'We still had the second period of extra time to play, but they were gone. Out for the count.' Dunne wished he could have come off. 'Come on, get it over with,' he thought. Benfica shouldn't have been able to come back from that, but Dunne still wanted the game to end. He hadn't enjoyed the final – there was too much at stake. He'd felt United were in control of the game but they'd had to work hard to keep it. Dunne was too tired to enjoy the last quarter of an hour.

'There were loads of goals to be scored,' says Charlton. 'If we'd gone at them in the second period of extra time we'd have got more, but it was over anyway.' By now the match was almost like an exhibition game. The remainder of extra time was notable only for the way the packed stadium chanted the name of the selfless Aston, so long the target of the boo-boys at Old Trafford, and for another fine save by Stepney who denied Eusebio yet again.

'Aston might have pondered on the fickle nature of football fans as he received treatment on the touchline after being assaulted by Henrique in a position where he might have anticipated a tackle from the right-back,' says Derick Allsop. 'John-ny Aston, John-ny Aston,' cried those who'd barracked him on not-so-good days. John Aston senior watched with pride and satisfaction.

First, though, Kidd almost added to his tally, while Eusebio tested Stepney with a header. Dunne was hurt in the challenge and Eusebio sportingly stayed with him until play was stopped and help summoned. The gesture won Eusebio warm applause.

Eusebio kept going until the end but Stepney continued to defy the Portuguese maestro. This time the United keeper made a remarkable save low down to his left to keep out a scorching shot, unleashed with virtually no backlift. Charlton, still working, fetching and carrying, got back to head clear. Green would have dearly loved to see a goal from Eusebio before the end 'as a tribute to his marvellous power and feline movement'. Even Stepney was to feel sorry for him after the match.

By now, Best had decided it was time to party. He audaciously flicked the ball up in the air and lobbed it into the penalty area. 'Goodbye, Benfica, goodbye,' sang the United fans. A couple of supporters thought it was all over. They ran onto the pitch but they'd arrived too early; there were still a few minutes to go. Even Stiles knew the end was near. After Eusebio ballooned a shot off high and wide Stiles sportingly acknowledged that the Portuguese star had outfoxed him to create a scoring chance. It was easy to be gracious now the job was done.

Then, at last, the referee blew the final whistle. Dunne's first reaction was, 'Thank God that's over'. It was a relief. Manchester United, the first English club to enter the European Cup, had become the first to win the trophy. 'For so long there were butterflies in the pit of the myriad stomachs and suddenly it was all over,' wrote Green. 'The barber shop critic, that powerful thinker, who said that United would win in extra time, was indeed proved to the hilt and I shall willingly submit to a shave from his razor.'

At the end, happy, laughing, crying crowds at Wembley and in many parts of London and Manchester partied. Busby had not been chasing rainbows after all. His was a dream to be lived. 'It was a triumph against adversity as well as a gladiatorial victory,' wrote Tom Tyrell and David Meek in *The Illustrated History of Manchester United.* 'Little wonder the tears flowed afresh, almost drowning the happiness of the winners.'

The scenes immediately after the match were charged with emotion, which was clear to see in the players' faces. Kidd was in tears, Charlton fell to his knees, Stiles performed a cartwheel. 'It was just fantastic,' he says. 'Manchester lad, United fan – and now I'm in the European Cup-winning team. That made it special to me. Very special.' Foulkes looked cool and calm, as if it had been just another game, but deep down he was as excited as everyone else. 'I was so relieved we had done it, and I looked at Bobby and I could see the same thing with him – he was drained. The feeling of, "That's it, we've done it". It was like a pressure had gone from me. I felt so relaxed, I was floating. I wasn't jumping around. People have accused me of being stone-faced, but I was ecstatic in my own way. It was different for the younger lads – they wanted to have a party. The ones who'd been at Munich wanted to do it more quietly.'

'Having won it, I thought Matt may have had enough, emotionally,' Foulkes went on. 'I wouldn't be surprised if it wasn't the same for Bobby. He was crying. I've never been as emotional as Bobby, but I felt it just the same, just as much. I didn't feel the others were outsiders, but we had a different purpose. I think they were worried about being so overjoyed.' Foulkes and Charlton certainly knew what the occasion meant to Busby.

The Boss, his number two Jimmy Murphy, trainer Jack Crompton and all the other officials raced onto the pitch to hug the players and express their delight at United's success. McGuinness, grinning wildly, unashamedly directed his excited applause towards the Boss. McGuinness wasn't alone in absorbing the personal meaning of this crusade. It was a bittersweet moment for Busby. Typically, he went to Benfica's players first and shook hands with them and the club's officials before turning to his own men, including his magnificent backroom team. Even Benfica couldn't deny United their moment of glory and, to their credit, showed they didn't want to. They, like the rest of the crowd, recognised that at long last the Reds and their manager had fulfilled a dream. Charlton would later say how sorry he felt for the Portuguese. 'They didn't know how much it meant to us,' he said.

Busby had a beatific look on his face that would last for days. Best thought he looked as if he should have had a halo over him. 'He had one of those faces that lights up, like the pictures you see of saints,' he says. It was something journalist Bryon Butler would never forget. 'If I remember one picture of the man it will be that period – the moments, the minutes after the European Cup final. He had a smile then that went twice round his face. That smile, that marvellous smile. It was also for the team that perished at Munich. You had the impression that they were there somewhere up in the rafters of the old stadium looking down.'

It was Busby's hour. He was the heartbeat of Manchester United. To have made his dream come true was reason enough for the players to celebrate. Suddenly everyone was clamouring for Busby. He was the first person all the players ran to, each one – especially Charlton and Foulkes – eager to give him a hug. Busby searched for Charlton among the growing crowd of people in the middle of the pitch. He was in tears as he headed towards his captain. 'They embraced in a moment that required no caption,' says Derick Allsop. There was sadness as well as joy when Busby and Charlton fell into each other's arms, feeling far more than the glow of victory. 'What images must have flashed through his mind,' wondered Charlton. 'Duncan Edwards, powering forward with the ball at his feet; Eddie Colman shimmying this way and that; the near oblivion of a Munich airstrip.' Charlton, too, was familiar with those images. Todd in *The Guardian* seemed to capture the moment: 'And did he [Busby] look up briefly at the heavens as if seeking – and getting, no doubt – the approval of the spirits of Munich?' It was the end of the journey, the climax to a great adventure that, like life itself, had contained both sorrows and successes.

One by one, the players hugged their Boss. Dunne was half running around; his legs were killing him. He saw Busby coming towards him and gave him a playful tap on the back of the head. Dunne felt strangely distant. He was going through the motions of people talking to him, blankly looking at them, saying things, but it was as if his mouth wasn't moving. 'I could just do with being with my wife and father,' he thought.

The players, the older ones still in tears, tried to break with Wembley tradition and persuade Busby to go up and receive the cup. He refused. He was never a showman, and his reward was the victory. 'If Munich was the low point of his career, then this was the highest,' says Crerand. 'He was like a little kid of five years old on Christmas morning.' Torres, waiting for the right moment, asked Charlton to exchange shirts. United's captain said he couldn't, not yet anyway. There was something he had to get first.

Charlton had a fresh spring in his step as he began to climb the steps to the Royal Box. He combed his wispy hair with his hand as he prepared to receive the coveted European Cup. Wembley rocked with a joyful noise, red-and-white banners waved and the whole place was transformed into a carnival. His happy but exhausted team-mates wearily dragged themselves up the steps behind their captain. There was a huge roar from the crowd as Charlton shook hands. He just about managed to raise the huge silver trophy chest-high. 'The moment Bobby took the cup it cleansed me,' said Busby. 'It eased the pain of the guilt of going into Europe. It was my justification.' While the Boss enjoyed the moment, Charlton was struggling with the huge trophy. 'The first thing I thought was how heavy it was, because at the end I was physically rather than emotionally drained. I've never known humidity like it in this country before or since.' But Charlton lifting the cup was the moment the crowd and the millions watching on TV had been waiting for, and the gesture was met with a wall of cheers as the fans expressed their delight. United's players were surprisingly subdued. 'Perhaps they felt an obligation to observe some perceived, dignified protocol,' says Derick Allsop. 'More likely, a psychological burden, intensified over the years, had taken its toll.' Kidd was less withdrawn than some of the others. He smiled happily and kissed his medal.

Charlton was too exhausted to carry the heavy cup around the stadium so he handed it over to the others. Busby looked on proudly as his players went on a lap of honour with the gleaming trophy. They put on a celebratory show, dancing and jigging around the track, for their besotted, delirious fans. The players then saluted the Stretford Enders stationed in one section of the stadium. Stiles produced his famous toothless grin once again as he performed a jig of joy for a delirious Wembley. But for some time the emotional ordeal was too much. Charlton slowly trotted along at the back, no doubt thinking of all the years that had gone to make up that moment of glory.

The satisfaction, public or private, would be with them for the rest of their days. 'It was a moment of high emotion, a dream come true, a pinnacle of exultation after a valley of dark despair,' wrote Roger MacDonald. 'It may not have been the greatest United team that took the trophy, but it had those priceless qualities of resilience and experience to do what no other Football League team had done.

As the new United paraded with the cup, one sensed the gleeful, whispering shadows of the old [United], flitting across a field they had graced in the sunshine. Busby, a man of deep compassion and understanding, remained the magnet of them all.'

Eusebio received more appreciation as he again retreated, the vanquished hero. 'It was nice for Matt Busby to win the European Cup,' he says, 'but I was not happy that night.'

The party went on in United's dressing room. As the players took the mickey out of Charlton for scoring with his head, Stepney was amazed to find his older brother Eric there. He'd blagged his way in. United's keeper sat on the bench under his peg fishing for a cigarette with tears – huge, baby tears – rushing down his face. The emotion of the occasion was just too much for him.

Busby sought out his fellow Munich survivors, Charlton and Foulkes. They shared unspoken perspectives on the victory that nobody else could fully appreciate or understand. Hugging Charlton, Busby said: 'This is the greatest night of my life, the fulfillment of my dearest wish to become the first English side to win the European Cup. I'm proud of the team, proud for Bobby Charlton and Billy Foulkes who have travelled the long road with me the last eleven years.'

Charlton felt he'd reached more than the climax of his career. It was the ultimate achievement, not just for the individual players, but for the club and for Busby. Charlton had been present as the curtain fell on an era that had started, more or less, with his debut in European football. He was a Busby Babe when winning the magnificent Cup of Champions would have been a novel and exciting triumph for a British club, at a time when European football was viewed suspiciously by the English.

It was the end of a marathon pursuit for Busby as well. 'I have chased and chased this European Cup with many disappointments, but here it is at last,' he said. 'I am the proudest man in England tonight. The boys have done us proud. They showed in Madrid that they have the heart to fight back and tonight they showed us the stuff that Manchester United are made of. I am proud of them all.'

'At last Manchester United have climbed their Everest and after 11 years of trial and effort their dreams have come true,' wrote

Geoffrey Green in his match report under the headline SEVEN MAGIC MINUTES THAT GAVE MANCHESTER UNITED THE CUP. 'So the crown sits on the heads of the first English club to enter this competition, seeing its wide horizons and the possibility of it on a world scale.'

David Miller explained why Busby deserved the victory in *Cup Magic*. 'It was belated reward for the courage with which he had pulled himself and the club together after Munich; reward for a vision of the game in which, in the main, he had tried to steer towards what was noble; a reward of sorts for the families of the Munich dead who had been invited to the match.' Busby always used to say that in memory of the lads who had died, it was right and proper that one day United should win the European Cup.

Benfica's proud manager Otto Gloria, magnanimous in defeat, said sincerely and quietly, 'The title is in good hands.' The Portuguese, as always, were very friendly and sporting, particularly the captain Coluna. But United, following on from the example set by Celtic the year before, had further loosened the vice-like grip the Latin nations had on the Champions Cup since it began in the mid-'50s. Few occasions, except perhaps the Matthews' final in '53 and the World Cup final in '66, had equalled the joy expressed at Wembley that night.

Crerand had always felt that United would beat Benfica. '. . . playing at Wembley was a big help. I had a little doubt when it was one each, and Eusebio went through on Alex. The first half was a bit scrappy – there were a lot of nerves. But in extra time we ran amok. John Aston was magnificent. David Sadler should have had a hat-trick – he missed chance after chance. And George maybe should have passed it once or twice.'

'As a game of football it was a non-starter,' recalls Foulkes. 'But for drama it would take some beating. The team wasn't as effective as it had been in the past, although in saying that I'm thinking of myself, really. George was great . . . Johnny Aston came in and played out of his skin . . . Paddy took a lot on his shoulders as well. But, to be honest, it was nothing like the side we knew, nothing . . .'

Aston felt a great deal of personal satisfaction; he was entitled to, after having such a difficult time in the League. 'People say it was the best game I had for United and I think I'd probably agree. I'm not being immodest, but if they'd had a man-of-the-match award I think I would have won it.' Aston had warmed the hearts of those watching, especially his father, the club coach. Perhaps United's all-blue strip had something to do with his performance. 'Blue is a good colour for the Astons,' he said. 'My dad wore a blue shirt when he won an FA Cup winners' medal with United in 1948.' Aston had produced a memorable performance (one he'd never match). It was a storybook finish to what had been a trying season for him.

Sadler was relieved after squandering so many opportunities. But he didn't really have cause to regret his profligacy in front of goal. 'I was ready to shoulder the blame of losing after missing a couple of early chances,' he recalled years later. 'I missed three really good chances in the second [half], but I always think that if I hadn't missed those we wouldn't have had extra time so it worked out okay.' Sadler had, in fact, made a great contribution to United's victory with his precise passing and the way he'd repeatedly turned defence into attack.

Stiles had been concerned during the build-up to the final, with some saying he might try to kick Eusebio out of the match. 'I was frightened before the game with all the ballyhoo about how I would mark Eusebio,' said Stiles. 'People were suggesting I was a clogger. One newspaper said he [Eusebio] had asked the referee for protection. I just don't believe he ever said that. I respect him and I find him all right. I have never gone out to kick him and I have played against him four times.' In those four games – three for United and one for England – Eusebio had scored just one goal, and that was a penalty. Stiles had once again played Eusebio fairly and with superb skill. His emphasis had consistently been on tactical positioning rather than physical contact.

The two fullbacks had enjoyed a good day. Dunne completed a hat-trick of cup medals by adding the European Cup to those he'd won in the FA Cup and the Irish Cup. Yet he wasn't entirely happy. 'We'd got to win it, and yet when we did it was a terrible anti-climax for me. I'm sure it was for other players too. Sometimes you win a game and think, "Yeah". Not that.' Still, Dunne did love winning the European Cup, because it was so important to him. 'I would have thought – and I'm sure a lot of us would have [too] – we were failures if we hadn't won. And what would have happened I don't know. It wasn't a situation where I was worried about my position, because the manager thought an awful lot of me. It's just that everything was geared to it.' Brennan was just grateful to have played at all. 'I lost my place just before United played in the final of the FA Cup in 1963,' he said. 'This time I came in on the last lap, so naturally it meant even more to me.'

Charlton believes he speaks for everyone when he says the players felt they'd performed a duty for the club. 'For some of us it was a family thing,' he says. 'We had been together for so long, and while people recognised that we had some great teams, there was nothing in the European record book until 1968 to show for it. Sir Matt had made us pioneers in Europe and winning the European Cup was not just a Manchester occasion, it was for the whole country.' Foulkes had never thought for a minute that United would lose. 'I think we were playing for Matt and for the boys. I've never spoken to Bobby about it, but I think he felt the same.'

The lads never asked Charlton about Munich. 'Even now there isn't a day goes by when I don't think about it,' he told Derick Allsop in *Reliving the Dream*, 'and, of course, I've since flown there many times. But it was always a private thing and they respected that. They were obviously aware of the history and the significance of the European Cup. They were aware of their responsibilities, as well. But they were good players in their own right, so why shouldn't they win the European Cup? We were never really going to be a *proper* football club until we won it.'

The sense of achievement was immeasurable to men like Busby, Murphy, Foulkes and Charlton. The Boss and his assistant had walked into numerous dressing rooms and bitten hard on many disappointments. Foulkes and Charlton had followed them through the door on most of those sad occasions. 'I'd lived through the gamut of emotions for the European Cup,' says Charlton, 'right from when we first played in Europe. It had been a long and painful journey. But we made it.' Now the champagne – vintage after being kept waiting so long – could be opened.

Eight

The Celebrations

While United's players hugged on the Wembley turf Denis Law, the forgotten man, was enjoying his own celebrations in St Joseph's Hospital having a few beers in the ward with his friends. After the game the players telephoned Law, who was by then in a drunken haze. The BBC had planned to take their cameras into his room to get an immediate reaction to United's triumph in a live interview with David Coleman. But Law was not in a fit state to appear on television. 'He's too emotional to talk to you,' the BBC were told by a nun. The interview was quickly cancelled. Law later admitted to Coleman that he was drunk on McEwan's lager. 'If you ask him now, he only laughs and says what a great night it was,' says Pat Crerand. At Wembley, Crerand went into the dressing room with a bottle of champagne and found Coleman telling the players what had happened to Law's interview.

Law wasn't the only one to miss out on the celebrations that night. Charlton was absolutely drained of all emotion and energy, and kept fainting. He'd been the same after United's come-from-behind draw in Madrid. On that occasion, while the lads had gone out on the town, Charlton couldn't face anyone or anything and had crept into bed hoping to get some sleep. Exactly the same thing now happened in London. As the excitement began to subside Charlton felt very tired and a little sick. The reception at Wembley was too much for him. He was very emotional, with no appetite for exuberance. He needed air, so he sloped off with Brennan and sat in the stand. Everybody else had gone except for some workers removing seats in preparation for the greyhound racing. 'Football is like that,' wrote Rick Glanville in *Sir Matt Busby – A Tribute*. 'Defeat requires bucking up, solidarity, a different kind of strength and brashness; victory often leads to a slump, an anti-climax, a time for other thoughts.' In the tunnel below, Charlton found Crerand, who was also suffering. 'Crerand was the same,' he says, 'sick as a dog even before we left Wembley.' The carpets laid out for the royal guests had already been pushed to one side. Charlton and Crerand sat on them, not saying a word. On the streets of Manchester people danced and sang the night away and planned the team's homecoming the next day.

United eventually left Wembley for the Russell Hotel in London's West End, where the club had arranged a big dinner-dance for the team and their guests, David Coleman and his wife among them. When the players arrived, Johnny Berry, Kenny Morgans and the families of the Busby Babes were already there; all the parents of the Munich victims had been invited. 'Great,' thought Charlton. 'This is going to be brilliant.' Sadler looked at Charlton and Busby. They both looked drained. In fact, the Boss looked very old, which he'd never seemed before to Sadler. 'There was a sense that this was the end of something momentous,' he says, 'there really was a sense of that and it was almost immediate, not something that came days or weeks later.' Sadler had another disturbing thought about the future: 'Is there anywhere to go from here, even in defending the Cup? I don't know . . .'

Charlton went upstairs with his wife Norma to get ready. He was dressed first and sat on the bed waiting for her. 'Right,' she said. 'Let's go down.' But when Charlton stood up the blood seemed to drain out of him. He felt fine lying down, but every time he tried to rise he felt nauseous and started to pass out before he reached the door. He attempted to get up five times but couldn't manage it. If he'd drunk water, as the players do today, he'd have been all right. Instead, he was completely dehydrated. In another room, Crerand felt much the same. Charlton told his wife to go downstairs and join the party. He'd join her when he felt better. But after nearly passing out at the top of the stairs trying to follow her, he realised he just couldn't face the official banquet. His stomach muscles were so tense. He went back to his room and slept, leaving Norma to attend the banquet alone. Crerand, on the other hand, recovered and accompanied his wife Noreen to the dinner.

The entertainment featured the United 'house band', Joe Loss and his orchestra. Busby and Loss were old friends. The band's former singer, Frank Rogers, was a driver on Busby's army team Italian convoy during the war. Each time a player came into the banqueting room Joe Loss got the band to play Cliff Richard's 'Congratulations'. The club had invited representatives of all the teams they'd played in the previous rounds as well as all the old players and the relatives of the lads who'd died in Munich. 'That gave an extra dimension to the evening,' says Crerand. It was a fantastic night, but in a sense also very sad.

Nellie Busby and Jimmy and Agnes Matthie were there from Old Orbiston as well as Matt's sisters Delia, Kathy and Margaret. So were Eddie Colman's parents and Duncan Edwards's folks. Crerand had a long talk with Edwards's dad. He didn't really know what to say. There were lots of tears. Crerand kept thinking that if Edwards had been alive he'd have played instead of him. Someone said he'd have been 31 on this very night. The parents of the boys who'd died at Munich were all delighted United had won but the occasion brought back sad memories. It was suggested that Charlton had failed to show up because he couldn't handle the emotion, but that wasn't the case; he was simply too ill to go. Everyone he wanted to see was there, including his former team-mates Harry Gregg, Kenny Morgans, Johnny Berry and Jackie Blanchflower.

Most players had a much better time. 'It was wonderful,' says Stepney. 'That was the pinnacle. That was everything. Ten years after the crash and he [Busby] had achieved what he probably should have achieved ten years earlier. And he just took over the evening.' Busby was presented with the Manager of the Year award and a cheque for £1,000. Joe Loss presented Kidd with a giant birthday cake in front of his mum and dad. The youngster thought it was a nice gesture. Perhaps surprisingly, Kidd also felt the evening was 'a bit of an anti-climax, but for a local boy it was still a wonderful experience'.

Later, Loss and the boys convinced Busby to sing. There was only one tune appropriate for the mixture of feelings Busby experienced that night. 'Play Louis Armstrong's "Wonderful World",' he laughed before launching into Satchmo's song of hope, beauty and togetherness, reflecting precisely the qualities Busby saw in the game he loved. Everyone joined in, applauding him. 'He was a better manager than he was a singer!' says Stepney, who saw Busby as an ambitious man who held this quality within himself. There was so much going on that Busby dropped his cheque during the evening and probably would never have remembered if someone hadn't picked it up and returned it to him. 'I think he'd had a few,' says Stepney. Aston thought it was a 'strange night'. Glorious, but strange.

Best enjoyed himself. He got drunk and later wouldn't recall much about the victory night. 'I was celebrating and I had every reason to,' he says. 'The skinny, shy little boy who came off the ferry from Belfast seven years before had done his job.' Foulkes said 'See you in the morning' as he went off to bed, but there was no way he intended to be there in the morning. He had to be at Davyhulme Golf Club in time to play in a competition that started at ten o'clock – less than 12 hours after he'd collected his European Cup winners' medal. Charlton's wife Norma returned to her room and told Bobby it was a pity he hadn't made it because the Old Man had sung 'What a Wonderful World'.

Meanwhile, the M1 motorway was thronged with fans that steamy night. The last of the supporters returning from London by train didn't arrive at Manchester Piccadilly until 4 a.m.

Best had gone his own way by the time the party moved on to drag artist Danny La Rue's nightclub. His friend Malcolm Wagner thinks Best probably went to see his girlfriend Jackie Glass. England internationals Stepney, Stiles, Charlton and Sadler were under strict instructions from Sir Alf Ramsey not to go out and have a late night.

They all had to be up bright and early next morning, to travel to Germany for a friendly before heading to Italy for the European Nations Cup. Charlton was too ill to go anywhere that night, but Brennan, Sadler, Alex Stepney and his wife Pam and Stiles were among the group that headed off to La Rue's club. The players enjoyed a long party – hardly anyone got to bed. Stiles and Stepney were among those who rolled in at 5 a.m. 'Alf [Ramsey] never knew,' says the United keeper. While the younger players partied the veterans enjoyed a quiet sense of satisfaction; relief was their main emotion. Busby stayed in his room for a while and thought about what he'd achieved. In the early hours he was heard walking along the hotel corridor crooning 'What a Wonderful World'. Sadler again wondered where United could go from here. 'It was a marvellous win and a marvellous night for all of us, but I think, if the truth be known, some of us, the younger ones or those who had come into the club after Munich, did feel slightly like interlopers, a little bit out of it. We were all in it together, it's a team game and we were all elated with the victory at Wembley, the achievement and significance of it all. But at the same time we were aware it was about Matt, Bill and Bobby, in particular, because of all they had been through. Bobby was drained. So was Matt, and for the first time he looked old, and you wondered what was left.'

It had indeed been a marvellous and yet tearful night. Foulkes decided not to stick around in the morning. At 6 a.m. he left with his wife and sons to drive back to Manchester. When Charlton heard more about the night's celebrations from Norma the next morning he felt the Boss was entitled to sing his favourite – 'What a Wonderful World' – it summed up what had been an incredible experience for them all.

Nine

Post-match Verdict

The players were overjoyed at their success, especially after beating the great Real Madrid and Benfica – two of the legendary European teams. Nobody could say United's path to glory had been easy. There was relief that after trying for so long the biggest trophy in club football was theirs. 'I knew it would come one day,' says Charlton, 'yet it was in the nick of time.'

'Wembley against Benfica proved the end of the rainbow, the moment of triumph for Sir Matt Busby,' says Foulkes. 'I had come the whole way with the Boss trying to become champions of Europe. I thought the destruction of our team at Munich would have been the end of it, but he patiently put together another team. I'm proud to have been a part of it and for those of us who had lost our friends coming home from a European tie in 1958 it seemed the right tribute to their memory.'

'It was a save from one of the fiercest shots ever hit in a football match that did as much as anything to bring the European Cup back to Manchester,' says Kidd. 'For had Alex not been able to hang on, it would have been 2–1 to Benfica. And I think that they would have won.

'It's the winning of the thing. It's the crash, the history. You felt like you were going down a tunnel, and every time you lost you felt like a flop. But to win the European Cup, that was going to take a great deal of pressure off you. Because now you were there, and you know when you've been there once, you can be there again quite easily. Because you're good enough and suddenly the flowers are blossoming. You're now the top team and it's taken this great weight off your back . . . you've won it at last.

'When you think that Matt nearly died at Munich and then, ten years later, had created another great side and won the European Cup, it is incredible. He had taken English football into Europe, way back in the '50s, and it was fitting Manchester United should become the first English team to win the European Cup. The Cup-Winners' Cup and UEFA Cup are good trophies, but the main one is the European Cup.'

The press were delighted United had achieved their date with destiny. WHAT A GREAT DAY FOR BUSBY the *Daily Express* splashed across its front page the next morning. 'At last, at last! We have done it,' said Busby in a ghosted article. 'It is Manchester United's European Cup, my dearest longing for the club. It is the greatest moment of my life.' Accompanying the story was a Roy Ullyett cartoon capturing the 'end of an 11-year dream'. Busby was sitting up in bed, smiling, in striped pyjamas with his left hand grasping the European Cup which was sitting on his bedside cabinet. 'I woke up and it was really there!' he's saying. The possible resignation of the French President, General Charles de Gaulle, was restricted to a short, single-column story. At the foot of the page was a report on Sir Ivor's win in the Derby.

BUSBY DREAM COMES TRUE AT LAST headlined *The Guardian*. BUSBY'S MARVELS WIN LIKE DREAM said *The Sun*. A picture of Busby holding the cup aloft filled page one of the *Daily Mirror* alongside the headline MATT'S MADE IT! 'It's bloody marvellous . . . I'm the proudest man in England,' he was quoted as saying. Frank McGhee introduced his match report in *The Mirror* with MANCHESTER UNNITED ARE THE NEW KINGS OF EUROPE. Elsewhere there was a picture of the emotional Law entering into the spirit of the occasion as he watched the first pictures of the revellers in Trafalgar Square on TV.

'In truth, it was not a vintage European Cup year,' wrote Derek Hodgson in *The Manchester United Story* some years later. 'Yet, as any champion will confirm, the crowning performance is to defeat all the opposition and that is what United did in a match of intense nervous excitement and spectacle, whatever the technical deficiencies may have been.'

Ten

The Homecoming

The next day the players got up very late. The United party and the European Cup were scheduled to travel back to Manchester on a private train from Euston Station. Unfortunately, United's four England players couldn't be with their team-mates.

For Stiles, not taking part in the victory parade through the streets of Manchester was the only sad part about winning the European Cup. 'All my life I'd wanted to come back with the cup in an open coach, through Manchester to the Town Hall,' he says. 'I didn't in '63 when we won the FA Cup because I didn't play in the final. And I couldn't in '68 because I'd gone off with England . . . That was a big disappointment, missing that. I'd have loved it.' Poor Charlton didn't even get to see the old players he'd missed the night before because he had to leave the hotel at 8 a.m. with his England colleagues. By that time David Coleman and his wife were travelling along the M4 to get back home and get the kids to school. (Years later Coleman wouldn't be able to remember too much about the night before!)

A few minutes before boarding United's train from London, Crerand met an old Scottish man and his friend when they came up to congratulate him and tell him what a great night it had been at

Wembley. They now stayed in Manchester and were die-hard United fans. Crerand thought they seemed like a couple of nice blokes who were obviously having a whale of a time. 'Are you going back to Manchester?' Crerand asked. 'Yes,' they replied, 'we're going back on the train.' There were a lot of trains leaving London that day for Manchester but Crerand was boarding a nine-coach 'special' laid on for United's players, officials and specially invited friends. The club had arranged that everything on the train was free. 'You're not getting on that one,' said Crerand motioning towards United's train. 'That's a private train.' The two men didn't say anything.

Crerand got on the train and sat down. A few minutes later he walked through to the bar. If you wanted a drink you simply asked for it and you got it. Crerand was playing cards with some of the boys to pass the time when he felt a hand on his shoulder and heard a voice saying, 'Hello, Pat, how's it going? This is a great train, isn't it?' Crerand looked up and saw the same two Scots who'd talked to him in the station. They looked the same as before, except that by then each carried a full bottle of whisky under their arm. Crerand had a laugh with them for a while and when they'd gone the boys naturally asked who they were. When Crerand told them he had no idea, they soon realised why he was laughing. They could imagine the two enterprising characters telling their friends what a generous club United were, giving you free food and drink and a bottle of whiskey as a souvenir.

Crerand soon forgot about the two happy gatecrashers towards the end of the journey. The players would never know how anyone knew the train was United's, but there were people waving to them at the side of the track and from the platforms of all the stations they passed through. At Manchester Piccadilly, United's victory train pulled into Platform 11. The party boarded a special 20-year-old red and white open-top bus which was waiting to take the team around the town to the Town Hall. The idea was that the players would be on top showing the Cup. But when Crerand ran up to the open top deck he nearly fell down again. His two Scottish friends from the train were already sitting down, quietly enjoying the view. While Crerand admired their ingenuity he felt this was going a bit too far and quickly pointed them out to United's secretary, Les Olive. He told them they had no right to be there and they left cheerily, clutching their bottles of whisky.

The scenes in Manchester were fantastic. The whole city was out on the streets. The newspapers estimated that a quarter of a million people had turned out to welcome their heroes home. Busby had always loved the fans and always found time to talk to them; now he was overwhelmed by their affection for him and his team. The coach proceeded at three miles an hour in a convoy of seven coaches and a security van, with the police forming a five-deep chain. It took the players to the Town Hall for a civic reception. (Charlton, Stiles and Stepney were missing because they were travelling with the England squad who were competing in the European Nations Cup and Foulkes was also absent after having come back to Manchester with his family.)

Thousands upon thousands of United supporters (250,000 by some estimates) lined Manchester's streets from the railway station to the Town Hall in Albert Square. Every street seemed packed and they got a fantastic reception when they arrived at the Town Hall, where they were received by the mayor before crowding onto a specially erected balcony to show off the European Cup and hear speeches by the mayor and Busby. Crerand was sure that no royalty had ever had a reception like the Boss got when he spoke to the crowd that night. At the civic reception Busby expressed his gratitude. 'I said that last night was the greatest of my life, but I don't know whether tonight is the second best or the greatest as well. I feel very deeply for the enthusiasm which the crowd outside has shown to the boys.'

Amid the celebrations Crerand spared a thought for players like young Francis Burns, who'd lost his place in the United side just two games before the end of the season to the more experienced Shay Brennan. Crerand told guests at the civic reception: 'We have a squad of first-team players and I would like you to thank from us those who were not on the park against Benfica but who helped us reach the final.'

After the cup had been shown again and again, the players turned to edge their way off the wooden platform. Then Crerand heard a voice behind him saying, 'What a night, Pat . . . What a night, eh?' He thought, 'It can't be. Nobody could talk their way onto that platform.' But sure enough, the two Scottish lads from the train were standing behind him, smiling all over their faces and still clutching their bottles of whisky. Crerand couldn't believe they'd got away with it. If he hadn't seen it himself he'd have said it was impossible for anyone without official passes to get aboard the train, the bus and the platform. 'Only after a hard night would you even try it on,' he says. In a way, though, he was secretly pleased they'd succeeded. He reckoned their story just about proved that if two Scots set out to get somewhere no amount of Englishmen can stop them!

A few hours later Busby went round to St Joseph's Hospital with the cup. He wanted to show the missing member of United's triumvirate what they'd won at Wembley. 'That was a great moment for me – and a very special one that I don't think many people either knew about or will remember,' says Law. 'Not being in the team for the European Cup final was very hard on Denis,' says Crerand. 'Even though he's got a winner's medal he is still likely to say, "Oh, I didn't win the European Cup. I wasn't in the team." But a lot of players appeared in some of the earlier rounds, including Law, and they helped United win the cup just as much as those who played in the final. Anyway, if Law had been fit he'd have been selected.'

The European Cup was to make a splendid sight as the centrepiece of United's glittering trophy room in the visitors' lounge at Old Trafford. They'd earned it the hard way. Shortly afterwards Busby was knighted for his services to football. It was wonderful recognition for all he'd done to develop the game at all levels. The boys he'd tragically lost in the snow at Munich would have been proud of the Boss.

Book Three
History

Prologue

Busby's Legacy

Manchester United had conquered Europe and were feeling on top of the world. But it would be more than 30 years before they would once again stand at the pinnacle of European football. The players knew Busby's quest was over. Charlton and Foulkes were also nearing the end of their careers. They lost their grip on the European Cup by 2–1 on aggregate against Italian side AC Milan in the semi-final after Charlton scored their only goal in the second leg at Old Trafford. 'It was the end of an era really,' says David Sadler. 'Soon afterwards Sir Matt Busby announced that he was stepping out of the front line to make way for a younger man.' It would be another seven years before United were back in European competition. Even worse was the shame of relegation at the end of the 1973–74 season. By that time Best, Charlton and Law had all gone. Ironically, Law had joined rivals Manchester City and his goal against United condemned them to the drop.

United went straight back up to the top flight as champions and got back into Europe via the UEFA Cup in 1976–77 by virtue of finishing third in the league. They lost to Juventus in the second round. An FA Cup win in 1977 saw them qualify for the European

Cup Winners' Cup. Porto knocked them out in the second round. In 1980 the UEFA Cup beckoned again but Widzew Lodz beat them in the first round, as did Valencia at the same stage two years later.

A glimpse of European glory came in 1984 when they reached the Cup Winners' Cup semi-final where they lost 3–2 on aggregate to Juventus. The following season saw a fourth round UEFA Cup exit to Videoton of Hungary. United finally tasted European success again in 1991 when they beat Barcelona 2–1 in Rotterdam with both goals from Mark Hughes, but they failed to defend the trophy after a second-round defeat to Athletico Madrid.

Torpedo Moscow beat the Reds on penalties in the first round of the UEFA Cup in 1993, but United won the first Premier League that season and returned to the European Cup for the first time since 1969. Turkish side Galatasaray controversially knocked the Reds out on penalties, but they won their first domestic double and had earned another crack at the European crown. It didn't last long as away defeats to Barcelona and Gothenburg put them out at the group stage.

Blackburn pipped United to the Premier League title in 1995 and Everton beat them in the FA Cup final, so the Reds had to settle for a UEFA Cup place. But their European ambitions were short-lived when unfancied Russian side Rotor Volgograd went through on away goals in the first round. United concentrated on the domestic programme and won another double of Premier League and FA Cup after beating rivals Liverpool at Wembley.

Their 1997 Champions League campaign prospered and they reached the semi-final for the first time in 28 years after qualifying from a group including Juventus and beating Portuguese side Porto in the quarter-finals. United were drawn against Ottmar Hitzfeld's Borussia Dortmund in the semi-finals and should have won. Instead, they were unfortunate to lose both legs 1–0 and missed the chance to play Juventus in Munich, scene of the devastating air crash 29 years before. It was Eric Cantona's last attempt to win the coveted European Cup, as he retired soon after. Another Premier League title was scant consolation for failure yet again on Europe's biggest stage.

Forty years after Munich and thirty after that wonderful Wembley night when Best and Charlton weaved their magic against

Benfica, United tried again to emulate Busby's team. They reached the quarter-finals once more but went out to Monaco on away goals after a creditable 0–0 stalemate in France and a 1–1 draw at Old Trafford. Monaco goalkeeper Fabien Barthez had little to do in either leg, which summed up United's increasing frustration in the Champions League.

One

Route to Barcelona

Arsenal had thrown down the gauntlet to United when the Gunners won their second domestic double of Premiership and FA Cup in 1998 to match the Reds' own achievement in 1996. Having been knocked off their domestic perch and with a fourth attempt to win the Champions League having already failed, United manager Alex Ferguson felt the Busby legacy slipping away. He watched that year's Champions League final between Real Madrid and Juventus full of sorrow in a bar in Tel Aviv.

'We had to thrust ahead of Arsenal again in England and we had to give ourselves the best possible chance of ending our frustrations in the European Cup,' says Ferguson. 'To achieve those aims, I had to strengthen my squad, and PLC (Manchester United's public limited company – in other words, the board) would have to be persuaded that providing the money made sense.'

The Old Trafford hierarchy knew they had to spend big to reclaim the domestic throne and succeed in their number one priority of winning the Champions League. Chairman Martin Edwards therefore sanctioned a trio of transfers totalling a massive £27 million as Ferguson twice broke the club's transfer record.

Towards the end of the season, while Arsenal were busy sweeping up the domestic prizes, United swooped for Dutchman Jaap Stam of PSV Eindhoven for a club record of £10.6 million. As the new campaign was about to begin, Ferguson's lengthy pursuit of Parma's Swedish international Jesper Blomqvist bore fruit when he signed for £4.4 million. And, finally, just six days after the start of the season the seemingly endless Dwight Yorke transfer saga ended when the Trinidadian with the infectious smile left Aston Villa after United agreed to pay a new club record fee of £12.6 million. 'Ideally I would have liked to add a further striker of international calibre to my armoury but at least I had pushed through the improvements to the squad that I saw as being essential if we were to have a successful season,' says Ferguson in his autobiography *Managing My Life*.

Stam soon became a rock in defence and Yorke's arrival spawned one of the most potent striking partnerships United had seen for decades as he teamed up with Andy Cole. The boys of '96 – Gary Neville, David Beckham, Paul Scholes and Nicky Butt – had the benefit of three more Premiership campaigns under their belts and all except Butt now had World Cup experience after England's campaign at France in '98, which had ended in brave defeat to Argentina. Schmeichel's mid-season announcement that he would leave at the end of the campaign was a distraction, but the Dane had recaptured his best form and was playing as well as during his phenomenal 1996 season.

United's challenge for the Champions League had begun in August when they played a qualifying tie against Polish side LKS Lodz. It was a legacy of their failure to win the Premier League. United completed Yorke's transfer just hours before beating Lodz 2–0 at Old Trafford with goals from Giggs and Cole. In the away leg they stifled their Eastern European opponents to secure a 0–0 draw and reach the group stage. The draw took place in Monte Carlo on 27 August and United were put in the 'group of death' alongside Barcelona, Bayern Munich and Brondby. It was by far the toughest of the six groups.

The draw had thrown up a trip to Bavaria to play Bayern in what would be United's first competitive match in Munich since the 1958 air disaster. The Reds met Barcelona in a thrilling 3–3 draw at Old

Trafford before travelling to Munich, a place that would always be a part of the club's history. An estimated 2,400 supporters followed United to the German city and took their places among a packed 55,000 crowd at the Olympic Stadium, where a minute's silence in memory of those who'd died in the air disaster was only broken by a lone bugler playing *The Last Post*.

United played well and were leading 2–1 until the last minute, when Schmeichel had a rush of blood to the head and completely misjudged a long throw from French international fullback Bixente Lizarau. 'I'm not making any excuses for that – it was plain stupidity,' said Schmeichel later. Brazilian striker Giovane Elber jumped with Sheringham at the far post and, although nobody knew who'd got the final touch, the ball ended up in United's net.

Bayern had salvaged a point and denied the Reds the distinction of becoming the first team to beat the Germans at home during the Oktoberfest beer festival. Sheringham's involvement in a last-minute goal was to become a key feature of United's Champions League campaign, but on this occasion it stopped them winning away against one of Europe's elite clubs for the first time.

Fortunately, their next away fixture was more rewarding as they thrashed Danish side Brondby 6–2 to top the group. The return leg at Old Trafford was just as convincing, with United winning 5–0.

The trip to Barcelona's Nou Camp was next on the agenda and produced another remarkable game. After falling behind to a Sonny Anderson goal, United equalised through Yorke and then went ahead twice, as Cole and Yorke were on target again. Barcelona pegged them back each time. Brazilian genius Rivaldo struck twice and the match ended in another 3–3 draw. 'You've got to admire Rivaldo,' said Ferguson. 'He was their star player and the man who made all the difference for Barcelona.' If anything, it had been even more exciting than the first game.

United had no idea what they needed to achieve in their last group match at home to Bayern. The six group winners qualified for the quarter-finals and would be joined by the two best runners-up according to points, then goal difference and finally goals scored. Ferguson was determined to go for victory to make sure the Reds qualified as group winners. Roy Keane put United ahead before half-time, but Hasan Salihamidzic equalised just before the hour mark. Then, with 15 minutes left Ferguson learned from Bayern coach Ottmar Hitzfeld that other results, mainly Juventus's 2–0 win over Rosenborg, had gone United's way. They would finish as the best runners-up with Real Madrid. Ferguson let his players know. The game was virtually over. Ferguson and Hitzfeld, who respect each other greatly and are good friends, shook hands with a smile as they congratulated themselves on reaching the quarter-finals.

United were drawn against Inter Milan in a tie to be played over two legs in March. 'I'd have thought Inter Milan were probably the favourites for this cup,' said Ferguson. 'If we get through that one you can make us favourites.' Two goals from Yorke in the first leg at Old Trafford put the Reds in the driving seat. A 1–1 draw in the San Siro, thanks to a goal from substitute Paul Scholes two minutes from time, saw United safely through to the semi-finals for the sixth time in their history. 'This could be our year,' said Bobby Charlton. 'If we get a little bit of luck and stay reasonably free of injuries, we can give it a good shot.'

But Keane had picked up a booking for dissent and was now just one yellow card away from a ban which would mean missing the Champions League final should United get there. Meanwhile, Bayern thrashed fellow German side Kaiserslautern, the previous season's surprise Bundesliga champions, 6–0 on aggregate after an impressive 4–0 away win.

United faced another Italian team in the semi-finals and Juventus would prove to be much tougher opponents than Inter. The teams drew 1–1 at Old Trafford after Giggs struck a half-volley into the roof of the net to save United with the clock on 90 minutes. They had a ray of hope. 'When we go across there the pressure will be on them in front of their own fans, they'll have to turn it on against us and you never know,' said Sheringham. The Reds travelled to Turin for the second leg in the Stadio delle Alpi, knowing they had to score to avoid being eliminated as a result of Antonio Conte's 25th-minute strike which had given Juve a precious away goal in the first leg.

One of Ferguson's tactics throughout the European campaign, and especially in the days building up to the second leg of the semi-final, was to repeat at press conferences and in interviews that despite playing away United would score. He put great emphasis on this, partly because he believed it but also to raise doubts in the minds of the Juve players. In Turin Ferguson said United would definitely get a goal.

The United manager tried to instil in his players the belief that they could win the return. 'Now I feel that we are capable of playing against anyone and I have a genuine feeling we will beat Juventus,' he said. 'We have more control and patience about our game now and hopefully that will carry us through. We know we have to score and if you look at our record away from home in Europe there is plenty of evidence that we can do that.'

Juve boss Carlo Ancellotti wanted his side to play at a fast pace straight from the kick-off to unsettle United. 'We should start the game as if it was 0–0,' he said. 'We will attack from the start. That is our only option. It will be very hard because of United's strength, but we too have the strength and the determination to get the result we need.' Ferguson was already wise to the Italians' tactics. 'Knowing Juventus they will try to finish the tie in the first half-hour, because that is the sort of side they are. The important thing for us is to remember that if we score over there that can change the whole thing.'

In 41 years of European football Juventus had only lost in Turin seven times. United had never beaten an Italian side away. But Ferguson took a positive attitude with his players. In his pre-match talk he told them it didn't matter if Juventus scored, because just one away goal would put United back in control. The team were calm and very confident. The players knew they had to take the initiative and were quite sure they could do so. More importantly, they were clear on how to approach the game.

Giggs had scored a fantastic goal by taking on most of the Arsenal defence single-handedly before firing an acutely angled drive into the roof of David Seaman's net to win the FA Cup semi-final the previous Wednesday night. But he'd left the match on crutches and would miss the game in Turin. Blomqvist replaced the Welshman on the left. Butt came in for Scholes to add extra bite in midfield.

Juve replaced their half-fit hardman Paolo Montero with Ciro

Ferrara, who was even tougher. Alessandro Birindelli came in on the right in place of Zoran Mirkovic. The rest of the Juventus team was an international assortment of superstars. Antonio Conte, Angelo di Livio, Didier Deschamps and Edgar Davids would grace the midfield, while World and European Player of the Year Zinedine Zidane was to partner Filippo Inzaghi up front. Daniel Fonseca and Nicola Amoruso were on the bench.

The match kicked off in a blanket of smoke from the flares lit by the home fans in a capacity crowd of 64,500. It was their first full house of the season. About 6,000 noisy supporters hailed from Manchester. The game began cautiously until Beckham made a recovering tackle after five minutes at the expense of a corner on the left. Zidane was allowed to play it short to Di Livio and pick up the return ball. He had plenty of time and space to improve the angle and delivered a perfect cross to the far post, where Inzaghi was more alert and decisive than United's defence. He got in front of Gary Neville, stuck out a leg and forced the ball into the net. Ferguson was 'disappointed and angry' at losing a goal after six minutes to a move concocted by Juventus at a corner. It was poor defending and Ferguson knew it. 'We should be above surrendering goals like that,' he said later.

After 11 minutes Blomqvist lost possession and Juve got the ball out wide to Gianluca Pessotto on the left. He laid it into the channel and Inzaghi raced down the side of the penalty area with Stam. The Italian found room for a shot, Stam stretched to block and the ball ricocheted off the Dutchman's boot and looped over Schmeichel's fingertips into the goal. Ferguson wasn't annoyed this time. He knew it was just bad luck. 'Although I had tried to ease their worries about conceding a goal, little did I anticipate that we would go two down, and in the first 11 minutes,' he says.

At this stage the possibility of a humiliating defeat was staring the Reds in the face. Teddy Sheringham, who was among the substitutes, says, 'It was horrible sitting in the Stadio delle Alpi knowing you could do nothing to help. We could identify with our pals out there, though, and we knew without a doubt what they would be thinking: that it would only take one goal to get us back into it and we needed no more than a 2–2 draw to get us through on away goals. Neither the team on the field nor the one in the stand ever lost its sense of optimism, that it was going to be OK.'

Ferguson felt numb, but he knew the match wasn't over. He'd always believed United would have to score twice and the Italians' second had confirmed that target. In a strange way the early goals were a blessing, since the Reds now had plenty of time to come back. Ferguson also recognised that Juve had a tactical dilemma. Should they attack and try to get a third goal to kill off the match, or close down the game to defend their aggregate 3–1 lead? Ancelotti recognised the problem. 'Funnily enough, our two-goal lead worked to their advantage,' he says. 'It gave us the impression it [victory] would be easy and we stepped back and didn't play aggressively enough.'

United just had to keep their composure and express themselves. Though Schmeichel was annoyed at having conceded two goals he felt confident that they could change the course of the game, and Keane still felt United could come back and reach the final.

At last the Reds began to get some momentum going. They carried on playing, sometimes in cavalier fashion, still believing they could turn the match around. They had a good rhythm to their play, as well as most of the possession, and felt comfortable on the ball. When they finally raised the tempo it was to prove too much for Juve.

On 21 minutes a clearance by Schmeichel was backheaded into Yorke's path by Butt. The striker beat one defender and dribbled into the box. As he prepared to shoot, Ferrara grabbed his shirt collar and Yorke fell. It should have been a penalty or at least a free kick on the edge of the area, but the referee didn't blow his whistle. The ball broke loose to Beckham whose shot from outside the area struck Ferrara's hand. At last the referee spotted an infringement, this time for offside.

Three minutes later Keane made a late run and rose above the Juve defence and goalkeeper Angelo Peruzzi to meet Beckham's corner and glance a powerful header into the top corner. 'Roy Keane with a captain's goal for Manchester United,' said ITV commentator Clive Tyldesley. Keane made it look as if such a header was the most natural thing in the world. Ferguson felt it was as though the

Irishman's will had given the ball no choice but to land in the net. The amazed Italians just stood and watched. The United party and the travelling fans went barmy. 'It was somehow appropriate that the man who put us back into contention was Roy Keane, our captain and an heroic figure all season,' says Sheringham. The Reds were back in the game, thanks to Keane. There was still hope.

Schmeichel felt that Keane's goal, his third in Europe, not only tilted the balance of the game towards United but broke the Italians psychologically. 'They could feel us breathing down their necks, and they knew it was only a question of time before we would equalise,' he says. 'And that would mean we would take over the game completely.'

Keane almost immediately turned away to run back towards the United half for the restart, showing the Italians that his goal was to be just the start of the fight-back. There was more to come. It also signalled to his team-mates that the game was anything but lost. He still found time, though, to acknowledge the part Beckham had played by pointing a finger at his midfield partner before gripping his hand.

The Reds now began to take control and Juve looked concerned. But they were still dangerous. Zidane ran down the left and crossed to find Conte in the area. Schmeichel had come to collect but got nowhere near the ball and the Juve midfielder looped a header over the Dane towards the goal. Fortunately, Stam read the situation perfectly and ran back to stoop and calmly head the ball off the line and away for a corner. Inzaghi inexplicably watched the United defender, instead of running in to score.

Three minutes later United's task was made harder when Blomqvist played a short pass to Keane, who let it run too far. Realising Zidane was about to take the ball off him, the Irishman made a wild tackle. Zidane was sent flying and Keane was booked, harshly in Ferguson's view. The skipper would now be suspended and miss the final in Barcelona, if the Reds got there. Keane would later reflect that maybe he should have taken the ball in his stride rather than let it run across him. 'It was just a mistimed tackle,' he says. 'I've had thousands of them, hundreds of thousands of them. Some people said it was a silly booking but we had pushed forward and were trying to hit them on the break, and if Zidane had got away from me . . .'

Keane knew the consequences of his yellow card, yet he became even more determined, if that were possible. His reaction was to roll up his sleeves and drive United on against all the odds. 'Pounding every blade of grass, competing as if he would rather die of exhaustion than lose, he inspired all around him,' says Ferguson. 'It was the most emphatic display of selflessness I have ever seen on a football field. I felt it was an honour to be associated with such a player.' Keane and Butt won the midfield battle with Deschamps and Davids, which allowed United to push forward in search of an equaliser.

In their next attack on 34 minutes Neville played another long ball towards the edge of the area. Beckham headed the ball back for Cole, who controlled it and looped in a perfect cross over Ferrara for Yorke to send a diving header past Peruzzi. He got to his feet with a smile even wider than usual as Cole congratulated him. It was Yorke's eighth goal in Europe that season, but his first for six weeks. United were level, but with two vital away goals Juve now had to score.

Yorke had a chance to put United ahead in the 38th minute when Neville played another long ball, which was headed away by Juliano. Yorke controlled it and beat a defender with his first touch before firing in a shot with his second. This time his effort hit the inside of the post and Blomqvist failed to capitalise on the rebound. 'All my life I have based my football creed on passing the ball, possession with rhythm and tempo,' says Ferguson. 'For 30 minutes of the first half against Juventus, my ideals were almost totally realised by United. That we had fallen two goals behind before we rose to that level of excellence only made the achievement all the more remarkable . . . it was the finest display I have ever had from United, with an intensity and speed of passing that was absolutely brilliant.'

The Juventus players were glad to hear the half-time whistle and walked off with their heads bowed. With the score at 2–2 the away goals rule meant United were halfway to Barcelona. 'I was thoroughly relaxed and couldn't envisage anything other than victory,' says Ferguson.

For the second half the tactically astute Ancelotti took a gamble by bringing on Montero, who wasn't fully fit, for Juliano. He also replaced right-back Birindelli with forward Amoruso. Di Livio was moved to right back and Zidane dropped into midfield. The Italians had adopted a classic British 4–4–2 formation, although Di Livio and Pessotto were sure to attack down the flanks.

The stadium was eerily quiet as Juve came back into the match. To keep their lead United had to play a defensive game in the second half, so Ferguson had changed the formation to a traditional back four rather than a three-man defence. The Reds' defending was therefore far from desperate and their counter-attacks, particularly through Beckham, stretched the Italians to breaking point.

When Scholes came on as a substitute for Blomqvist after 68 minutes, United were immediately more fluid in midfield. Three minutes later Scholes continued a polished move involving 13 passes by finding Irwin charging into a space on the left. The Irishman dribbled into the area, got past Di Livio and found space for a shot across Peruzzi, which unluckily hit the inside of the post. Scholes then engineered his own personal tragedy with a two-footed tackle on Deschamps, who had also gone over the top. This resulted in a booking, though Ferguson thought it was a fair challenge. Like Keane, Scholes would now also miss the final in Barcelona if United held on in the Stadio delle Alpi. Their semi-final performance was winning all the plaudits, but if they survived they'd have to play in the Nou Camp without their strongest midfield player.

Juve began to tire in the final 20 minutes as United's constant probing stretched them. Ferguson knew that whoever scored next would come out on top. With just six minutes left Montero failed to control a long clearance by Schmeichel and the ball broke to Yorke. He played the ball between Ferrera and Montero and ran through the straining defenders, making the most of a lucky rebound. Ferguson could sense a goal was coming. Yorke jinked to Peruzzi's right as the keeper dived at his feet and dragged him down. But the ball broke to Cole who slid it into the net from a tight angle. According to Ferguson, Cole had 'coolly completed as good a night's work as any team had ever done in Juventus's backyard'. With the Italians needing to score twice in the last few minutes United's place in the final was secure. 'Full steam ahead Barcelona,' said ITV's Tyldesley. 'Manchester United are in sight of a European Cup final again.'

At the final whistle Keane showed no sign of the dejection he must have felt as he celebrated with his team-mates. The Italians hung their heads and walked off despondently to their dressing-room. Back home in Cork, Keane's mother Marie had been watching on television. 'My heart is cracking over Roy,' she said. 'It's always been my dream that he would lift the European Cup one day. I thought . . . a lot worse things which happened on the pitch went unpunished.' It was only when Keane was leaving the field that his face finally betrayed his true feelings. His downcast look was in sharp contrast to Yorke's beaming smile as the Trinidadian put a consoling arm around his sad captain.

After the match Ferguson called United's achievement 'the greatest performance ever produced by a team under my management'. His only regret was sending Scholes on as a second-half substitute, since he would now miss the final. 'It was heartbreaking for Paul, who is not only an outstanding player but a wonderful lad,' says Ferguson. Keane and Scholes would have to settle for playing in the FA Cup final. 'It said something about our season that an appearance in the old showpiece at Wembley could be considered a mere consolation prize,' adds Ferguson.

Keane was asked how he felt about missing the final, which would be against Bayern Munich who had beaten Dynamo Kiev 1–0 in the Olympic Stadium for a 4–3 aggregate victory. United's skipper replied that he wasn't emotionally upset, just frustrated with himself, because of his booking against Inter Milan more than the yellow card which had put him out of the final. 'Ultimately, you can't help getting booked for tackles but I was annoyed I got booked for arguing [in the Milan match],' he says. Denis Law, who'd missed the 1968 final because of a knee injury, had some encouraging words: 'Keane is young. I'm sure he'll get another shot at the final.'

United's first-team coach Steve McClaren analysed every match and marvelled at Beckham's stamina. He watched the game in Turin and measured how many runs Beckham had made and how far he had travelled compared to the other players. Beckham ran 14.1

kilometres – the furthest distance by a long way. 'His contribution was enormous,' says McClaren. Beckham's stamina would be desperately needed to help compensate for the loss of Keane against Bayern Munich in the final. 'The Germans have this daunting reputation of being physically strong and well-organised, but we are both of those things, even without Roy Keane,' said Beckham. 'They'll get a game.'

Two

The Build-Up

United wrapped up the Premier League title with a come-from-behind 2–1 win over Tottenham at Old Trafford on Sunday, 16 May. Beckham and Cole scored either side of half-time. There was no margin for error. The Reds finished on 79 points, while second-placed Arsenal had 78. The FA Cup final the following Saturday began with an injury to Keane, but was all over by the 52nd minute when Scholes added to an 11th-minute strike from substitute Sheringham to sink Newcastle at Wembley. The United players were delighted to secure another double, although there was little time for celebration. The bigger prize was still out there waiting to be won.

On Sunday, United moved out of London to the peace and quiet of Burnham Beeches in the Buckinghamshire countryside. They had a fun training session at Bisham Abbey in the morning. The players looked remarkably fresh. Ferguson thought they were 'buzzing', and put it down to the way they had conserved energy in the FA Cup final by playing a simple passing game. Their high spirits were also further proof of how well they'd coped with a hectic fixture programme in which almost every game was like a cup final.

After the FA Cup final, Ferguson had all the information he needed to select who would play in the Champions League final. His thoughts on the matter had been almost clear by the Saturday night, but he couldn't decide for certain where to play Beckham and what role he should give to Giggs. He was still mulling over the problem during United's morning training session. Ever since the Juventus game, which had left Keane and Scholes suspended for the final, Ferguson had intended playing Giggs in central midfield. His speed and penetration would be a handful for the Germans, especially the veteran Lothar Matthaus, whom Ferguson wanted to put to the test.

'I envisaged Giggs giving us penetration from the middle of the park,' he says. 'The only problem I had about that was that, if Bayern sat deep, I'd expose myself to the counter-attack.' Opting for Giggs's surging style in that area would also mean surrendering an essential part of United's game – the controlled, sustained possession that calls for a player who can hold the ball and spray calculated and accurate passes around the pitch. 'I was concerned that we base our game on passing and getting a rhythm to it,' says Ferguson. 'I thought that, with Beckham in the middle, we could maintain that. He was so up for it in the FA Cup final, and controlled the game so much, that I felt he would be inspired. I knew I'd be sacrificing his crosses, but something had to give.' Ferguson knew Beckham was again eager to play in his favourite position in centre midfield. He kept thinking that the lush, green Nou Camp pitch would suit Beckham perfectly. Giggs would play on the right and Butt could do his usual midfield job, leaving Beckham to control the passing.

As Ferguson pondered the make-up of his midfield, he was soon made aware that UEFA had ordered the pitch to be narrowed by four metres, to what it called 'standard' size. The Nou Camp playing surface was normally 72 metres wide, the measurement for all Barcelona's games that season. It would now be 68 metres wide, less than Old Trafford but surprisingly enough the same as Bayern's Olympic Stadium. It was surely more coincidence than conspiracy, but nothing had so far been officially reported to United about the change. It certainly might be expected to help the Germans, who respected United's wide players because of the damage they could do if they were given space.

After dinner on Sunday evening the players watched highlights of United's Champions League group games against Bayern for 45 minutes. 'That was the only video they were going to see,' says Ferguson. 'A mass of film evidence, like a bombardment of tactical theory, can be more confusing than enlightening.'

The staff they took to Spain reflects the thoroughness of United's preparations for their biggest challenge in 31 years. They tried to leave nothing to chance. The party included Jesper Jesperson, the Old Trafford chef, nutritionist Trevor Lea, Doctor Mike Stone, two physios, David Fevre and Robert Swire, Jimmy Curran for massages, two kit men, Albert Morgan and Alec Wylie, and two stalwarts from the club's administrative office – club secretary Ken Merrett, who handled the organisation of the trip and made sure that Ferguson, Steve McClaren and Jimmy Ryan were not distracted from their work with the squad, and his assistant, Ken Ramsden, who dealt, as usual, with the media.

On Monday, after some light morning training, the United party assembled at Manchester's Ringway Airport. Naturally, the press were out in force. The cameras did not, at first, seek out the man who had a key role to play against Bayern – Nicky Butt. Too often in the shadows, he didn't cost millions, have a pop star girlfriend, score hat-tricks for England, play with a brother for club and country or score incredible goals in FA Cup semi-finals. Of all United's youngsters, Butt was the least well known – but he wasn't complaining. He'd won lots of medals, been capped by England at every level, drove a Porsche and lived in a £700,000 house without making much impression on the tabloid news pages. He was happy to keep it that way. As Beckham walked past surrounded by microphones and flashing cameras, Butt was asked if he envied his team-mate's profile. 'I couldn't handle that,' he replied. 'I admire people who can.'

Eventually, though, the spotlights turned on Butt. He had no choice but to take centre stage. Butt said he was ready to embrace it. He'd have to marshall the midfield if United were to impose themselves on Bayern. Although Butt would have Beckham alongside him against Effenberg and Jeremies, he knew the onus was on his shoulders. Butt had featured in 45 of United's 61 matches, 13 as a substitute. That put him in the top 11 appearance-makers that season, although no outfield player had appeared in more than 54 games. Butt was a prodigious goalscorer at youth level, but had only hit the net twice all season.

'I know what my responsibility will be,' he said. 'We're young men now, not kids, we've got to stand up and be counted. We have got to stand up and say: "This is our time now." We are not 18 or 19 years old, we are 24 and 25. We know we have got to perform well for the club. It doesn't bother or daunt me: it excites me.' Butt's anticipation was tinged, though, with sympathy for the players from whose misfortune he'd benefit. 'I felt for them. When it gets to the final they should just cancel [suspensions] out. It's so harsh to miss the biggest game of their lives because of a mistimed tackle.'

Keane certainly felt United's squad was big and strong enough to beat Bayern without him. 'There are other players who can come in and do a job and we have top international players who are sitting on the bench. The squad rotation system has been criticised at times, but we said from day one that we are in this together.' Turning to the threat posed by Bayern, he said, 'They are a very powerful team physically, they all look massive, about 6ft 2in. They have talent as well. But we are a fit side. Maybe that is underestimated, but the manager and Steve McClaren put a lot of emphasis on it and we always seem to be able to run and run. Maybe that is why we get a lot of late goals.'

In Munich, Bayern were holding an open day for the English media at their training ground on Unter Sabener Strasse. The Germans seemed to think they were on easy street as they prepared for the final. 'Even if it would be wrong to deem them complacent, the visitor to their premises . . . could not mistake their poise,' says Kevin McCarra of *The Times*. Outside the clubhouse they practised nonchalantly in front of the cameras. Instead of training with the balls provided by the club's official sponsor, they were using a rival UEFA-endorsed product. Bayern's coaches wanted them to get used to the special ball which would be used in the final. They'd been practising with it for weeks.

Roast beef was being served inside the clubhouse because Bayern thought that would put the English press at ease. Hitzfeld patiently answered questions about the final. Bland compliments to United were rolled out with the red carpet. 'None of that respect, however, was paid at the cost of trust in themselves,' says McCarra. 'At the Nou Camp, United [will have to] contend with a side that is absolutely convinced of its capacity to accomplish a given task. Where Bundesliga footballers are concerned, the term arrogance is often bandied around, but it is a poor fit for the true mental state. Arrogance rests on miscalculation, whereas the Germans have thrived on being absolutely correct in their calculations.' The combination of professionalism, attention to detail and carefully considered public appearance was the secret of Bayern's success.

The Germans had hinted at their line-up for the final at their last training session. In one team Hitzfeld fielded the 11 players who'd beaten Kiev including two strikers, Carsten Jancker and Alexander Zickler, supported by Mario Basler. 'There are good reasons for making that team play,' said Hitzfeld.

By the time the United party boarded their British Airways Concorde plane for the flight to Barcelona, Ferguson, true to his gambler's instincts, had made up his mind. He would play Beckham in centre midfield with Giggs on the right flank, Blomqvist on the left and Johnsen at the back alongside Stam. It was the boldest of the options available to him and the biggest gamble of his 13-year career at Old Trafford.

At two o'clock United left Manchester in style on Concorde, 'a touch designed to bring a sense of occasion to our preparations', says Ferguson. He'd told them about the arrangements a few days earlier. 'It was like winning another medal,' says Yorke. 'I hadn't been on it before, and I don't think most of the players had. Apart from Becks. He might have been. I'd heard so much about it, so I knew it was quite small inside. But not that small. It was brilliant.'

Although Keane couldn't play against Bayern Munich because he was suspended, he wouldn't have been fit enough in any case because of the injury that had forced him off at Wembley in the FA Cup final. Still, his presence in the squad that flew out to Spain was welcomed and appreciated by the other players. 'Keane had played twice against Bayern Munich in the group stages, he had observations to offer and his innate will to win was infectious,' noted Stafford Hildred and Tim Ewbank in their biography *Captain Fantastic*. 'His colossal presence would be missed out on the pitch, but the FA Cup final had proved to the team that they could win the big game without him.'

Ferguson went to Spain convinced that despite being seriously weakened by the loss of Keane and Scholes, United could win the trophy they coveted most of all. And yet the European Cup had been so cruelly elusive that he had to steel himself against the possibility of yet another disappointment. 'In each of the two previous seasons we had seemed good enough to win it,' he says, 'only to have our hopes crushed in the late stages of the tournament by a combination of injury problems and our own lack of the absolute conviction needed to finish off the highest calibre of opponents when we had them at our mercy.'

It was reported that Ferguson would collect a £350,000 bonus if United won the treble. Chairman Martin Edwards wouldn't officially reveal the amount he was ready to pay, but he gave a clue to its worth. 'The manager will think it's well worth him winning on Wednesday. He won't be disappointed. Don't worry about that. Winning the treble is like getting 100 out of 100 in an exam. It's an achievement that will never be topped.' Ferguson's reward would dwarf the £150,000 each of his players would pick up, probably as much as United's boys of '68 had earned in their entire careers. But money wasn't on the players' minds; instead, they wanted to know if they'd made the team for the most important club game of their lives.

As United's plane winged its way towards Barcelona the football party nobody wanted to miss was already exercising its compulsive pull. Fifty hours before the final hundreds of United and Bayern fans wandered around outside the Nou Camp weaving between the TV engineers who would relay live broadcasts to 200 countries. Dozens pressed themselves against the walls and fences of the stadium in homage to Catalonia. It was hot and quiet, but humming with a sense of the drama to come. The supporters mainly talked about their team's chances and where they could get tickets.

The thousands of United fans who filled the Placa Catalunya, Barcelona's main square, were mostly afraid that Keane's absence would be a crucial factor in deciding who won. The camaraderie that had developed among the English fans was overwhelming and a competitive edge had emerged. They injected some humour into the proceedings by singing 'Come for the shopping, you've only come for the shopping,' to Bayern's big spenders in Las Ramblas, the main pedestrian area of Barcelona. It was a typically Continental street the like of which you could never find in England, full of popular outdoor restaurants, bars and designer stores.

The fans had come by any means of transport they could find. They slept where they could. Some were staying in luxury Barcelona hotels, where prices had been bumped up considerably. But the hotels were home only to the lucky few who secured a room before everyone realised United would be in the final or that Barcelona was hosting the Spanish Grand Prix, a technology conference and a fresh fish festival in the same week. Others had found cheap *pensions*. The city's hostels were full days before the game, but there were alternatives. Due to the lack of accommodation in Barcelona, supporters were scattered along the Costa Dorada and Costa Brava in resorts such as Reus, Salou and Lloret de Mar. Many had booked reasonably priced, week-long packages to the coastal resorts, hoping to buy match tickets on arrival. The police also found quite a few tired revellers trying to sleep on the five-kilometre beach that lies between the vibrant city and the sea. One group of United fans had booked accommodation on Majorca, only to find there were no ferries and no flights from the island in time for the final. The authorities were anxious about friction in the resorts because hoteliers had ignored police requests to let rooms to either British or German fans, but not both. They needn't have worried.

United's plane arrived an hour behind schedule and was met by a huge crowd. The official party was transferred immediately by coach to the luxury five-star Melia Gran Hotel in the trendy seaside resort of Sitges, some 20 miles south of Barcelona, accompanied by a large security escort.

The hotel was set on a rocky bluff and the players could see the Mediterranean below. It was ideal. 'Our hotel at Sitges was perfect, with a lovely outlook over the sea,' says Ferguson. But when the party arrived there they were mobbed by United fans crowding the lobby. 'I must admit I was taken aback by the number of our supporters staying in the hotel and eagerly waiting to greet us,' says Ferguson. His mind firmly fixed on preparing the team, he dreaded the distracting effects this might have on them if it were to continue over the next two days. 'I let my guard slip,' he says. 'In fact, I did more than that, I lost my temper.' Ferguson had anticipated a secluded preparation and shouted, 'Why don't you give us a bit of peace?' He told the fans that if United didn't win they'd be the first to complain and asked the security staff to clear the place.

After Ferguson's action the fans were not a problem to the players, but he regretted blowing his top. Ferguson cherished his affinity with the fans who'd made United the greatest football club in the world. Several of the groups of supporters included children and afterwards he was sorry he'd disappointed them, feeling he may have been too brusque. 'I place great importance on supporters, and I was out of order,' he says. But the United boss hoped those who were ushered out of the hotel understood that when he was focused on winning, everything came second to his players' welfare. He later apologised to the supporters. 'It was a difficult moment but we quickly put it behind us,' says Ferguson.

Rumours abounded, and the best was that United had a deal with an Italian label to wear its suits for their off-field appearances at both the FA and European Cup finals. Everything was fine until Victoria Adams told David Beckham they should be wearing Versace. 'David, who is allegedly under the well-manicured Spice thumb in matters of personal style, insisted this be made so,' reported Richard Benson of *The Guardian*. 'Victoria got on the phone to Donatella, with whom she and David are thick, and there was a bit of double-quick designing.' This apparently explained why, to their surprise, the players had Versace suits waiting for them in their hotel rooms. 'Of course, this could only be a preposterous rumour,' wrote Benson. 'Such a ludicrous thing would never really happen.'

United didn't have time to use all the facilities at the hotel since they were locked in the private world of the travelling football team. The favourite meeting place, as usual, was the physio's treatment room. It seemed to Ferguson that when they gathered there, the atmosphere of United's Cliff training ground had been transported to Sitges. 'There was the familiar good-natured savaging of [kit man] Albert Morgan,' says Ferguson, 'the only Manchester-born member of the backroom staff and a rabid fan who just happens to be an employee.' Morgan was great at cheering up the players and Ferguson as well.

At the time, Cole felt United's players might have been enjoying a holiday instead of preparing for the most important game they were ever likely to play. Looking back, he thinks that was deliberate: 'Put us in a prison, locked away from the rest of the world as we were for three days, but make sure there is an element of paradise about it.' Away from the media hype and the tension and expectation generated by thousands of fans, the players could calm down and relax at last, with time to play cards and pool. Still, Ferguson and his coaching staff had to keep an eye on the players, watching out for anything that could upset their preparation, such as sunbathing. 'I had to chase David Beckham off his veranda a couple of times,' he says.

The canny Hitzfeld surprisingly announced his team on the Monday, 48 hours before the final. He wanted to give his players time to prepare. They were without injured striker Elber and World Cup-winning full-back Lizarazu, but Hitzfeld stuck by his usual 3–4–1–2 formation. The team was Kahn, Linke, Matthaus, Kuffour, Babbel, Jeremies, Effenberg, Tarnat, Basler, Jancker and Zickler. Unusually, given the multinational mix of stars in most top European teams, there were ten Germans in the line-up. 'I can't play hide-and-seek and that's why I have named my team,' said Hitzfeld. But he'd left the door open for one or two changes. 'There is still the final training session tomorrow. Normally the only purpose of this is to get to know the pitch. On the other hand, Mario Basler was not in the team that played Manchester United in December and that happened after the last training session before the match at Old Trafford.'

Somewhat surprisingly, Hitzfeld had chosen to play Babbel instead of Thomas Strunz, because of his defensive qualities. Babbel, earlier designated for a place in the back three, would be shunted forward to the right side of midfield for the challenge of restricting Giggs, seen by the Germans as one of United's main dangermen. 'Giggs is more of a striker than a midfielder, hence we need stability in defence,' explained Hitzfeld. That would leave Thomas Linke and Samuel Kuffour playing on either side of the indestructible Lothar Matthaus at the back. Tarnat expected to face the thankless task of marking Beckham on the left. Bayern had dubbed Beckham '*Flankengott*', which literally means 'god of the flanks' but more easily translates as 'crossing god'.

Beckham's crossing had been carefully cultivated over many years and owed much to his determination as well as the natural skill with which he'd been blessed. From his office on the first floor of United's training ground, complete with three picture-lined walls and a large window, Ferguson would often swivel round in his chair to look out towards the practice pitch. He could always hear the sounds of his players talking with a satisfied air in the canteen along the corridor after training. But usually a lone figure remained outside on the pitch, still practising, still trying to perfect his technique. That player was Beckham. Sometimes the England midfielder stayed out there so long that Ferguson would have to tell him to stop training and get some rest.

Says Beckham: 'I stay out for an hour hitting balls if the manager lets me. Sometimes he sends me in. I have tried to sneak out but the manager's office has a view of everything so I can't get away with it. I practise all the time. If I didn't practise, I wouldn't be able to put the ball on a sixpence. Sometimes I don't get it right but I have always been able to strike a ball well, even as a youngster. What I've learnt since then is technique. The crossing is a natural thing. It's getting noticed more because the games are bigger and more goals have been scored from them. If I put a ball into the box and Yorke or Cole get on the end of it, we win the game and we all look good. It's nice to be talked of as the best crosser in the game but I don't think too much about it.'

The Germans were well aware of United's strengths down the flanks and intended to cut off the supply. 'It is important that the wide positions are closed off,' said Babbel. 'If we can do that then we will have a very good chance of winning.'

Jens Jeremies and Stefan Effenberg would have the pivotal roles in central midfield and Mario Basler was to occupy the crucial area just behind the front two, Carsten Jancker and Zickler. Effenberg, with his surprise passes and powerful free kicks, was Bayern's brains and would have his usual licence to roam and make the killing pass. He was the man United had to mark closely. Ferguson had sent his brother Martin to watch all Bayern's Champions League matches. The United boss had studied the German side meticulously, using the information his brother had brought back. Martin would have told him that Jeremies, who'd had a good World Cup in a poor German team, was likely to be deployed behind Effenberg. Jeremies was the driving force, the tenacious marathon man who never stopped running and tackling. But if there was one player who could inspire the Bavarians to victory it had to be the old warhorse Matthaus, who dearly wanted to end a fabulous career by becoming one of the oldest players to win the Champions League.

Hitzfeld had tasted European Cup success two years before with Borussia Dortmund after they beat United in the semi-finals. He claimed that nothing compared to it. 'To win the Champions League is something very special. The whole world will be watching and the players can become heroes.' Hitzfeld was now bidding to become the only man to win the trophy with two clubs.

The media couldn't predict what United's line-up would be. Some thought Johnsen might be best suited to partner Butt in central midfield, since his defensive qualities would enable him to snuff out the threat posed by Effenberg. The other options were to put Phil Neville in a similarly destructive role, or Giggs, who'd already shown he could play in the centre. Some thought Sheringham was sure to start after his impressive man-of-the-match performance in the FA Cup final when he'd come in cold for Keane in midfield. In the previous few weeks he'd played better than at any time in his two seasons with United – including the early months of 1997/98, when he was scoring a few goals. He felt he'd proved he was a big-match player who could rise to the occasion. At the same time, he prepared for the possibility that he might not get a place. The 50-goal Cole–Yorke combination was Ferguson's preferred option up front, even though the two players hadn't been on top form recently. Sheringham's only chance of starting was therefore in midfield; otherwise he'd be on the bench. 'You can only do what you do and then leave the decision up to the manager,' said Sheringham. 'He knows what it's all about and what it will take to beat Bayern. That's the way it goes; it's a tough thing. I've been out through injury, wasn't in the side at the start of the season and the lads have done unbelievably well, so I've got no qualms about that. Having said that, in the last month or so things have changed around, I've done well and hopefully my name will be on his mind when he picks the team.'

At 11.30 a.m. on Tuesday United's players went for a walk together, followed by the first of three team talks at which Ferguson told them all who'd play and why, and how United could win the game. At the second session they went through Bayern's tactics based on how they'd played against Dynamo Kiev in the semi-final, scoring an early goal and shutting up shop. They discussed the German side's threat in the air – they were a big team physically although, Ferguson insisted, not big enough to beat United. In the third team meeting McClaren went through United's organisation at set-pieces, both when attacking and defending.

The first team talk had been eagerly awaited by the players since they found out who'd been picked for the biggest match of their lives. Ferguson told them Beckham had been selected to play the central role he'd filled so well in the cup final. His task would be to direct the play. There were concerns before the match about playing Beckham in central midfield, with some arguing that it would prove to be less a blessing than a curse. 'A bit of a chance, that, bit of a gamble, not having Beckham doing what Beckham had been doing all season,' journalist Hunter Davies was to reflect in his biography of Dwight Yorke.

Beckham had only started one game all season in central midfield for either his club or his country and that was against Luxembourg, which hardly provided a proper test. Although he'd switched to the middle in the FA Cup final, his opponent was Gary Speed. Matthaus, despite having 'the mobility of an old tank' according to Matt Dickinson of *The Times*, would prove to be a far tougher adversary. But one man, arguably the best player the world has ever seen, believed Beckham could easily play in the centre. He rated him as 'one of the very great players of this year'. 'Rivaldo is the best footballer in the world,' said Pele. 'Next is Zidane. And there's David Beckham. He has played very well this season. He's a different style to the other two but he's very important to Manchester United. He's such a hard worker. He's got vision and he's an exceptionally good passer of the ball. With a player like Beckham you must give him his freedom. Some coaches might try to put him in one position. I would not. I would organise the team and let him free. Leave him, because he knows what to do. He understands the game and he knows when to change it.' Giggs would move to the right wing, where Ferguson felt his pace could give Michael Tarnat, Bayern's left-sided defender, problems quite different from those he anticipated from Beckham. Blomqvist, who with Butt was the other replacement for Keane and Scholes, could play in Giggs's usual position on the left. That would provide width in United's attack, vital against opponents who'd shown how afraid they were of that quality by successfully lobbying to have the pitch narrowed. Such admirable adventurous intent would also allow Ferguson to play Johnsen instead of May at centre-back. May was playing well, but Johnsen had greater tactical awareness and mobility. United would need those defensive qualities.

Jaap Stam had done enough in the 13 minutes he'd played against Newcastle at Wembley to suggest that his Achilles injury would hold up for one more match. He would partner Johnsen in the central defence. Irwin, who'd missed the FA Cup final through suspension, and Gary Neville were the obvious selections at left- and right-back. Ferguson, as expected, stuck by his first-choice front two of Cole and Yorke. 'The gaffer said I was playing – but I knew that already,' says Yorke. 'Before the [FA] Cup final, he had made that clear. He was saving me for this one. Teddy was upset, but it was expected that me and Coley would be up front. Teddy had done well in recent games, but all season my partnership with Coley had been so good. I don't think any of the lads were surprised.'

Sheringham's name might have been on Ferguson's mind, but it wasn't in the line-up. The day before, Ferguson told Sheringham and David May that they wouldn't start but should prepare for anything. They both put a brave face on it, but were terribly disappointed. 'I felt for Phil Neville, Teddy Sheringham and Ole Gunnar Solskjaer starting on the bench,' says Ferguson. 'There would have been even more heartbreak had Roy Keane and Paul Scholes been available.'

At the first team talk, Ferguson also told Yorke and Gary Neville they'd be taking questions at the final pre-match press conference on Tuesday afternoon at the hotel.

There was just a sprinkling of United and Bayern supporters in Sitges, where United were based. The beautiful seaside resort was half-an-hour and a world away from the capital of Catalonia. Stephen Wood of *The Times* was enjoying the atmosphere of Sitges before heading off to Barcelona in search of a ticket for the match. 'The sun shines, the Mediterranean laps gently on to the golden shores and the locals spend hours on the beach volleyball courts; you have to wonder if we are all here for a football match . . . the touts can wait,' he wrote in *The Times*.

Thousands of United fans continued to arrive on the Costa Dorada on Tuesday morning, taking the total to about 50,000. Just under half did not have a ticket for the match, and this was their main concern. The capacity at the Nou Camp had been cut to 92,000, partly because UEFA rules – which state that everyone must be seated for Champions League matches – had closed off a section of terracing. Two-thirds of the tickets had been split between the finalists, with the rest going to UEFA, Barcelona supporters and officials, foreign associations and sponsors.

It was clear that the Reds would enjoy most of the support. Although Bayern had sold their entire allocation of 30,000, the club said there had been demand for only another 500 to 1,000 tickets. For many United fans, this was their first experience of following the team to a European Cup Final. Those under 40 would have struggled to recall the last time the Reds had graced such a momentous occasion, in 1968.

The 30,000 United fans without tickets had a difficult time ahead. Members of the Barcelona Supporters Club, which had received about 7,500 tickets, made no secret of their intentions. United supporters watched as Barcelona fans bought tickets legitimately for £28. They quickly resold them outside the Nou Camp for up to £400 right under the noses of Spanish police. The touts familiar from Old Trafford every Saturday were also enjoying their place in the sun. Since few Bayern fans had travelled without tickets, those sold on the black market were being snapped up almost entirely by United supporters. But the prices in Barcelona were a bargain compared with those demanded in England by the agencies, who were asking £1,000 for a flight and ticket package.

Another risk for fans was forged tickets. Up to 1,000 originating from Britain were believed to be circulating. According to one British police source, the fakes were good quality but did not have a watermark and there was a misspelling of the word 'Gradaria', with an extra 'n' after the first 'a'. Genuine tickets had a watermark bearing the words 'UEFA Champions League'.

One fan, dubbed Michael R. by the police, gave a Spanish tout 7.1 million pesetas (£28,000) for 116 tickets to be collected the following day. Predictably, the tout never showed up.

Despite the problems finding tickets, there was a carnival atmosphere in the Catalan capital in the days before the match. The downtown area was taken over by Bayern and United supporters, who mixed in friendly fashion. Songs and chants echoed across the main boulevard of Las Ramblas. Lightly armed police, who stood against a wall with their arms crossed watching the screaming, drunken fans, predicted it would get worse on Wednesday. 'This is just the beginning,' said one, shaking his head as he watched the fans stagger by with huge cups of beer. 'Wait until the game . . . then we will really see some action.' By Tuesday lunchtime English and German fans were gathering in heat of 26 degrees outside the Nou Camp – or the new camp, as intoxicated Mancs tended to call it – getting angrier by the minute as Barcelona fans tried to sell their tickets at extortionate prices.

Bayern were due to answer questions from the press inside the stadium that afternoon but, unusually, they were late. Finally, at about 2 p.m., Beckenbauer, Hitzfeld, Matthaus, Kahn and Effenberg walked into the press conference. They all wore club blazers, except for Kahn who was casually dressed in a T-shirt. Hitzfeld showed he had a sense of occasion. 'We want to win this game for the people; it will be for the history of Bayern Munich,' he said. Beckenbauer echoed those thoughts: 'Our game in Germany has suffered terribly. Because of the lack of success in recent years, this final is important, not just for Bayern, but for all German football.'

Bayern's goalkeeper and captain Oliver Kahn sat next to the microphone. He made the surprising suggestion that he thought United were interested in him as a replacement for Schmeichel. 'I'm proud to be named by United as a possible replacement,' he said, quickly adding that his first priority was to shut out the United forwards. He knew the final would be close and expected a long, drawn-out affair. 'We've been asked a hundred times over in the last few days what will be the deciding factor and all I can say is luck. There is no other answer. It will come down to luck, luck and luck again. We know about the strengths of Manchester United. Their strongest points are Beckham and Giggs. But if we play clever tactically, they cannot play to their strengths.' Kahn also knew it would be an exhausting encounter. 'The first two games were very close and, of course, we're prepared for extra time, or even penalties.'

His sentiment was echoed by Effenberg who acknowledged that United had enough 'big players' to cope with the nerves. He agreed that it could be a super feast of football, providing the players did not freeze under the pressure. 'We're going to do everything possible to win inside 90 minutes but we're ready for anything and we'll fight for as long as it takes.' But, his guard down for just a second, Effenberg admitted that nerves would play a part, even for him. Still, he sounded in the mood. (He had asked his wife earlier that day to name her heart's desire for her birthday. 'The European Cup,' she replied. 'OK, darling,' he told her.)

Effenberg and Kahn both smiled when they heard a question involving the words 'English' and 'penalty complex'. 'We haven't practised penalties ahead of this match – you can't,' said Effenberg. 'But we've got great forwards and a fantastic goalkeeper. That's as much as we can do.' He added that there was little to choose between the two sides. 'Both teams are on the same level and tomorrow there can only be a lucky winner.' Effenberg sportingly admitted it was a great shame Keane would miss the final, as he would have relished the chance of playing against him once more.

'I'm a big admirer of Keane,' he said. 'He's one of the best midfield players around. He defends well and can also get forward and score, as he showed against us. I enjoyed our battle in the two previous games. But his absence will not weaken Manchester too much because they have a very good squad.' Nevertheless, Kuffour was relieved Keane wouldn't play. 'That is good for us,' he said. 'He is such an important player. He holds the midfield together . . . he is their driving force.'

Beckenbauer said the match was an important milestone for German regeneration. England manager Kevin Keegan had said something similar a few nights before when he suggested that if United won it would prove a shift in the balance of power towards England. But since the Reds had so many foreign players in their line-up that comment rang a little hollow. Bayern's team was almost entirely made up of Germans so Beckenbauer's statement had more of a ring of truth. 'Beyond that,' said the Kaiser, 'this is a once-in-a-lifetime prestige match for football.' Matthaus, cold-eyed and matter-of-fact, had a blunt answer for the English inquisitors who questioned his team's strength. 'There's no clear favourite for the final,' he said. 'We know each other very well after playing two tough games against them already. But I remember it was Gary Lineker, one of the heroes of English football, who said: "Football is a simple game. It's just 22 players running after a ball – and in the end the Germans always win."' But Matthaus conceded that players like Schmeichel and Stam, Beckham and Giggs, Yorke and Cole were worthy of wearing the famous red strip. 'This team shows that the legend of Manchester United is still living,' he said.

Hitzfeld concluded by having a dig at United's status as a plc. 'Manchester United are a financial business, quoted on the stock market. We are more of a football club.' United were unaffected by Bayern's attempts to wind them up. 'The cheap talk never penetrated the United camp because every player kept himself deliberately focused on what we needed to do,' says Cole. 'We knew it was a massive game. It was the European Cup final, for pity's sake, and you might never get the chance of appearing in it again. More than that, though, it was *the* game which would determine whether United could secure the greatest, most monumental treble of all.'

As the tabloids put it, the treble was United's three steps to heaven, but did they have the nerve to make it?

At 5 p.m. Ferguson, Gary Neville and Yorke ran the gauntlet of United fans jostling outside the team hotel for a glimpse of their heroes as they made their way to meet the press, who had been driven to Sitges that afternoon. They looked completely relaxed as they faced the packed hall of reporters and cameramen. Yorke was impressed with the turnout. There seemed to be journalists from every country in the world. 'It was mega,' he says. 'I thought my first press conference, when I signed for Manchester United, was big, but this was enormous. Oh, well over 100 journalists, from all over.'

Gary Neville was so laid back he was munching on two rounds of jam on toast. 'You can take the kid out of Bury, but you can't take Bury out of the kid,' said the *Manchester Evening News* reporter. 'It's a wonder he wasn't getting stuck into a black pudding.' Ferguson looked calm, though unusually red-faced. 'He obviously decided to mix his Champions League business with a spot of sunbathing,' thought the reporter.

They fielded questions between them before leaving. Yorke was asked about the pressure of playing in the Champions' League final. 'Of course, there is tension but I'm a light-hearted guy anyway,' he said, displaying his infectious smile. 'At this stage of the season we have to believe that if we get it right on the night we are capable of beating anybody. But I imagine the Germans have exactly the same thoughts.' Admirably, Yorke then put the match into perspective. 'Pressure is Kosovo, when people aren't getting any food and their country is being bombed. Playing football isn't pressure, it's enjoyment. I express myself and get paid a fantastic amount of money to do things I always dreamt of doing.'

Ferguson, who as a 26-year-old had watched United win the European Cup at home in Scotland, tried his best to avoid comparisons between the present side and the boys of '68 or between himself and Sir Matt Busby. He remembered the goals from that Wembley final and the fact that Denis Law didn't play. ' . . . I was disappointed about that,' said Ferguson. 'Being a Scotsman he was my number one hero and he still is my hero.' He insisted that equalling Busby's achievement was not his main concern. 'You may not believe it, but I don't think it's so important matching Sir Matt Busby, the more important thing is to give the club the success that we all hope we can. If we do win it, then it is up to the critics to sit back and assess us.' Nevertheless, if he could emulate Busby's achievement then he would be indisputably recognised as the greatest manager of all time with 13 trophies, a record three doubles and a historic treble.

Denis Law reckoned that Ferguson had already achieved a status equal to that of Busby and Jock Stein. He didn't need Barcelona to confirm it. Law didn't like to compare the side he had played in with the current stars, but said that Yorke, Beckham and company had surpassed the Busby Babes in terms of domestic success. 'We had a great team and this is another great team but they are on the verge of a treble and we never even managed a double,' said Law. 'They probably have a stronger squad of players but the philosophies of Busby and Ferguson are similar.'

Ferguson was determined to restore the European Cup to England for the first time since Liverpool beat Roma on penalties in 1984. 'It's significant. I've always said that a national team is the focus point in the country and the next stage is the European Cup. The English teams in the 1980s were fantastic and you could say they dominated the competition really. I think we've progressed to that level and we're as good as any English team that has been here before. So that must give us a great chance to change the pattern. There is a difference between us and the teams of the past in that we've not won it yet, but we can do that now . . . I'm sure that we're as diligent as those sides were, and we've done our homework.'

Ferguson admitted that outsiders might have preferred Bayern's more laid-back build-up to the final but he insisted: 'I know how my players have developed over the past two months. Don't forget the number of challenges, one after another . . . My players are not tired, they are still sharp. They seem to thrive on it. The more the games come at them, the better they like it.'

Ferguson told the reporters he'd already picked his team for the final the previous Sunday. He even dropped some hints about who would be in the side, the main clue being the prospect of Beckham joining Butt in central midfield. But he wasn't saying what the team was. They'd have to wait until the day of the game for confirmation. He was indulging in his favourite pastime of playing mind games with the opposition.

'It seemed fitting that Ferguson appears to have decided to stick with his principles right to the bitter end in the European Cup final,' wrote Oliver Holt of *The Times*. 'Most expected him to play it safe in the centre of midfield . . . Instead, the United manager has put his faith in flair and verve. He has not picked the conservative Ronny Johnsen to play alongside the attritional Nicky Butt, the predicted move that would have signalled his intention to nullify the creativity of the Bayern Munich midfield in which Stefan Effenberg excels. That has not been Ferguson's way this season, nor will it be his way . . . when United play for the biggest prize in European club football, the prize that will transform their reputation from that of a very good team to one of the greatest in the modern history of sport.

'It is the boldest of teams, a radical change on the most important night of every United player's life. It heaps immense pressure on Beckham, of course, and shows just how much store Ferguson sets by the player who has been his most consistent, explosive performer this season. It throws him back into the heart of the side, back into the position in which he was playing when he was sent off for England against Argentina in the World Cup. A year on, Beckham . . . is much better equipped to deal with the responsibility that has been heaped on his shoulders. His battle with Effenberg is now likely to be the decisive factor in whether United lift the trophy for the first time in 31 years and break the hold with which German sides appear to have gripped opponents from England in recent times.'

Ferguson picked out United's away win over Inter Milan as the game in which his team generated their enormous sense of self-confidence. 'That result in the San Siro was the one that did it for us. After that, Juventus held no fears. The boys believed in themselves completely and it was no problem to fall a goal down.' Asked what his final thoughts would be when he went to bed the night before the final Ferguson replied: 'I think I will just turn over and go to sleep . . . I hope. That is usually the best thing to do. There will be a lot of things racing through my mind, but with experience you know you cannot let that encroach on to your players.'

The previous weekend Yorke had revealed he'd dreamt about United completing a treble in his first season. 'I've dreamt about it,' he said. 'I've woken up at night in a cold sweat and I know I am touching those winners' medals. If ever a club deserves to rewrite the history books, this club does and nobody will stop us.'

By Tuesday evening what was believed to be the biggest exodus of football fans to leave British shores continued flooding into Barcelona. Police sources in Manchester now estimated the number of United supporters travelling as high as 100,000 – more than three times the number of tickets available to the club. Tickets for the match had by now been changing hands for as much as £1,000 on the black market. Flights were also expensive, with supporters paying more than £300 for a seat on a budget airline. A Manchester airport spokesman said: 'We expect to handle 33,000 fans on 225 flights with the busiest day being Thursday, when they all return.' The airport was a mass of red as supporters took charter flights.

On the Tuesday night Bayern arrived at the Nou Camp first for a routine hour-long workout under Hitzfeld's watchful eye. They worked out grimly and their goalkeeper Kahn, 'wearing an undertaker's countenance' accoding to Graham Spiers of *Scotland on Sunday*, slogged through routines with Effenberg. The players eventually sloped off 'as if heading for coal mines', thought Spiers.

After the Bayern squad had finished it was United's turn to train on the pitch. 'The Nou Camp stadium is everything you could imagine and more,' says Sheringham. Each United player had a locker – Sheringham's belonged to Sergi, the little Barcelona left-back. 'It was a wonderful playing surface, like a bowling green,' recalls Sheringham. He knew that if he didn't get to play on this 'field of dreams' the following night he'd regret it for the rest of his days. 'In these circumstances, knowing you would get a medal if you were an unused substitute was just beside the point,' he says. 'Playing in a match of this calibre at such a terrific arena is the pinnacle of a footballer's life at club level. It doesn't get much better than that.'

Some United players wore plain black T-shirts whilst others had been given flash tops with luminous lime-green sleeves. It wasn't until the smiling players began training in the Nou Camp that Keane realised what he was missing. He was on the pitch in his tracksuit like the others, but mostly kept away from them. The Irishman was there in mind, body and competitive spirit but, unusually, his footballing skills weren't required. He'd endured a mental picture of what it would be like to miss out on the biggest occasion of a footballer's career at club level for almost six weeks. Now he was experiencing it first hand, and it wasn't pleasant.

As they trained Ferguson stood at the edge of the pitch, paying his own homage by wearing a '60s replica shirt (red rather than the blue United wore in the 1968 final) as he presided over training. Before pulling it on he spoke movingly about how special the current team were: 'I'm proud of my players, I trust them and I'll be trusting them tomorrow.' He thought back to his lonely night watching the Champions' League final in Tel Aviv. 'Disappointment can either kill you or inspire you,' he said. 'We all shared the disappointment of last year [when United won nothing] and we've all done something about it this time.' His cotton replica shirt must have shrunk in the wash, because it was very tight-fitting!

'Ferguson's choice of shirt was heavy with a touching kind of symbolism,' says Holt of *The Times*. 'He stood out as he watched his players put through their paces because he, alone, was wearing the red top with the round white collar that will always be associated with the wonder years of Best, Charlton and Law. Perhaps it was a little too small for him, perhaps it emphasised the spread that has come upon him in late middle age, but, in everything that he has done this season, in everything that his astonishing treble-chasing side has achieved, he has shown that the spirit of Busby and his team lives on at Old Trafford.'

Ferguson wore the shirt to gee up his players, but that hardly seemed necessary. Their competitive edge, the craving that had driven them through a season of gathering glory, meant there was no easing off even in the warm-up. Unlike the calculating Germans, there was a lightness of spirit about United. Ferguson even summoned onlookers in the stand to come down for an anecdote.

There were two brief injury scares during the hour-long training session, involving Beckham and Phil Neville. Beckham received brief treatment with an ice pack on his thigh, but it was merely a precaution. Giggs twice clattered into Phil Neville during what was supposed to be a light-hearted routine. Neville's left ankle needed a swift icing but after a few minutes' attention from the physio he resumed training. Beckham was able to walk off at the end of the session apparently unhurt.

Former Tottenham and Barcelona striker Steve Archibald had been watching United train. He went down on to the pitch he'd graced as a player and spoke to Ferguson. The brief conversation was to have a major impact on United's players the following night. Archibald, who had been in Terry Venables' Barcelona team, beaten in the 1986 European Cup final, recalled his dismay after losing. He told Ferguson it was agony looking at the European Cup on the table waiting to be presented to the winners, knowing he couldn't touch it or hold it. 'I know son, I know,' said Ferguson.

Meanwhile, in the city centre United's fans continued to enjoy themselves. 'By Tuesday night the streets had become slick with spillages of one kind and another and crowded with clinging figures who, dazed and rouged by the unhappy combination of too much cheap beer and too much hot sun, looked unlikely to make it through to the final, or who, at the very least, would be undergoing late fitness tests,' wrote Giles Smith in the *Daily Telegraph*. There was no trouble in Barcelona, but three English fans were arrested in the beach town of Lloret de Mar after a scuffle with Bayern supporters. Otherwise all was calm and the only real trouble the fans had was finding their way back to their accommodation. At least the alcohol meant they'd sleep well.

Unlike Dwight Yorke, who had another dream. This time, unusually, it was terrible and woke him up at about 2 a.m. Yorke had a vague sense something was wrong but couldn't remember what the dream was about. He switched on the TV and tried to find an English channel. He'd been watching *Sky News* all evening, but now he couldn't find it. Instead, he watched a programme in Spanish. He didn't understand a word. He rang a friend in Australia but couldn't get through. Yorke sat and thought, 'Who else can I ring at this time of night?' He couldn't think of anyone. Eventually he went back to bed, but he didn't sleep well.

Cole had no such troubles. 'The only thing that really bugged me was waiting for it all to happen,' he says, 'no nerves, no nightmares and certainly no fear, only the sheer frustration of wanting to get the final job done.'

On the morning of the match *The Sun* ran a story saying Ferguson would be knighted if United won. It all added to the pressure. Sandy Busby set off for Barcelona knowing that a United victory would eclipse the legendary accomplishments of his late father. Under Sir Matt, United had won the league, the FA Cup and the European Cup but, as Law had noted, never two in the same season, let alone three. Nevertheless, Ferguson was usually one of the first to point out how awesome Busby's achievement had been in rebuilding the club with the help of his assistant Jimmy Murphy out of the ruins of the Munich crash.

The Boss had died in 1994 after hanging on just long enough to see his beloved club become league champions for the first time since 1967. But the 1993 championship-winning side did not have the flair of the present team. 'My dad,' says Sandy, 'would have drooled over this side. Him and Jimmy Murphy, they'd have drooled over Beckham, Giggs, Scholes and Butt.' Sandy clenched his fist as he said of Scholes, 'He's got a little bit of that . . . Jimmy liked a player to have some steel. And Solskjaer; he reminds me a bit of one of the players who died in the crash, Billy Whelan. He used to look slow, he'd drag and drag, and suddenly he'd be round the player and away.'

It was another Munich survivor, Bobby Charlton, who'd first suggested the appointment of Aberdeen manager Alex Ferguson as United boss. After he arrived Fergie enjoyed seeing Busby at Old Trafford. 'They had great respect for each other,' Sandy recalls. 'My dad had a little office, where he mainly answered letters, and Alex always used to look in and say "How are you, old yin?" My dad would say, "I'm all right son; come in" and they'd have a natter. Alex told him he wanted him on the team bus. He said, "I want the kids to see you when they're getting on." And so he did go to a few away games with them, which was lovely.'

Manchester Airport was swamped in red again on the Wednesday as another 10,000 fans prepared to jet off to Barcelona. Extra staff were employed as Ringway handled hundreds of flights during one of the busiest mornings in its history. Airport managers praised the patient fans who faced lengthy check-in queues for more than 30 jets to northern Spain. Former United skipper Steve Bruce was one of the first to head to Spain that morning. He was taking his son to the match.

The thousands of fans arrived in Barcelona stone-cold sober. The Civil Aviation Authority had ordered that no alcohol should be served on any of the flights. If Ringway Airport was chaotic, Barcelona was even worse. Hundreds of coaches jostled for position outside the main terminal, waiting to transport the United supporters to their hotels. The fans were drawn towards one coach with horns painted on the front and were having a great time waving their red banners in front of it like a matador's cape. Fortunately, the driver had a sense of humour. All the new arrivals could see when they landed was a sea of red and white. There were so few Bayern fans that the Red Army wondered which airport the Germans were using. The coach journey to the hotels confirmed that Barcelona was packed with United supporters. In the build-up to the final the city, heaving with holidaymakers, was a blaze of red on every main road and on the Ramblas thoroughfare throughout the day. The sound of Mancunian chanting echoed from every corner as the fans enjoyed their day in the sun. 'Championes, championes,' they sang, their voices ricocheting deafeningly from the tall buildings. They made their presence felt in the pulsating heart of the city as they strode up and down in a purposeful, thrilling tide. Drink was consumed in huge quantities, but the fans did their best to charm the locals. 'Takin' over, takin' over, takin' over Bar-ce-LON-a,' roared the Stokey Reds, Stoke-on-Trent's branch of the United supporters' club, cans of Stella Artois clasped firmly in their hands.

Spanish police were deployed in a massive show of force in an effort to prevent violence between English and German fans. They began patrolling around the Nou Camp early and would number at least 5,500 by the end of the day. The police said they were worried that already tense relations between rival fans could heat up during the day as English and German supporters celebrated before heading to the game. Local newspapers said police had been given the order to exercise a 'strong hand' in dealing with possible violence to prevent a repeat of scenes like the disastrous 1985 European Cup final in Belgium, when 39 people died in the Heysel Stadium disaster.

Barcelona looked more like Cold War Berlin as the police set up roadblocks splitting the city into British and German zones to keep the fans apart. The action was part of an international police operation to prevent any serious outbreak of hooliganism. Police intelligence officers said they had identified 500 United fans and 300 Bayern supporters who were potential troublemakers. Eugenio Pino, chief of the central anti-riot brigade, said '700 bad people is a lot of bad people'.

Officials were also worried that black market tickets might have scuppered efforts to ensure rival fans would not be in the same area of the stadium. Some United supporters had already paid £500 for tickets which they later discovered were in the Bayern end. Barcelona residents, who had marvelled at the alcohol capacity of the visiting fans, were warned to stay away from the stadium. 'If I lived in Barcelona, on Wednesday I would try to leave my house as little as possible,' said Pino. Reassuringly though, the relaxed mood among the supporters at the airport was transferred to Barcelona. By Wednesday afternoon United fans were ten-deep on the pavements outside almost every café bar. In one part of the city four Bayern fans stood outside a butcher's cornershop chewing on whole, spit-roasted chickens. Nearby, United fans sang 'Ooh-ah, Cantona' and drank lager for Britain. The whole of north-east Spain seemed to be bouncing to the United beat.

According to Cole, the mood in the United camp was such that it was almost like the preparation for a third-round Milk Cup tie at a Third Division club. The team didn't do anything special until lunchtime when Ferguson gave the last of his customary pre-match team talks that seemed to get longer every season. He was well known for digging into his dossier for European matches so he could outline the strengths and weaknesses of the other side. He always focused on different players and provided a general breakdown.

Cole was given instructions about Bayern's central defender, Samuel Kuffour. Ferguson told Cole to play Kuffour the way he had at Old Trafford in the qualifying round. He said if Cole moved

Kuffour around the big stopper wouldn't stand a chance, adding that if Yorke and Cole were busy and mobile and kept their heads down United would win.

Ferguson went back to his room and sat on the veranda. He looked out over the sea and wondered if perhaps the European Cup was one trophy fate would keep out of his reach. 'If it did,' he thought, 'I would still have reason to be satisfied with my career in management . . .' That career had begun 25 years ago at East Stirlingshire when he took over a club that didn't have enough players to put out a team. He'd won 10 major trophies in Scotland and 11 with United, having taken the European Cup Winners' Cup back to both Pittodrie and Old Trafford. Ferguson didn't even count 'extras' like the Charity Shield and European Super Cup, won with a single victory. The question now was whether he could add the most precious trophy of all to his collection.

Three

Champions League Final

Wednesday, May 26, 1999 was the most important day in the history of Manchester United Football Club. There had been many special days since the club was formed in 1878 as Newton Heath LYR by Lancashire and Yorkshire Railway workers. But this one could establish the Reds as the only team ever to win the coveted treble by adding the title of European Champions to those of Premier League Champions and FA Cup winners. Not even the mighty Liverpool side of the 1970's and '80's, or indeed United's own great teams of the '50s, '60s or '90s, had managed that. If they could pull it off the Reds would become the best European team bar none.

The quest for ultimate glory in English football began in the League's first season in 1888–89 when Preston North End won the 'double' of League Championship and FA Cup without losing a single game or conceding an FA Cup goal. Eight years later Aston Villa repeated the feat. But it wasn't until the great Tottenham side of 1960–61 that the double was achieved in the 20th century. Ten years later Arsenal matched their north London rivals. The only way to top the double was to add the League Cup and/or a European trophy. No team had ever won all three domestic trophies, but Liverpool managed the League Championship, the League Cup and the European Cup in 1984 and followed that with their own double in 1986.

From 1993 United began to dominate domestic football when they won their first League championship – and the first Premiership – since Matt Busby's great team of Charlton, Law and Best had captured the title in 1967. The Reds followed that with doubles of their own in 1994 and 1996 inspired by the wonderful skills of the idolised Eric Cantona. But Arsenal matched United by securing their second double in 1998. The only way for the swashbuckling 1999 United side to establish themselves as the best of the 20th century was to win the 'impossible' treble.

Cynics could argue that the Champions League had produced an Also-Rans' Cup final since both United and Bayern had qualified by finishing runners-up in their leagues (to Arsenal and Kaiserslautern) in 1998. The purists and traditionalists, who relished the simplicity of a contest between national champions, might be disappointed. But with both clubs having already won their domestic titles and going for the treble such protests just didn't stand up. Ajax and PSV Eindhoven from Holland and Celtic's pioneering team of 1967 had all won the treble. But neither the Dutch nor the Scottish leagues could be compared with the Bundesliga or the Premiership. No team from one of the big five European countries – Italy, England, Germany, Spain or France – had ever won the treble. Whoever triumphed would deserve to be remembered as the most successful club side in a single season in Europe (Bayern still had to win the German Cup final but were hot favourites). History was about to be made and the English press hoped the team from Manchester would make it. 'Now United can win and win in style,' wrote David Lacey of *The Guardian*, 'and although they will be pressed to revive the script of 1968, they have it in their power to give the 20th century one last European final to remember.'

The enormity of the occasion may not have been getting to the seemingly relaxed Ferguson or his players but the Press sensed a different atmosphere in Barcelona, among the fans at least. Paul

Hayward of the *Daily Telegraph* summed up the change: ' . . . already there is a feeling here that United's third league and cup double has retreated into the pages of Rothmans. Among United's eager but edgy followers there is not the proprietorial air that can be seen when they travel to Leicester or Wimbledon.'

As Ferguson watched a group of United supporters playing around in the pool at the team hotel there was a part of him that wanted to be as light-hearted as they were. The fans were relying on the players and staff and Ferguson to deliver happiness. But United's manager knew it wouldn't be honest to envy their carefree mood. He'd always craved the pressure of responsibility, of being asked to make things happen on the pitch. All his working life had been a preparation for the challenge awaiting United a few miles up the road in the magnificent Nou Camp.

Gary Neville thought this was the biggest match of his life. ' . . . because of the way I was brought up, because I have been a Manchester United fan since I was four years old, because of where I'm from, nothing could be bigger than the match I am going to play in the Nou Camp tonight.

'We know that if we achieve what the [1968] team did by winning the trophy, we will take our place alongside them in the history of the club. There is a feeling that we need to complete a jigsaw against Bayern Munich tonight.'

Thousands of miles away in the Caribbean the day of the most important game in the career of Dwight Yorke, Tobago's prodigal son, began like any other. The only sign of football frenzy in his village was the Rastafarian sitting by the barber's shop wearing a Manchester United shirt with number 19 on the back. Chun was one of Dwight's best friends. The strip was a present. Chun made sure the whole island was hyped up for the game, even if it didn't look that way. 'We are a Third World country,' he said. 'We are a relaxed people.'

'The Red Army expects – Can Man U deliver?' asked ITN's Trevor McDonald as pictures of hordes of pink United fans cavorting in the Spanish sunshine were beamed home. The entertaining Red Army brought a broad smile to the faces of the locals in Barcelona. Tea-time commuters on the metro were squashed by the fans but cheered up with a full repertoire from the Stretford End.

By now the streets of Manchester were deserted as fans crammed into pubs and gathered around TVs at home. Hundreds of fans flocked to the Lower Kersal Social Club next to United's Salford training ground. There were two giant screens in the men-only games room christened the Vault of Dreams by the regulars.

In the Welsh seaside town of Mumbles 61-year-old Munich survivor Ken Morgans, affectionately nicknamed Tiger, settled down to watch the match in the local tennis club. The irony of United playing a team from Munich in the European Cup final was not lost on the club's former winger.

Back in Tobago only family and friends had been invited to watch the match at the Yorkes'. Dwight had grown up in a modest bungalow in Robert Street, Canaan. His mother, Grace, still lived there. Dwight's other school friends went to watch the game a few blocks away at the house of Gymbuck, an ornithology student at Warwick University when Yorke was at Aston Villa.

Yorke had been desperate to join United. He'd cried and begged to get his dream move to Old Trafford. Twice in three months he went to the home of Villa chairman Doug Ellis to ask whether the club would release him from his contract. Each time Ellis had refused. Then one morning the Villa chairman opened his curtains at about 7.45 and saw Yorke's BMW. It was the last day players could be signed to register for the Champions League. Yorke had been sitting there for hours. He told Ellis it was his ambition in life to play for United and in the Champions League. But again Ellis said he wouldn't let him leave Villa. 'He was very distressed, let me leave it at that,' says Ellis. The Villa chairman felt 'pretty horrible'. He called a meeting with his other colleagues and manager John Gregory. They decided Yorke was perhaps not going to give his best if he was kept at Villa against his will. 'We decided if (United chairman) Martin Edwards was prepared to go to £12 million we would let him (Yorke) talk to United,' said Ellis. Within 10 minutes Edwards called back. 'Done,' he said. Yorke was finally on his way to the Theatre of Dreams.

United's reacquaintance with their status as the team players dreamed of joining owed almost everything to a certain Frenchman whose Gallic flair had reawakened the sleeping giant and set the club on a trophy-collecting spree in the 1990's. 'Ooh' and 'Aah' would forever rhyme with his name at Old Trafford. Eric Cantona was in Barcelona to see his old team achieve what even his remarkable skills had failed to deliver: the European Cup. He sauntered around the white marquees that ringed the stadium with the air of a man who had helped to create United's new-found invincibility. Cantona reminded everyone what the club had so recently achieved, but it was another majestic player from an earlier era whose presence did so much to embroider the occasion with its sense of history – Sir Bobby Charlton.

By now, United's few days in their hotel hideaway had left them feeling good. Cole sums up the mood: ' . . . we ended up so relaxed and laid back that we were almost falling over by the time they had us in the lobby, boots and kit packed, and ready for a bit more action with those rather impertinent, err, cocksure chaps from Munich.'

Ferguson made his way to the team coach for the short journey to Barcelona for the biggest night of his professional life. 'Dad,' said his son Jason, 'if you don't win tonight it won't change things. You will still be a great manager and we all love you.' As Ferguson admits in his autobiography *Managing My Life*: 'Who could fear anything after hearing words like those?'

The players and backroom staff boarded the coach and were soon heading along the motorway. 'I tell you, it was unreal,' says Cole. 'It was like a trip to the beach with Spanish music playing on the coach's stereo system. There was the odd bit of banter, too, but – boy oh boy – were the troops relaxed. To a ridiculous degree, I would say. If anybody was feeling uptight and screwed-up it didn't show at all. History beckoned and we almost treated it with a yawn.'

Suddenly, the rising splendour of the Nou Camp – the home of Barcelona and Catalonia's cathedral of football – appeared surrounded by a mass of red. The police outriders nudged the coach through a crowd of United supporters the size of which was almost beyond belief. 'Thirty thousand tickets, that's what they suggested we had as the allocation,' says Cole. 'Double it, then add the number you first thought of, and you might be close. Even then, the importance and impending drama of such a massive occasion didn't even penetrate. It was as if we were in a dream.'

Despite having played more than 350 European matches between them, United and Bayern had never met in a competitive game before the group stage of the Champions League. Bayern were one of only four clubs to have won each of the three European club competitions along with Ajax, Barcelona and Juventus. United had won the European Cup in 1968 and the Cup Winners' Cup in 1991, when they beat Barcelona 2–1, but had never lifted the UEFA Cup.

United had lost just one match out of 20 in their last two seasons in Europe – a 1–0 defeat to Juventus in Turin almost 18 months ago. Bayern's only defeat this season was a surprise upset by Danish side Brondby, who won 2–1 in Copenhagen with two goals in the last three minutes. Only four times in the past 21 seasons had both European Cup finalists scored. Everyone hoped this year would be different. United had scored 126 goals in all their matches so far this season, including 29 goals in Europe, while Bayern had scored 93 with 24 in European competition.

Ferguson had been excited rather than apprehensive as the match, which was being beamed live to more than two billion people around the world, got closer. But he was glad when the quiet hours of playing the game through in his head were replaced by the noisy, colourful reality of the Nou Camp which had been chosen to stage the final in honour of Barcelona's centenary celebrations. The players were simply in awe of the place. 'When we got to the Nou Camp, you just stand there, looking up at the stands and think bloody hell, it's unbelievable,' says Yorke. 'I'd been there once before, when we played Barcelona. And I thought the same thing – fantastic.'

Schmeichel's 398th and last appearance for United, equalling Bill Foulkes's 30-year-old club record of 35 European games, was potentially the most epic. Six months had passed since he'd announced at a press conference in Manchester that this would be his last season at Old Trafford after eight 'contented and successful years'. But now he was so focused on winning that he didn't think about it being his last appearance in a United shirt. 'There was no room for sentimental reflection within the ring of concentration I have always built up around myself in the lead up to a match,' he says.

When they got inside the dressing room Yorke thought the atmosphere was fine. 'Cool, quiet, but I'd say quite relaxed.' The players had been through pressure games before. It wasn't anything new to them. Cole slouched about for a while. He wasn't usually the type to walk out onto the pitch in his club suit and tie. This time, though, was different. He was tempted up the steep concrete steps leading to the arena along with his team-mates and, suddenly, he was inside the fabulous Nou Camp, 'a huge canyon of a place but never too daunting, just inspiring'. He looked around at the thousands gathering on the towering terraces. That's when the realisation of what it was really all about, the immensity of the next 90 minutes, hit him for the first time. It wasn't quite butterflies, or the panic of big-match nerves, but he'd definitely got a feeling of how important the match was.

It was soon time for the players to return to the dressing room. As they filed back in Ferguson looked, as he always did, for signs of how they were coping with the demands facing them. There was a calm, matter-of-fact, do-the-job atmosphere as they gathered in near silence with one purpose on their minds. They all quietly understood that it was time to get serious. There was a strong sense of determination in the room and little for Ferguson to do but wish them well. Before the match he gave what Schmeichel describes as 'one of his more beguiling and emotional team talks'.

'There isn't a team in the world who play as well as you do,' said Ferguson. 'And that's why you mustn't be afraid. There's no reason to be. No team can beat you if you play at the level you are capable of – and of course that's what you'll do. I am very proud, and honoured, of what you've already given for me and the club. The only thing I regret is that I can't send you all out on to the pitch. As you know, we're only allowed to play with 11 men, but all of you without exception deserve to be out there today.'

Ferguson didn't mention the suspended Keane and Scholes but he did refer to United's rivals Arsenal. 'You are playing a team who are not as good as Arsenal,' he told them. And Ferguson sincerely believed the Gunners were a better side than Bayern. But he had to tell his players that anyway because the Germans had a similar mentality to an English team. The message Ferguson gave them was:

'You've got the better of Arsenal this season, so you can certainly beat Bayern.'

The teams for the final were:

MANCHESTER UNITED: 1 Peter Schmeichel; 2 Gary Neville; 3 Denis Irwin; 4 Jaap Stam; 5 Ronny Johnsen; 15 Jesper Blomqvist; 8 Nicky Butt; 7 David Beckham; 11 Ryan Giggs; 9 Andrew Cole; 10 Dwight Yorke. Substitutes: 17 Raimond Van der Gouw; 20 Ole Gunnar Solskjaer; 12 Philip Neville; 10 Teddy Sheringham; 24 Wes Brown; 4 David May; 34 Jonathan Greening.

BAYERN MUNICH: 1 Oliver Kahn; 25 Thomas Linke; 10 Lothar Matthaus; 4 Samuel Kuffour; 2 Markus Babbel; 18 Michael Tarnat; 16 Jens Jeremies; 11 Stefan Effenberg; 14 Mario Basler; 19 Carsten Jancker; 21 Alexander Zickler. Substitutes: Bernd Dreher; 7 Mehmet Scholl; 17 Thorsten Fink; 20 Hasan Salihamidzic; 5 Thomas Helmer; 8 Thomas Strunz; 24 Ali Daei.

Only four Englishmen were in United's side – Beckham, Butt, Cole and Gary Neville. The others were from Denmark, Eire, Holland, Norway, Sweden, Tobago and Wales. By contrast, Ghanaian defender Kuffour was the only foreign player in Bayern's team, given the absence of Bixente Lizarazu and Elber. There were five internationals, including a couple of foreigners, on the German team's bench. Unusually, both sides were captained by their goalkeepers: Schmeichel and Kahn.

UEFA regulations stated that both teams should change their strip if there was a colour clash unless the finalists reached an agreement. The clubs felt it would be a shame not to allow one team to wear their usual colours and agreed to toss a coin. United won and would play in their traditional kit of red shirts and white shorts. Bayern, whose first-choice strip featured a white and red shirt and white shorts, would play in their silver-grey second colours.

There wasn't an empty seat in the stadium. The 90,000 fans – the largest crowd ever for a Champions League final – produced an incredible noise. Most United fans were grouped in the Nord Gol part of the ground. But many neutral areas were also filled with Reds fans from all over the world. They clearly outnumbered Bayern's followers. Banners showed United's appeal from Aylesbury to Zurich, while the flags on the German side of the ground were of a local flavour.

United had invited the 1968 European Cup-winning team to Barcelona as their guests. Denis Law, who didn't play at Wembley, and Shay Brennan couldn't go. But Pat Crerand, George Best and almost the whole of the rest of the team had made the pilgrimage to the Nou Camp. 'That is tremendous that the club would do this,' said Crerand. 'It was a huge night for us back in 1968 but this is even bigger now because the lads could win the treble and I just hope that they do.'

'Those of us who played that day still see each other regularly, but we regard the invitation as an appropriate way of acknowledging the achievement at Wembley,' said Bobby Charlton. 'It is, after all, a long time since we have been in this position. We are as well prepared as we will ever be. I hope we can do it, for this is such a showpiece for us and we want to do it right.'

Alex Stepney, who'd written his name into the club's history with that last-gasp save to deny Eusebio in the 1968 final, had somewhat ironically been given 24 hours' leave from his job as a goalkeeping coach by his employers and United's rivals Manchester City.

The match was being played on what would have been Sir Matt Busby's 90th birthday. Crerand wondered if that might be a sign. 'You have to think about that,' he said, 'but you can never be sure about such things. What you can be sure of, though, is that Matt would have been proud of this team, not just for the success they have had but for the way they play the game. It's what he always believed in, attractive and attacking football.' That had been United's trademark and Ferguson had carried on the tradition established by his fellow Scot.

Charlton sat nervously in the stands alongside the club's other directors and a group of FIFA delegates who'd help to choose the venue for the 2006 World Cup. He was hoping and praying for a United victory and a second European triumph after 31 years. There were also visiting celebrities and dignitaries including several politicians and many football personalities, among them two former Barcelona coaches in England's Terry Venables and Dutch master Johan Cruyff.

As the teams walked out into the evening sunlight for the 44th European Cup final, the crowd rose as one and generated a wall of sound. The German fans held up a mosaic of cards spelling out BAYERN MUNICH. Cole just couldn't believe what was waiting for them:

> ' . . . not just a cacophony of noise, a wall of it, in fact, but so much eye-blinding colour and, then, brain-bashing numbers; it seemed as though the whole planet was there to watch the game and they had all turned up in United red. I've never witnessed anything like it in my life. Never will again, most probably. There was only one reaction in my case. Goosepimples, from the top of my head to the end of my big toe, they just covered me. Along with a shudder down the spine that might well have raised a sizeable measurement on the Richter scale. And I'm not supposed to be the emotional type. But, in that instant, I understood, no matter what happened to me in the future and without any shadow of a doubt, that this was the most significant night of my life in football. Nothing could ever compare. Whatever fate had in store in the years ahead, even reaching a European Cup final again, for instance, would not be able to compete. It couldn't even come close. This was the first time, the best time. I felt as though my heart was going to explode under the intensity of the whole experience. There was first a rumbling noise, then a roar, then an explosion on a deafening scale as our fans backed their team like never before.'

United's supporters had often been too quiet at Old Trafford and were frequently drowned out despite outnumbering the away fans by more than ten to one. But nobody could accuse them of not backing their team vocally at the Nou Camp. ' . . . this was something else,' recalls Cole. 'This was the hard core. And did they make a racket. It blew my mind, it blew me away.'

The announcement that Jesper Blomqvist would play in a United team with two wingers delighted the red-shirted hordes as their team warmed up for the match. 'On a perfect Catalan evening of blue skies, a dipping sun and a sense of both great theatre and expectation, it was an early and positive psychological step by the English champions against their German counterparts,' thought Timothy Collings of Reuters.

The dew on the grass made it a perfect surface on which to play. Bayern aimed to make the most of it and attacked as soon as bald-headed referee Pierluigi Collina, a 39-year-old financial consultant, blew his whistle to start the game. He was the first Italian to referee the final since Larese took charge of the 1991 Red Star Belgrade versus Marseille match.

United supersub Solskjaer sometimes got feelings it was going to be his night and he was going to score. When that happened he'd call one of his friends in Norway. Solskjaer had already made that call. Just before the game started he turned to reserve team coach Jim Ryan and said: 'I think this is going to be my night.'

The game kicked off to ear-bursting songs and chants from the excited Red Army. The disappointed Keane had to just sit up in the stand, alongside United's reserve team manager Jim Ryan, with Scholes and Berg. All of them wished they were out on the pitch. Before the match Ferguson had offered some advice to the fans who had tickets. 'Don't hold your breath and get a grip of your seat and make sure you're tied down quite tight because it could be a roller coaster of a match.'

In the opening minutes the weight of history and expectation all seemed too much for United. It appeared to be a crushing burden and Ferguson's players looked as if they were frozen with tension and the realisation of how close they were to the prize they had pursued for so long.

Bayern played exactly as Ferguson thought they would, relying heavily on long balls up to their front men, Jancker and Zickler. Sheringham thought Bayern's tactics were strange for a German side. 'It was a bit at odds with what we had come to expect of German football, with its considered, practical approach to the game and its nuances,' he says. 'Organisation was their watchword, and they usually played solid keep-ball, moving the ball through the midfield and getting the opposition running about. And here they were playing like Wimbledon.' What Sheringham and Ferguson could not foresee was that one such unsubtle attack would have disastrous consequences for United. Then again, the Reds had an alarming habit of making life difficult for themselves in Europe. Barely five minutes had gone when Johnsen ran into the back of Jancker, knocking him over on the edge of the penalty area as Irwin came across to try to cover. Collina blew for a free-kick in a very dangerous position. United thought Johnsen's challenge was accidental. ITV's commentator Ron Atkinson agreed. 'I think they were very fortunate to get that free-kick, Bayern Munich,' he said. 'That looked a genuine collision for me between Johnsen and Jancker.'

Bayern eyed up the situation, 20 yards out. The ball was to the left of Schmeichel's goal. Basler and Effenberg weighed up the options. United quickly gathered six men in a wall that should have been unbreachable. 'We thought we were set up,' says Cole, 'we thought we had it right, it should have been no bother.' Unfortunately, United's keeper had positioned himself in no man's land.

The Germans were past masters at finding openings. Jancker and Babbel made the key moves. Jancker, marked by Stam, joined United's defensive shield as Basler, the flamboyant midfielder, loitered menacingly over the ball and Effenberg moved away leaving the kick to his team-mate. As Basler approached the ball, Jancker moved away from the wall taking Stam with him. Then Babbel leaned on Butt, giving his shirt a slight tug as he peeled backwards and ducked behind the red sentries in a classic ploy that effectively took the United midfielder out of the end of the wall. Ferguson was itching to run on to the pitch and stop Butt falling for the ploy, but he was helpless as United's cover was blown and the gap was created.

Basler, having bided his time, half-hit a low curling shot into the space. Although he scuffed it, the ball came at an angle Schmeichel hadn't anticipated. It skidded around the wall as the big keeper, who was badly unsighted, hardly moved. He was stuck in the middle of his goal, as if his feet were set in clay, while the ball crept into the bottom left-hand corner of the net. The hole-in-the-wall gang had struck and the Germans had a precious 1–0 lead after just five minutes. It was Basler's fourth goal of the campaign and a brilliantly worked strike straight off the training ground. United's players looked around, their faces filled with horror. They couldn't believe what had happened because it was a poorly struck free-kick. Schmeichel clapped his hands together in frustration. The goal had spoiled the opening of the final engagement of his farewell tour and meant he would not keep his 180th clean sheet in eight seasons with United. 'Manchester United as they've done time and time again on this European run have made it hard for themselves,' said ITV's Clive Tyldesley. '[They've] been trying to cram everything into 10 dizzy days. This is a handicap race they are trying to win and now they have given themselves one more handicap.'

Accusing glances were aimed at Schmeichel who was a picture of abject misery. '. . . one would have thought that a keeper of Schmeichel's experience and guile would have ensured that he had the angle covered,' wrote Mark Lawrenson in *The Irish Times*. United's players were understandably angry. 'Yes, there was a bit of shouting at each other,' says Yorke, 'but there always is when you concede a goal. Players say, "Why didn't you clear it? Why didn't you do this or that?" Pete never has anyone on the line for free kicks. He's so good. He doesn't need them. So I don't know what happened, how it got through the wall.' Schmeichel stared back at his defence and said: 'I just couldn't see it'. He thought it should never have been allowed to happen. 'I think that pissed off a lot of our chaps,' says Cole. 'If our goalkeeper, the best in the world at that, couldn't see the strike, he was left with one option. He should have adjusted the wall until he could.' If Keane had been there surely they would have organised themselves better.

United were used to coping with adversity and Yorke was philosophical. 'It was nothing new, as we'd gone through the championship chasing games, having to fight back from being behind. But it was very disappointing. But you do what you always do – think positive. You have to think ahead, tell yourself there are still 80 minutes to go, we can still get back.'

Nevertheless, from such a demoralising, disappointing beginning it looked a long way back. ' . . . we were plunged into the nightmare of chasing the game against opponents who could emphasise their strengths and hide their limitations by applying a policy of unambitious containment,' says Ferguson. 'If we had taken the lead, we would have tried to kill off the opposition. The Germans were concerned with killing the game. With such a barren philosophy, they did not deserve to win . . . '

Ferguson put United's early vulnerability down to 'edginess'. They were used to crucial games but a European Cup final was another level. The weight of the club's history and all the heady speculation about the treble was on their shoulders.

The Mancunians were there to see the lads lift the cup . . . but now they had to lift the team. They were disappointed rather than dismayed. 'Stand up for the Champions' began to filter around the Nou Camp as the fans reacted to the goal by redoubling their chants. They got louder and louder and within seconds more than 30,000 United fans were standing.

United didn't create a clear chance until the 21st minute when Yorke took a hopeful swing at a bouncing ball at the near post from a deflected Beckham cross and caused panic. Kahn stretched above Cole to punch the ball away and Effenberg completed the clearance. It was the first time the German keeper had been forced to make a save.

United clearly weren't at their best without Keane and Scholes. ' . . . our football did not approach the levels of fluency and penetration that had distinguished our best performances during the season,' says Ferguson, referring in particular to the way United had demoralised Juventus in the semi-final. 'But at least we were the only team with a positive attitude.'

Graham Spiers of *Scotland on Sunday* agreed with the United manager. 'Alex Ferguson's team gnawed away at Bayern without appearing able to crack their resolve, but the Germans, with their goal advantage, were self-punishingly cynical and negative.

Following Mario Basler's opening strike, the way Bayern sought to stifle this game's creative ebb and flow was quite depressing.'

United's failure to turn possession into clear-cut chances was partly due to their unfamiliar formation. Both sides of Ferguson's normally wide-flowing team were emasculated. Using his left foot as he galloped down the right, Giggs was carried inside rather than outside his marker and wasn't as effective. On the opposite flank Blomqvist was clearly no Giggs as he lacked the pace needed to go past Babbel. Ferguson's gamble simply hadn't worked. 'It was not Beckham's fault,' wrote Oliver Holt in *The Times*. 'When he did get possession, he used it wisely and well, spraying passes right and left towards Andy Cole, Giggs and Blomqvist, but far from being discomfited by the sight of Beckham occupying his unfamiliar role, Bayern seemed to be encouraged by it.'

When United had the ball Bayern pushed Matthaus into midfield where Beckham already faced the formidable twin obstacle of Effenberg and Jeremies. Thus play became congested in the centre of the pitch. It was simple enough, but it had the effect of swamping Butt and Beckham and denying them the time or space to operate. Bayern's tactics were clever. Their wing-backs were the string tying Yorke and Cole into a sack created by the three central defenders.

Paul Hayward of the *Daily Telegraph* was disappointed with the impact of the Reds' formation. 'For once there was no howling dervish from United, no unstoppable force ripping into a foreign defence, just uncertain, crab-like incursions that lacked the usual fluency and conviction.'

Yorke looked more nervous than Ferguson had ever seen him. But Bayern's defence deserved credit for their close-marking and quick tackling, especially the brilliant man-marking job done by Linke on Yorke. Ferguson thought Kuffour was even more impressive. Cole and Yorke, the most prolific scoring partnership in the Premier League, were subdued. 'Yorke, in particular, appeared to have allowed his mind to drift at times back to West Indies beaches, and he treated possession like loose pesetas,' says Matt Dickinson of *The Times*. Sheringham could see all too clearly that United had yet to fire on all cylinders. ' . . . we were not at our most convincing in the first half,' he says. 'Sure, we were taking the game to them, but we could not quite seem to make it gel.'

Although Bayern were in front, their President Franz Beckenbauer had been watching the match in the agitated state of somebody who was afraid his team were going to lose. But at least the 'Kaiser' was 100 per cent behind them. In a pub in downtown Cologne a German journalist was watching the match among equal numbers of Germans and Englishmen. There was a lot of singing, but it all sounded very strange, off-key and halting. That was because all the Germans supported United and sang in English, while all the Englishmen rooted for Bayern and tried to sing in German. Bayern and United really did have a lot in common. When they played it was hard to be neutral.

The half ended with United looking as though they'd recovered from their early loss. Both Ferguson and Hitzfeld felt the Reds were the better team in the first half despite being a goal behind. Ferguson had shown great restraint in not tinkering with the team before the second half. He had to hope his patience and sense of calm would filter down to his players.

Schmeichel knew Ferguson's half-time analysis would be interesting. United's manager grabbed hold of the big Dane and let him know they had played a bloody awful game from the start. He wanted to know what the hell had happened, giving away a goal like that. Schmeichel clearly wasn't in the mood for an argument so Ferguson said to the team: 'But in the last 20 minutes you played fantastic. Do you realise how many times you could have scored?' The players knew they hadn't really been anywhere near Bayern's goal. But Ferguson had planted a seed of hope.

He told Sheringham that if things hadn't changed and United were still 1–0 down he should get ready to go on after about 20 minutes. Sheringham had mixed emotions. 'I wanted to be involved, but I wanted us to get back in it as well,' he says.

Just before they left the changing room Ferguson tried to rally his players. He decided to use the line Steve Archibald had given him the day before. The United boss stood in the middle of the dressing room and turned slowly to look each player in the eye. It was 9.35 p.m. and he was about to change the course of history. 'Lads, when you go out there if you lose you'll have to go up and get your medals,' said Ferguson. 'You will be six feet away from the European Cup, but you won't be able to touch it, of course. And I want you to think about the fact that you'll have been so close to it and for many of you that will be the closest you will ever get. And you will hate that thought for the rest of your lives. So just make sure you don't lose. Don't you dare come back in here without giving your all.'

Ferguson's oratory was Churchillian. He'd spoken quietly and from the heart. He thought that although it was a simple bit of motivation it nevertheless stressed the gulf between winning and losing such an important match. 'You have got to find a way to affect people's lives through motivation,' Ferguson would tell reporters later. 'But you have to have players who can be motivated. Some people can just melt.' Schmeichel knew the boss had made a very shrewd point, albeit almost recklessly bold. Sheringham thought it was a great speech.

To Schmeichel, at least, it certainly seemed as if United had been transformed when they went out for the second half. Gary Neville trotted towards the fans, gritted his teeth and raised both fists showing the spirit and bond between players and supporters. But Bayern must have been surprised and delighted when United continued to persist with their unbalanced formation. And Ferguson's team-talk did not bring an immediate change of fortune since Bayern started more positively.

Ferguson's forecast that it would be an open game was at last coming true. United were moving forward in their efforts to regain ground and Bayern, instead of sitting back, were also ready to attack and threaten the Reds when the opportunity arose.

United were still finding it difficult to make chances. Bayern knew another goal would kill them off. But the Reds were showing more fight and 10 minutes into the second half they put together their best move of the match so far to create their first clear chance. After a long spell of possession Giggs curled over a cross with his left foot from the right and found Blomqvist, who'd got in front of Babbel on the edge of the six-yard box. The Swede had a wonderful chance to score but couldn't control his touch as he stretched to reach the ball and fired over the bar. He'd missed an excellent chance. The disappointment was all over his face.

A few minutes later, Giggs was about to set off into the heart of the Bayern defence when he was brought down by Effenberg who became the first player to be booked.

The Reds still hadn't broken Bayern's resistance 20 minutes into the second half. By now Sheringham was straining at the leash to get on. The Germans were already showboating. Bayern won a corner. Sheringham watched as Basler dropped the ball and walked over to the corner flag. United's number 10 was warming up right next to the Bayern midfielder who was so confident of a Bavarian triumph that he waved his arms to orchestrate the German fans as they went through their celebratory anthems. Sheringham couldn't believe what he was doing. Basler often waved to the fans but this time it was as if he thought Bayern had already won. 'It was probably in his mind at that point that he had been the match-winner with his free-kick,' says Stam. 'I doubt whether anyone in the German camp had considered the possibility of defeat.'

Sheringham watched Basler 'giving it large'. 'I wasn't best pleased,' he says. 'I still wasn't on the pitch and he was doing that. That's not good to see. The Germans were getting very flash and a bit cocky and it was only 1–0. It gives you more of an incentive.' Basler's actions had clearly stirred up the United forward. 'I saw what he was doing and it wound me up,' says Sheringham. The Germans obviously didn't respect their English opponents. Unwittingly, Basler had helped spur the Reds, and Sheringham in particular, to take swift revenge. The United striker was now on a mission. 'It gives you a sweeter incentive to get on and get a result out of it,' says Sheringham.

Ferguson knew he had a proven goalscorer in Sheringham on the bench, but most people doubted the former Spurs striker could again slip out of his tracksuit, Clark-Kent style, and re-enact his Wembley heroics. Having come on after nine minutes in the FA Cup final to replace the injured Keane and scoring within 96 seconds before setting up Scholes for United's second after half-time it was a tall order to expect anything remotely as dramatic in the Nou Camp. Ferguson realised it was a risk bringing Sheringham on but United had to take risks. He kept the striker waiting for a couple of minutes on the touchline. 'Come on, get me on now,' pleaded Sheringham.

By now, the United supporters were crying in sheer desperation: 'Oh Teddy, Teddy . . . ' They needn't have worried.

Ferguson, with his customary intuition, knew he had to make a change. In the 66th minute the ball went off for a United corner and Ferguson bowed to the inevitable. He took off the ineffective Blomqvist and sent on Sheringham. 'Go out there and get us a goal,' he whispered in his striker's ear. As well as the substitution he changed the formation to 4–3–3. At last Giggs and Beckham were restored to their rightful places with the Welshman moving to the left and the Englishman to the right, while Yorke dropped deeper to form the apex of a diamond midfield.

Sheringham had come a long, long way for this. He had endured ridicule from Spurs fans all season with their chants of 'Oh Teddy, Teddy, he went to Man United and he won fuck all' after a barren first campaign when the Reds ended up without a trophy. But he'd silenced the critics and had two medals in his pocket already. Could he now help United to a third triumph and get his hands on the most valuable medal in European football? The 33-year-old, whose career was born in the unfashionable surroundings of Millwall's Cold Blow Lane in south London, was playing in one of the most fabled stadiums in world football, part of a team that was competing for one of the great prizes in the game. And it all looked as if it was going to end in agonising anticlimax. 'Were we going to end this season of seasons, in which we had already achieved so much, with the crushing disappointment of defeat at the last hurdle?' he wondered. The signs weren't good. But as he ran on to the pitch Sheringham wanted United to win so much it almost hurt.

The Reds reacted well to the change and Sheringham's shrewd runs on the left began troubling Bayern. They looked better balanced. Hitzfeld, sensing United were gaining an advantage, decided to make an astute one of his own in the 70th minute. He sacrificed pace for guile by taking off Zickler and replacing him with German international midfielder Mehmet Scholl who'd suffered with injury all season. Jancker – 'the man for whom we reserved another name', says Cole – was now left to battle on up front alone. Immediately, Scholl made a difference as he formed a creative axis with Effenberg that threatened to finish United off. 'Until then, it had been a pretty even match,' says Effenberg, 'but once Mehmet and I were playing together we made a lot of chances.'

On 72 minutes Scholl found Jancker in the area and he put Effenberg clear on the left with a brilliant first-time chip over United's defence. The 33-year-old midfielder tried to half-volley it over Schmeichel who spread himself like a giant starfish to turn a certain goal into a corner as he reached up to make an outstanding fingertip save. It was a tremendous leap by the Dane, but United desperately needed to reach similar heights at the other end.

Sheringham wasn't impressed. He thought Bayern were arrogant and self-satisfied. 'We had watched as the Germans put the trophy in their cabinet long before they had any right to. We had watched as they played to the crowd with 25 minutes [remaining] as though they had it in the bag. We had watched as they betrayed their reputation for playing calm, coldly logical football by getting more flash than we thought any German side would ever get. We hated all that.'

But Bayern were still in the driving seat. In the 78th minute Scholl almost scored the goal that would have killed United's challenge. Basler, running 40 yards, turned United's defence in knots as he burst down the right, hurdled Beckham's flying tackle and raced towards the penalty area. Scholl, who had run in from the other side, took the ball off him on the edge of the area. Everyone expected a shot. Instead, Scholl delicately chipped the ball over Schmeichel. The Dane watched as the ball floated towards his goal. The delightful chip hit the inside of the right-hand post and bounced into Schmeichel's grateful hands. It was the best move of the match.

With 10 minutes left Hitzfeld took off the tiring Matthaus and replaced him with Fink. 'I was finished but I could have played on,' says Matthaus. Scholl would later criticise his captain, saying he could have finished the match. But Hitzfeld defended his sweeper. 'Lothar was exhausted,' he said. 'You can drive with a flat tyre but you can't drive fast . . . He wanted to play the whole 90 minutes, but he didn't have the stamina.' Yet his departure robbed Bayern of a player who would still have marshalled the defence and helped his team to keep their concentration.

Ferguson now made his last throw of the dice by bringing on Solskjaer for Cole. He felt the fresh legs of Sheringham and Solskjaer were always liable to score. 'I believe in myself and my abilities and if I can come on in the last 10 minutes, the rest of the players are very tired so I'm more likely to score then,' says Solskjaer. 'Has he got a goal up his sleeve?' asked ITV's Clive Tyldesley.

The failure of United's strike force was shown by the fact that Kahn knew tension for the first time nine minutes from the end. Within a minute of coming on for Cole, Solskjaer got his head to a fine Gary Neville cross with his first touch forcing Kahn to haul himself across the line to keep the ball out. It was the closest United had come to scoring. It was also eloquent testimony to the manner in which Matthaus had orchestrated his defence with Linke and Kuffour either side of him.

The match was simply exploding into action. But while United had finally mustered their first serious goal attempt, it was still Bayern who looked more likely to add to their lead. With seven minutes left Basler's corner was cleared but Scholl headed the ball back into the box. Jancker, with his back to goal, elegantly struck an overhead volley that crashed against the underside of the bar and he just missed the rebound with a similar attempt. United should have had the Germans pinned in their own half. Instead they were on the rack and living on their nerves. 'Bayern Munich can't finish them off,' said Tyldesley. 'United's name is on the Cup,' declared Atkinson.

After their lucky escapes United continued to be the more confident aggressors and Bayern's most distinguished cheerleader in the stands, club President Franz Beckenbauer, was not alone in suspecting his troops were still in danger. United chairman Martin Edwards would later tell Ferguson that Beckenbauer gave the impression of being uneasy during most of the match. 'He [Beckenbauer] was apparently agitated, as if he felt that something was not quite right, that they were going to lose,' says the United manager.

But ITV's Atkinson hadn't lost faith in his former club. 'I'll tell you what, if they can equalise, and I'm not betting against them, I think they'll win this,' he said. Yorke was not so sure. ' . . . as the game went on, I have to admit I didn't see it [a United goal] coming,' he says. 'It wasn't a classic game. We didn't play as well as we can. No, I'm not saying I personally didn't play well. You don't think that at the time. I felt great during the game, no problems. But sometimes, when you are trying to be a hero, so eager to score the winning goal, it just doesn't work out. You have already played the game in your mind. Then when you get out there, you're thinking, "If ever I want it to go well, this is the time, this is the one." Then if it doesn't go well . . . things get worse . . . But during the game, I felt fine. I wasn't aware of playing any different from usual.'

The Germans still couldn't find the self-belief to try to outplay United. The Reds had to make every yard of the running. 'Bayern Munich tried to back into the winner's enclosure,' says Ferguson. Graham Spiers of *Scotland on Sunday* agreed. 'In the second half, this cynicism then assumed a ridiculous stereotype of German dourness, Basler at one point even shepherding the ball from the point of attack back to his own half, and every intermittent Bayern corner thereafter taking an eternity to tee-up and deliver. For a side who had twice proved themselves capable of striking United's woodwork, this was pitiful pragmatism.'

The fact was, however, that Bayern were still in front. Even Bobby Charlton thought the season had caught up with United. Somewhere along the line he feared one test would be beyond them. Rob Hughes of *The Times* summed up the mood. 'After Basler's goal we waited, we hoped and, towards the end, we ran out of belief. This was because the German champions had, at times, passed the ball with greater finesse than those of England. It was because German tackles, seldom rash, always brusque, were being timed to a near-perfection that drummed their apparent superiority into the night. David Beckham was the exception. Sometimes his passes, angled, long and perceptive, transcended his team and, indeed, most of the opposition.'

Despite Beckham's heroics, the Reds were still a goal behind and seemed to be looking down a blind alley. Sensing they had the game under control and were heading towards their first European Cup final victory since they won three in a row from 1974–76 Bayern's fans began celebrating noisily. They even included a mocking version of Three Lions with the refrain 'football's coming home' among their anthems in the closing stages as United battled to find an equalizer.

But whatever the views of the Press, and even the doubts raised by the likes of Charlton, the players never lost faith. Stam looked at the electronic scoreboard and saw that United had two or three minutes left to save the game. 'There was no urge in the team to surrender,' he says. Stam couldn't believe it when he saw some of the German players waving to the crowd and that made him even more determined to do everything to get the equaliser. 'Bayern were already taking it easy. They had the look of people who believed the game was already won. They ought to know us better.' Basler was replaced by Salihamidzic as the countdown to the final whistle began. As he was leaving the pitch to the applause of the fans Basler motioned to them to roar the team to victory.

'I thought we'd lost the game,' says Scholes. 'With four minutes left I started to feel a bit sorry for myself. I stopped looking at the stadium clock.'

George Best, the maestro from another era, left the stadium. He believed United's treble dreams were over and dashed off because he didn't want to see his beloved Reds lose. He also wanted to avoid the masses of autograph hunters who always seemed to follow him around. 'We had both thought they were going to lose and didn't want to see that happen,' said his spokesman Paul Hughes. 'Also we had to get George out early because there were about 6,000 supporters trying to get his autograph.'

As Best was leaving RTL commentator Marcel Reif thought it was time to wheel out the traditional line about Germany always beating England. He told RTL's 13.6 million viewers: 'Yet again in the crucial game the English team has proven inferior to the German team.'

The British Press were already scribbling criticisms of Ferguson's tactics. 'As the final whistle approached most of us in the press box were polishing regretful paragraphs pointing out the error of Alex Ferguson's decision to start the match with his wingers occupying unfamiliar positions,' says Richard Williams of *The Independent*. 'Fergie, we were thinking, had gone into the biggest match of his career by making the biggest strategic mistake of his life . . . To imagine that Ferguson would have escaped censure would be unrealistic. But most of us were concluding that, after leading United out of the wilderness to three Doubles in six years, he had earned the right to commit one almighty goof. He would deserve sympathy rather than condemnation.'

Ferguson would later feel the need to defend his decision to use Beckham in central midfield and Giggs on the right. 'Anybody who doesn't think Beckham was the most effective midfielder on the park was taking a strange view of the action,' he said. 'By comparison, Stefan Effenberg was anonymous. The suggestion that Giggs had little impact is hard to square with the frequent demands for back-up that Tarnat directed at his bench. The strain Ryan put on the opposition was one of the factors that steadily drained them in the second half. We had so much of the ball that their strategy of protecting their flimsy lead became an exhausting one and by the end several of them were out on their feet.'

Despite the contributions of Beckham and Giggs United still faced defeat. ' . . . for much of the contest with Bayern, for all Beckham's heroic efforts, we were living on the edge and we knew it,' says Cole. 'Time, and patience, were running out in equal measure as the last two minutes of normal time approached. We needed an act of desperation, we needed a miracle, we needed some sort of intervention from above.' Sheringham also realised they'd have to produce something special quickly.

The tempo hotted up as the final whistle got closer. United never lost their belief. They knew they were a good side and should win, but it didn't look likely. They were unbeaten in 33 games stretching back five months. It was a record waiting to be broken. They'd made a habit of coming from behind to win, but Ferguson had already begun practising to be a good loser.

Even United's players started preparing for the inevitable defeat. 'At 1–0 down with a minute to go, I did think it was all over,' says Beckham. Yorke, too, thought United's chance to equalise had gone. 'As it got near the end, I did think that was it. At the 90th minute, I thought we couldn't come back now. Not this time. It's too late. No one watching could have thought we would do it. Nor did we. We were dead and buried. That didn't mean we gave up, whatever was in our minds. That's not the Manchester United way. You might have doubts. But you don't give up.'

Twelve seconds before the end of the 90 minutes the ball went out of play for a United throw and was caught by a big, dark Hungarian called Birka Tibi, a Reds fan who'd travelled from Budapest for the match. He held it up ceremoniously, kissed it and shouted something totally unintelligible. But whatever he said seemed, finally, to do the trick.

There had been very few stoppages in a clean game. Effenberg was the only name in the book. Red flares illuminated the Nou Camp clock that had stopped to show the end of normal time had been reached. Anxiety grew. 'We are in the last of the 90 minutes,' said ITV's Clive Tyldesley. Ferguson was still out on the touchline when the official flashed the board that spelt hope for United. There were three minutes of added time for them to get the ball past Kahn.

As the stadium clock stopped at 45:00 minutes UEFA General Secretary Gerhard Aigner made his way down to the dressing rooms. He had the job of tying the red-and-white ribbons with the Bayern logo on to the European Cup. As the seconds slipped away the Germans sniffed victory and their 30,000 fans massed at the north end of the stadium whipped up a deafening roar.

Even Sheringham and Solskjaer had so far failed to make their typical intervention. There were glances of frustration among the United players as balls went astray and half-chances weren't taken.

As Neville came over to take the throw few people in the Nou Camp could have expected the game to do anything but revert to Anglo-German type. 'We would have had no reason to be disappointed after the season we had had,' says Ferguson. Nevertheless, he was gearing up to face the final and inevitable question: 'Do you think you will ever win it?' 'You have to address that,' he says. 'But I was refusing to interrupt my way of life in a sense. I wasn't going to let it obsess me. The European Cup was always going to be the thing that you strive for but . . . I was so relaxed about it. I was accepting we were going to lose. I was not going to get myself twisted inside about it because I have got a life to live . . . I hadn't thought the treble was possible. I just felt the FA Cup was one step too many. To get to the semi-final, then a replay and then extra-time. That was the killer for us. I had to juggle the balls. Tried to relieve the pressure. But deep down I didn't feel the treble was really on.'

And so with time almost up Ferguson, the man responsible for the collective self-belief in his players, had effectively run up the white flag by composing himself to take defeat on the chin. It wasn't just a fleeting emotion. He was so convinced United were about to lose that he was already deep into the mental process of preparing himself for defeat. 'I was reminding myself to keep my dignity and to accept that this was not going to be our year after all,' says Ferguson. His assistant Steve McClaren had similar thoughts. 'I have to admit I was beginning to think it would go against us too.' But United's players refused to admit defeat. 'We are the team that never dies,' said Gary Neville. 'If we had been able to stay alive against Juventus in the first leg of the semi-final with an extra-time goal and if, in the FA Cup, we had also beaten Liverpool and Arsenal when they were about to turn the lights out, then why not again here? We were not going to lie down. There was just a refusal to give in.' Schmeichel got the feeling United could score because they were a team who never gave up.

The game was moving into stoppage time when UEFA President Lennart Johansson stood up and headed past the row of VIPs to make his way down to the presentation ceremony. His journey took him past Sir Bobby Charlton and Johansson paused for a polite word. 'Bad luck, Bobby,' he said and disappeared into the bowels of the stadium. Outside as many as 30,000 United fans waited in the streets hoping and praying to hear a tumultuous roar from their soulmates inside the Nou Camp that would signal an equaliser.

Ferguson had said recently: 'At our club you tend to accept that somewhere deep down in the make-up there's something that seems suicidal at times. The players can thrill you and exasperate you at the same time. You're never safe even if you're winning two or three nil. That's the nature of the club and it's not something you can halt. It's ingrained in the fabric. You have got to go with the flow. They will take you right to the wire. They will wait until the last minute while I'm on the bench having three heart attacks and contorted with stomach pains.' His words were about to become prophetic.

Four

The Greatest Two Minutes in the History of Sport

Giggs retrieved the ball from Tibi, the Hungarian fan, and handed it to Neville. He took a long throw into the heart of Bayern's 18-yard area, which was headed out by Kuffour. 'There has been half-a-minute of injury time,' said ITV's Tyldesley. Beckham picked up the ball on the edge of the box, produced a mesmeric dribble just when it was required, including an outrageous dummy, and fed Neville who fired a low cross into the crowded area. Basler was waving to the fans again on the touchline as Effenberg cut out the cross at the expense of a corner on the left. It was United's 11th of the match and perhaps the most important in their history.

'Can Manchester United score?' said Tyldesley. 'They always score.' He should have known. Tyldesley had statistics at his disposal that would have made John Motson jealous. United had only failed to score once all season. For those who thought they still had a chance, this was it. RTL's Reif knew a German victory was very close. 'It must be the last chance for Manchester United and the last danger for Bayern,' he said. Effenberg reckoned it would be the last corner of the match. 'If we can only get the ball away the game is over,' he thought as he prepared to defend.

Schmeichel knew something pretty extraordinary had to happen. He decided to gamble everything and race up the pitch into Bayern's penalty area. It was the last throw of the dice. He realised he could be caught in no man's land. There was a collective groan on United's bench as they saw him lumbering forward. It was hardly the sound of approval. The last time the big man had made such a desperate move he'd torn his hamstring against Arsenal. But he *had* scored with a header against Rotor Volgograd in a UEFA Cup tie at Old Trafford four years earlier.

Out of the corner of his eye Ferguson, still on the touchline, caught a flash of the green-clad 'mad Dane' running past him. The image would stick in his mind. 'He [Ferguson] must have felt like the Saxon facing the gallows spotting Robin Hood, bow at the ready, in the execution crowd,' wrote Townsend of the *Independent on Sunday*. United's manager turned to his assistant Steve McClaren and said, 'Can you believe him [Schmeichel]?'

The Dane believes Ferguson had already virtually accepted United would lose when he saw him running towards Bayern's goal. He thinks his manager had simply lost his overall view of the game. McClaren's previous clubs had never considered taking chances like this, and Ferguson's assistant wasn't completely satisfied with what Schmeichel was doing either. But McClaren had only been with the club four months and the big keeper sensed he didn't yet feel in his soul what it would mean to United to lose a game like this.

Schmeichel ignored Ferguson's vigorous body language, which signalled unmistakably that he should get back to his goal immediately, without worrying in the slightest. (They would laugh a lot about it afterwards.) The possibility of the Germans breaking away and scoring in an open goal didn't cross his mind. 'Schmeichel, look, Schmeichel is coming up into the box for the corner!' said an astounded Reif.

Yorke saw the big man moving into the area. Schmeichel knew he'd make a nuisance of himself, since there's always something unsettling about a keeper in the wrong penalty area. He hoped to get in the way, get a touch on the ball, anything to upset Bayern's defence and go out still trying. 'I suppose you couldn't fault Peter,' says Ferguson. 'After all, there were only two minutes remaining in his last game for United – he probably expected to score.' Beckham approached the left corner flag in front of the United fans in the 14,000 peseta seats. As he shaped up to take the corner, the TV cameras honed in on Sheringham at the near post. Out of the corner of his eye Beckham noticed the cup being carried down the stairs with Bayern's colours already on it. That made him dig a little bit deeper.

Beckham knew United's time was almost up. Stam looked at the big digital clock on the front of the stands ahead of him showing the full 90 minutes was over. Bayern were seconds away from winning the European Cup for the fourth time and the first since 1976. The atmosphere at the Trafford Centre in Manchester, where about 5,000 fans had packed in to watch the action on the giant screen, was more wake than carnival. United were cutting it so fine that Lynne Truss of *The Times* couldn't help but draw a parallel with the last-gasp endings so often seen at the movies. 'The chap with the reprieve who so often bursts in with a one-second-to-midnight message from the governor appeared to have either lost his way in the Ramblas, or got distracted by the Gaudi architecture,' she wrote. 'Either way, he was very late.' But United's players kept the faith. 'We still didn't think it was too much to do,' says Stam. 'But at the end we had to give everything to get the chance.'

As Beckham swung in the corner, Schmeichel's appearance distracted Bayern's defence. 'My green goalkeeper's jersey managed to cause considerable confusion,' he says. 'They didn't know what the hell I was doing.' United's keeper drew three defenders as the ball passed over Sheringham's head. The big Dane caused the kind of chaos defenders dread. 'He got a touch, yes he did, because I saw it,' says Yorke. It was Schmeichel's last contribution as a United player. The ball glanced off a defender's head towards the far post. For Sheringham time stood still for a moment. The whole of his career flashed before him in the blink of an eye. Yorke, so important, so influential in this already historic season, headed weakly back towards the goal. Fink tried to clear but panicked and sliced the ball straight to Giggs on the edge of the area. It was 40 seconds into added time. The Welshman had a chance to write himself into the history books. He swung his right foot with more hope than accuracy and miscued towards the left-hand post.

Sheringham had been allowed to make a diagonal run to the front of the six-yard box – no marker followed him. The closest defender was Effenberg. Solskjaer was also unmarked next to Sheringham and was played onside by two defenders too slow to come off the line from marking the goalposts. It was very lax – very un-German.

The ball ran to Sheringham, with his back half-turned to the goal, in a yard of space. He didn't really know where he was. He knew the ball was coming towards him and thought it might hit the post or go wide. All he had to do was help it over the line from four yards out. 'It didn't have to be pretty or spectacular,' he says, 'it just had to reach the net. If it did that, it would be the most important goal in the recent history of Manchester United . . . '

Sheringham wanted to really smack the ball so that it would rocket over the line like a bullet. But he knew he had to get something on it. He spun as the ball came past him, swung his leg and got the slightest touch off his ankle. He managed to steer it to Kahn's right just inside the post, giving the keeper no chance. Time seemed suspended as all eyes turned to the linesman. Sheringham knew he wasn't offside because a defender was running towards and past him as he scored. But he still glanced at the linesman to make sure. The official's flag stayed resolutely by his side. At last, United were level. 'Name – on – the – trophy,' said Tyldesley as his Geman counterpart Reif was spluttering, 'It cannot be true! Teddy Sheringham! It must not be true!'

The United bench erupted. 'It was a place of total anarchy and madness,' says Cole, 'with the boss going absolutely berserk. Why not? Two minutes left, we should have been doomed, it should all have been over, and yet here we had the salvation of a second chance at lifting that famous tin pot.' The red section of the Nou Camp erupted and flares lit up the night sky. In Manchester it was pandemonium. At the Trafford Centre fans who'd been urging their team on with increasing desperation jumped for joy, leaping into an ornamental pool and hugging everyone in sight.

Reif tried to analyse how Sheringham had been allowed to score. 'Mehmet Scholl was with him, tried to step up and play him offside, but that is a dangerous game to play in the six-yard box. Teddy Sheringham has taken this final to extra time. Bayern already had their hands on the silver . . . I don't believe it! Paralysing dismay now on the right side of the stadium, and on the left side they are singing.'

In 17 years as a footballer Sheringham had never experienced a feeling quite like it. 'We had been virtually dead and buried; now, with a suddenness that was almost scary, we were back in it. And I, a player whose emotions and aspirations had been well and truly put through the mangle of disappointment in this my second season at Old Trafford, had played a central role in grabbing the lifeline we thought we would never see.'

Schmeichel's gamble had paid off. He'd become the only goalkeeper in a European Cup final to claim an assist. 'I have no doubt whatsoever that my sudden rush up the pitch was a contributory factor in that goal,' says the big Dane. 'I went up to create chaos and confusion and, at 6 ft 4 in, I probably did it. They had been very strong at set-pieces, so we had to try something different. Maybe that was the thing that worked.' He enjoyed the goal celebrations. 'It is not very often that I get to be in the penalty area when all the players are celebrating, so that was different and great,' he'd say later. But Schmeichel looked deadly serious as he walked back to his goal.

Yorke couldn't believe they'd equalised against the run of play. 'Bloody lucky,' was the first thought that came into his head. 'Can't call it a miracle. Miracles are usually deserved,' he says. Cole had a different perspective. 'It was the finest, most exquisitely scuffed equaliser I am ever likely to see. Absolutely brilliant, Ted, it was, even if we are still not speaking. The gaffer, in making those late substitutions, was looking for no more than a goal to take us into extra time. There it was, the miracle had happened, and he had been granted his wish.'

Ferguson would have bet long odds-on that the European Cup was now United's. 'I knew immediately after Sheringham scored that Bayern were beaten,' he says. 'There was certainly the odd hint in their body language to suggest as much, but I felt we had a sniff of victory, and they couldn't possibly lose the scent. I knew that that was it. We couldn't lose it after that.'

The haunted look etched across Matthaus's stunned face summed up the devastation felt by the Germans. Their world had just fallen apart. Hitzfeld said later that the equaliser had put his team into a state of clinical shock. Schmeichel too was aware of the psychological boost the equaliser had given United. 'That goal seemed to shatter the Germans, perhaps understandably, and certainly gave us that extra motivation to draw on our very last resources.'

Best was outside the stadium getting into a car with his spokesman Phil Hughes when Sheringham scored. He was delighted to hear that United had equalised and they made a dash for a local hotel to watch the rest of the game on television.

By the time UEFA President Lennart Johansson re-emerged by the side of the pitch United's players were trotting back to take up their positions for the re-start. The Hungarian fan Tibi had staged a one-man pitch invasion but it was quickly brought under control. A couple of Bayern's players remained slumped on the turf, devastated. United were watching a team crumbling before their eyes. 'The self-satisfied smirk had already left their faces,' says Sheringham. 'They were frightened men.' This was the defining moment of the match, the instant when most of United's players knew they would win – 'and, I suspect, the moment they [Bayern] knew they weren't [going to]', says Sheringham.

Effenberg believed the game was virtually over when United struck. 'Then suddenly it was 1–1 and the referee told me there were still two minutes to play,' he says. 'I could see we had problems. I was even worried about extra time because it was obvious Manchester's morale had soared while ours had sunk . . . We were just wishing the game over, so we could think about what had to be done in the extra 30 minutes . . .'

Yorke was also preparing mentally for an extra period. 'When Teddy scored, I thought "now we'll be having extra time proper",' he says. 'We'd saved ourselves, just in time.' But Yorke still felt the Germans had the upper hand. The goal was a reprieve, 'if only temporary', thought Yorke. 'For surely Bayern will win in extra time, having clearly been the better team.'

As play began again most of United's players thought they were the only winners now, whether the game was settled in normal time, extra time or a penalty shoot-out. Cole expected the full-time whistle at any moment. Stam was also aware of how close to extra time they were. 'We scored that first goal and straight afterwards we felt there was a chance of another one. But we knew that the 90 minutes had been played, so the chances were we would have extra time.'

As Yorke thought of an extra period and tried to remember if it would be golden goals and sudden death, what he calls 'a second dollop of bloody luck' landed at United's feet. The remaining 100 or so seconds would surely remain with Sheringham for the rest of his life. 'They seemed to be played in super-slo-mo; every move, every pass, every grimace, every tackle, caught in infinite detail. No 100 seconds have ever passed so slowly – it was as though our whole footballing lives were contained within it.' Through it all Sheringham held in his head a vision of what was to be. The European Cup would be United's and he would play a part in the taking of it. He wasn't going to let the biggest prize of all slip away now.

McClaren's thoughts immediately turned to getting United ready for the extra period that would surely follow. He tried to talk some sense into Ferguson. The gamble had worked, he argued, and now the game was square. United should change their high-risk 4–3–3 formation. As McClaren spoke, only 23 seconds after Bayern had re-started the match, the Reds were getting themselves into another scoring position. 'Now let us sit back and try for it in extra time,' McClaren said as Giggs won possession. 'Go back to 4–4–2.' At that moment the ball dropped to Irwin in the middle of United's half. 'Hang on a second, Steve,' said Ferguson. 'Something's happening out there. This game isn't finished yet.'

For those who had no idea what would happen if the match was drawn ITV's Tyldesley provided the answer. 'As things stand we will go into extra time with a golden goal hanging like a massive shadow over this final,' he told the 18 million viewers as Irwin pumped a long pass down the left wing deep into Bayern territory towards the corner flag. From the half-hearted way the Bayern players retreated it was clear they were already playing for the whistle to take them into extra time. Solskjaer, who like Sheringham had been one of United's men-in-waiting all season, chased it and picked the ball up. Only Kuffour raced back to mark him. Tyldesley took up his sentence again like an old friend. 'Unless' – another pause as he contemplated the astonishing possibility – 'Ole Solskjaer can conjure up another.'

The Norwegian ran at the Germans before sending in a cross but Kuffour charged it down. Another corner. A huge scream of anticipation went up from the banks of United fans behind Solskjaer. 'Once again, Manchester have a corner,' said RTL commentator Reif. 'We are in the 93rd minute, though only the referee knows why.' Tyldesley seemed to sense what would happen next. 'You have to feel this is their year,' he said. Even Ferguson was aware that fate seemed stacked in United's favour. 'There was almost a feeling of inevitability about what we were seeing, as Bayern wearily tried to regroup,' he says.

The television cameras focused on a young fan with a painted face clutching a furled flag. Breathless with anxiety, he was shaking with the tension as he looked on. The youngster was panting, desperate and pleading as he watched Beckham run across to the corner flag. He'd probably never lived life so intensely.

'They must be playing defensive,' joked Atkinson, 'Schmeichel's not coming up for this one. He thinks he's done enough.' But United did fill the area with players. Referee Collina was looking at his watch to herald extra time. Bayern were reeling as Beckham hit one of his special in-swingers from the left into a jostling, jousting mass of bodies at the near post. Sheringham, having made a late run to the front of the box, got ahead of the static Linke, rose above him and sent a glancing header down across the goal towards the far post. It may have gone in, though even Sheringham doubts it. Towards the far post Kuffour was so desperate to mark Solskjaer that he clung desperately to his shirt. Then, inexplicably, he moved forward the moment the ball approached and left the Norwegian free.

The ball was flying across at such pace that Solskjaer had no right even to get close to it, but he instinctively stuck out his right foot. With unfailing certainty, the 'Baby-faced Assassin' inspirationally poked an incredible winner into the top corner of Kahn's net. He had been on the pitch for just eight minutes. 'Manchester United have reached the promised land,' gasped Tyldesley. 'And what must Matthaus be thinking? With the greatest of respect, who cares?' An emotionally drained Beckham nearly had a heart attack when the goal went in. Ferguson thought the chance couldn't have fallen to a better man. 'He has such quick feet,' he'd say later. Solskjaer's strike was not a classic one and Bayern's defence had been on holiday, but United had struck the killer blow. The meticulous Germans had amazingly been beaten by two set-pieces.

United's fans went berserk. Total strangers hugged and danced on the Nou Camp terraces, although many of them hadn't seen the goal because they were still cheering and embracing each other after the equaliser. At the Trafford Centre in Manchester children who'd spent most of the second half in tears were grinning. Staff were swallowed up in hugs. Inside the Nou Camp, Schmeichel performed a surprisingly graceful cartwheel for such a big man at the other end of the pitch. The dignitaries around Bobby Charlton were speechless and in shock.

United's bench was still in a state of uproar from the first goal when Solskjaer scored. Cole's view was therefore obstructed and he didn't see the *coup de grâce*. ' . . . The greatest goal I never saw', is how he would describe it. 'Not everybody is smiling,' said Tyldesley. 'It is going to cost the bookmakers about £10 million. They were 80–1 for the treble at the start of the season.' But even the bookies took it well. 'At a time like this you just have to lie back and think of England,' said William Hill spokesman Graham Sharpe.

Back home 18.8 million people – one in three of the population and by far the highest viewing figures for a sporting event all year – saw the goal. 'Many people tuned in for the result and they got that marvellous finale as well,' said an ITV spokeswoman. In the studio Terry Venables, the former England manager who'd suffered the anguish of watching his side lose to Germany on penalties in the semi-final of Euro '96, couldn't stop laughing when the second goal went in. It was revenge of sorts for the Londoner.

'At the moment of triumph it felt as if nothing else mattered,' says Cole. 'The whole night was distilled into that one moment,' recalls Stam. Every one of the United bench was on the pitch. It was complete and utter bedlam. 'The celebrations begun by that goal will never really end,' said Ferguson later. 'Just thinking about it can put me in a party mood. At the time, all of us associated with the team were blissfully demented.'

Solskjaer, the angel-faced hero, jumped over the advertising hoardings and headed towards United's ecstatic supporters. The rest of the playing staff followed, 'a breathless bunch of crazed humanity roaring down the pitchside track for fully 60 yards', says Cole. Solskjaer had almost reached the corner flag when they caught him. Cole was surprised Collina didn't book them all. 'Yes, the mayhem was that bad. I have never experienced a football moment like it and I don't think I ever will in my lifetime.'

It was Solskjaer's 18th goal of the season and he'd only started 15 games. The Norwegian would already have been the leading scorer at 14 premiership clubs.

Two goals in two minutes of injury time. It was the most incredible ending in the history of European club football. 'This was the greatest comeback in European football, possibly the history of the game,' reckoned the *Daily Telegraph*'s Paul Hayward. Yorke had revised his view of miracles. 'I hadn't believed we would draw level, so when we scored again, it was just, well, another shock. Must be a miracle now,' he thought. 'No other word for it.' Cole also believes Solskjaer's goal was divine. 'That, I swear, was . . . intervention from above,' he says. 'God blessed us that night, no doubt about it.'

'He [Solskjaer] made the shot look so easy,' recalls Schmeichel, 'but actually that kind of timing and direction demands the finest touch of technique – not to mention composure.' Yorke's emotions had been turned upside down. 'One moment I was feeling so disappointed. It was the big occasion, the one we'd waited so long for, and we hadn't pulled it off. That was still in my mind. I'd got used to that feeling, that we were out. The next moment was this enormous relief. But it all happened so quickly. I just felt stunned.' The ultimate footballing fairytale was complete. 'Unbelievable! Ecstasy!' was how Sheringham described the goal and his feelings.

RTL's commentator Reif couldn't believe his eyes. 'Solskjaer! It's happened, though it should never have happened. Bayern have only themselves to blame. You can't score a second goal from a corner seconds before the end of a Champions League final. But, you see, you can. Look at the scene in front of the Bayern goal, they are lying there, the vanquished.'

There were still 13 seconds left, but the Germans didn't want to know. 'So this is what it takes to break the spirit of the Germans,' thought Kevin McCarra of *The Times*. While the television cameras and the eyes of 45,000 United fans were focused on the men in red celebrating Solskjaer's remarkable goal, there was just as much drama at the other end of the pitch in the penalty area where the Norwegian had just scored. Several Bayern players were on the ground, disbelieving, horrified. 'The sight of grown men crying, or flat out and wasted on a football field, will always live in the memory,' says *The Observer*'s Brian Oliver. 'Seeing grown Germans in this state was the sight of the night. On one of the greatest sporting occasions in history, it was a picture that will live forever.' Stam's emotions were at the opposite end of the spectrum to the Germans'. 'There was complete euphoria as we ran past German players frozen in shock,' says the Dutchman. 'Such a great feeling.'

Bayern's players were totally devastated. 'I don't have the words to describe such a sickening moment,' Effenberg would say later. 'It is too brutal,' Williams of *The Independent* wrote: ' . . . the portion of the pitch occupied by Bayern Munich players looked like a Giacometti sculpture garden. The footballers stood or sat or lay, suddenly frozen in postures of despair.'

Four of the players in grey, a colour that matched their mood, were still on the ground when the game was ready to restart. The prone Effenberg would not have continued, could not have moved a muscle, had Collina not helped him up on his feet, telling him there was still some stoppage time left. Kahn, on his knees behind his goal line, curled himself into a ball. As hard as he tried, he could not make himself small enough. Tarnat slumped against one post. Babbel sat resting his head against the other. And then there was the inconsolable Kuffour. At first he lay on the pitch, stunned and motionless like Effenberg. Then he bayed with fury and punched the turf with incredulous disgust. He had to be dragged to his feet by his team-mates. After that came tears and Collina gave him a shoulder to cry on. Then he was angry, chopping his arms and marching towards the halfway line screaming at himself.

Collina went around picking up several stricken Germans by their limp hands to get them to kick off and play out the last few seconds so he could blow the final whistle on the most remarkable ending to any of the 44 European Cup finals. 'For once, this formidable race of footballers could not be persuaded that any hope remained,' says McCarra of *The Times*. 'The Germans, rightly renowned for their powers of recovery, accepted that time had run out on them.' Only reluctantly did they respond to the pleading of their captain Oliver Kahn to restart the final. 'They knew, all of them, that by all the normal criteria they had deserved to win,' says *The Independent*'s Williams. 'They'd done enough – more than enough, actually – to prevail in what was not, in truth, a great game of football.'

Sheringham couldn't believe Bayern's reaction. 'Had it been us, we would have been desperate to get back into the thick of it, well aware that no game is over until the final whistle is blown. We would have reasoned that if the opposition could score twice in a matter of seconds, it was possible for us to score once in the time left. It's a difference in attitude, I suppose, but it was one that didn't reflect well on Bayern.' RTL's Reif gave the German perspective. 'For God's sake, let's face up to the truth here. Bayern had all the chances, they were almost through, they were presumed to be the team with the greater stamina. But that's how English football pros are.'

Even United's players seemed in shock, dazed and confused. 'Their emotions, settled into the acceptance of defeat, had been churned up, chopped up, chucked in the air and hadn't quite come down,' says Hunter Davies.

In the Nou Camp press box in those closing moments the British press, who just minutes earlier had been scribbling down their criticisms of Ferguson's tactics, had to hastily revise their opinions. Among the German press, too, stories were being quickly altered in the sort of instant revisionism that turns heroes into villains. Familiar stories of German tactical discipline eclipsing English enthusiasm had already been filed down countless telephone lines. All that had changed in the blink of an eye. Presses had to stop mid-turn because of United's ingrained never-say-die spirit. They'd been out-thought but never out-fought. It was 'a climax so astonishing even Roy of the Rovers would discard it as unbelievable', says Glenn Moore of *The Independent*.

Three minutes after UEFA General Secretary Gerhard Aigner had walked down the stairs to the dressing room to tie Bayern's ribbons on to the European Cup an aide came rushing after him. 'Change the ribbons,' he said. 'Are you crazy?' a clearly stunned Aigner responded. He was unaware, as Paul Hayward of the *Daily Telegraph* put it, that 'in the time that existed only in some alternative cosmic dimension, Manchester United went from 1–0 down to winning the European Cup'. It was the most dramatic end to a European final since Bayern lost to two late goals in the last 10 minutes of the 1987 final against Porto in Vienna. But even that finish paled into insignificance compared with United's comeback.

'With Manchester United, it is never over until the Fat Lady has a heart attack,' wrote McIlvanney in the *Sunday Times*. 'Wherever the current representatives of Old Trafford stand in the all-time league table of great football teams, they yield to nobody as producers of drama. That is a distinction which can only consolidate their status as the club with the most genuinely global following in the game.'

Bayern's fight was over. The match restarted and they got the ball into United's area before losing it almost immediately as Butt headed clear and United booted it as far away as possible. Collina had seen enough and blew to end one of the most dramatic finals ever played. When he heard the final whistle Giggs knew he was going to celebrate all night.

'A thousand flashbulbs recorded the moment,' wrote Oliver Holt of *The Times*. 'When the final whistle went . . . they lit up the Nou Camp as though it was noonday in the Barcelona sun and froze the Manchester United players with their arms in the air. It was the instant they passed into legend.' Basler stood on the touchline in stunned disbelief. Matthaus, who thought he'd seen it all, was also at the edge of the pitch with despair etched across his face. The 38-

year-old walked away shaking his head in the knowledge that his long-harboured dreams of European glory were finished.

Tyldesley summed up the evening for those watching at home. 'History has been made. Manchester United are the champions of Europe again and nobody will ever win the European Cup as dramatically as this. United have everything their hearts desired. The only question that people will ask in the future is: "Where did you watch the 1999 European Cup final?" Fifty thousand English fans will never forget they were here in Barcelona.'

Reif saw things from a different perspective, but he also recognised the enormity of United's achievement. 'Bayern are in mourning and with good reason. They had more, and better, chances to score. They were already the winners. Manchester were finished, down and out, but then try telling this to an English professional . . . Manchester United have won the 1999 Champions League in a finish such as I have never seen before. Manchester have won the treble, they are immortal.'

David Miller of the *Daily Telegraph* called upon a literary giant to put things into perspective. 'Imposters, Kipling called them. Triumph and Disaster. Seldom, if ever, in sport have such joy and cruelty simultaneously been so explosively creative in the space of 90 seconds, nor so late in a final that was volcanically turned upon its head. While I celebrate for Manchester United, throughout the modern era always so positive in attitude, how anyone's heart should ache in sympathy for Bayern. Never in the history of the game, it can safely be said and without exaggeration, has there been a team so ecstatically, so unexpectedly victorious, no opposition so destroyed as if by some thunder-clap from heaven. Was it from Sir Matt Busby on his birthday?'

Reuters football editor Mike Collett called it 'one of the most astonishing victories ever seen in a match of this stature. If it had taken place in a Sunday morning league match in a local park it would have ranked as quite some achievement. That it should happen in front of 90,000 incredulous fans in the Nou Camp stadium and an estimated 500 million television viewers around the world lifts the game into the realms of folklore.'

Collina's whistle was the cue for United's fans to go wild. 'The noise that reverberated around the Nou Camp stadium would have drowned out a space launch from Cape Canaveral,' according to Frank Malley of *PA Sport*. Back in Manchester, pubs and bars that moments earlier had been mired in gloom erupted into uncontainable joy as victory dawned. One banner hanging from the Nou Camp said it all: 'Spirit of '68, Class of '99'. It was brilliant and breathtaking, a finish that defied belief. United were fortunate to win, but deserved their success. They hadn't lost in 13 European ties and their exciting attacking approach had brought them 31 goals.

The Germans inside the stadium were in a state of shock. 'Behind us, a knot of Bayern supporters slumped to their seats in stunned disbelief,' says one United fan. 'Then, in an amazing act of sportsmanship, they came across to us, shook our hands and said, "Well done".' In Germany there was widespread rejoicing among the other clubs' fans at Bayern's humbling. 'Bayern are so arrogant. It's wonderful. Now they will be famed worldwide for this stupid defeat,' said Kaiserslautern supporter Christina Otte.

On the pitch a clearly overwhelmed Ferguson was ecstatic as he danced and emotionally hugged and kissed almost everyone surrounding the United outfit. Every second of joy was thoroughly deserved as he claimed the only prize in club football he had never won. Schmeichel, tears welling up in his eyes, was swamped by his team-mates, who threatened to crush the Dane under their combined weight. As they lost themselves in their own joy Ferguson looked up briefly at the cloudless Catalonian sky as if seeking – and getting no doubt – the approval of the spirits of the Munich disaster. It was a fleeting but poignant moment. 'There are mighty football men up there somewhere, revered Scots like Shankly, Busby and Stein, who would have been bursting with pride,' wrote James Traynor of the *Scottish Daily Record*. 'Ferguson is of their ilk and although he would never be so presumptuous as to say so himself, he has gone beyond even their achievements . . . the man from Govan had become the best British manager ever.'

When the beaming Ferguson faced the cameras moments after the final whistle he beat his hands against his head in disbelief. ITV's Gary Newbon tried to interview the Scot, who'd been left breathless by the sea of emotion ushered in by his team's sensational victory. The United manager was sure Newbon got a flood of gibberish for his pains. All the flabbergasted Ferguson could say was, 'I can't believe it. I can't believe it. Football, eh? Bloody hell.' Not that he minded sounding foolish. 'There was no happier idiot on the planet,' he says.

Not that everyone thought Ferguson was talking rubbish. Ian Bell of the *Scotsman* was quite impressed with his reaction. 'The first recorded words of Alex Ferguson in Barcelona on Wednesday night were more eloquent than anything offered before or since on miracles, answered prayers, bolts from the blue, or what hysterical commentators deem unbelievable. Vindicated, the Manchester United manager had only three words, fans' words, sufficient for ineluctable mystery.'

Four and a half years earlier United had slunk out of the Nou Camp in shock after losing 4–0 to Barcelona, their defence torn to shreds by Romario and Hristo Stoichkov. They had been traumatised by a thrashing that questioned their ability to compete at the highest level. Restricted then by the limitations on foreign players, they'd been outplayed so comprehensively that the scoreline was flattering. With the Spaniards playing on a different plane to that seen in the Premier League, it was debatable if United, or any other English team, would ever catch up. Since then each European experience had increased the players' knowledge and the team was now full of worldly wisdom on young shoulders. It showed in their gritty performance. After 31 years of trying, especially during the Cantona-inspired 1990s, United had finally returned to the throne of European football. More than that, they'd won the treble, '. . . the mythical treble that everybody had said was impossible', says Sheringham. 'Except for us: we had always believed in ourselves and our club.'

The fact they'd won the treble didn't even register with Cole at the moment of exhilaration. 'It was mind-blowing,' he says. 'I might as well have been on Planet Zog.' He tried to think, but couldn't. All he knew was that the European Cup, the great prize he'd seen teams play for and win on television as a boy, was now United's, and therefore his, for at least a year. The achievement left him almost zombie-like as he wandered around the pitch in a daze. 'How could we have won it? How the hell did we win it?' he thought. Cole couldn't absorb it all in a few minutes (or during the partying that night or many of the summer days ahead).

Sheringham was more philosophical. 'We would still have had a marvellous season even if we had lost in Barcelona, but defeat would, nevertheless, have been a massive letdown,' he says. 'To have come so far along a road no English team had ever travelled only to lose our way with our destination in sight would have been gut-wrenching. But, thank goodness, it was not, in the end, an experience we had to endure. Instead the Nou Camp was transformed from our temporary workplace to a stage where we could share our moment of glory with our fans.'

George Best wasn't one of them. By the time he arrived at a nearby hotel to watch the end of the match, Solskjaer had scored United's second goal and the final whistle had gone. He should have expected as much. 'Shame on Manchester United supporters who sneaked out before the dramatic denouement,' wrote Matt Dickinson of *The Times.* 'They should have known that, in this year of living dangerously, Alex Ferguson's team would conjure their most extraordinary comeback yet.'

The 52-year-old Best, who had played 361 times for the club, was so upset he'd missed the triumph that he had to console himself with a glass of Rioja. 'George was absolutely gutted,' said his spokesman Paul Hughes. 'But, of course, he was delighted United had won.' Best would stay up until 3 a.m. watching highlights of the match on TV.

Five

Receiving the Cup

For the next ten minutes there was pandemonium on the pitch and in the stands with a huge contrast between the jubilant Reds and Bayern's devastated heroes. Sheringham thought of looking for the non-plussed Basler 'to give him a little wave'. Matthaus was bent over the bench dejectedly. Jancker was a broken man and wept unquenchable tears as he crawled on all fours across the pitch. The 23-year-old Kuffour was left on his knees banging his hand on the ground. He shed more tears because he knew he'd cost his club the cup. Kuffour, a religious man, didn't even have the strength to pray as his team-mates lay on the ground all around him.

Matthaus, one of the truly great players of his generation, took it upon himself to return to the battlefield to console his shattered troops. 'To watch Matthaus, so often the symbol of German superiority, walking slowly back on to the field to console his team-mates in such shocking defeat was not to glory in revenge but to mark another notch in the career of a great player,' wrote Andrew Longmore in the *Independent on Sunday*. Slowly Matthaus went to each player in turn, exchanging a brief slap of the hand with Hitzfeld, patting the gangling obelisk Jancker, who was staring into nothing, on the head, shaking hands with centre-back Linke, and then hugging Italian referee Collina, an old sparring partner from Matthaus's days with Inter Milan.

A European Cup winners' medal was the one honour missing from Matthaus's collection. His doomed search for the one medal he craved was a romantic quest. He'd even brought along his new girlfriend to see him finally get his hands on one. Now, the time for filling the gap had pretty much run out. 'I feel for Lothar, because he made a great contribution in the period when we established control of the match,' Hitzfeld said. Not that United's players offered much consolation to Bayern's defeated team. 'They said nothing to me,' says Effenberg. 'And I'd have been the same. When you win a final you are too busy celebrating. Anyway, for the loser, at a time like that, it's better to be alone.'

But for the winners came the spoils. United were the souls of jubilation and wild celebration. Giggs was the first player to rush towards Ferguson. 'We go back a long way,' United's boss said later, 'to that day when I first saw him as a 13-year-old, floating over the turf at our training ground with the unmistakable aura of a boy who was born to play football.' Ferguson then hugged every player. In fact, they all embraced in a living red mass of delirium. They formed a line and jumped up and down with joy. As they stood in front of their supporters, Sheringham mimicked the action of sweeping in his equaliser and Yorke and Cole danced a samba of delight in the centre circle. 'If there was any poignancy among the English,' wrote Oliver Holt, 'it was sympathy for Roy Keane and Paul Scholes, the men who had missed out because of suspension.'

The Germans, who not long before had been strutting their stuff, stayed flat out on the pitch. They were staring into space or just sobbing. Cole noticed men erecting the presentation stage. 'The Bayern lads, clearly out of it, couldn't have cared less,' he says, 'come to think of it, neither could we.'

After the final whistle United Chairman Martin Edwards, beaming from ear to ear, and Sports Minister Tony Banks, waved a teary-eyed Charlton down to the front of the directors' box for a better view. Edwards was all smiles and so emotional that Banks gave him a big hug. 'It was a magical moment and I was not the only one with a tear in my eye,' says Charlton. It was a bigger deal for Edwards than the last time United got their hands on the trophy. 'This means more to me than 1968 because I am now the chairman of the club,' he said. 'I was at Wembley 31 years ago when my father, Louis, was chairman, but I was there as a fan. What happened then will always be special because it was ten years after Munich and Sir Bobby, Sir Matt Busby and Bill Foulkes, who were in the air disaster, were part of the Wembley triumph. The two European Cup wins are fantastic achievements. But the demands are greater now. In '68 we had to play nine games to win it. This season we've had 13.'

The heroes of 1968 looked on with pride even though the present stars had just eclipsed their triumphant legacy. Up in the stands, along with Charlton and Stepney, were Tony Dunne, little changed from that heady Wembley day all those years ago, Shay Brennan, Nobby Stiles, still peering through bottle-top glasses, Bill Foulkes, white-haired and grandfatherly, the irrepressible Pat Crerand and the dependable David Sadler.

Down on the pitch Bayern's players wearily got to their feet to collect their medals, 'aware they had felt like winners, and now they were just a bunch of losers', says Cole. 'They took it bad, real bad, as well they should.' Matthaus was especially distraught. UEFA president Lennart Johansson grandly put the silver medal around his neck. ' . . . As he goes up to get his loser's medal, which he keeps on for precisely three seconds, he looks like Charlton Heston', thought *The Independent*'s Chris Maume. 'He's a Roman general about to fall on his sword.'

ITV showed a fantastically expressive shot of Matthaus from behind as he walked away, looking up towards the Bayern fans, their eyes either filled with bitter tears or blank with post-traumatic stress. Kuffour walked slowly towards the Bayern fans, removed his shirt, folded it and presented it to a supporter. There was little left for Bayern's players to do but trudge off the pitch and, with the exception of Kuffour, leave United to bask in the glory. Oh, how they wished it was them.

Schmeichel was bursting with pride as the Reds prepared to mount the podium Maume described as 'the piece of cast-off *Blake's Seven* scenery UEFA use for presentations' to finally receive the

European Cup. ITV's Tyldesley ran through the names of previous British captains who'd lifted the trophy: 'Billy McNeill . . . Bobby Charlton . . . Emlyn Hughes . . . John McGovern . . . Phil Thompson . . . Dennis Mortimer . . . Graeme Souness'. For Schmeichel, winning the trophy ranked alongside the European Championship Denmark had won seven years before after a fantastic final when they beat Germany in Gothenburg.

Ferguson's heroes crowded onto the space-age podium, kissed the huge cup and settled back for the symbolic moment of triumph. Schmeichel, captain for the day because of Keane's suspension, having just played his 398th and final game for the club, was suddenly holding the trophy. It was his last official act for United and he couldn't have wished for a better climax. 'What a way for Schmeichel to go,' wrote Paul Hayward in the *Daily Telegraph*. 'For him, there can be no turning back now. How could he improve on this? He might be better off never laying a glove on another ball.'

In November, when announcing he was leaving, Schmeichel had promised to help the club conquer Europe. He'd kept that promise. He gave the trophy a huge smack of a kiss. United's fans followed his every movement with bated breath. The big Dane wrapped his massive fists around the handles of the cup. He then ordered 30,000 people to be as quiet as church mice before asking Ferguson to help him lift the huge three-foot high trophy. 'He [Ferguson] has been working hard for 25 years to get to lifting this trophy,' Schmeichel would say later. 'The way that he has been driving us every year, but particularly this season, he is the catalyst for what we have done. He has come in before every game and made us believe that we are the better team. He has given us the belief and trust to go out and express ourselves. That is why I thought it was fitting to ask him to lift the cup.'

A hush descended before Schmeichel and Ferguson held the trophy up towards the black Barcelona sky 'like a war souvenir for the fans,' says Cole, 'ripping a huge roar from the throats of the teeming throng' in the words of the *Daily Telegraph*'s Henry Winter. There had been wild enough scenes when United lifted the premiership trophy and then the FA Cup, but nothing compared to this. Thousands of flash bulbs lit the Catalan night. When the elated supporters erupted, Schmeichel felt like he was at Old Trafford. 'You don't really feel normal on an evening like that,' he says. It was the crowning moment to Schmeichel's United career and he couldn't have wished for a better one.

Behind United's cavorting winners, the inconsolable Matthaus, Hitzfeld and two other stunned Bayern players summoned the dignity to stand and applaud as their opponents received the trophy. It was a sporting acknowledgement of United's remarkable fight-back. (Although disliked by English and German football fans alike for being arrogant, Matthaus had been the one German player with the sensitivity to acknowledge the losing England players after their heart-breaking defeat on penalties in the 1990 World Cup semi-final. Now he was experiencing the emotions for himself as United celebrated.) Others, spread-eagled on the pitch, could not bring themselves to look up. Jeremies, who'd sweated all night to restrain United's midfield, seemed dazed, his arms folded and senses shredded. Kuffour, the athletic stopper, was inconsolable, tears reddening his eyes.

'It's difficult to explain the feeling that rushes through your body when you lift up the most important trophy in Europe in the direction of 45,000 ecstatic fans,' says Schmeichel. 'In a way, you can compare it with being handed your newborn child in the delivery room. And then you have to multiply that by a factor of two. There aren't many things that surpass the sensation of seeing your child for the first time, but that is the sort of experience most people have the opportunity to savour at least once in a lifetime. There are not many people who get the chance to hold aloft the European Cup to a roar of excitement. That is what makes it a little bit more special.' Despite a shaky start, Schmeichel had made some truly wondrous second-half saves and he deserved to be the first United player since Bobby Charlton to lift the European Cup.

Ferguson and Schmeichel danced a jig of delight on the platform, but Cole deliberately stayed at the back during the presentation. He literally and figuratively wanted to take a step back. He wanted to remember every second of that moment of history. He felt the whole staggering experience should be locked away in his mind and this was the only way of doing it. He witnessed the look of pride and elation on the faces of his team-mates, and a celebration that was close to hysteria. That mental picture was never going to fade. Cole was gobsmacked, numb, tearful, intoxicated, and through all those conflicting emotions he knew that as long as he lived he'd never know anything like it ever again. 'And to this day I know I won't,' he said afterwards. 'That's how moving and special it was to me.' He dubbed it an 'epic, quivering, goosepimply night'.

Schmeichel was the centre of attention as he lifted the trophy, but the next morning it would be one of United's unsung heroes on the front pages of papers across Europe. The photograph they carried showed a beaming David May seizing the historic moment. United fan David Carlin described the picture in all its glory in the *Independent on Sunday*. 'There he was with the winner's medal around his neck, arms aloft like the statue of Christ the Redeemer – or Ronaldo – over Rio, forming the triumphant apex of a beautifully framed triangle from whose base the rest of the players seemed to be looking up at him in wonderment and adoration.'

Schmeichel felt an intense mixture of immense personal pride and joyful humility. 'It truly was a marvellous evening in Barcelona: a historic achievement for Manchester United, and for myself a completely unforgettable conclusion to eight wonderful years . . . I was delighted that I was able to play a part in re-establishing Manchester United where they belong: at the very top.

'It may be true that the final was not a particularly spectacular football match. Finals seldom are, because everything has to be decided on the night. This often leads to a tight, tactical confrontation, but the final minutes of this game are surely destined to be written up at some length in football's history books.' Ferguson bestrode the pitch like a senator with his winner's medal glinting against his grey suit. He was enjoying the greatest moment of his life after picking up the 24th trophy of his remarkable career. The old refrain from *We Are The Champions* by Queen rang out, 'We'll keep on fighting to the end'. It seemed a particularly appropriate line.

One man who'd unknowingly helped inspire United's fight-back rejoiced at their victory, much to Ferguson's delight. 'I was moved by how emotional Steve Archibald was when we won,' says United's boss. 'When he played under me at Aberdeen our relationship wasn't always cosy but I liked the lad, always felt a lot of warmth for him. Seeing how he reacted really increased my pleasure in the greatest occasion of my career.'

The flash bulbs continued as the elated United players embarked on one of the most elaborate celebrations ever witnessed at a football match. ITV's Tyldesley and Atkinson celebrated with every United jig as the players took their applause around the pitch. The United supporters didn't want to leave. Cole described it as 'that grand, manic, three-ringed circus' of a parade around the pitch. That's when he let his hair down and began to go berserk like the rest of the team. 'We tossed the cup around, hugged it and loved it, and generally behaved like a bunch of four-year-olds,' says Cole. 'It was pure playground behaviour, but why not? It might be something we are never blessed to enjoy again.' The players danced in delight, Stam resplendent in a wig of wild black, white and red-striped curls. 'Somebody at United must be trying to tell me something about my hair because every time we win something I get handed a fuzzy wig to wear,' he says. 'People obviously prefer me that way.' Schmeichel got hold of Cole, 'and you don't get free of him [Schmeichel] unless he chooses to let you go,' says Cole. They rolled around on the grass, along with Yorke, laughing, screaming and hollering like a couple of madmen.

After Cole had got his hands on the trophy for the first time he sauntered off with McClaren. They ended up beneath the now almost deserted seats at the Bayern end. It was moving to watch those German fans who remained applaud the United team on their lap of honour. They seemed to take their abrupt reversal of fortune with enormous grace. 'The nature of the defeat had sucked the wind out of them, but their mood was one of contemplative hope for the eventual recovery of their powers of speech, rather than one for car rolling,' noted Giles Smith in the *Daily Telegraph*.

'Turn around and look at that, Coley,' said McClaren as they gazed towards the United end. They stood there for at least five minutes marvelling at the swirling, sweating, leaping mob of United fans. It was 'delighted mayhem on a grand scale', Smith observed. It only became clear just how many United fans there were in the Nou

Camp when most of the Bayern supporters had drifted away, stunned, into the night. More than half of the 90,000 crowd remained and most wore United's colours. As the players carried the cup towards the largest gathering of Reds fans in the stadium, the applause was deafening. 'We must have walked around the pitch about eight times,' says Butt. 'I was totally knackered at the end. That is a feeling you remember for the whole of your life. I saw the faces of my friends and family in the crowd. I couldn't stop waving to them. It was brilliant.'

In the moments after his greatest triumph, while the players were still passing the big silver trophy around, Ferguson was in the tunnel about to do one of the many television interviews that were beamed around the world when he recognised an Aberdeen fan. The supporter had followed Ferguson's career since he left Pittodrie for Old Trafford in 1986. The sudden reminder of his native Scotland touched him and the water that had been brimming up in his eyes leaked out. They were tears of sheer emotion, pride and joy. 'He wept at the enormity of what he'd achieved in the still-fabulous setting of the Nou Camp,' reckoned James Traynor of the *Scottish Daily Record*. 'People whose lives are governed by powerful desires to be the best can, in a sense, be weak. Sometimes they are unable to keep a lid on their emotions and they bubble, as Ferguson did in the tunnel of the Nou Camp.'

Outside, Samuel Ofei Kuffour's tears were at the opposite end of the emotional spectrum. He hadn't been able to cope with leaving the pitch alongside his team-mates and had stayed on the damp turf alone. After what seemed like an eternity the other Bayern players finally reached the sanctuary of their dressing room. After the most devastating experience of their professional lives, they felt numb, as inert as the stone-cold floor. There was no noise except the clacking of studs as the last stragglers arrived from the arena now left to United's celebrations. Many of the distraught players held their heads in their hands as they tried to come to terms with the disaster that had befallen them. Nobody spoke for 20 minutes. The club's suave, efficient press officer Markus Horwick felt as if he was gatecrashing a funeral. 'It was like a morgue,' he says. 'Some players were crying, others you could come up to within half-a-metre and they wouldn't see you, some just began to pack their shirts away in their bags without seeing or thinking.'

Nobody deserved more sympathy than Kuffour. By now, he'd been out on the pitch for such a long time that there was no route back to the dressing rooms. He had to ask the police to stand aside and let him through. Of all the losers on a night for winners, some lost more than others and Kuffour was one of them. He eventually reached the dressing room, where he joined a sombre group of players. Later, when he briefly showed his face outside the dressing room it was creased with streaming tears.

Hitzfeld came in and spoke to them. 'Yes,' he said, 'it's terrible, but life must go on.' Then the awful silence descended once again. 'Hitzfeld could have said anything he wanted,' recalls Effenberg, 'because nobody was listening. We were in no state to take anything in. I have never known a feeling like it in my career. Never. It was the worst . . . we were the better team – and yet we lost in a manner that stripped us of our dignity. It was a very bad defeat.'

Roy Keane now decided it was time to leave the pitch. The modest United captain didn't want to take the limelight from his team-mates. As they continued to celebrate, he walked to the dressing room and waited for them to return. It was to be a long wait.

None of the other players wanted to leave and, even if they had, the fans wouldn't let them go. They stayed out on the pitch for almost an hour, though it seemed like an eternity. 'It was one of those occasions you pray will last forever,' says Cole. His sister Lorraine gave him a wave and his girlfriend Shirley blew him a kiss. He could see the look of elation on the glowing faces of all his friends up in the stands having a ball. The players did stop-start victory laps, lifted Ferguson and enjoyed the screams and chants of the supporters who also let off smoke flashes. 'We were like the top-of-the-bill act being repeatedly called back for encores and yet another standing ovation,' says Sheringham.

Long after the game had finished, the official ceremonies were over, the photographers had gone and the opposite end of the stadium had emptied of the 30,000 Bayern supporters, the United players found themselves on the pitch in the Nou Camp alone with their fans. John Carlin described the scene: 'One half of the stadium was empty, and seemingly in darkness, save the occasional flickering shadow of what must have been a crushed remnant of a Bayern fan contemplating doing the honourable Prussian thing, you imagined, and self-immolating right there. In the dazzlingly illuminated half of the stadium, where there were more red shirts than you could fit into Old Trafford, we United fans – gathered from all corners of the globe – were having the mother and father of all parties. The players were there on the pitch, alongside the goal that gave us the two minutes that shook the world, facing the euphoric Red army. But not so much revelling in the adulation as sharing in the general excitement, as if they had come off their pedestals and become fans for the night. No longer heroes, but lads, who no more wanted to leave the hallowed grass than the fans wanted to abandon the terraces where they had witnessed their finest hour.'

The hundreds of pounds supporters had spent on black market tickets now seemed like the bargain of the century. David Wilson, 33, of Salford, summed up the feelings of every United fan: 'It's going to be the best night of my life. I thought the treble was gone – I can hardly believe it. We are going to have a massive party.' His ticket had cost £275. 'It was worth every penny.'

Half an hour after the final whistle, the mood suggested that the party might just be dying down. A hoarse Old Trafford announcer tried in vain to coax the fans back to their coaches, notifying them that hundreds of planes were lining up on the runways of the Barcelona airport. Ignoring the announcements, the fans chanted for Alex Ferguson. It was at this moment that May displayed his amazing ability as a crowd choreographer and a master of imagery. He had what Carlin describes as 'a talent for moving masses that would have been frightening in the hands of an unscrupulous political leader'. He grabbed the giant Champions League trophy and walked a few steps away from the other players to face the massed red ranks who braced themselves to let out another mighty roar. But May did not raise the cup above his head. Instead, he placed it carefully on the pitch and, looking sternly at the supporters, put his right index finger to his lips as he tried to quieten the crowd. Not everybody got the message so he repeated the gesture. Then he stretched out his hands and motioned slowly downwards. 'Sshh,' he urged the crowd. 'Red devils transformed into lambs, we obeyed,' recalls Carlin. About 45,000 fans fell amazingly silent. For a few seconds you could have heard the proverbial pin drop. Then May, with an almighty flourish, lifted the cup high over his head. ' . . . I swear, the Ramblas rattled, the Pyrenees shook, to the sound of our roar,' says Carlin. Andy Cole agreed. 'The bellow of noise from those terraces was quite unbelievable,' he says, 'huge waves of it filling the stadium again.'

Where May led, the other players followed. 'Like toreadors, they took turns raising the giant cup in teasing theatrical jerks,' wrote Paul Hayward of the *Daily Telegraph*. Each player came forward in turn to have a go at the new game. As the cup was paraded and passed among them each one got the same long, thunderous, deafening response. But the nature of the pauses in between differed from player to player. Yorke performed a deliciously tantalising little Caribbean jig before bringing the fans to yet another climax. Schmeichel pretended to hoist the cup high but stopped abruptly at waist height, turning to laugh at the supporters' confusion, to 'mock the vast *coitus interruptus* he had triumphantly engineered,' in Carlin's words. All United's players – about 20 – went through the same ritual in their own unique style.

In the extraordinary elation of a victory so totally unexpected and so emotionally destabilising, the fans had not forgotten Keane. 'It was all great fun until we realised there was someone very important missing from the party,' says Carlin. 'Or rather two people [Scholes was the other], though one was more in our thoughts.' They wanted to stage their own tribute to 'Captain Fantastic' as Keane had become known and refused to leave until he came back on to the pitch. Bathed in the glow of red smoke flares, the supporters began calling for their idol. They struck up the song that used to be known as *Blue Moon* but now went by the name Keano. There was no sign of him, since he'd disappeared down the players' tunnel long ago. 'Keano, Keano' began reverberating around the Nou Camp. The chants became more insistent and by now even his team-mates were refusing to leave the pitch until he reappeared. Eventually, a runner was sent to give Keane the message that 40,000 fans wouldn't leave the stadium until they'd given him the acclaim he deserved. Keane had played a vital role in the 12 matches leading to the Champions League final, but number 13 had proved cruelly unlucky for him. It had been hard to sit on the touchline when he should have been leading his team to their greatest triumph. 'I watched him. He was gutted,' Ferguson later revealed.

Keane didn't really want to return to the pitch as he was a bit embarrassed by the adulation. But, 45 minutes after the match had ended, he finally re-appeared to a tumultuous reception after insisting the suspended Scholes and Henning Berg go with him. Keane moved sheepishly forward, while repeatedly casting glances back towards the United officials and the players who hadn't appeared in the final as if seeking permission to sample some of the ecstatic applause. An equally tentative Scholes was also waved forward. Together they inched towards the United end of the Nou Camp. What happened next was another stroke of choreographic genius. It must have been May who plotted it. The players out on the pitch, who had by now sat down for a rest, stood up on weary legs and formed a guard of honour with their arms around each other, at the end of which they placed the European Cup. Finally, Keane, Scholes and Berg reached the group of broadly smiling players, some of whom had joined in the chants from the crowd. Keane and Scholes passed side-by-side through the guard of honour, accepting the solidarity of fellow titans transformed into ordinary mortals for the night, to reach the cup that Keane should have lifted. The stadium fell strangely silent until they raised the trophy to a cacophony of sound from the players and their grateful supporters. It was a bittersweet moment for Keane. The adulation made him feel uneasy, but United's captain was also deeply touched and viewed the episode as a great compliment. 'Some players might only play a few matches, some might play more than 50 but we're all in it together,' he'd say later.

By now the players just wanted to get back to the dressing room to congratulate each other. Only when they'd finally trooped off the pitch, more than 45 minutes after the game ended, did the first few gaps begin to appear in the stands.

The chief football writer of Barcelona's *La Vanguardia* newspaper wrote that the United supporters had crowned themselves as the best in the world. Carlin didn't disagree. 'The desire of the United players is at one with the desire of the fans,' he says. 'That is not always as common as one might think. Spanish writers, grown weary of the prima donna-packed teams that rule their league, have been unanimous in their admiration for that rare mix of humility and ferocious pride that defines the United spirit. In that uncannily intimate communion between players and fans, long after the cameras had gone, you had a glimpse of the divine energy that made possible what will go down in football history as the Miracle of Barcelona.'

Back in the dressing rooms another incredible sight awaited the players. 'I think you would call it a champagne lake and the lads were quite content to drown themselves in it,' says Cole. The party was about to start. As soon as they were inside the champagne corks were popping. Keane grabbed a bottle and showered his team-mates with bubbly. Naturally, he shared their excitement and jubilation. After all, as he'd said himself, it was the squad that had lifted the trophy and he was part of the squad. But to Keane at that moment, it didn't feel that way. Somehow the contrast between his smart-suited appearance and the sweat-soaked kit of the players around him who'd earned such a famous victory said it all. While Keane considered his mixed emotions the rest of the lads were enjoying the bubbly. Because they hadn't eaten anything the champagne went straight to their heads. 'I wished I had been close to a camcorder because the video would have been a bestseller in the Megastore, no doubt about it,' says Cole.

Neville reflected on how the Germans had dominated England during recent encounters. 'I told the players in the dressing room afterwards that it looked like a German team were going to do us again. I remember Euro '96. I remember Borussia Dortmund when we missed all those chances [in the 1997 semi-final when United lost both legs 1–0]. Bayern were unlucky. To win three trophies, you need an element of luck and we've had that this year in Europe. In the past, we hadn't.'

Schmeichel talked to Ferguson and McClaren about his sprint into Bayern's area. He was a little disappointed with Ferguson, who'd always given him the impression he'd consider it a lack of winning instinct if he didn't go up at the end of a game that was slipping away and try to decide it in United's favour. Ferguson admitted he just hadn't been able to see any way United could get back into the match; in other words he'd all but conceded defeat when he saw his keeper rushing up the pitch like a madman. Schmeichel had a little friendly chat with McClaren. The big Dane hoped he'd made him realise that it was worth taking chances if you're good enough and the stakes are sky-high.

Many people would later ask Schmeichel how he'd had the nerve to run upfield with two billion people watching, given that he would have looked foolish if Bayern had scored in the open goal. The possibility didn't cross his mind. 'If they had scored immediately afterwards, it wouldn't have worried me at all,' he says. 'A 2–0 defeat is no worse than a 1–0 defeat in a final. And this was a major final – it had to be won. When you're losing there is only one way to go, and that is straight towards your opponent's goal. Manchester United's duty was to score, to get a draw, and perhaps even a win. And that is what you have to try to do at all costs!'

It was estimated that United would pick up about £15 million in prize money, TV revenue and gate receipts from their Champions League campaign. Ferguson's reported £350,000 bonus for winning the competition appeared almost modest alongside an £800,000 salary and a reputed £5 million deal to continue at Old Trafford for another 3 years. The rumoured £150,000 bonus for each of the players was pocket money to most of them. Beckham had recently spent that amount on a Ferrari Maranello. He was also about to move into a £2.5 million Shropshire home with Victoria Adams and their son Brooklyn. Giggs, who was earning £20,000 a week, owned a similar Ferrari along with 13 other vehicles.

Meanwhile, in the depths of the Nou Camp, Markus Horwick, engulfed in his own misery, found that his passion for Bayern and his job as a press officer clashed. He had to persuade the players to talk to the waiting press when all he really wanted to do was cry with them. 'I've only known an atmosphere like that twice,' he says. 'Once was after the 1987 European Cup final when we lost to Porto. But this was worse. I'm searching for the right English word.' He looks through the pages of his dictionary. 'Yes, here it is. Cruel. That's it. That's the word I've heard most.' Eventually, the old troupers,

Basler, Matthaus and Scholl, were persuaded to answer the questions for which at that moment, in the middle of an anonymous concrete tunnel faced with a barrage of notebooks and cameras, there were no answers.

Graham Spiers of *Scotland on Sunday* observed the Germans in their moments of despair: ' . . . Beneath the concrete edifices of the vast stands, a couple of the Bayern players could be found freshly showered and smoking cigarettes in their fragility . . .' While Basler, Matthaus and Scholl faced the press the rest of the players slipped past the waiting reporters into the comforting shadows of the team coach, 'and long will the image linger of many of them limping like emotional basketcases to their bus', says Spiers. Poor Kuffour, their fine Ghanaian defender, had sprained his wrist thumping the grass with frustration. He was still whimpering as he walked past Spiers a full hour after the game.

Ferguson was driven to the media centre in the back of a white golf buggy for the post-match press conference. The triumph was perhaps sweetest for the United manager, who was still wearing his winners' medal around his neck. He could now retire knowing he'd achieved the fulfilment he deserved. It was his triumph more than anyone's and he could hardly take it in. Ferguson says, 'I didn't like most of it. The most important factor is you cannot deny people with spirit and the will to win that exists at this club. That's what won the trophy for us tonight. It is the greatest night of my life. I am still stunned by what happened at the end. Bayern tried to lock up the match, and that's a dangerous game to play. We always tried to attack, and then we had to risk playing three strikers through the middle. I don't think we deserved to lose it because as a team we were trying to win it all the time. We rode our luck in the last 15 minutes when they hit the woodwork twice, but that was a lot to do with the way we were playing then, because we had to take risks to get back in the match. But my team play the right way. They embrace every concept I have of football and Manchester United.

'Sheringham and Solskjaer are goalscorers and they are good at their job. They are terrific substitutes. I am proud of my players, proud of my heritage, proud of my family. My players never give in. You always expect they can do something. But this time I thought we were beaten. I was starting to adjust to defeat near the end. I kept saying to myself, "Keep your dignity and accept it is not your year." But football's such a funny game, you never know. And then look what happened. The players won't rest on this because they're young. It's fantastic. They never give in so you always expect something from them. The players are incredible human beings . . . their spirit is unbelievable. I haven't said anything to them yet and I was just hugging and kissing them and slobbering all over them.

'We got off to a bad start but kept at them and got our reward. We had a bit of luck in the last 20 minutes when we got caught on the counter-attack but you've got to gamble in a European final and we deserved it. Bayern tried to shut up shop after the goal, like they did in the semi-final against Dynamo Kiev. But we had a much better mental strength than Kiev . . . and shutting up shop is a very dangerous game to play.'

Explaining the thinking behind playing Beckham in a central role, Ferguson said: 'I felt we were a passing team so I put David in the middle because he is a great passer. I knew we would miss his crosses but I had to do it.'

Ferguson had reckoned the treble was possible in January when United started their 33-match unbeaten run. He kept the dream alive by rotating his large squad. 'I felt the only way we could do it was by exercising my pool. I felt a case in point was the [FA Cup] semi-final replay [against Arsenal] at Villa Park when I left out Andy Cole, Dwight Yorke and Ryan Giggs simply because we had Juventus the next Wednesday. I wasn't going to risk a European Cup semi-final and possible place in the final for a semi-final [of the FA Cup].'

But Ferguson admitted United could never better their achievement. 'You can't top this because it is the pinnacle. You can equal it and we can try to maintain our high standards. There is always going to be a question mark over the team and me when you win a trophy like this. A lot will be written saying that we'll be taking it easy. That's true and I will take it easy – until we lose the first game. The players are made of something special and you saw that against Bayern. They will go on because I want them to go on. I just want to relish the evening. I want to let it sink in and understand what happened out there.'

Earlier in the season Ferguson had rejected the suggestion that United were somehow fated to win the Champions League, arguing that you get what your effort deserves and not what you read in your tea leaves. You could not have peddled that line in Bavaria on the Wednesday night. Ferguson had said a few weeks before that he hoped there was some meaning to the final being on Busby's birthday and against Bayern Munich. By the end of an emotional evening the remarkable events on the pitch had forced him to cast aside his scepticism about the notion of help from above. Ferguson could tell Busby was looking down on him and the delighted United boss nodded heavenwards to a divine helping hand.

'I was starting to believe we were going to lose . . . But it's a fairytale really, coming on Sir Matt's 90th birthday. I think he was doing a lot of kicking for us up there in the last couple of minutes. I suppose you could say we have come out of his shadow now but, with all the team has achieved this year, they could not have had any question marks against them. This team plays the right way . . . What they have achieved is unprecedented. Nobody has ever done it. They deserve it.' Journalist Graham Spiers felt that Ferguson, in speech and demeanour, resembled someone who was once more conquering the very summits of life, and when he spoke about 'my heritage' and 'where I belong in life' you knew you were listening to someone savouring that rare experience of complete accomplishment. 'Being mined out of the old Scottish working-classes, as Ferguson himself is the first to proclaim, shouldn't necessarily be the opening gambit of any assessment of his quality as a man,' wrote Spiers in *Scotland on Sunday*. 'On the road to excellence, this football coach has absorbed many episodes, of varying character, and his chief gift has probably been in learning and strengthening himself amid each of them.' In this context, late into the night Ferguson reflected on there being 'some things that suddenly change the pattern of your life'. In the case of his team, he said, it was their quarter-final victory over Inter Milan in the San Siro that finally made them believe they were in possession of something untouchable. That night also proved one of the last catalysts in thrusting Ferguson himself towards glory.

The way the press viewed Ferguson varied considerably

depending on the journalist, the paper, the country (the Scots were usually more generous since he was one of their own) and the circumstances. But in the wake of United's triumph there seemed to be a softening in attitude towards the man who was 'out on his own as not only Manchester's but Britain's most successful manager', to quote Paul Wilson of *The Observer*. 'One of Ferguson's most endearing traits is humility,' wrote Wilson, 'and in what has been a magical time for United and a special treat for English football, there has not been a trace of personal triumphalism. Even in the glow of victory at the Nou Camp, Ferguson never attempted to deflect credit from his players, or to deny that he had been worried about defeat. He simply sat back and allowed the club's restored mantle of greatness to rest on his shoulders.'

When Ferguson got up to leave at the end of the press conference the room erupted in applause and the cameras started flashing. The glow of fame was shining brightly. Ferguson clambered back into the buggy that had transported him to the waiting journalists. Fifty yards down the carpeted walkway, it buzzed past the night's biggest loser, the loser of losers. Samuel Kuffour was scuffling around in the grey dust, uncertain whether to climb aboard the Bayern team coach as it waited for the last few players to emerge. An hour after the game the Ghanaian defender, who by now had told reporters that he blamed himself for both United goals despite a marvellous performance at the heart of Bayern's defence, was still trying to calm himself down, still trying to answer the question: 'How?' A German media friend decided to show him.

Off they trudged to the replay machine in the broadcast journalists' centre where Kuffour watched the two goals over and over again. While he watched the equaliser, his friend pointed out that others were at fault, not Samuel. Kuffour's fingers darted to various points on the screen. Him, him, him and him – a finger for each man out of position. Another replay, and this time the finger of guilt was pointed at Fink, whose sliced clearance led to the goal. Kuffour looked to the canvas roof of the media centre, rolled his eyes and sighed. But Kuffour was partly to blame for the next goal. He was marking Solskjaer and a half-hearted tug at his shirt was never going to be enough to stop the goal. 'For me personally,' says Kuffour, 'this is . . . a great injustice. I am very sad. Very sad.' He felt he had let down himself, his team-mates, his country and the whole African continent which, he says, had only produced four players in Europe's champion teams. 'The game was ours. We were progressing, playing so good.' Kuffour is a religious man. 'Maybe God knew better,' he said before dawdling back to the coach. When Schmeichel was wheeled into the press tent on a golf buggy he was asked if he felt sorry for the Germans. 'Of course I felt sorry for the Bayern players. You put yourself in their position and to lose like that was cruel. But in football you sometimes have beauty and cruelty together, and I think that's why we all love the game as much as we do.'

Schmeichel was more concerned with United's stunning victory. 'Not even Hans Christian Andersen could have written a fairytale like that,' he said. 'Of course you believe you have a chance until the final whistle goes and I never stopped believing we had a chance – although I admit, not much of one. But the late goals exemplified our team spirit. One thing I have learnt throughout my time at United is that we never give up and we proved that tonight. This is absolutely fantastic for me and I just feel on top of the world. When I announced I was leaving at the end of the season I vowed to myself I would do all I could to help the club finish at the top – and you cannot get higher than this. Tonight is the night for Manchester United – Manchester United and champagne.'

Ferguson had already made it clear that he was very sorry to see his Great Dane leaving United. 'It is sad that he is leaving us but he could not go out in a better way,' he'd said. 'We wish him well – he's the greatest goalkeeper Manchester United have ever had.'

Ferguson sat talking to Bobby Charlton in the dressing room long into the night. They pondered heavenly intervention as his mind flashed back to the legends who had brought the first European Cup to Old Trafford. He and Charlton chatted about just how great the latest European achievement was. Charlton said Matt Busby was probably looking down on them. 'There had to be some meaning to it all,' says Ferguson. 'Matt's birthday. Playing a team from Munich and all that. The number of times we have won games like that and, of course, Peter Schmeichel's last match.'

Six

The Celebrations

The Bayern fans had long ago melted into the night when the crowd burst on to the streets of Barcelona. The United supporters filing out of the stadium ready to celebrate seemed both astonished and delighted. 'Incredible', 'unbelievable', 'fantastic', were some of the words repeated over and over by the wave of bodies. They'd seen history made.

The party then made its way across Catalonia's elegant capital. United fans from the stadium joined thousands of others who'd been unable to get black market tickets and had watched the final on TV. They inevitably headed towards the Ramblas. The city's famous avenue was turned into a sea of red elation as 30,000 fans danced in a good-natured flow of passion that would continue until sunrise.

Back in Manchester, joyous fans flooded on to the streets to launch a party that would last 36 hours. Streets that for the best part of three hours had been almost silent came alive with red-shirted revellers. The city was driven by the drama of the night. A crowd of 4,000 gathered outside Old Trafford and up to 6,000 people jammed the city centre. Peter Street, Oxford Road and Albert Square were all packed. By 10 p.m. streets in the city centre were blocked by traffic and fans leapt into fountains.

In Barcelona, United supporters draped themselves over every monument in the city and sang their hearts out as a diminishing police presence looked on. Some supporters hung out like branches from trees. One lady peeled off her clothes, down to panties and bra. The Mancunians strolled up and down the Ramblas shaking hands with strangers.

It was well after midnight when United's players emerged from their champagne-soaked dressing-room. The game had ended at least two hours earlier. 'Either Manchester United take extremely long baths, or they had found something to celebrate in there,' mused Giles Smith of the *Daily Telegraph*. Most of the team were half-cut, which seemed to provide the more likely explanation. 'Maybe that's one of the reasons why it took us forever to get away,' confirms Cole.

The players, most with their winners' medals around their necks, made their way from the dressing-room to the team bus, stopping briefly to talk to waiting journalists. 'The Germans have been so lucky in the past against us that I think we deserved this bit of luck,' said Giggs. 'I always said we would never be judged as a great team until we had won the Champions League. We've done that now and I think we deserve to be ranked along with the Liverpool team of the '80s.' Giggs also gave an insight into the mood of a team that was still unbeaten in 1999. 'We go into every season thinking we can win everything, win every game and every tournament that we enter.' Giggs reckoned it was United's never-say-die spirit that was the difference between glory and glorious failure . . . It hasn't sunk in yet, the atmosphere, the fans, just unbelievable.'

As Giggs spoke, the neatly suited figure of Gary Neville appeared. 'I can't explain how we won the game,' he said. 'It just happened. In a way it was supernatural. It was like nothing I have ever experienced before in my life. The manager sets the work ethic here, and if you let that slip you will be out of the club. This team never gives up. It fights to the end and that reflects the manager's spirit.'

Beckham sauntered past with a very classy-looking sponge bag in one hand and the European Cup in the other, which was no mean feat given the size of both the trophy and the bag. But it didn't appear to be a strain. The smile on his face looked like it wouldn't melt for months. As if to rub salt into the German wounds Effenberg emerged from the routine doping test just as Beckham was strolling by cradling the big silver trophy. He'd never forget the thoughts running through his mind at that moment. 'I really felt this should have been our cup and I don't want to experience that pain ever again,' says Effenberg.

Neville, soon to be best man at Beckham's wedding to Victoria Adams, laughed at the suggestion the trophy had been on the wedding list. He then picked up on Giggs's theme that United never give up. 'We've shown that this team never dies. It keeps going right until the end and we've shown it on the greatest stage. We didn't play our best ability-wise or skill-wise, because too much of what we tried just didn't go right. It was something else that won us the game. We were not going to lie down. Our guts took us through. There is a refusal to give in, a will that we've got to win because nothing else is accepted at this club. It mirrors the manager's thoughts, the manager's ambitions. He has got that into the players' heads. Come the first day of pre-season, the manager will be at us again. When you see your manager, who has been there, seen and done everything in the game, and you see his motivation and determination, how can I fail to have it at 24?' Sheringham agreed. 'It stems from the manager. He gave a great speech at half-time telling us . . . just don't come back in here without giving your all. We certainly gave our all.'

Neville then spoke about the widespread obsession with United's 1968 European Cup winners among the fans and the media. '1968 was never a burden. The '68 team were a fantastic team. People will probably say we've surpassed [them] but I wouldn't agree with that. We've just won the same competition. It's nice that people will look upon us in the same way. They had world-class players. We have said all season that we don't have a priority, that we play each competition as it comes along. But the European Cup has always been the big one for us.

'We have given people so much entertainment. We've done it

with style. We are a disciplined side. People have to admire us even if they don't like us. And we have set ourselves a standard tonight.' But who, he was asked, had celebrated the wildest in the dressing-room afterwards? 'Any one of 40 people,' he replied.

Winning the Champions League had capped an incredible year for Beckham, both on and off the field. 'I've had a big year with the birth of my son and that was the most special thing that could ever have happened to me, but this is next,' he said. 'It's been an amazing 11 days for the team, for the manager and for everyone. Alex Ferguson deserves everything he gets. We owe him everything. I certainly do because he brought me into football and made my career. But this victory wasn't just for the players on the pitch but for everyone involved in this great club. You could tell at the end when the boss wanted Roy Keane out there holding the trophy. He might not have played but, believe me, he was there in spirit. It's the same spirit between the players that's made us complete this wonderful treble.'

His sentiments were echoed by Yorke, who was overcome with the emotion of it all. 'It is unbelievable,' he said. 'I grew up as a kid thinking of these matches. Lothar Matthaus is a hero in my eyes, a legend. To play against him in a Champions League final shows what a life I've had. I was close to tears just thinking about it.'

Yorke had been at United less than a season but was familiar with the team's dressing-room camaraderie. 'It's all down to good management, good team spirit. My private life has been published a few times and my team-mates and manager supported me. That has made me stronger. There's a closeness in this team, a bond in the dressing-room, and we have proved that over the season . . . To be part of Manchester United is the best feeling that any footballer can have.' Before setting off to celebrate, Yorke added: 'I hate to think what is going on back in Tobago. I felt that if there was anything to compare with what Brian Lara has achieved, then it was to do the treble.'

The players staggered out of the Nou Camp and headed for the team bus. Solskjaer was always likely to try to slip away unnoticed – that is his style. 'We just had to score goals after the pressure we had,' he said. 'Someone had to do it. Fortunately it was me. To lose in that way must be terrible. But to win it that way is that much better. The team spirit is unbelievable. Everyone works for each other, we're all in this together. It's unbelievable and it's very difficult to describe how I feel just now, but if anyone wonders why I stay at Manchester United, they can see why here.' As the other players received the backslapping of the fans, Solskjaer seemed to be clinging to the wall. The self-effacing striker had recently bought his own boots at the local sports shop because he didn't want to trouble anyone at the club's sponsors, Nike. 'To come into the final of the Champions League as a sub and to score in injury time is what you dream about,' he said.

Beckham, appropriately enough, lugged the cup onto the bus 'with the insouciance of a Costa Brava reveller with a sombrero-clad toy donkey', according to the *Independent on Sunday*'s Nick Townsend. 'It's one of the best feelings in the world, especially with being 1–0 down with a minute to go,' said Beckham.

Cole's mobile phone rang continuously as he sat down. Congratulations came pouring in from his parents in Nottingham, and many friends. 'Eventually, the team coach got underway,' says Cole, 'although some of the boys might not have noticed because we were all steaming by then, and we headed for the big bash.' As Beckham sat cradling the cup he told Ferguson, 'Don't worry about me – I'm staying for good.'

Ferguson and his players were taken to the plush £250 a night Hotel Arts, near the Olympic Village in Barcelona, where they would soon be joined by family and friends. 'I didn't really take it all in,' said Ferguson later. 'I didn't really feel a lot to be honest, but when I got back to the hotel and was with my family I really enjoyed it.' All of his family were there, except his grandson who was only five.

Cole went up to his room, dropped his bags and left immediately for the buffet reception. The tables were buckling under the weight of all the food. It was, like the FA Cup final dinner, a celebration for the club and everyone associated with their success. 'We were finally able to throw a party without thinking about the next engagement,' says Stam.

United had played 63 matches, losing only 4 and scoring 128 goals. They'd earned their party. Nearly 300 people – including players, management, directors and select guests – were there to celebrate through the night at the hotel's famous Grand Salon. The European Cup took pride of place on a table in the corner of the plush function suite. Solskjaer sat just yards from club football's most glittering prize. He looked as though he was scared to touch it. In fact, none of the players went near the trophy. After all the emotion of the Nou Camp – the singing, dancing and hugging – a strange calm had descended around United's heroes. The enormity of what they had just achieved was slowly sinking in.

The champagne was flowing and the players had gathered their families to party. Sheringham's girlfriend Nicola was there and his son Charlie was allowed to stay up to enjoy the celebrations. Beckham sat next to his fiancée Victoria and stole furtive glances at the European Cup. 'Maybe he was double-checking that the ribbons were in his club's colours,' says Ferguson's niece Laura. She remembered Beckham's glance at the cup with Bayern's ribbons on it in the dying seconds of the final that seemed to spur him on. 'Now he seemed content just to know the trophy was there. In the same room as him. With United ribbons on it.'

All around the room the smiles were getting wider by the minute. Eventually, players began to sidle up to the cup. Family members followed them. Pictures were taken – memories to cherish. 'And it was at moments like this that you saw that these players – household names throughout the world – are really just like everyone else,' says Laura. United were like a family and that was one of the reasons they were so successful. They shared a bond far deeper than friendship.

Ferguson and United's Chairman Martin Edwards made formal speeches. But the closeness of the players became clear for all to see as the party started to rock. Even Edwards redeemed himself in their eyes by dancing on a table while smoking a big Cuban cigar. The players themselves were soon parading the cup and posing for madcap photos. They gathered in a huge circle, singing the songs that the fans had created in their honour. 'You are my Solskjaer, my Ole Solskjaer . . .' and 'Ryan Giggs, Ryan Giggs running down the wing . . .' 'The party just didn't stop,' says Schmeichel. 'But it was a once-in-a-lifetime achievement. I don't think anyone would begrudge us enjoying ourselves. We're all kids, we're like the fans. We sang terrace songs, we laughed at one another . . .'

The players took turns at dancing with the cup in the middle of the circle. As they entered the circle their team-mates chanted their name. 'You could see the relief, the joy in their faces as they sang,' says Laura. And in the middle of them was Keane, with the biggest smile of the lot. He refused to let any personal disappointment at cruelly having to sit out the biggest game of his life from getting in the way of the party. He was so obviously proud of his pals for completing the job. As the night wore on the cup rarely left his hands. Ferguson wandered from table to table, chatting happily to his heroes and their families. He stood back, beaming from ear to ear, as his players raised the roof.

In another part of town at the Hotel Santsa more subdued banquet was being held to honour the vanquished in front of 800 guests. Etiquette demanded that Bayern's players attend the official post-match UEFA bash, though Oliver Kahn paid lip-service to tradition by not showing up. In truth, the only company the players wanted to keep was their own. But in recognition of the major part Bayern had played in a remarkable final they were given a deserved two-minute ovation.

Bayern President Franz Beckenbauer had done many things for German football, almost all of them with style and grace. But never had those qualities been called upon more than in the hours after his club's defeat in Barcelona. He rose to speak and told the guests and the players: 'It is hard to find the right words. But I will try. It is a game, was a game and will always be a game. We have not lost a battle, nor a war; nobody has lost their lives. We have lost a game.' Then he turned to the players. 'I am proud of what you have done,' he told them. 'I am proud of how you played and the whole of Germany will be proud too. But we have seen tonight how cruel football can be.' Beckenbauer went on to praise the club's performances in winning the Bundesliga and reaching the Champions League final against the odds. The audience listened, even if they did not quite hear. The events of which he spoke were still beyond their comprehension. Most of the players remained distraught throughout the evening. Some sought solace in the bottom of a beer glass.

Jordi Cruyff, who'd been on loan from United at Celta Vigo, had already been in touch with Yorke to arrange a night on the town. Cruyff and two friends took Yorke to a Barcelona nightclub where they danced and had a great time. Before the final Schmeichel had ordered some cigars for after the match. Yorke had asked for the biggest Havana he had and took it to the nightclub. He didn't smoke, but the cigar was in and out of his mouth all evening.

Bayern's general manager Uli Hoeness was in denial. 'We have achieved all our goals for the year,' he claimed. 'We wanted to be in the final and we achieved that.' Most of the time Bayern's people wandered around looking, according to the *Suddeutsche Zeitung*, 'as if they had just lost someone close to them'. Mehmet Scholl felt especially low. 'There is only emptiness inside you, boundless emptiness,' he said.

But by around 3 a.m. even the Germans were starting to let their hair down. Having decided the self-pity couldn't go on forever Mario Basler and Hasan Salihamidzic climbed on a table to dance the salsa, then mounted the stage with several team-mates to sing *We Are The Champions*.

Back at United's hotel Keane enjoyed the official party into the early hours. 'Those Irish boys, I can tell you, are Super League when it comes to enjoying themselves,' says Cole. 'When they talk about pushing the boat out, it's the whole damn fleet that goes to sea.' When somebody tried to shut the bar and close down the disco at three in the morning it wasn't the most diplomatic of discussions. 'There was a barney, the chaps just wouldn't tolerate any friendly persuasion, and we carried on laughing, and joking, and drinking until around five, what you might call a respectable hour to end a party,' adds Cole.

Barely a crumb of food was eaten as everyone knocked back the alcohol. By 4.30 a.m. the guests were all toasting each other when a United player shouted for nightclub owner Frank Pearson, known as Foo Foo, a drag queen and confirmed bachelor famous throughout Manchester, to make a speech. The lifelong Red had done charity work with most of the players and knew them quite well. Tonight he was dressed in ordinary clothes. 'You don't attend a soccer match in a frock if you want to stay healthy,' he says. Pearson thanked the players for winning the treble. He later told the *News of the World*: 'It was a great night and a great party. Everyone had a marvellous time. When I left everybody was laughing.'

By now, many of Bayern's players were laying awake in bed tormenting themselves with the thoughts of what might have been. 'My players will need days and weeks to recover,' Hitzfeld had said. Ferguson stayed up until 5 a.m. when United's players were still partying. They celebrated so long and hard in their hotel dining-room that when dawn crept over Barcelona and turned into morning the celebrations still seemed to be in full swing. The party only broke up when the hotel staff begged the players to wind things up because they wanted to set the tables. They had to start laying out the breakfast around them at 7.30 a.m.

Eventually, some of the European Cup winners, still wearing their medals, gave in to the exhaustion that adrenalin had kept at bay. They just about managed to find the lift back to their rooms before crashing out. Others wandered into the deserted streets and walked towards the port. They met some Bayern fans who were as downhearted and devastated as the German players had been on the pitch just a few hours before. United's players graciously offered their condolences and talked about the incredible drama of the previous night. Then they walked back to the hotel to get ready for the flight home, still barely able to believe the nature of their dramatic comeback.

As the sun rose in Spain those fans who'd spent the night on the streets blinked and wondered if it had all been real. They stumbled down to news-stands where huge headlines in the English newspapers that had been flown over especially told them the dream had come true. The Spanish media said a big thank you to their celebrating visitors. *La Vanguardia*, the Catalan 'national' newspaper, even managed a cheery sentiment: 'Problems? Not one. They are ugly – but they are good people.'

Yorke didn't return to the hotel until 9 a.m. 'It was a tremendous evening,' he says. When Yorke arrived back Keane was *still* partying. The Irishman eventually went to bed at about 9.30 a.m., which didn't surprise Cole at all.

The next morning Cole felt rough. He wasn't the only one. Some of the players' wives and girlfriends headed for the shops. 'They could have had any kind of plastic they wanted off me,' says Cole, 'just so long as they promised to leave me alone.' He stood in the shower for a good half-hour trying the 'Niagara' hangover cure.

Seven

Returning Home

Bayern's players had to prepare for a league match away to Bayer Leverkusen and returned to Munich airport at 2 a.m. on Thursday. They broke up without a word. Friday's edition of *Die Welt* had rolled off the presses with the text of Beckenbauer's speech to Matthaus, Effenberg and company published under the Kaiser's own byline. Top to bottom, president to playmaker, Bayern were baring their tortured soul as if to do so might somehow be therapeutic.

In Barcelona, United's euphoria was collecting itself for a renewed assault on the senses as the street cleaners worked overtime and the tired heroes enjoyed a lie-in. When they finally woke up to a clear, bright new day they did so in the knowledge that United were the first English team for 15 years to win the European Cup.

'They are their own men now,' wrote Oliver Holt in *The Times*, 'they have gone from excellence to greatness, they will be fêted as the most resilient, adventurous English side of all time. They have developed a reputation for coming back from the dead, but this was beyond anything we could have expected. Now, we will talk about the moment when Sheringham scored, about the disbelief at

Solskjaer's strike in the same breath as we talk about Best's goal against Benifca at Wembley all those years ago. Nothing could equal the drama of what United achieved here.'

The empty champagne bottles had barely been cleared away and the famous trophy had only been in Ferguson's possession a few hours, but as he sat in the morning sunshine against an exotic background of fountains and palm trees in Barcelona's modern, elegant waterside Hotel Arts, it was already business as usual for the manager. Ferguson treated hype with the same disdain he reserved for those who couldn't match his desire to be the best. As he faced the press for the first time since guiding his team to immortality Ferguson beamed the smile of a contented man. He looked fresh and alive after having his nerves shredded on a night of unbelievable tension.

Everybody wanted to offer Ferguson their congratulations. 'If he hadn't already considered it the previous night, he must have thought he had been transported to nirvana, everyone wanting to shake the Scot's hand, genuflecting and paying homage like Nubian slaves at the feet of King Rameses,' wrote Nick Townsend of the *Independent on Sunday*. Ferguson sat outside on a first-floor terrace, the noise of water from a roaring fountain below calming his racing thoughts. He was, understandably, more than happy to answer questions from the assembled journalists about the Miracle of Barcelona. Oliver Holt of *The Times* was among the throng.

> His [Ferguson's] voice was hoarse with elation and fatigue,'
> says Holt. 'His words, though, were clear and emphatic.
> Perhaps it was a trick of the mind, but they seemed to carry
> even more authority than usual. It was as if he had taken the
> final leap into greatness with his team the night before. He
> spoke of the drive that he still had, of his determination not to
> go quietly or without further success in what he said will be the
> last three years of his career. Yet there was a sense of
> peacefulness about him, too, a sense of completion and
> fulfilment. And for us, there was an inkling of what it might
> have been like to have sat and listened to the wisdom of Sir
> Matt Busby the day after George Best and Bobby Charlton had
> helped him to the European Cup 31 years ago.

'Ferguson will not dwell in anyone's shadow any more. His domestic achievements had already brought him most of the way into the sunlight. The fact that United had just completed an unprecedented treble, and that they had done it by performing a miracle of footballing resurrection, completed the transformation. It made it more special that it had happened on the day that would have been Busby's 90th birthday, that United will now be able to associate the name of Munich with something that is a symbol of the club's rejuvenation and rebirth, not just a lasting reminder of the tragedy and misery of an air disaster.'

Ferguson knew that his chance of making history would never come again. 'I honestly felt that last night was my best chance,' he said. 'Next year, you've got 17 [Champions League] games on top of your domestic programme in England, plus internationals, and . . . it's going to be a mammoth task.' He then revealed how he had anticipated progress through Europe. 'I thought that with Cantona in the side we might do it. He was a talisman and had the presence to convince players they could compete at this level. Three years ago there was the [Borussia] Dortmund game which should have been the final. It was a gutting experience, but it told you we weren't far away. Our form in the Champions League has proved that with incredible performances against the Juves, the Bayerns and the Barcelonas . . . then you think to yourself, maybe it's not going to come to you.'

Some of the hacks felt United were lucky to collect the last piece of their treble jigsaw with victory at the Nou Camp. 'Those two late goals cannot conceal the fact that Ferguson was out-manoeuvred by his counterpart, Ottmar Hitzfeld, his team outplayed by a side superior collectively if not individually,' wrote the *Independent on Sunday*'s Townsend. But even he admitted that while the treble wasn't achieved in the style that might have been desired, 'the record of Manchester United, losers of 4 of 62 matches this season and scorers of 128 goals, counters any argument that a unique treble is not just reward'.

'You can talk all you like about tactics,' said Ferguson. 'But tactics didn't win that game last night. It was sheer will; maybe luck, too. They [United's players] never stopped and you have to give them credit for that. Even Bayern accept that. For that equaliser, we had nine bodies in the box.

'The ability of the players has always been the most important thing to me. But I told them they had to have the mental toughness of the 1994 team. There was a challenge for them to match guys like [Bryan] Robson, [Steve] Bruce and Cantona. Now they've done that I think we will see them bring an authority to their play. When a player is 24 he doesn't know how to control a game. When he gets to 27 or 28 he can develop that part of his control on the field. We're still, in many ways, playing off the cuff but I hope that will change now.'

Back in Scotland on Paisley High Street, close to where Ferguson had once managed St Mirren, the conversation at the back of the bus on Thursday morning ran along familiar lines. There was the same old shake of the head, followed by the obligatory 'imagine sacking Fergie' before several passengers agreed with a collective sigh.

'That sigh has carried across the 21 years since St Mirren sacked Alex Ferguson, gathering fresh impetus from each of the 21 trophies he has won for Aberdeen and Manchester United,' says Douglas Alexander of the *Sunday Times*. 'Each time that famous trophy-burnished grin breaks out below those trademark ruddy cheeks, a St Mirren supporter winces with regret. The stigma of sacking Ferguson runs so deep it could be ingrained in the club badge.'

One man felt its presence more than most. Willie Todd was an affable, 79-year-old grandfather. He was also the chairman of Scottish club St Mirren who, on 31 May 1978, told Ferguson he was sacked from his £15,000-a-year job as manager. Despite having led the club to promotion to the Scottish Premier Division, Ferguson was dismissed for what was described as 'breaches of contract', including the payment of extra bonuses to players and his trip to watch the European Cup final between Liverpool and Bruges, both without the authority of the St Mirren directors. A statement issued by Todd said it had been agreed that because of 'a serious rift' between the board and Ferguson his contract should be terminated immediately. Fergie, then 36, accepted the news calmly. He joined Aberdeen just two days after he was sacked. Ferguson took St Mirren to an industrial tribunal for unfair dismissal and lost. Since then he'd been the winner and St Mirren the losers. 'When the divorce came,' says Alexander, 'Ferguson was granted custody of success.' Now a multimillionaire, and having just signed a new three-year contract at Old Trafford worth about £5 million, Ferguson probably had enough money to buy St Mirren twice over.

But Todd had no regrets and cheered on United from his armchair on the Wednesday night as he celebrated Ferguson's triumph. He was delighted that Ferguson had achieved his ambition of winning the Champions Cup. 'I've met him several times at football matches since then and our relationship is quite amicable. He did a lot for St Mirren and it was clear even then that he was very good. He was very ambitious and had great ability to get the best from his players, as well as a good eye for talent. Of course, you do think about what we might have achieved had he stayed for longer, but that's life.'

In Barcelona, after midday, Phil Neville was the first United player to emerge from his room. Neville's angelic girlfriend, dressed all in white, looked as if she'd come from the heavens rather than an all-night party. As the couple set off down the corridor for breakfast they held hands and actually started skipping. It was that sort of day. Schmeichel was the last player to leave the hotel. He was mobbed by grateful fans. 'I've got to go,' he said, trying to fight his way through the crowd.

Eventually, a very tired United party assembled at the airport for the return trip to Manchester. Cole thought most of them could have managed to get back without an aircraft. 'We were flying anyway,' he says. 'How much can a footballer drink? Endless supplies, it seemed, as long as you have won the European Cup. Those air stewardesses should have been sponsored by Nike for running up and down the aisle carrying trays of drinks.'

Keane sat by himself at the back of the plane, alone with his thoughts. 'It was frustrating not to be able to play in the European Cup final,' he'd say later. 'But I still felt a part of our success. We had to play a dozen games to get this far. It wasn't just won on the night. And I have a medal to show I was part of it, which is nice. But of course it doesn't feel the same as it would have if I'd played. Scholesy and Henning will tell you the same.'

Thousands of bleary-eyed supporters had begun arriving home in good time to attend an all-night jamboree in Manchester's streets as the reality of their team's achievement sank in. Further south at London's Heathrow Airport the baggage-handlers had programmed in a special message on the screens for those passengers arriving on flights from Munich. 'Manchester United 2, Bayern Munich 1,' it read. 'Welcome to England, home of the European champions.' But Manchester was the place to be. Fans were travelling to the city from all over the country to welcome their team. One train from Taunton in south-west England was packed with hundreds of United fans and when it stopped in Birmingham more supporters got on. So many passengers were wearing United shirts that the train resembled a Red Army special.

In Manchester anticipation of the players' return had already brought business to a halt. Some workers were told to leave at 2.30 p.m. Three supporters shinned up Prince Albert's statue in the city centre and couldn't get down. They were left clutching the Prince's coattails until one called the fire brigade on a mobile!

The contrast in Germany could not have been greater as the country slipped into the national equivalent of clinical depression. Television news cameras panned around the empty Olympic Stadium in Munich where the previous night more than 40,000 fans had been cheering and singing as they watched the final on a huge screen. The TV coverage was fittingly accompanied by funeral music; it was as if the country was attending a wake.

No side had ever inflicted such a shocking defeat on Bayern. United's late win had changed the feelings of a nation towards the German club everybody except its supporters usually loved to hate. Bayern's switchboard flickered with messages of sympathy all day. Supporters of rival clubs from Frankfurt to Hamburg and Schalke to Kaiserslautern, where Bayern's glamour was loathed and envied, rang just to say sorry. 'Maybe three-quarters of those who hate us were crying with us,' said Bayern's press officer Marcus Horwick.

'The day after they would hate us again, of course, but for the day I think they understood.'

Not that everybody in Germany was sympathetic. There was widespread rejoicing among some supporters at Bayern's humbling. 'It's wonderful,' said Christina Otte, a Kaiserslautern fan who worked at the Frankfurt Stock Exchange. 'Bayern Munich are insufferably arrogant. They have more money than anyone else and they go round ruining other clubs by buying up their best players.'

But the anti-Bavarian feeling, tempered by sympathy for the awful unexpectedness with which the game had turned, made the reaction of the losers themselves all the more admirable. Beckenbauer had said United deserved to win and Hitzfeld believed they'd earned the victory every bit as much as his own side would have done. 'The Germans have become a nation of good losers,' wrote Andrew Grimson in the *Daily Telegraph*. 'They are not always chivalrous about each other, but they know how to take defeat at the hands of other countries in such tournaments as the World and European Cups.'

Absenteeism in Bavarian offices was unusually high, rivalling the Friday before a Bank Holiday. Roger Boyes of *The Times* thought it would take some time for the Bavarians to recover from their sickness. 'This particular bout of flu will be difficult to shake off. Unable to blame the ref, lacking the German phrase for "we wuz robbed", Germans raged against the Nordic god of football . . . Germany is the most insured nation in the world, Germans book their holidays a year in advance; they are not the kind of nation given to scoring last-minute goals. Perhaps that will have to change.'

United's players arrived in Manchester at about 4 p.m. for what Sheringham describes as 'the most emotional few hours of the lot'. By then, with the rush hour dash home already underway for the best part of an hour, red shirts began to outnumber suits and office gear in the city centre.

Butt returned a hero. 'I'm so proud, I'm going to give my medal to my father, Terry. I owe all this to him,' he said. Butt reckoned having the medal proudly displayed in his dad's trophy cabinet was the biggest thank you he could give the man who'd backed him every inch of the way to stardom, never missing a game on the windswept, rain-lashed council parks where he was raised. 'My father helped me throughout,' said Butt. 'I will look back on all this when I am retired and have grandkids.'

Butt was still in a daze after the incredible night before, but he was clear-headed enough to dedicate the European trophy to the fans, his kind of people, from the same Manchester background. 'This victory in a way was better for the fans than the players . . . We don't care who we beat. We have just won the European Cup. But it could be the local Royal Oak pub team. I don't care as long as we win things.'

The celebrations began as soon as United's plane touched down. Hundreds of airport staff cheered and applauded as Schmeichel paused at the top of the plane's steps to hold the cup aloft. Then the players were whisked away across a red carpet patterned with footballs that had been laid down to greet them at the airport. Their wives, girlfriends and families had already left the plane by an air bridge.

Some 500,000 people were expected to be waiting for the team at the civic welcome in the city centre. United were to parade through Manchester on a balloon-covered open-top double-decker bus with their three trophies. The destination on the front said 'Match' and the route number proudly announced the European Cup final result: '2–1'.

Some fans had taken up their positions eight hours before the bus was due to leave Marsland Road in Sale's comfy suburbs at 6 p.m. From there to the rebuilt bomb sites by the cathedral and on to the backwaters of Ceylon Street, the city would soon experience the 'mother of all homecomings'. The supporters waited in warm sunshine for a glimpse of the 'greatest team in the world'. They formed a ribbon of red and did not so much line the route as engulf it.

The bus was to travel down the A56 to Stretford, along Talbot Road and into the city via Deansgate. The seven-mile journey would finish at the MEN (*Manchester Evening News*) Arena at 9 p.m., where Ferguson and his players would parade their trophies before a sell-out crowd of 17,000 ticket holders, those lucky enough to gain entry after thousands had queued for tickets the previous day.

Sheringham had been looking forward to the bus journey. Some of the lads had told him it was a great experience, but it was to exceed his wildest expectations. His son Charlie and some of the other players' kids were also going along for the ride. Twenty minutes after landing the team boarded the bus. Beckham and Yorke were swinging the Champions League trophy between them as the Trinidadian chomped on his cigar from the night before. He wasn't exactly sure why, but having a cigar appealed to him. 'It gave me a buzz, putting a cigar in my mouth. Where I come from, the image of smoking a big cigar is that you are now successful. So that was it, I suppose.'

By the time the bus reached Sale the Red Army had re-created the atmosphere of the Stretford End. United were still four miles from the city centre when the players saw the first supporters out to cheer them on. The European Cup was propped up front like a huge hood ornament, while the FA Cup and the Premiership trophy were precariously balanced on the top railing. As they travelled down the A56 the number of fans steadily increased. '. . . For the cynics who regularly suggest United's fans don't hail from their home city, there was the ultimate argument lining the streets,' says Cole.

The supporters were six deep and growing in number all the time as the bus made its way towards the heart of the city. The nearer they got to the centre the slower it went. United's late goalscorers were lapping up the adulation. Sheringham was joined at the front by Charlton, while Solskjaer smiled and waved from the back to the screaming fans. The crowds let out a roar as they caught a glimpse of Ferguson. The noise went off the register when the bus suddenly left the Manchester A–Z map on to 'Sir Alex Ferguson Way', a previously unknown street near Old Trafford, marked with suspiciously new-looking signs. 'We had to do something dramatic,' said Danny, one of those responsible for the new road.

Thousands of fans walked behind the bus while others started running as soon as it went by to try to catch a second glimpse of their heroes. As well as the universal 'Sir' Alex, titles were also showered on the players from banners and placards reading 'Becks for King' to 'Prince Schmeichel Please Stay'.

On this sultry north-western afternoon, there was justified

gloating about the weather too. According to Martin Wainwright of *The Guardian*, 'you could have made a Spanish omelette, nicely browned, on the pavement outside Trafford Town Hall'.

Wainwright captured the atmosphere nicely. 'The sense of a city on top spread well beyond the long scarlet snake approaching half a million people and taking the bus over two hours to pass to backwaters like Ceylon Street, half a terrace standing like broken red teeth off Oldham Road. Renee Drinkwater's inflatable FA Cup in front of her nets and banner slung between bedroom windows had a special significance – pointing over a wall graffitied with MUFCs at a mess of lank grass, she said, "That's where the Loco Sheds lads first played".'

Nicknamed The Heathens, the Loco Sheds XI were the very first Manchester United, billed as the Newton Heath Lancashire and Yorkshire Railway FC until they almost went bankrupt in 1902, and a rescue consortium of Manchester businessmen demanded a snappier name. The area is rinsed in red – across Oldham Road, most of the streets on the Heathfield estate are named after Busby Babes who died in the Munich air disaster. Across the railway sidings a plaque marks the site of the first Manchester United clubhouse on the wall of Moxton Brook comprehensive.

By the time the United party arrived at Deansgate, the main shopping street in Manchester, it had taken them almost three hours to cover the seven-mile journey. The rest of the city centre, which had been crowded with celebrating fans, suddenly emptied as the supporters thronged the route of the victory procession.

The street was so crowded that a policeman in a helicopter used a public address system to plead with the fans to make way for the bus. Even then eight police horse riders had to gently prise apart the crowd to allow the bus to get through. It all seemed too much for Roy Keane, who was slumped in the corner of the bus as the celebrations reached fever pitch around him. It was the biggest sporting street party Britain had ever known. 'In Deansgate, it was unbelievable,' says Yorke. 'Players who'd won the double said they'd seen nothing like this – all these hundreds and thousands looking up at us on the coach. You just wanted to thank them back for what they'd given us.'

Those who couldn't get onto Deansgate were crammed into the side streets. They only saw the bus for a couple of seconds, but were satisfied they'd honoured the team they lived and died for. 'The ovations we received were overwhelming . . .' says Schmeichel. Cole correctly thought there were twice as many fans as the expected 500,000; he was later told that at least a million had turned up. 'I didn't even know that many lived in the place, never mind supported us,' says Cole.

It was a family affair. Dads carried toddlers in miniature United strips on their shoulders. But it wasn't only the die-hard supporters who turned out. There were office workers in their pinstripes and elderly matrons who looked as if they'd be more at home in a concert by the Hallé. Shredded ticker-tape showered down from offices and beer was sprayed around with shrieks of celebration. The revellers toasted each other as well as the team. Young girls kissed complete strangers – as long as they were wearing the right T-shirt. When the crowd applauded United's bus the players clapped back. The fans took photos and the players got out their video cameras to film the crowd. Old-fashioned civic pride was in the air.

It was an intensely moving experience. Sheringham had a huge lump in his throat and tears sprang to his eyes. He was a bit prone to outbursts of emotion at the best of times. Sometime before he'd had to stop singing the national anthem on England duty because it always made him cry. 'I'm not embarrassed to admit that things like that tug at my emotions,' he says. 'Indeed, I am proud of the fact that I love my country and my club enough to be affected that way.' Sheringham thought the kids on the bus were very lucky. 'It must have been wonderful for them to be a part of it. I know Charlie [Sheringham's son], for one, will never forget it.'

By now it had taken almost four hours for the bus to wind its way through the masses from the outskirts of Manchester to the downtown MEN Arena. *The Times* described it as 'the moment Alex Ferguson's team passed into footballing legend'.

If the players thought the fans on the streets were deafening, nothing could have prepared them for the screams and flashes of a thousand cameras when Ferguson and his men reached the arena for the grand finale. The supporters had been blowing whistles, singing, chanting, cheering and holding European Cup balloons in a carnival atmosphere for nearly two hours to get into the arena for the all-ticket, sell-out event. Inside, the auditorium rapidly turned red as mums, dads and their children created a family carnival, waiting for United to make their final appearance with the three trophies.

The players entered the arena to fireworks and a wall of ear-splitting noise. 'Welcome the greatest soccer team in history,' shouted the announcer over the Tannoy system before being drowned out by cheering fans. The thumping of the disco music was unbelievable as the United party of players, management, backroom staff and directors was greeted by an ear-splitting standing ovation from 17,000 flag-waving fans. Children with battery-operated Red Devils horns and pitchforks waved flags and sang the team songs.

The players walked up the red carpet to the centre of the arena like kings. Ferguson, proudly clutching the European Cup, received the biggest cheers as he strode to the stage. He was followed by Keane with the FA Cup and Schmeichel holding the Premiership trophy. The fans screamed their names and sang *Glory, Glory Man United* over and over again. The players lapped it up.

Ferguson later admitted he had been overwhelmed by Manchester's magnificent reception. He wanted to thank the whole world. One by one the players held the European Cup above their heads as the fans went wild and screamed for more. Ferguson told the cheering crowd: 'I can't talk. It is just beginning to sink in now and we are all very emotional. We've had a terrific reception right from Sale through the streets to here. It has just been a marvellous occasion and we have the best fans in the world and an absolutely fantastic bunch of players. Someone had said there would be a quarter of a million people. It feels like a million. Well done. I thought we needed a miracle, and we got one.'

When the master of ceremonies turned to Schmeichel and said, 'You're leaving us now, sir?' he was drowned out as people whistled their disapproval. It was a negative response, but an emotional Schmeichel knew they were expressing feelings of loss. They desperately wanted him to stay. 'I hoped I might get one trophy, but to stand here with all three is fantastic,' he said. 'I'm sad to be leaving Manchester United. I've played for the best team in the world and I'll always remember you. This side is going to win these trophies for many years to come. Thank you very much.'

Then Keane took the microphone. 'I think we deserved to win all three trophies because we have played some great football,' he said. 'The Man United fans have been superb all season,' he added, giving his thanks for the passion of the Red Army.

As the evening ended those outside listened on their radios while Ferguson said it was the proudest day of his life. He seemed to be speaking for an entire city. Ferguson also paid tribute to Schmeichel. 'Peter is a fantastic goalkeeper . . . the best the club has ever had,' he said. 'Are you ready for one more sing-song?' the fans next to the stage were asked. The faithful responded by shouting 'Champions, Champions' with one voice. They shouted louder and louder until they were nearly hoarse, an amazing wall of sound enveloping everyone and everything. Just when everybody thought they had no more energy, the fans began dancing the samba, waving their flags and kissing each other.

After their appearance at the arena the players had to endure a long wait on the bus. 'That little interlude, I have to say, seemed a complete waste of time, but maybe I am being a bit churlish,' says Cole. 'It would have been better, following the civic parade, if they had allowed the players just to get on with the party . . . very quickly we were split up, packed off home, and suddenly there was a huge feeling of anti-climax,' he adds. 'We knew we wouldn't be seeing each other for a few weeks and, after the greatest moment of our lives, we just headed off like ships in the night. But, let's be honest, we had just been through an incredible 24-hour whirl of emotion and achievement, a day in my career that can never be surpassed.'

In the suburbs of Munich on Friday morning a sense of disbelief still pervaded Bayern's handsome headquarters in the Sabener Strasse as the players went through the motions to get ready to face Bayer Leverkusen in a Bundesliga match that had arrived far too soon. The enormity of Bayern's failure against United began to sink in, but they knew they had to pull themselves together because the double was still on the cards. Bayern searched deep into their soul and found enough strength to defeat Leverkusen 2–1. A fortnight later they beat Werder Bremen on penalties to lift the cup and complete a double. It was scant consolation for missing out on a historic treble.

Horwick knew Bayern had missed the chance to make history against United after a night of football drama unlikely to be equalled. 'This is a big club and we have had many great nights, but that was the perfect event, the sort of moment you wait a lifetime for. If you'd made a film, you would have come down to Manchester United against Bayern in front of 90,000 people. Two top teams, both on an equal level, both going for a treble. But you got a result and scenes no film would dare . . .' Fantasy football on a grand scale. United were still pinching themselves in case it was all a dream.

Eight

What have we done?

United had become the first team from one of Europe's five major leagues to complete the treble. They were unrivalled in England, France, Germany, Italy or Spain. There were bound to be comparisons with the teams produced by their great north-west rivals Liverpool.

'Before Wednesday night no English club had ever won the League Championship, FA Cup and European Cup in a single season,' wrote David Lacey of *The Guardian*. 'United's astute sense of timing has ensured that the 20th century will never see its like again.

'The only comparison with the present United side which has some validity involves the Liverpool team of the late '70s and early to mid-'80s that never achieved the double but narrowly missed out on the treble in 1977 and did, in fact, win three trophies in 1984 ... In terms of consistent excellence over a long period Liverpool, with nine titles in 13 years, are still ahead of United.'

Brian Glanville of *The Sunday Times*, in an article entitled 'United Still Not Truly Great: Alex Ferguson's team have some way to go before they join the ranks of European legends,' assessed whether the present team were better than the '68 vintage and looked at where the team stood among the great European sides of the past. Glanville wrote: 'It would be unfair to judge this Manchester United side merely on the basis of what went on in Barcelona, where we did not, could not possibly, see the real United. How could it be otherwise, with Roy Keane and Paul Scholes torn out of the midfield? Yet I submit that the 1968 United team was superior to this one, not least because it had three great players: Bobby Charlton, Denis Law . . . and the incomparable George Best. You might even say that Alex Stepney was a more reliable if less spectacular goalkeeper than Peter Schmeichel . . .'

But Ken Jones of *The Independent* gave Ferguson's side the edge over Busby's.

> In the build-up to last night's match . . . much emphasis was placed on the importance of Peter Schmeichel who some see as the greatest goalkeeper in history. This may be carrying things a bit far but nobody, not even Eric Cantona, has contributed more to the progress United have made under Ferguson's astute stewardship. Alex Stepney . . . had plenty going for him, but not enough to come ahead of the big Dane.
>
> It does not take much for the big names of '68 to heap praise on the team's defenders: the dogged thoroughness of its centre-half Bill Foulkes . . . the tackling and expert covering supplied by full-backs Shay Brennan and Tony Dunne, together with the influence of Nobby Stiles, who grew in stature and confidence after helping England win the 1966 World Cup final.
>
> If there is not much between the full-back pairings, adaptation to modern auxiliary attacking gives Gary Neville and Denis Irwin an edge.
>
> Combative, quick and a much better footballer than he was given credit for, Stiles would be a strong candidate for inclusion in midfield if a holding player was called for. Crerand's lack of pace would be a serious drawback in modern football, so despite superior passing ability he would be unlikely to replace Roy Keane or Paul Scholes.

Nobody played better for Manchester United in 1968 than their left-winger John Aston, who had the game of his life before slipping into obscurity. But Aston ahead of Ryan Giggs? Hardly.

Even though they were talented footballers, both England internationals, it is hard to make out a case for David Sadler and Brian Kidd, which brings us to an issue any manager would kill for. That of accommodating Best, Law and Charlton. Best and Law as twin strikers, Charlton the thrusting midfielder, Giggs and David Beckham out wide. What an attack that would be.

Rob Hughes of *The Times* also felt Ferguson's team was better than the '68 side, at least in one respect. 'When the pulse is allowed to rest, when the pleasant shock of this magnificent victory seeps into the consciousness, we might begin to ask how this United compares to the team of 1968. In matters of merit, we might have to question it, but for sheer human spirit, that will never be in doubt.'

Holt of *The Times* felt United's achievement would be almost impossible to copy. 'In two astonishing, almost surreal, minutes at the end of the last European Cup final of the 20th century, the gilded youth of the most famous of clubs left excellence behind them and found the greatness they have been searching for. The treble is theirs now, as well, something unprecedented, something that even the great English sides of the past have always fallen short of. It is unlikely that it will ever be repeated.

'By coming from behind to beat Bayern Munich with two goals in the final minutes, by transforming what seemed like certain defeat into glorious, glorious victory, this United side escaped once and for all from the shadow of Sir Matt Busby and the team that won the trophy in 1968. The problem for future United teams, for future teams of all nations for that matter, will not be in trying to recreate the magic of George Best and Bobby Charlton, it will be in the impossible task of trying to surpass the unsurpassable, of bettering a finish that could not be imagined.'

Ferguson agreed. 'I don't think it will ever happen again. I believe Manchester United's unique treble will remain exactly that for all time. So many things have come together, and the odds of this happening a second time with today's increasingly intensive demands seem to me to be stacked so high against as to make it well-nigh impossible.'

But did the Reds' victory testify to the virtues of the Premiership? Not according to Rob Hughes of *The Times*. 'The fact is that United had been second to the ball, second in their game plan and tactics of football for 89 minutes. So please let us not draw false conclusions that this testifies to the strength of the FA Carling Premiership. It is the strength, singular, of Manchester United, the culmination of that combination of talent, desire and sheer team effort that Ferguson has breathed into his teams. It has taken 13 years at Old Trafford, taken 35 unbeaten matches this season and taken an absolute triumph over the British system. For United had been handicapped, as English sides before them, by the priorities that make England's one of the biggest leagues in the world and which cram into the final weeks of the long marathon three such dramatic peaks as this.'

The Germans and a number of journalists thought Bayern deserved to win. Even Andy Cole called United's victory 'sheer piracy'. But, as Mark Lawrenson wrote in *The Irish Times*: 'European finals aren't stages for individuals to go out and embellish reputations, they are games for teams to consolidate their place in history.' In any case, United's buccaneering spirit deserved to be rewarded with victory. 'You can easily make out a case that during the 1998–99 season Manchester United played the most entertaining football that has ever been seen in the Champions League,' says Schmeichel. 'I certainly don't remember ever having seen another team that played such attacking football and took so many chances in order to capture the title.

'This conviction was allied to the underlying philosophy of our team, which was the simplest of all: we just need to score one goal more than the opposition, irrespective of how the balance of possession, or any other irrelevant statistic, reads after the 90 minutes. In this manner we managed to do what no team before us had done.'

Ferguson's place in history was beyond doubt. He was a hero, according to James Traynor of the *Scottish Daily Record*. 'If he does nothing else in his lifetime this man will be a hero for ever more because on a balmy Catalonian evening destiny did come calling. He knows that Manchester United should never have beaten Bayern Munich, who were much the better side on Wednesday night, but it was meant to be. Simple as that.

'This is not to say, though, that Ferguson's side are unworthy. Far from it because the team he has fashioned have at their very core the qualities which were always likely to ensure he himself would stand alone as the finest of his own and other generations. If United hadn't been influenced by Ferguson's tenacious desire, if they had become just another bunch of Hollywood footballers in pursuit of riches, they would never have recovered from the loss of an early goal against the Germans.'

Ferguson felt United's approach deserved a reward. 'The truth is we were by far the more convincing team for the bulk of the hour and a half, and we were infinitely more ambitious . . . Those observers who thought [Bayern] were in smooth, sophisticated control were imagining things.' Even Beckenbauer had said United deserved to win. 'He wasn't wrong,' says Ferguson, who had become the manager with the greatest span of years – 1983 to 1999 – separating the winning of two European club trophies.

United's boss says he'll remember the final weeks of the season until the day he dies, adding 'Those moments at the end of the game at Nou Camp when Teddy Sheringham and Ole Gunnar Solskjaer scored will never be far from my thoughts . . . Everyone will have their memory of those last few minutes. I know I have mine. When I close my eyes they flash into my mind. The unique treble has been achieved.'

'In roughly a millionth of a second my life changed utterly and completely and forever,' says Cole. 'It was Barcelona and bliss. Nothing would ever be the same again. I had won the most historic treble of all time, sharing in a Manchester United achievement unlikely ever to be repeated because of the growing intensity and increasing demands of the modern game.'

When United ended their 26-year wait to win the championship in 1993 Ferguson allowed himself no more than a few hours to soak up the glory. If the players retained their hunger, he said, there was no limit to what they could achieve. The journey that ended with Schmeichel and Ferguson lifting the European Cup in the Nou Camp began in Budapest on 15 September 1993. That was the night Ferguson's United took their first faltering steps in the quest to emulate Sir Matt Busby's legendary team after years of exile from the Continent's premier club competition.

Six years, two doubles and a treble after their first league title for twenty-six years, it was clear Ferguson had succeeded in ensuring the players remained ravenous enough to conquer Europe. He'd always said he'd wait and reserve the right to compare his present team to the outstanding double-winning side of 1994. Now he had no doubts. 'The '94 team had mental toughness. So many of them. Real tough bastards. Mentally tough that is. I said this present bunch could only be judged on what they have achieved. Now they have achieved and now they are the best. There is no question about that. These players . . . have established themselves on a new higher level. In the pantheon of George Best, Denis Law and Bobby Charlton. They can't be ignored now in that respect. I don't think the '68 side will deny them either. They are proud of them. The old team did their bit all those years ago. They were men of other times. Now these lads have established something by themselves. They are the legends now.

'This European Cup is always something you strive for. I was never obsessed by it though. Now I have won it, I do feel a sense of fulfilment I did not feel before. There is no question about that. You look at the cup and the managers who have lifted it and the teams that have won it recently. There was Ajax, Juventus, Borussia Dortmund, Real Madrid and now Manchester United. You see those names and you think that's what this is all about.'

Afterword

Manchester United's 'Impossible Treble' may prove to be just that since the club has failed to get close to the success they enjoyed in their amazing 1998–99 season. The mixture of last-minute goals and luck every team needs to turn a good season into a great one has been sadly lacking, especially in Europe's leading club competition.

United have picked up three more Premier League titles (2000, 2001 and 2003) and the FA Cup (2004) since their treble season but the Champions League trophy has been missing. Their record in Europe shows a loss to Porto in the first knockout round (2004), three quarter-final defeats – two to Real Madrid (2000 and 2003) and one to Bayern Munich (2001) – and a semi-final defeat to Bayer Leverkusen (2002) on the away goals rule. The luck just has not been there.

United manager Sir Alex Ferguson is desperate to repeat his 1999 success in Europe after missing out on the two finals he would have loved his team to play – in his home town of Glasgow in 2002 and at their own Old Trafford ground in 2003.

However, the odds are stacked against them ever enjoying such a successful season again. They may have already fulfilled their destiny.

Ken Ferris,
London, 2004